Tatiana

Princess Tatiana Metternich's first memories are of herself as a small child in St Petersburg in the closing years of Tsarist Russia – a world of English nannies, of comfort, space and beauty which is rudely shattered by the coming of war and revolution.

She and her family escaped aboard the *Princess Ena*, sent by King George V to rescue his aunt, the Dowager Empress Maria Feodorovna, and faced the nomadic life of émigrés – a life which took its toll through separation, cramped discomfort and total destitution as they travelled across Europe to her father's estates in Lithuania.

The outbreak of war in 1939 finds Tatiana on the German border with Poland – a witness to the despair and tension preceding the German invasion. Her unique account of life within the Reich during the war years is graphic in its description of the horror and deprivation endured by the civilian population, and sharply critical of the Nazi regime. As she chronicles the tragedy of the Russian front, to which her dashing young husband, Prince Paul Metternich, was sent, we feel the full depth of her fear and concern for his safety, and that of her sister, Missie, and their friends involved in the 1944 plot to assassinate Hitler – only narrowly escaping themselves from being implicated.

Tatiana is also the story of two houses: Königswart and Johannisberg – both Metternich family homes. From Königswart they are forced to flee ahead of advancing Russian troops to face a hairraising trek in an open cart across a dangerous and lawless Germany to Johannisberg which they find has been bombed out of existence.

This sensitive and human account of a harrowing period of history closes on a note of hope for the future as Tatiana faces the task of rebuilding Johannisberg and yet sadness for the fate of Königswart, now a state museum in Czechoslovakia.

This edition includes a previously unpublished memoir of life in the Vienna of the armistice, the setting for Graham Greene's *The Third Man*.

Cover shows 'The Ball' by Victor Gilbert

Tatiana Metternich

TATIANA

Five Passports in a Shifting Europe

CENTURY
London Melbourne Auckland Johannesburg

Copyright © Tatiana Metternich 1976

First published in Great Britain in 1976
by William Heinemann Ltd

This edition was published in 1988 by
Century, an imprint of Century Hutchinson Ltd,
Brookmount House, 62–65 Chandos Place, Covent Garden,
London WC2N 4NW

Century Hutchinson Australia Pty Ltd,
PO Box 496, 16–22 Church Street, Hawthorn,
Victoria 3122, Australia

Century Hutchinson New Zealand Limited,
PO Box 40–086, Glenfield, Auckland 10, New Zealand

Century Hutchinson South Africa (Pty) Ltd,
PO Box 337, Bergvlei, 2012 South Africa

Set in Garamond

Printed and bound in Great Britain by Richard Clay Ltd, Bungay, Suffolk

British Library Cataloguing in Publication Data
Metternich, Tatiana *Fürstin von*
   Tatiana: five passports in a shifting
   Europe.—(Lives and letters).
   1. Metternich, Tatiana *Fürstin von Metternich*
   I. Title II. Series
   947.084′2′0924   CT1218.M/

ISBN 0 7126 1877 5

Contents

To Missie, my ally and companion
in good and bad moments.

It is an experience of tremendous liberty; the extreme limit of what one feels and what one does . . . A man who has gone through fire is another being. Teilhard de Chardin on 'Nostalgia for the Front'

Illustrations

Preface

Childhood is often supposed to be an illness from which one never recovers: for us our childhood was mostly our parents' life. As a matter of course we accepted the fact that the loss of their country was an amputation which deprived us of the right to be thoughtless or inconsiderate, but we looked forward to our own life with eager expectation. It was therefore not those earlier years of emigration which left a scar, but the second world war.

This account of it is based on diaries and notes dating from 1939 to 1945, and is an attempt to give an entirely personal impression of the atmosphere in Germany as we experienced it at that time.

Life under a dictatorship is difficult to grasp for those who have only known democracy, whereas for us the years under Nazism have made the shadings of existence in a totalitarian country easier to understand: once the elementary principles of morality and law have been abolished, it becomes almost impossible to break away, for no one is then any longer free from fear.

After the French Revolution, those who had survived appeared almost suspect to returning émigrés. Confronted with the contrast between concentration camps and everyday life in Germany, the Allies were not far from taking the same view. We had come to realise however, that one cannot dwell on 'real' horror. After any catastrophe, life, normal everyday life, resumes almost immediately; unless every man builds his own refuge, he would go down in the storm.

As the long months went by, these refuges shrank like melting icefloes until for many, moral independence could only be asserted by a final gesture of defiance or even of mockery, the last resource being one's own inner strength.

Until put to the test, who can tell how far this can be counted on?

When all was over, we learnt that horror was not the sum of human experience. Those who survived would only remember the flashes of light in the darkness: the warm comradeship, the selfless gesture of love or courage which seemed the last reality in a world gone mad, where finally simplicity and gentleness remained the only valid sounds in a man's heart.

No one could be quite the same again, yet at no time since then, has the feeling of living been more intense.

Tatiana Metternich

Part One

Early Years

I

Returning to Leningrad for the first time in 1963, the house on Fontanka 7 seemed to have shrunk. So many buildings tend to loom larger in memory, perhaps in proportion to one's smaller size. The erstwhile capital had been lovingly restored, a whole district was still named 'Petrograd' – it was as familiar and as distant as a glimpse into a previous life.

In fact, I was barely two years old when we left, so I recalled the house only in sudden disjointed flashes . . .

I remember squatting on the first of three steps at the end of a winding and panelled corridor, waiting philosophically while Irina and Alexander (my older sister and brother, seven and five years of age) tussled over who was going to hold my hand down the steps and round the turn to Mamma's room.

It was my second birthday. (The first is always ignored in Russia.) Mamma was in bed; lacy and soft to touch, smelling of lavender and roses, like handkerchief sachets. Piled on the quilt were my presents: fluffy toy animals, and slippery satin-like pages of English books. (Soon afterwards imported toys were no longer to be had. Russian hand-made ones were wooden and gaily painted, but we did not like them as much.)

In the afternoon there was a party at our house. A large black cup-board was set up at the end of the ballroom, and Punch and Judy popped up and down jerkily on top. Rows and rows of doll-like children sat on thin spindly gold chairs: little girls with bows in their hair and smocked eyelet embroidery dresses over pink or blue slips, and small boys in sailor suits, with a whistle on a cord under their flappy square collars.

Then we climbed a stair to the tiny platform above a polished wooden slide. A sharp shove: whish! Down to Nannie, waiting to catch me below, sharply admonishing jostling boys:

'You must behave like little gentlemen!' to be answered by the hapless howl: 'I don't want to be a little gentleman!' repeated by generations of children all over Europe, as their Nannies never gave up trying.

What a bitter disappointment next morning! The great room was quite empty and all the little boys and girls had vanished. I had thought they belonged there.

Soon there appeared a tiny, red, crumpled new baby, wrapped in frothy pink as if it were a chocolate.

'Why a clothes-basket and no cot?'

'It is wartime and there are none to be had, but Nanny has made it pretty with ribbons and frills.'

It was so much more exciting than any toy, and coming so soon after my birthday, belonging specially to me – just as the bigger ones considered I belonged to them.

Towards tea-time, we would be led into the drawing-room to be 'shown' to the afternoon guests, and given one of the tiny pink or green cakes I could see on the lowest tray of the three-tiered table. All I remember at that time seems to have been at waste-paper basket level: pedestal of columns, the lower rail of stair-balustrades, tables and chairs seen from underneath, until teasing uncles swung one high into the air.

There seems to have been a forest of these uncles. I remember them more by their touch – the prickle of a moustache, when caught up and kissed, the smell of tobacco, eau de cologne and scented soap and leather – than their faces, which blend into the photos we still have. There were Oleg, Papa's sister's husband, who was in the Navy, and Papa's brother Nikolaï, who played the cello beautifully. His younger brother, George, had already been killed in the War. He was so handsome, and too tall, they said, too good a target for the enemy. His servant, Ivan, had carried him back under fire, and been awarded the St. George medal for valour.

Mamma had three brothers: Boris, my godfather, Dimitri who was her special friend, and the greatest tease of all. Adishka, the youngest, looked after the stud of race-horses, one of which, 'Wilburn M.', had won the Derby and a huge cup too.

Except for Uncle George, they had all been recently married, so there were plenty of aunts too, but they were quiet and gentle, smelt delicious, and having babies of their own for the most part, did not play with us as much.

Tall and gay, mostly in uniform, the uncles were rather overwhelming. They talked and laughed while dogs leapt about their feet. The large white Eskimo-dog, a 'Laika' called Norka, sat under a marble-topped table in the hall, staring straight at me with black unwinking eyes, while I uneasily watched his bushy tail swishing gently to and fro, like a great feather. I clutched some tall grown-up's hand, hoping to be whisked out of reach should that ominous tail stop swaying and Norka, rising slowly, stretching to immense size, decide to lick my face.

On a hot sultry day in Lotarevo (Mamma's home in the country near Tambov), I sat on my godfather (Uncle Boris Wiazemsky's) knee, his white linen Norfolk jacket, plastered with pockets, cool to touch. His cropped copper hair was a shade darker than Mamma's, his smiling eyes chestnut brown. Armed with a pipe-cleaner, he carefully wound a tick out of my ear, with the sure and gentle touch of long practice on his dogs. Irina and Alexander lost the list of names from their animal Lotto, but he wrote it all out for them again, without having to look them up. He had brought a baby lion back from India, and at first it roamed at large in the park, but soon it grew so big, it had to be given to the Zoo, and was called 'Lev Wiazemsky'.

The uncles would suddenly turn the full beam of their teasing attention on to some squirming victim. They never scolded, but treated one as a full grown person, capable of bantering repartee, just as they were used to joking with one another. They were delighted if questions produced a good answer, but if cheeky or affected, we would be ignored, gently pushed aside, feeling immediately stupid. It hardly compensated for the relief of being left alone.

Some years later, Missie, looking like a cherub off a Christmas tree, tongue-tied, spun-gold hair hiding her face, rosebud mouth drooping, would gradually boil over into flowing tears at the least remark. They were deeply concerned and showered her with presents, but nothing helped. She would only answer them (and even Mamma) through me. But she soon grew out of it, and could laugh with them. When half grown-up, they still teased her about it:

'Well Missie, will you speak to me, or are you going to cry?'

Our grandmother Gaga's (Mamma's mother's) home was called 'Ossinevaya Rosscha' (now 'Levachovo'), near St. Petersburg on the Finnish frontier. It was a small château of the early XIXth century, a half-circle of tall columns rising to the roof from a pedestal of shallow steps on the garden side.

A stone's throw from the capital, it was always full of guests, and the children lived a life of their own. Small wicker open carriages would be driven in the afternoons, but the ponies were restive, and young grooms held their heads while Nannies walked alongside. A tea basket was carried along, strapped to the back of the carriage, and presently we got out and walked in the park. Peeping through long high grass, we watched the bisons in the distance. We were not allowed to go too close for they were wild, and charged if they had young with them. Huge and grey, they stopped munching to stare back at us, and we wondered which was the mother and which the aunt, for the father never came near his family. Irina would get very nervous.

Soon Mamma was all in black, her face so white, framed in long dark veils, which could not dim her copper hair. At night we were told to pray for the uncles who had been killed, but the list got ever longer: George, Oleg, Dimitri, Boris.

Papa's first cousins, Sergei and Nikolaï, had already been killed at the Front, and their father (who was Granny Wassiltchikoff's brother) would turn up my chin and say wistfully:

'Nikolaï! She has Nikolaï's eyes.'

Then Aunt Mary Scherbatoff, her daughter Sandra and son Dima were murdered in the depths of the country where they lived. Papa was on the point of going there to persuade them to leave.

There seemed no end to it. But we did not know what it meant to be dead: it was only another classification in our prayers. Neither did we realise how young all our uncles were – under thirty for the most part. But there was the sadness of absence, and Mamma so still, so unlike herself. She would come to the nursery all the time and Nannie and she talked in low voices:

'It is from here that I get all my strength!'

We tried to be good and made up small surprises, but she hardly noticed and stroked our hair as we sat on her knee in turns, the bigger ones gathered close.

A lump grew in our throats when we noticed grown-ups crying, especially if they pretended not to. We kept as quiet as mice. I was always cuddled on somebody's knee, pressed against a hard military belt-buckle or frothy lace, but nobody had time any more to laugh at the funny things Irina said, and she and Alexander would break into sudden pent-up explosive bickering when alone.

Uncle Dimitri, Mamma's favourite brother, was killed in a car as a bomb was hurled into it, and Mamma's first cousin, Aunt Maroussia Veliaminoff's sister, was shot dead as she stood by the window while people fought in the street. It was therefore considered wiser to move children and Nannies to the Crimea until those troubled days were over. There, they would be safe from street-shooting and uprisings.

Great clouds of steam came belching through the black wheels of the engine under the glass-domed tunnel of a station. An entire first class coach had been booked for us and was hooked on to the main express train to the Crimea. Our two English nurses, Miss Thompson and Miss Menzies, Irina's governess Miss Scott, the Russian nursemaids (though in fact our favourite, Eva, was Finnish), the servants and the dogs were all coming with us.

We were lifted up the high steps of the coach, and soon the train rumbled away into the night. The sheets were smooth and cool, but the 'posy' so shaky, it led us a dance. During the day spotless white coverings, edged with rough cotton lace, were spread over the padded seats, which smelt of horse-hair and ancient dust. It was like being in a house of our own on wheels, and we dashed up and down the corridor visiting everybody. The dogs were in a special compartment, and we went to talk to them and hand them pieces of sugar through a small grating, but I had to be lifted to peep through.

After a long, long journey, there came a burst of heat and warm sunshine, palm trees gently waving, scented flowers, stark stony mountains and a shimmering sea.

The entire household, including our fox-terrier Billy, and Baby Missie's stuffed dog called 'Cat', moved into a villa, which the Dowager Empress, Maria Feodorovna, had lent Mamma. It was on the edge of a large garden around her own house and was called 'Charaks'.

We soon settled into the familiar routine of regular hours and insipid English 'Benger's baby food', all mashed and slushy, relieved by copious teas, Beatrix Potter stories, nursery rhymes and long walks.

We played in secluded corners of the large, dusty garden, its bushes all in flower. Two neat ladies, dressed all in black, would often come and watch us dig in the sand-heap. Dead crows seemed to be laid out on their plate-like black hats, claws and feathers spiking the air. They were the Empress, who had a crumpled face, and bright, kind eyes, and her lady-in-waiting, who hardly seemed to be there at all – like a shadow.

Our Nannie, Miss Menzies (Miss Thompson was no longer with us), and Irina's governess, Miss Scott, stood us up, dusted us down, and subsided in deep curtsies, hastily whispering how good we had to be. Patting us on the head, the Empress gave us large lumpy sweets in tasselled paper, like small crackers. She spoke to us very kindly in an abrupt and husky voice. We were not shy at all and liked her.

Although frequently away journeying north, Mamma and Papa spent more time with us than ever before whenever they were at home. Mamma would let us play with her chains of jewelled Easter eggs, their enamel bright as flowers, set with tiny sparkling coloured stars: they were more beautiful than any toy. Papa had just brought them from Petrograd. He had walked into our house there, which was being plundered: anyone could walk in and take whatever they wanted. Even the front door was no longer shut. Papa found the eggs in a drawer of Mamma's dressing-table, and put them in his pocket. As everybody else was stealing, nobody noticed or stopped him.

Irina loved jewellery and told us that all Mamma's bigger things had been put away in a 'Bank' until the shooting was over and we could go home again. It sounded like something between a prison and a fortress, and could not be plundered as easily as our house.

While the maid coiled Mamma's long hair, we learnt our letters in Russian and Latin writing on large squares of cardboard. Alexander liked the letter 'Z' for 'Zaitz' (hare) so much, he would take it to bed with him.

In the evenings, Papa played the violin to Mamma's piano. Guests often filled the house, and the grown-ups made music together, or talked and talked far into the night. There was no laughter as in Lotarevo. With our doors wide open, we could hear them from our rooms. Although so young, we were well aware of all the underlying tension and excitement.

On her last trip north, Mamma had been accompanied by Uncle George's (Wassiltchikoff) orderly Ivan, who had carried him out of the Front line of battle, mortally wounded. Although he could not save his master's life, everybody was grateful to him, and had treated him as one of the family.

But when officials appeared in the train to check their papers, knowing Mamma's were false, he whispered: 'Give me a thousand roubles, or I will say who you are!'

Stopping off in Moscow, Mamma went to find her younger brother Adishka (Wladimir), who was in hiding. She got him out of town with Ukrainian papers just in time, for all officers were being rounded up in the riding-school and shot out of hand if they did not join the Red Army and fight against their own people.

She then went on to Petrograd, but there she was recognised, arrested and brought to the Bolshevik prison, the 'Tcheka'.

She was pushed into a crowded cell, chance prisoners and thieves all mixed up together. Somehow they made room for her, and she found herself next to Countess Brassoff, Grand-Duke Michael Alexandrovitch's wife, whom she had never met before. (His morganatic marriage to her had been the reason for his refusal to accede to the throne after the abdication of his brother, Nicholas II.) She was beautiful, and kind too, sharing all she had, especially handkerchiefs and soap with Mamma, who, picked off the street, had nothing with her but her handbag.

At night they were taken in turns to be questioned by the terrible Uritzky, who was known to show no mercy to anyone. Never had Mamma seen such despicable-looking creatures as those now lounging behind a long table to judge her. It was like a vision of Hell. She got so angry to see Uritzky and his colleagues fingering her Bible and sneering at some hand-painted pictures marking the pages inside, that she turned on them:

'They were given me by my brothers, you and yours have murdered. It is not pleasant to see filthy hands pawing what is holy to us.'

Surprisingly they said: '. . . not so dirty', but she had meant stained with blood.

Perhaps the Ukrainian passport helped, for they returned the little book, and after three days, thanks to urgent intervention from outside, released her.

We listened as she told Nannie all about it, and how when she was in prison, at night, they started the engines of the lorries standing in the courtyard, so as to drown the sound of prisoners (mostly officers) being shot.

'They do not shoot women in the prisons yet: that is why Mamma got out again,' Alexander explained.

We were very frightened and began to have terrible nightmares, so the grown-ups were afterwards more careful not to speak in front of us.

But one night we were put to bed fully dressed, our boots buttoned right up with the horn hook, coats and all – as if going for a walk. Luckily we were at least spared the silk padded quilts under our coats and the *valenkis* (felt overboots) we wore in winter, but it was still dreadfully hot and stuffy to sleep in.

We dozed fitfully, disturbed by strange sounds: an approaching roar, like a great wave, feet running, shouts and calls. Then lorries came grinding up the hill and the yelling got louder and louder.

Nannie tiptoed in. Then Mamma. They whispered together.

'I hope they don't wake the children,' said Nannie.

The roar came right up to the house, then died away up the hill. Short crackling whacks followed, and then silence.

Next morning we heard that Papa had been on guard all night with a gun, pacing the garden. That sounded very exciting, and somehow reassuring too.

'Was it loaded? Did you shoot?'

Next day General Wrangel and his Army came marching in to save us. He was a great friend and often came to visit us. Alexander went around with shining eyes, quite bemused, for the General gave him his signed photo and a small white-blue-red flag, which he then hung over his bed, next to his icons.

The White Army brought order again, and hanged those who had committed crimes, like throwing the officers into the port of Yalta, rocks tied to their feet. The diver, let down to identify them, went mad, as they stood swaying around him. There was much discussion about this, also about the hanging.

The grown-ups forgot all about us again, and we listened as we played in a corner, and later tried to imagine whether it would have looked like Alexander's tin soldiers standing at the bottom of the bath. But Mamma was shocked when we explained and said:

'Nobody dies any more: they are always killed.'

The sailors on guard at the nearby lighthouse often sat in our kitchen and then the maids squealed more than usual. But their friendship with the sailors kept the bad ones away on the night Papa had stood on guard. They came to ask him to tell General Wrangel that they had done us no harm, which Papa did. Lists had been found, carrying all the names of those who were to be killed that night. Even baby Missie was included. We were thrilled and felt very important not to have been overlooked, tiny as we were.

People began to smile again. Spring was coming, and the air smelt of flowers, of earthy greenery and salt. In the mornings we could go down to the beach once more. The waves were lazy ripples, and splashed with a lapping swish over the smooth flat grey stones, sprinkled with tiny pointed or dishlike white shells. It was difficult to run, for they crunched and slid away under our sandals. Mamma swam out and we held on to her shoulder like small fish. It was wonderful to look back at the steep coast, houses and gardens climbing over each other as if to get a better view.

Afternoon walks with Nannie were resumed too. They often took us down a wide high road to Aloupka, near Yalta, where our equally small cousins, the Worontzoff grandchildren, lived. Sometimes we stayed for the night, and I slept on a green silky sofa, turned around against the wall, as snug as any cot.

Mamma photographed us all astride on the great stone lions, which flanked the wide steps leading down to the sea. Uncle Georgie Scherbatoff-Stroganoff, who was Uncle Oleg's younger brother and about fifteen, helped to hold us on.

Mamma said we and our cousins spoke the English our respective Nannies did, Jim and Nina, Uncle Adishka's children, having a special twang called 'Cockney', like their Miss Macklin. Our Miss Menzies, who was Scottish, would not allow us to copy them, although she was also very fond of dear 'Mackie'. Leonide and Sandra Wiazemsky, Uncle Dimitri's small children, spoke a rather affected 'Oxford' English, thought Nannie.

Walking down the long high road one day, Alexander and I lagged behind, clinging to the wooden telegraph poles to listen to their mysterious humming. We thought it was the sound of messages being sent, the buzz of distant voices urgently calling.

The golden road led away into the sky, and it was suddenly darkened by a cloud of dust rising from a green mass of soldiers, their helmetpoints and bicycles glinting in the sun as they came. Germans!

Panic stricken, we ran breathlessly to catch up with Nannie so far ahead, pushing the pram, Irina good as gold at her side.

We were not fast enough. They were on us as we dashed across the road. Alexander managed to reach the other side, but with a thud and a crash, I found myself lying in the ditch, entangled in spikes and whirring wheels. The sky was the wrong way up and there was a big bump growing on my head, cuts and bruises everywhere.

An orange-bearded, red-faced burly man, smelling strongly of boots and uniform and a hot day, set me carefully on my feet and mopped the cuts with a large chequered handkerchief.

'Ach, ich war immer ein Unglückskind!' (Ach, I was always a child of misfortune), he moaned, while flustered Nannie reassured him, and the whole company stood around in a sea of bicycles and sympathy.

Later Nannie told Mamma:

'I never thought my first words to a German after this terrible War, would be words of consolation.'

There were now rumours that the Tzar Nicholas II, the Empress and all those lovely children had been murdered by the Bolsheviks. It seemed too awful to be believed, and at first the Empress Dowager would not accept this as true.

With great difficulty, it appeared, King George V of England, first cousin of the Tzar and nephew of Empress Marie Feodorovna, who was Queen Alexandra's sister, had succeeded in persuading the Prime Minister Lloyd George to send a warship to the Crimea to save his aunt. When it arrived, she refused to embark unless all those who wished to leave were taken along too. As they had received the order to save the Empress, the British Fleet was only too glad to stretch a point, and send in as many ships as were available to embark a large quantity of refugees, including us, without asking for further permission.

So we were leaving! Leaving Russia.

There was a tremendous surge of packing, and the maids streamed wet with tears.

'Only essentials,' said Papa.

'I will abandon what we can't take on the pier, then,' said Mamma.

'No toys?'

'One each and a few books. Lesson-books, too.'

One trunk was filled with that boring 'Benger's Food', for Missie was only two and there was a baby on the way. I secretly hoped he would be called Tommy, but Alexander declared he would prefer a donkey with a brush to keep it clean. A baby would be too small to play with, and no use to anyone just now.

'But you couldn't take a donkey along either.'

'Perhaps they will let me have one later,' he sighed hopefully.

The fox-terrier Billy, black patch over one eye, his head cocked on one side, followed us around everywhere dolefully. We were very sad to leave him, although the maids promised to be good to him. He could not come with us because of something called 'quarantine'.

Mamma did not have to leave her trunks on the pier after all, for there was plenty of room in the hold of the ship waiting for us. Sailors ran up and down thin ladders, as agile as monkeys, as they balanced huge boxes on their shoulders.

On a sunny April day in 1919, we embarked on the *Princess Ena*.

We tore up and down in great excitement, for all our cousins were here too and we had never been on a ship before. Distracted Nannies could easily be evaded. They only found us hours later, preferences firmly established as we sat on our favourite sailor's knee, sniffing the lovely smell of tar-soap and rough serge, as we shared their thick black tea out of enamel pots, and crunched dog biscuits.

Nannie said our doll-like appearance in broad-brimmed floppy hats and our English surprised the crew.

I became the special pet of the burly Commander, Commodore Unwin. Sitting on his knee, I rubbed my face against his coat and played with his medal ribbons.

'What is this one?'

'The V.C.'

Alexander explained it to me afterwards: it was the same as in 'Misunderstood', where the Dying Child holds the hand of a War Hero, a 'V.C.', and does not even cry, although we wept with rapture at the harrowing tale. Alexander said a 'V.C.' was something quite special, universally respected and admired.

There were no more lessons, no more rules. We chased each other all over the ship, and then stood at the stern to watch the ink-blue waves churning into a wide creamy fan behind us. Nothing had ever been such fun before.

Presently we entered the Bosphorus, which seethed with busy little steamers, chugging up and down. They hooted to one another, ending in a dismal wail in the far distance across the sea, like strange birds calling. Stocky towers were set at regular intervals all along the coast. Alexander said they were fortifications for or against the Turks. They looked just like his treasured toy fortress, regretfully left behind.

Irina and Alexander were taken to visit the Mosque of Haghia Sophia, the largest church in Constantinople.

They went ashore in a tiny motor boat leaping out of a tail of spray, soon shrunk to the size of an insect as it wound its way among the curling puffs of smoke from other boats. The town lay waiting for them like a great humming bee-hive, spiked with sharp towers.

When they returned, they told us they had seen the bloody hand of the Sultan, high on the wall of St. Sophia, when he rode in over the pile of corpses after the siege of Constantinople.

It seemed to us, the Turks must have been like the Bolsheviks, smashing and killing wherever they came.

Calling it Constantinople, Visantiya or Novy-Rim (New Rome), grown-ups became dreamy when they spoke the magic name. They deplored Constantinople's squalor and dilapidation, but nothing could dim its golden associations in their minds.

Many refugees on board our ships disembarked on the Prinkipo Islands in the Marmara Sea. Later, many of the children were to catch virulent influenza (the 'ispanka') and die, leaving their unfortunate parents with nothing but a snapshot of their graves to remember them by.

Papa still owned estates in Lithuania, which had become an independent country. We were therefore not quite as 'refugee' as so many others, and were allowed to proceed to Malta. In a smaller group, we transferred to a ship called the *Bermudion*. We were soon told she had been twice torpedoed, salvaged and put to sea again. So the solid water beneath us was not so dependable after all! At any moment we might suddenly be swallowed in a huge gulp, as in the story of the town of Kitez.

The *Bermudion* was probably not too sea-worthy anyway, for as the journey proceeded, we tossed up and down on choppy waves and all the grown-ups disappeared from sight, violently sick.

For several days, no one came to dress or look after us. Our Finnish nursery-maid, Eva, would burst in with a pan of sticky porridge, plump it down on my knees, and with a handkerchief to her mouth, vanish as suddenly as she had come, like a Jack-in-the-Box. I then ladled the stuff into Missie's mouth, sweeping it up from under her chin and behind her ears with the large tin spoon. Stranded high on our cot, we played and then slept a lot, until huge chains rattled and there was much shouting and the sound of running feet.

We had reached Malta.

The sea was smooth at last, blue as the sky, sparkling under brilliant sunshine, the world washed clean. The streets led steeply up the hill and straight down to the sea again between tall houses. No gardens were to be seen, although we discovered one later. The proprietor's son at the hotel where we stayed was called Harry Cini. He was very kind and showered us with sweets and presents. He would help to feed us, and soon wanted to marry our pink-cheeked Eva.

We went for long walks every day. Guinea-pigs and flowers were sold at every street corner, and we gazed into the cages at the furry piebald little blobs and fed them salad leaves. The mules wore pointed straw hats adorned with artificial flowers or red pompoms, holes in the brim letting their long ears through, so as to twitch the flies away. Like a river swirling at the bottom of a deep chasm, singing processions under waving flags flowed down the narrow streets. Little boys in surplices shook bunches of tinkling bells, and statues of many-coloured Saints wobbled and jerked past. One of them depicted a Saint being bitten by a lion, but it could not have hurt much, for he smiled cheerfully.

A kind English lady gave Alexander a painted model of a Maltese boat. We had never seen anything so beautiful, but he only let us look at it. No touching.

Irina and Alexander seemed to be constantly locked in combat. Nannie said: 'Like cat and dog.' One night, they upset the lamp and the curtains of their room burst into flames. They rushed downstairs in their nightgowns, right into the dining-room where Mamma and Papa were having dinner with the British Navy.

The officers all ran to put out the fire and then stuffed Irina and Alexander with ices and cakes, so luckily they were not punished, as was usually the case when the fright was big enough. Besides, Harry Cini was so fond of Eva he would never let his father be cross with any of us for long.

Later Eva returned to Malta to marry him, and one baby after another was called after us.

2

We then left for France.

'Will we never stay anywhere as long as in Charaks again?' we asked sadly, for two years there had deluded us into thinking it was to be for good. A home.

We were now going to Beaulieu, and were soon installed in a pretty house set in a garden full of palm trees and sweet-smelling feathery mimosa.

Kind ladies kept us painting pictures all afternoon and when we got home, Mamma was in bed and there was a new baby.

He was kept in a wicker cot, often placed on two chairs in the garden. Missie and I had not seen him properly yet, so we climbed on to the chairs to get a good look. His nose was round and pink like a button, but quite soft to touch. Something over-balanced, and down we went: chairs, cot, baby and all. Nannie came running and there was a fearful commotion. The baby rolled cleverly into the hard hood among lots of pillows and was not hurt at all, but he howled so loudly, we were put to bed in broad daylight as a punishment.

Alexander was right: a donkey would have been easier to handle.

Both Grandmothers were often with us. Gaga Wiazemsky was tall and slim, and Grannie Wassiltchikoff soft and podgy. Their eyes were sad when they smiled at us, for their sons were the uncles we prayed for, who had been killed.

They would bring us presents, some carefully chosen toy, and jackets and caps they had knitted. They also read fairy tales to us by the hour. Aunt Lili was like a Tsarevna in one of them: huge black eyes and ivory pale. She had been married to my godfather, Uncle Boris, who had been killed. 'So young!' the grown-ups would say, but she was really twenty-two which seemed quite old to us. She was gentle and still, and never smiled, but she often came with us on our walks and picnics, and we were glad, for it was as if she visited us from another world.

The Nannies would not explain what had happened. Alexander implied darkly that it must have been worse than anything we could imagine, but we were too small to be told.

Grandpapa, Papa's father, 'The General' Nanny called him, was a grumpy old gentleman with a square white yellow-streaked beard. It smelled of tobacco and tickled when he kissed us. He would often come to play chess with Alexander and draughts with me. We had to do it in turns to please him. He snorted and chewed before pushing his pawn, and nearly always won. Afterwards we had nothing to say to him and were relieved when we could run out into the garden again and go on with our own games.

There were other grown-ups around us, but they seemed blurred in outline, like trees or houses from a fast-moving train. We were aware of them, but they did not catch our attention for long enough, and yet we understood everything instinctively without having to be told. As if we had known many things before: why people felt the way they did, and what they would do. The reasoning and explaining came much later, and then nothing was as clear again.

In great secrecy, Alexander told me of his plan: he would build a house in the middle of a field, mining it previously with a keg of gunpowder, to which a fuse and a long thread were attached. Lenin and Trotsky would be lured to it with the promise of secret information. Then they would blow up with a great bang, and no longer would awful things happen in Russia.

The sound of lorries at night still gave us nightmares, but walking with Nannie, we were sometimes passed by American Army vehicles, full of laughing soldiers. They threw us chewing-gum, and waved to us. Nannie took it away at once, but it did show us that nice men also drove around in lorries.

One morning we heard Irina had run away, and Miss Scott went to find her. We thought it very daring of her, just like the heroine of a book she was reading.

Tall for her nine years, with long black hair and a lovely peach-coloured skin, Irina was very alert, wide-awake and had been the centre of attention until we and our little cousins came crowding along on her heels. By then so much else was going on, that beyond a pat on the head and a quick kiss, there was no time for her. Perhaps she resented being pushed back into the nursery, for our games bored her, and she was only interested in the grown-up world; perhaps Miss Scott was too strict, and lessons never interested her anyway.

Towards lunchtime she was brought back in deep disgrace. She had left a letter to say she was going to stay with out Scherbatoff cousins in Nice, so Miss Scott took a tram there, and walked back to meet her. Afterwards Irina told us she had been followed by a man with an open knife in his hand, so it was a good thing Miss Scott had found her.

'Your poor Mamma, with all the things she has to cope with! How could you go and do such a wicked thing?' said Miss Scott. We did not quite understand why she had done it either, for she was happy to be back and enjoyed the fuss. Besides, Mamma now took Irina with her whenever possible.

Miss Scott was leaving soon anyway.

There was to be another journey: to Germany this time.

'Why Germany, since they are enemies?'

'Because Papa must go to Lithuania, which is quite close to it.'

The family house in Yourburg, near Tilsitt, had been burned down by the Germans in 1914, and the estates of Yourburg and Tauroggen were to be confiscated. Because of all he had done for Lithuania in previous years, the new Government had let Papa know that as far as he was concerned, this measure would be put off for two years, so as to enable him to provide for his big family. Besides ourselves, there were Grandpapa and Granny, Uncle Nikolaï and Aunt Sonia (Oleg's widow), and her four girls.

The newly declared independence of the Baltic States was still shaky. Perhaps they were far enough from the Bolsheviks to get away with it, but Mamma did not want to return there until this was certain, preferring to stay within reach of Papa at a seaside resort in East Prussia.

She was worried about him, for he had suffered a sort of nervous collapse in the Crimea, just before we left. The loss of Russia affected him like a lethal wound, sapping his strength.

At last we reached Rauschen by the sea near Königsberg. It turned out to be quite a nice place. In the afternoon the guests at our hotel ate huge fluffy cakes, which tasted of gritty flour and sweetish foam, a congealed cherry or two poised precariously on the surface. We could not understand a word they said, and Nannie sighed deeply to be in Germany.

Presently Mamma arranged for us to go for long drives in a lovely creaking carriage over sandy roads winding among pine trees, and soon we were as happy as crickets again.

A great turkey blocked our way to the beach, but Alexander bravely shooed him away with a stick. The beach stretched forever along the grey-green sea and was quite deserted. We made sand-castles and waited for Papa.

One day, horrid boys attacked Alexander, and for years I could not forgive myself for running away and leaving him in the lurch, but he forgot all about it. They threw stones and jeered, shouting:

'Russland kaputt!'

But Nannie said: 'Deutschland is kaputt too.'

We were all getting over whooping-cough and still whooped away. Irina would say sad things about herself: 'I will not live till morning, for my throat will tear!' Missie went purple coughing, but she hardly ever cried when there was a good reason for doing so. We clutched at every second tree for support, retching violently, and the Germans stared and stared at us until we had finished.

In the small hotel, Irina always knew who slept with whom, because of the shoes set in pairs at night in front of every door. She was getting very inquisitive.

At times there were violent storms, with crackling flashes and rumbling thunder. We wondered whether God was moving furniture around in His heavens. We thought He must be so clever to know all our needs – so very useful, too. Alexander worried about St. George, for how could he kill a dragon, since Saints only existed after Jesus Christ, and there were no dragons then. He knew this from visiting the prehistoric animals in the Berlin Zoo Museum, while I was ill with earache.

Papa joined us at last, and I went for long walks with him. More than one of us at a time tired him.

Presently we were all on our way again to a place called Baden-Baden, which sounded ridiculous until we got used to it. At first we lived in a hotel like a huge white cake called Brenners-Kurhof. We made great friends with the lift-boy, who wore a beautiful blue uniform, plastered with shiny buttons. He went all the way down to the dark and smelly hole under the lift, to fish out Missie's golliwog, hurled there by the Baby. Missie then wanted him to bath her, but Nannie did not think this such a good idea.

Baby Georgie had become Mamma's favourite now, which we understood. He looked sweet in his white rabbit fur jacket and cap, and said funny things. We kissed and hugged him constantly, for he was so soft and appetizing. He did not mind that a bit. He also smashed all our toys and was far too small to whack, so we could do nothing about it.

After much searching, Mamma found a house, a lovely house at last! She told us all about it: there was a view, and a large garden with enormous trees. It was being cleaned and painted, and we were to move in at once.

Flanked by two squat white towers, the single-storeyed house had a wide balcony thick with wistaria like a moustache.

Krippenhof reminded Mamma of the Crimea: Livadia, Ay Todor. For us the soft scent of wistaria and azaleas in flower pervaded our childhood from then on, later to bring whiffs of spring and cheerful memories.

Rambler roses drooped on the hill behind the house and caught at our clothes when we ran to pick raspberries in the hedges. Great cedars and a red beech stood on the lawn sloping towards the town and tempted us up, like monkeys, to their topmost branches. Escaping once from Alexander, I climbed one in no time, but he was hot on my heels. Edging away along a thick branch, I can still remember the vast view of Baden-Baden spreading below, its patchwork of roofs and twinkling lights at dusk, clearly framed between the leaves. Anger changed to horror on Alexander's face peering out of the tree, as the branch carrying me dipped, and gently dropped me safe on the ground, slithering down the slope.

Clutching tall glass jugs, we would run out in turns before lunch to pump icy fresh water from the spring in the wood, just outside the wide wooden gate. One of us held the jugs, while the other swung out on it, for it was too heavy for us to push.

Returning from church one Sunday, nose in the air as I guessed at the weather, I collided violently with the voluted iron corner of a protruding letter-box. Too stunned to cry, I trailed home behind the others, but at lunch, as she looked down the long table past the gaily-talking guests, Mamma noticed I was not eating.

'What is it?'

'I banged my head and now I can't see you any more.'

I was rushed to bed in her room, and then Mamma sat for many hours in the dark, a chink of light falling on her book through the drawn curtains, while the doctor came and went, and ice-packs were put on my head.

Meanwhile I lay half-conscious, at times aware of the golden gleam of her 'Breguet' clock, and the tiny cog wheels turning behind the rounded glass door, as it gently ticked the time away.

The numerous Russian colony, converging on Baden-Baden after the Revolution like migrating storks, brought colour and life to the daily scene, which would otherwise have been reduced to a crop of elderly couples taking the waters, or walking their dogs.

In later years, the small town would never forget this period, which seemed a reminder, a flickering renewal of those happy pre-revolutionary days, when Prince Menschikoff drove his Troïka of white horses down the Lichtentalerallee. Tourgenieff lived opposite the Brenners' Park-Hotel, and a Grand-Duke travelled with his Italian fountain, set up to play each time anew in front of his windows. Still more surprisingly, his personal doctor never moved without his own grand piano, 'as if Germany could not have provided him with one' people sniffed, reluctantly impressed by the grandiose lavishness of it all.

In the 19th century, a number of resorts in Germany were adorned with Russian churches. Either a Grand Duchess married abroad, with a church as part of her dowry, or as in Baden-Baden, Russian tourists soon collected the necessary funds, for, eager travellers as they were, they nevertheless could not bear to be without one for long.

As the wave of refugees rolled over Western Europe these churches became centres around which they converged, and in Baden-Baden émigré life was soon entirely organised around theirs.

Surrounded by a small enclosure, it stood like a much-loved toy. The star-dotted blue onion dome carried a twin-barred golden cross, anchored by light chains, as if it might fly away. Inside, behind the golden ikonostas, deep voices boomed in incantation or prayer, answered by waves of soaring song from the 'kliros', the recess, where the choir stood, Mamma's mellow contralto at times clearly discernible.

The members of the choir were all friends, and they greatly enjoyed both the rehearsals and the long services, which seemed to give them some inner joyous strength to face the waning hope of return to Russia which had sustained them so far. Love of their country was part of the marrow of their bones, and deeply attuned to the orthodox religion.

On Sundays, and especially at Easter, the sound of pealing bells hung in the air around the windows of our house high on its hill, quite separated from the Catholic churches in the valley they proceeded from.

We would then trudge to the Russian one down the Lichtentalerallee, day after day, all through the orthodox Holy Week, dawdling on our way to sniff the blazing yellow and reddish-orange clumps of flowering azaleas. Great banks of rhododendrons gave an air of luxury and opulence to the ankle-deep river Oos as it trickled over moss-covered paving. It was a river in proportion to a child, impossible to drown in, even boasting of a succession of step-high waterfalls, which were spanned at frequent intervals by lacy ironwork bridges, draped in wistaria. Sometimes these were even wide enough for two grown-ups to cross abreast. We leaned over, throwing bread-crumbs to tiny fish.

The long services taxed our strength, and Alexander and I, growing fast, after an hour or so on our feet, would keel over, pea-green, without previous warning. Seated outside on some step or tombstone, we then recovered gradually. There was not much sympathy proffered or expected, for we were supposed to pull ourselves together and never complain.

Eight-years-old was considered old enough to reason, and therefore mature for confession. In fact on my eighth birthday I had been discovered dissolved in tears, suddenly realising the weight of passing years, and the appalling fact that all those I loved would die one day, so there was something to it.

On Ash Wednesday we tore around the house, asking everybody's forgiveness for misdemeanours. The rule was 'to be at peace with the world' before confession, but we had discovered that we were not scolded for past misdemeanour if we went about it with enthusiasm.

Queuing up for confession in the dark church, head bent, clutching a melting candle, one suddenly felt humble and sincerely sorry for unkindness 'in thought or deed' (those ominous words), truly understanding 'God's judgment' was a state of being, like a dark cloak, to be thankfully laid aside now.

We returned home as night fell, subdued but relieved. As our spirits revived, we jostled and teased each other, hard put to remain sinless, even until communion next morning, and for once glad to get to bed early.

Next day we were careful not to swallow any water while brushing our teeth and, skipping breakfast, we donned our best smocked dresses and Alexander his sailor suit.

But once, abandoning all control, he ate some 'Passcha' before leaving. Gripped by remorse, he went up to the altar to confess again. He emerged soon after red as a beetroot, and went to kneel three times in front of the central icon, while all the congregation watched. We were so sorry for him, but nobody commented on it. Later the priest told Mamma he thought it would make him remember that a vow is a holy thing.

At last the red curtain jerked back, the golden gates were flung open, and we advanced to communion, arms crossed over our chest. Delicious gulp, and a wave of beatitude engulfed us. The Holy Week culminated in the Resurrection Service on Saturday night, starting with a burst of joyous singing which unfortunately sometimes trailed off into hesitant discordance, for the hymns were seldom sung and very intricate. We were close to bursting into untimely giggles.

Everybody then kissed everybody else without discrimination and we returned home to a copious spread, joined by guests of all ages, including of course our cousins. Groggy with weariness though we were, we would not have missed it for anything.

Mamma then added another small Fabergé egg from her collection to our chains.

With money melting away as the months went by, Russian spending was much reduced. Ever more incongruous jobs had to be accepted. Émigré children thronged to two schools, the Realschule and Gymnasium. They often achieved top marks, for no vicissitudes could dampen Russian passion for knowledge.

Smiling, plump, energetic Mme Pouschine organised picnics for the young, ending in exciting and terrifying games of 'Cossacks and Robbers', where one team searched for and chased the other through the woods.

Children were included in all the entertainments, and in winter joined in theatrical performances of fairy-tales.

Mamma collected all the available musical talent, and one house-concert followed another. Papa took no active part, but his brother Nikolaï played the cello to Mamma's accompaniment, and we were often allowed to stay up and listen. Bazaars, lotteries, balls, mushroomed in help of poorer refugees, and soon organisations in their aid were to become a major preoccupation.

In Krippenhof, a room in one of the towers was at our disposal. Our cats bred kittens there; cocoons, carefully bedded on salad leaves in perforated cigar boxes, burst into miraculous butterflies; seedlings sprouted in window-boxes for our individual patches of garden, on which our names were sown in water cress.

In fact, there was never an instant of boredom, so it always seemed odd to us when children hung around listlessly: as if a day was not a very limited time at one's disposal, starting with the extraordinary exhilaration of waking in the morning, feeling part of the world, the sun shining into one's heart; impervious to Nannie's gentle nagging.

When our Miss Menzies returned to her Scottish family, whom she had not seen for years, Mamma wrote her a recommendation as for a subaltern returning from the front line of battle: '. . . Cool-headed and resourceful when in danger, tireless under stress, indomitable courage...'

We missed her fearfully at first, then got distracted with the advent of Baby Georgie and Nannie Hillyard.

'Fräuleins' – which was what one called a nursery governess – came and went. One of them barely had time to smack us in the face before she was out again. The Swiss tutor, Monsieur Falletti, was expected to concentrate on Alexander. We had inherited him from the Gortchacoffs, and later they were amazed to hear what a saintly halo had grown around their mischievous heads, for according to M. Falletti 'Constantin et Michel' could do no wrong. It took us a long time to discover that they were quite human after all. Considering gastronomy part of a well-rounded education, Monsieur Falletti would take off with his pupil for copious meals in expensive restaurants. But when Papa got the bills, this practice was abruptly discontinued.

Soon there was constant talk of 'inflation', everybody counting in billions and trillions, clean notes given to us to play with as they became worthless from day to day. Gaga sent me a five-franc note for my birthday: I exchanged it for one million Marks and acquired a perfect 'Schwarzwald' doll's house.

There was no longer any question of buying Krippenhof and we moved to a small house on the erstwhile estate of the Prince Menchikoff who had shaken Baden-Baden out of water-sipping Kurort placidity so many years before.

Our rooms were small and musty, padded and upholstered in red and white 'Toile de Jouy': one felt as if inside a cushion. When all was quiet, mice scuttled cheekily up and down the hangings, almost within reach. We did not mind if we could see them, but felt uneasy when they nibbled and gnawed in the dark.

The garden ran even more wild than around our beloved Krippenhof. Roses trailed over disused buildings and hung in swathes, mixed with honeysuckle, from the lower branches of great cedars.

Exploring an old barn, Missie and I unearthed a toy motor-car, once painted bright-red, and a large elephant on wheels, shedding straw from mortal wounds in its woolly, moth-eaten hide. In spite of its tendency to tip forward, we raced each other down the steep drive. Both our steeds were quite uncontrollable, even when guiding the front wheels with our feet. Weak with laughter, we usually ended in a heap at the lower gate, our ankles scraped raw and bleeding.

This house soon closed down too, and we then spent some weeks in a tiny village perched near Lake Constance, the 'Bodensee', beyond Meersburg, a town like a toy model: clock-tower astride the arched entrance, fortified walls and all. The little train puffed, rattled and shrilly piped its way past half a dozen hamlets to our destination: Heiligenberg.

We were installed in the local inn, baths became a weekly event, but nearby there was a 'Schloss' towering over the spreading valley – anchored to the hill by its drawbridge like a ship stranded after some cataclysmic flood. Soon Papa and Mamma made great friends with the family which lived there.

The place seethed with a dozen grandchildren and their friends – all under or around ten years of age as we were, governesses and tutors in imposing numbers; we were delivered into their care and never saw much of our parents again as long as the holidays lasted.

They were, however, at a loss to understand why we returned every evening beaming, but in a sorry state of disrepair: cut and bruised, our clothes torn and dirty, for hardly were grown-ups out of sight or ear-shot, before hostilities erupted. Quite without bitterness, war had been declared. A few cousins joined our side to balance the rival factions, but beyond this initial concession, no mercy was proffered or expected.

We slid down the steep lawns on sofa cushions in hot pursuit of, or full flight from the enemy, trying to reach the underground passage below the hill, where in the dark, one side pelted the other with fine white stinging sand. Armed with pillows requisitioned from innumerable guest-rooms, ambushes lurked at dark corridor turnings. On Thursday, the great 'Rittersaal', across whose polished parquet floor admiring tourists plodded in felt slippers all other days of the week, was handed over to the 'dear children' to play in. In hobnailed boots, the two factions galloped from opposite ends of the vast hall to collide slithering in laughing heaps in the middle.

Next morning carpenters repaired the damage, and visitors shuffled about for a peaceful week again.

Picnics around bonfires were organised whenever possible, and baked potatoes, blackened to a turn, were first tossed in play, then hurled in earnest to smear as they landed with a dull smack.

'Kinder, Ruhe!' was the mild admonishment, holidays and doting grandparents ensuring impunity. But every now and then, an uncle or an aunt strode in and removed a combatant to cool his heels in solitude. For a while, truce was then maintained, and the hatchet buried for some harmless pastime: haymaking, or riding pillion on the Secretary's motor-cycle.

It all ended one day in a huge birthday party, towering cakes, and presents for all.

It was an unforgettable and wild holiday, which for us was never to be repeated again. When had we paused for thought in all our rampaging games? . . . There had always been someone to clean up behind us. We well knew this was a luxury beyond reach from then on . . .

3

Grown-ups and children all sat on any available chair, crowding together, satchels and bags packed ready at hand.

'Close the door.' Silence. A short prayer. 'Cross yourselves; the youngest must stand up first.'

Although this was the usual custom before any trip, we faced a momentous journey, for we were leaving Germany for good and heading for Paris, where our cousins had settled.

Sad as we were to go, the empty house disowned us already; the choice of what to take and what to leave had kept our minds off it until then. Only one toy basket had been allowed – all other playthings to be given away!

'It will make other children happy': meagre consolation.

'We couldn't take anything when we left Russia,' we proudly told the little ones. Missie was too small to remember and Georgie felt for ever thwarted by being born after emigration and thereby deprived of a 'past'. However, when talking to strangers, he would invent harrowing tales, as long as we were not within earshot to cramp his style.

For some unfathomable reason, the journey ground to a halt in Strasbourg. The trunks which had not been left in storage at 'Devant's' in Baden-Baden, waited for us somewhere, while Mamma with Nannie and five children settled in the Hotel National opposite the station. Papa had gone on ahead to prepare for our arrival.

Our windows looked out on to the Place de la Gare, shrouded in November fog, heavy with soot and smoke. The trams moaned and ground around the turn, to the insistent tinkle of the mushroom-like bell under the conductor's tapping toe. Street lamps winked and dipped in gusts of wind and rain.

Nannie at once reinstated the ordered routine of nursery life: long walks, lessons, tea and scones – or at a pinch, French brioches and madeleines.

Fresh air was a fetish, much encouraged by Mamma, who lived in dread of TB, that dragon in wait of youth, indiscriminately mowing down so many in previous generations. We would be marched off in any weather, sometimes boarding a tram to reach the canals on the outskirts of the town. It would bang along merrily at what seemed great speed, until the rod connecting the electric wires overhead jumped free with protesting sizzles. Quite unperturbed, his satchel with its scale of coloured tickets swinging as he leaped down, the conductor would cleverly jerk it back, bringing down a shower of sparks.

Reaching Paris at last, we moved into a small hotel on the Rue de l'Université. In the mornings, we bigger ones breakfasted at the corner bistro: a large bowl of delicious coffee, foaming hot milk and a long crisp ham sandwich smeared with mustard.

'Good clients!' said the owner admiringly.

I learned to play hopscotch in the courtyard with the little daughter of the neighbouring concierge, who was about my age.

There was a sense of waiting. Waiting for what? We did not know. Perhaps hope of return to Russia still put off final resignation. The months went by, and nothing seemed to get decided.

Meanwhile we frequently visited our grandmother and our cousins, meeting more and more Russian children, whose parents were friends of ours. An undefined line curiously divided those from Petersburg from the Muscovites, although they were for the most part related. The latter converged gradually in the suburb of Clamart, living in ever more reduced circumstances. Mamma was, however, often exasperated at their easy acceptance of symbols of penury, such as drinking out of jam-pots instead of glasses ... 'When both cost exactly the same ninety centimes!'

Most of the Petersburg group were still flanked by their nannies, some of them would stay on for ever with 'their' family without pay, sturdy support against the buffets of fate.

The Moscow children hooted with derision at our smocked dresses, over-polite manners and what they called our 'accent': 'Anglichani!' they jeered. But soon all clan rivalry would be forgotten in boisterous round games, choral singing and charades.

Long walks took us to the Luxemburg park, past a succession of 'Défense de ...' signs and rows of tawdry shops filled with icons and Fabergé baubles, acquired from pawnshops nearby, last resort for so many émigrés.

But we much preferred to cross the river to the Tuileries where shiny chestnuts burst from their shells on hitting the dusty ground, as if delivered perfectly wrapped for our benefit. Children ran through the neat piles of fallen leaves when the guards looked away, or squawked loudly at the ready slap of 'excédée' (exasperated) French mothers sharply snapping: 'Tu veux une gifle?'

The hum of distant traffic and pungent smell of petrol surrounded the square of gardens as if it were an island. At one end the palaces turned pink, while at the other the Place de la Concorde shone golden in the blaze of setting sun: it was so beautiful, we could hardly imagine the guillotine slicing off so many heads in such a setting.

Then came the tired return. But once I tripped in my hoop and lay down flat under a huge oncoming green bus. Brakes screeched, frightened faces looked down from all sides. Picked up, shaken, brushed down, home we went.

Having lost all his remaining money in the inflation of the German mark, Papa returned ever more frequently to Lithuania. As the political situation there was still far from stable, it seemed wiser for the time being to leave us all in France, but drastic economy meant goodbye to Nannie whom we loved. From then on Mamma, whom we more than loved, filled our lives, indomitable defence while we found our feet in an alien world.

Green eyes, thick bronze hair (lightening to copper as the years passed) cascaded to her waist when she brushed it in the mornings. Her back straight, head held high, every moment of life seemed to her fraught with exciting adventure.

She never lost her zest for living, which also included an excellent appetite. She fought to maintain her waistline with sporadic fits of austerity: a milk day, a fruit day, loathing both.

As a girl, her lovely complexion and smooth 'décolleté' – much appreciated before the first World War – made up for irregular features, too wide mouth with strong white teeth, indefinite nose – despair of so many Russians – and determined chin.

Her vitality and wide range of interests fascinated, sometimes exasperated – but never bored. She could turn from clownlike mimicry to deep and sincere sympathy for anyone meeting with injustice or misfortune, and searing inconsolable sorrow, when she lost someone she loved: her father, her brothers (especially Dimitri), and later – Alexander!

She was fearless, physically and morally, incapable of envy, hypocrisy, vanity or selfishness. But she could ride rough-shod, armed with the best intentions, over the susceptibilities of others.

We loved to hear stories of her childhood, and, as far as we were concerned, it did not diminish her authority in the least to hear that she had been rather a handful, often playing really naughty practical jokes.

In St. Petersburg in the early nineties, Countess Levachov, sipping tea with a circle of old ladies, was visited one afternoon by her small granddaughter, appearing for the ritual presentation and kiss.

With a deep bow, she removed a wide-brimmed straw hat in a mousquetaire-like flourish, and out hopped a group of startled frogs which had been nestling on her head, recently shaved after typhoid (a drastic measure, supposed to ensure luxuriant growth of hair after strong fevers).

Several years later a large Eskimo dog she owned, which only answered to the shrill blast of a policeman's whistle, escaped.

Ignoring the rule that no young girl should leave the house unaccompanied, she rushed out and jumped into the first passing *isvostchik* (open cab). Holding on to the burly coachman's shoulder, she stood behind him, a flying mane of flaming hair streaming behind her, and dashed through the streets of the capital, blowing her whistle.

Commotion, traffic jams! The police brought her home insisting they would find her dog, but would she please hand over her whistle:

'Barishnya (Miss), one cannot do such things!'

Her father, A.D.C. of the Emperor, Member of the Council of the Empire, Minister of the Apanages (Crown lands), was fascinated by his gay, violent, clever, mischievous and so warm-hearted little daughter, and spoiled her greatly. But he was also the only authority she recognised. One word:

'*Dilka, dovolno!*' (Enough), would stop her in mid-air.

Her mother, gentle, erudite, treated with great respect and loving consideration by all her family, had completely retired from social life at a comparatively early age, thus avoiding any friction with her husband, so charming and brilliant. Also for others.

She presided over the education of the children, as the household moved at regular intervals from the capital to the country and back again.

English nurses, French Governess and a Swiss tutor; a German maid. They were engaged to ensure that all three languages would be spoken at once and in that order: nursery English, literary French and rather rocky German. Perhaps also to restrain and temper violent, often contradictory temperaments and excessive (according to Western standards) intensity of feeling, latent in most Russians.

Music, catechism and reading were taught in the nursery. All three brothers and Mamma then went to Gymnasiums, girls and boys separate but all in uniform. They were expected to finish with gold medals, which they did.

Discipline was rigid, both at school and at home, to counterbalance privilege and luxury. There was a certain emphasis on ceremony, which was considered important to fix things in one's mind and breed respect.

Still far from the era of apologetic authority, they were preparing for active and responsible leadership, taught from childhood to face any challenge and to love and serve their country. But national conceptions and aims were kept to politics, people being treated as individuals and never lumped into nations.

Heads no longer rolled at a king's whim. Secure in their position, their duties clearly defined, there was no need of 'status' confirmation, and this ensured spiritual independence of opinion, a detachment which went hand in hand with a certain indifference of the soul to material belongings – to stand them in good stead when their fortunes took a downward dive.

The more sophisticated pre-revolutionary French aristocracy seems to have treated God as a highly esteemed ally, deserving consideration and even filial devotion in return for furthering their fortunes and advancement. This was not at all the case in Russia, where religion was a sincere and essential spiritual and ethical basis of conduct, however fallible one might be as individual sinner.

This attitude did not change in the least with emigration or reversed circumstances, but their careful training which had made them incapable of subservience, of monotonous uncreative work, even of routine, left them singularly untalented for money-making.

Perhaps aware of this blind spot, and in view of the fact that Mamma would inherit a considerable fortune in her own right, a school for orphans had been founded, and here, guided by her English Governess, she learnt to teach children hardly younger than herself. All their extra expenses were met out of her substantial pocket-money. But in spite of this, she failed to acquire a conception of the worth of money, and always freely spent whatever she had – though never on herself.

At home, Mamma and her brothers were expected to listen to and also talk to the prominent guests: historians, writers, travellers, statesmen. They were taken to see all major events, and frequently sent to concerts, the theatre and ballet.

A few years later, she finished the 'Conservatoire' for piano and singing, entering Oxford University in 1906. She was one of the first Russian girl-students there at the time, under the tuition of Miss Moberly and Miss Jourdain in St. Hugh's Hall. (These tutors were later to write that curious story set in Versailles, *An Adventure*.)

This well-ordered plan was interrupted and lightened by boisterous high spirits, culminating as they grew up in a blaze of balls and festivities during the winter season. Mamma then became the leader of a group of young friends, calling themselves the 'Schaïka' (gang). They would go together to dances and parties or organise their own. They formed an orchestra, each one playing his instrument, acted in theatricals and skated at balls in the depths of the winter. They sometimes adopted lame ducks on the way and gave them a whirl, as with Olga P. Mamma maintained that they never ganged up on others – nevertheless we could not help thinking how sad it must have been not to belong to that enterprising and brilliant group.

But we were happy to know she had had such a marvellous youth, before all the ensuing horrors broke over her head. We well knew this would all be out of the question for us.

She was passionately interested in the theatre, so her family breathed a deep sigh of relief when she became engaged to be married to a friend and colleague of her elder brother Boris.

My father's estates and main activities were centred in Lithuania. As the Governor was unmarried, Mamma found herself plunged into a range of duties far beyond her years: entertaining, charities, minority problems. One baby followed another, hardly slowing her down.

She got on beautifully with her delightful mother-in-law, but her congenital unpunctuality drove her poor father-in-law to distraction. As General of the Army, he was a martinet used to being obeyed. There was nothing to be done however: he strode up and down, watch in hand, shaking it significantly as she rushed in with an ever more unconvincing excuse and a lively tale to explain it all.

Grandmamma loved the soothing sound of gravel raked during the afternoon siesta. So after lunch, when the house retired to rest for a while, gardeners raked up and down within hearing. It did not really matter whether they did this then or early next morning, but years later, in New York, Russian émigrés now toiling at some menial job, would sigh nostalgically remembering this idiosyncrasy, symbol of another order: 'To think that your Grandmamma . . .'

In spite of total unpreparedness, in Russia World War I seemed to have broken out on a wave of euphoria and patriotism. Ladies leaving for the Front where they would work devotedly as Red Cross nurses, took their jewels along to be ready for receptions and balls in Berlin when the victorious Allies entered the capital of defeated Germany for the ensuing Peace Conference. The Congress of Vienna a century earlier seemed a reasonable precedent to fall back on.

With her usual drive and strong practical sense whenever others were concerned, Mamma reorganised and headed a hospital train on the North-Eastern Front throughout the War, barely interrupted by the advent of one baby after another. By-passing red tape, enrolling the highest authorities, she obtained the best equipment and conditions for both her wounded and her nurses. To all accounts her Red Cross Train functioned with remarkable efficiency in spite of the general débâcle.

Then came the murder of her brothers and of so many dear to her, the collapse of their entire world, departure and emigration, complicated by four small children and a fifth baby on its way.

Without money, without property abroad, she could count on no real support from Papa.

By nature already inclined to pessimism, he was never to recover from the defeat of emigration, which broke his self-confidence and impaired some vital spring. Not only had a useful and promising career been cut off in its prime – for he had been trained to statesmanship in the widest sense – but he had dedicated his whole life to service to his country. Member of the Douma for many years (and this was no sinecure), Papa had also been deeply involved in projects for the development of the outlying provinces of the Russian Empire, and after their marriage our parents travelled to French North Africa to study the systems of colonial government in practice there. In 1912 these were considered a three-scaled model of exemplary administration.

He enjoyed telling us of his journeys to Turkestan and Boukhara. All the local sheiks came to meet the official train bringing the inspecting commission: standing high in their saddles, whooping and brandishing scimitars, their brocaded and golden robes flashing in the setting sun, they galloped across the desert, like a many-coloured magic carpet.

But in Boukhara's half underground dungeons, prisoners stretched up their hands through iron railings in the pavement begging for food, for the cruel Emir still ruled as in the Middle Ages.

Papa had been a neighbour, disciple and colleague of the Minister Stolypine, whose reform programme extended in every direction. Above all his land reform would allow every peasant to own his individual plot. This was comparatively feasible in prosperous regions, such as the Ukraine, where no great acreage was required to feed a family. Whereas in greater Russia, although villagers already owned land communally, the main problem remained personal ownership, transferable to descendants, whatever the size of the family.

Co-operative agricultural centres seemed the answer. Owning property in Lithuania, Stolypine himself sponsored the model centre of Datnovo, which Papa had built there.

To apply the same principle all over Russia would have required a number of years for beside other problems, the backward peasants had to be taught to accept modern methods of exploitation.

Understandably, the Bolshevik opinion of Stolypine is that of 'a reactionary of the worst sort: dangling the devilish temptation of property before the eyes of the People, thereby distracting them from their Duty to the Community'.

No wonder they murdered him.

During the 1914–18 War Papa was a Staff Officer, and we were fascinated to hear that the enterprising young aviator Sikorsky had on occasion piloted him from one commanding post to another. Later Sikorsky emigrated to America, and apart from a passion for 'collecting' volcanoes (he visited them all!) applied his inventive mind to the improvement of helicopters, considering them to be the only form of aviation which would bring nothing but good to humanity.

Between the Revolutions of February and October 1917, Papa had still taken part (as layman) in the Holy Synod, which elected Patriarch Tichon as Head of the Orthodox Church. At the same time, he re-established the Red Cross as a 'Soviet' (i.e. Council), including minor employees in its board of Governors. He believed that the survival of these two poles of moral evolution would be the saving of Russia at some future date.

He never regretted lost possessions, to which he had not attached much value, except as field of action. 'Things' did not interest him, one or two beautiful objects within reach sufficing for aesthetic pleasure. But he now had to support his family. The income of his estates, which had been his for two years after the War, had melted in the inflation of the German mark, and although the Lithuanian Government had stretched their confiscation law in his favour, allowing the return of a small brewery, the endless transactions this involved wound through labyrinths of frustration.

At least the illusion of space in Lithuania gave him a feeling of being almost in Russia again, for he could never get used to foreign landscapes. He felt hemmed in by mountains or fences, and remained deeply nostalgic for the monotony of endless 'steppes', for Russians seem to feel that the soul flourishes in vast expanses. They are oppressed without 'prostor' (space) spreading around them, as if this brought them closer to the sky.

When at home, Papa was often either listless, or paced his room like a caged bear.

There was nothing we could do to make up for it.

Although rather remotely fond of us, he had viewed us as part of Russia's future. Now that this could not be the case, we were somehow no longer of much interest to him.

For women, the collapse of man-made laws holding the framework of Government together was perhaps less of a personal failure. Much more than institutions, Mamma regretted people, things, the country, and above all, Petersburg!

It was so much more than a town to them, part of the fabric of their lives. Papa maintained that the heart of Russia would always be Moscow, but Petersburg seemed a symbol of civilised Russia, their creation, their gift to the country.

However, she refused to accept defeat.

'Your mother, with her lion's voice, roared!' a friend once joked, for her ringing laugh and deep contralto voice had far-reaching resonance. With her joyous vitality and so generous nature, she often gave more than people were capable of receiving. Trained for a wider range of giving, her present restricted horizon must have irked her too, like a shrunken coat. Perhaps as an outlet, from then on, she would rear and defend us, like a lioness its young. We were slapped, bullied, taught . . . and deeply loved.

When we were ill or hurt, there was nothing she would not do for us, sitting through whole nights in our room, reading or sewing under a lowered lamp, for she could never be idle.

Soothing sounds of four-hand piano playing with Irina put us younger ones gently to sleep. Her intense interest and participation in all our concerns encouraged any spark of initiative.

Much in need of an outlet, we were wildly exuberant at times, and would invent games unsuited to the plushy, stuffy atmosphere of rented rooms: four chairs balanced precariously on a table, pushed energetically around the room, and we were a carriage pursued by galloping enemies, the driver cracking his improvised whip. But the rickety table collapsed in a heap of wreckage, and in consternation we tried to put the bits together with string and seccotine. An impossible task.

Another fascinating game was to chase one another in wild leaps from chair, to table, to bed, without putting a foot on the floor. Bumped and bruised, in gales of laughter we slithered between them, while neighbours rapped stormy protest on walls and ceiling.

Poor Mamma on her return would have to face the irate proprietor, patience all the shorter for the long overdue bill. The fact that Mamma then tried to rent one small house after another with surrounding garden, may well have been due to the fact that our progression through several provincial 'pensions de famille', where children and dogs are an oppressed minority on principle, was often fraught with such disasters.

These houses were chosen according to their view and the plumbing: the rest could be improved on afterwards.

The Russian priest would be called – even if the stay was short – and a crucifix and bowl of water placed on a table covered with a white cloth. Walking in procession from room to room, each one took up a stand next to his bed, and the new home was blessed and an icon hung in the corner of the dining-room.

We then took over.

Irina proved a talented cook, and I was soon entrusted with most of the odd jobs, such as taking up the inventory of the house we had just leased. (I was supposed to be endowed with 'an ordered mind', and these labels tend to stick for ever.)

Three bespectacled, ageless gentlemen in stiff collars arrived one morning to go over the terms of the contract. Tall for my eleven years, socks pulled up, satchel under one arm, I awaited them. Swallowing their initial surprise, they proceeded to dictate one item after another, which I dutifully jotted down in my school copybook. To be duly signed and countersigned by them and me.

I was also the packer, and plunged head foremost into huge deep trunks, barely reaching their bottom. They were relics from another world, brown and black, bound in copper and belted by painted stripes: the 'Family' colours.

When left to ourselves, we dressed up in Mamma's last 'Doucet' clothes, which she had not yet had the heart to discard, and huge 'Reboux' hats with trailing veils, mauve and green. We peered into the high glass, hanging in the dim corridor; startled to see ourselves so changed, suddenly beautiful and mysterious.

There was still some fine linen, embroidered with crowned initials, remains of Mamma's 'trousseau' – a word evoking brides, carriages, palaces – as in a fairy tale. We understood it must be precious, and soon I learnt to mend the thinning sheets, inserting huge squares with the help of a rickety child's sewing machine.

'She is clever with her hands. As good as any ladies' maid . . .' I was quite proud to overhear it.

Unfortunately, I then developed a talent for dealing with a satanic contraption called the 'calo'.

The 'calorifère' was the main furnace, heating radiators and bath water. If neglected for an instant, it was liable to peter out surreptitiously. First the hard 'scorie' of coal had to be shaken out, without the small iron door promptly jamming inexpert fingers. Then came layers of paper and 'margotins' – magical slivers of wood dipped in resin and tightly packed in great wheels compressed by knife-sharp wiring. Then wood, then coal. Both damp. So the only solution was to splash petrol into the yawning opening.

The French passion for saving probably induced patience with their 'calo's' moods, certain to ensure economy of fuel, but for me it meant hours in the cellar, poring over my school books, while I waited for the odious stove to start off with a reassuring roar.

Missie, my staunch aide-de-camp, once came to help, and nearly blew up with the calo, adding petrol when it was already alight. The flame shooting out of the open door singed off both eyebrows and fringe, but she held on to the can, averting disaster.

There followed a moment of panic lest she be disfigured, for she was a lovely child, with cameo-like regular features (much admired by the grown-ups), which we had been taught to respect. During nursery battles, she would cover her nose with a small fist, squealing: 'Mind my profile!' This was not out of vanity, for she never bothered at all about her appearance, but from a sense of responsibility towards a gift she was expected to preserve.

It was in all our interest to do so, for should 'the' nose get scratched during one of our tussles, or, God forbid, punched, punishment ensued for all concerned.

Fortunately within a few days, she stopped looking like a white rabbit, and was herself again.

When Mamma was away, we were supposed to keep a watchful eye on Georgie. He was an amusing and charming child, but difficult for us to control or box into bed at reasonable hours. We must have been brutal to him at times, partly to counteract Mamma's indulgence, but that did not prevent the most affectionate solidarity between us. Since our move to St. Germain-en-Laye, on the outskirts of Paris, we were rather cut off from other children, and much dependent on each other's company and inventiveness. We would make up long stories, to be told in endless instalments of hair-raising and romantic episodes, and combine our own games. But one summer evening Georgie escaped our vigilance, and we last glimpsed him climbing over the high garden gate, while with one hand he held the bell to prevent its warning tinkle. He was out of sight before we could reach the street.

As time passed, we waited anxiously, but were at length disarmed, when he finally returned flushed and self-satisfied, brandishing a parcel. He had gone to buy Missie a namesday present with all his savings. He could not resist exhibiting the dolls' ironing board with requisites, insisting:

'Promise to forget it, so it is a surprise to-morrow!'

Inevitably, we tackled any chore as a matter of course, wilting once however, at having to fetch a table from the carpenter's, and face classmates' derision on the way.

Mamma was not to be persuaded. She would not hear of such silliness. As we trudged along, encumbered with what seemed to be sixteen conspicuous legs and corners, we felt immensely foolish, and also ashamed for minding. There was however no question of backing out, for self-consciousness was considered affected or vulgar, to be put down firmly: one should treasure one's own values, expanding them whenever possible, but no predicament should be allowed to get one down or embarrass. Inner independence from any outward occurrence was an axiom. We did not really question these standards, but were occasionally submerged by waves of weakness, as we doubted our capacity to uphold them.

A guardian angel must have had us in his care, for any disciplined sport was far too expensive and we would compensate by undertaking the most hare-brained adventures without mishap. Anything reasonable we might want to do was out of the question and we never owned skates or a tennis raquet. But we could not help dreaming about bicycles.

We were too proud to ask, but sometimes other children lent us theirs, and we skimmed blissfully down the terrace of St. Germain, savouring the speed and the wind in our hair. Once I led the owner's large dog on a leash as I rode, hands free. He leaped for a cat across the way, with dire results. For days I limped to the doctor and sand and pebbles were scooped out of a deep hole in my knee.

Two fair little Canadian brothers, called Whitmore, Georgie's boon companions, had acquired the habit of smashing their bicycles shortly before Christmas so as to be sure of getting new ones. They went at it hammer and tongs while we watched, incapable of comment.

Years later, with my first earnings, I bought Missie the finest one I could find. By then she was fifteen, but it still came in time.

4

I was ten and Missie eight years old, when we entered the French Lycée of St. Germain-en-Laye, near Paris. Mamma had chosen it thankfully, charmed by the building's large windows and the flowering chestnut trees in the grounds.

Although we had haphazardly accumulated knowledge on a variety of subjects, we had never been to school. Missie and I found ourselves catapulted into the eighth and tenth class of the ink-chalk-Eau-de-Javel-smelling red-brick Lycée. We were not used to so many strange children, and were overcome by fits of shyness; quite unable at first to deal with rudeness.

It took us a term to get on to an equal footing with the others. Helped by a retentive memory, we could soon reel off entire pages in perfect French without an inkling of what the text meant. Missie gabbled, unquestioningly:

'The Gauls, our ancestors . . .' as she repeated her lesson to Mamma, who cried exasperated: 'The child is an idiot!' Towards the end of the school year a long list of questions was set before each pupil. The first ran: 'Profession du père.'

We were nonplussed: what could we put? 'Member of the Douma', 'Statesman', 'Maréchal de la Noblesse' (an important function in the Russian Empire, but so obviously irritating to a French Republican!), 'Ministre-adjoint'. It all sounded hopelessly incongruous.

All around us, earnest pen-sucking little girls jotted down in violet ink: 'Marchand', 'Tapissier', 'Avocat' and other enviably simple terms.

'But you must not be ashamed!' said the uncomprehending teacher, as she gathered up the sheets and saw the blank line. Visions of 'shameful' occupations floated in our puzzled minds. A question mark must have remained in hers, for when things went wrong, she would turn on us:

'Do you think you are still among the moujiks here?'

Could she really have imagined us wielding a 'knout', a cossack's whip?

Nevertheless among the almost overwhelming pile of often useless information instilled in us, there emerged one asset: the entire system of French schooling awoke curiosity of mind, taught one to think, where to find knowledge and how to sift it, and above all how to use their beautiful language.

However, even if it trained him to reason, it could not make a fool clever.

Transfers of money from Lithuania reached us in fits and starts, making it extremely difficult to budget for anything. The feeling of impending doom as bills accumulated brought us round Mamma in conclave. We were, however, too small to be of much use, either in counsel or as breadwinners.

When we were told in school to produce some requisite, the first elation at the prospect of a new pair of gym shoes, a pinafore, above all new books, was dampened by the knowledge that any additional expense was unthinkable. Without even mentioning it at home, in class we would invent excuses: the shop was closed, Mamma away, the right size out of stock. We sighed inwardly at the boredom of it, at first embarrassed, then exasperated at the teacher's obtuse insistence. Soon we were defiantly uncaring, for such minor vexations were out of proportion with what lay behind their cause.

As our school fees became overdue, we would be called out of class to be admonished severely by the 'Econome', cold eyes staring accusingly at us over silver-rimmed pince-nez.

Mamma then kept us at home as if we were ill and went over all our lessons with us herself for fear our studies would suffer.

'But the exams! we cannot miss those.'

We then slipped back, delivered our paper and stayed at home again, feeling like thieves but studying harder than ever. Unexpectedly my marks were so high that I won a scholarship. But we were 'foreign': it could not be awarded after all. I did not mind as much as Mamma thought, for it eased my conscience as to the unpaid fees.

Mamma tried to make the most of our talents; Irina rattled away diligently on the piano, Georgie and I painted and drew with facility but also without conviction, fearing this would not be the path to riches, Missie had a charming voice and a repertoire of songs in several languages, but gathered in a group around Mamma at the piano, we would all join in the meatier Russian ones.

While we worked, she read to us, sitting straight in a hard armchair, knitting at the same time, for she made all our jerseys. Her mellow voice and perfect diction giving the story or poem life and reality, we listened to her, and as naturally as breathing, became familiar with great Russian writers and poets: Pushkin, Lermontoff, Gogol, Tolstoy etc., the historians Karamsine and Platonoff, and Schilder's biographies of 19th-century Russian Emperors. Dostoyevsky was taken in minor doses: he was too dark for her sunny nature.

Our parents and their friends felt the responsibility of their failure acutely. In her childhood, Mamma said they used to sigh: 'Nothing ever happens nowadays: no more Wars, no Revolutions!' almost regretting not to live in more exciting days. They seemed to have had so much time at their disposal and filled it without hectic haste, planning ahead for generations. Highly educated themselves, they had always distrusted the 'professional intellectual'. They well knew however that they had been engaged in a race against time, the rising level of prosperity and progress in Russia just before the First World War had led them to hope they could win against the revolutionaries. Had not Stolypine himself declared: 'Twenty years more of reform, and the battle is won.' (But perhaps after all, only a small minority thought as they did?)

Learning Russian history, we were repeatedly reminded that any discomforts we might encounter were as nothing compared to what the Russian people were suffering.

In the story of 'Tarass Boulba', the famous Cossack 'Ataman' (chieftain) of that name slunk back into the Polish stronghold, where his son Ossip was being tortured to death on the main square.

Dying in agony, the boy cried out: 'Father, do you hear me?'

Out of the watching crowd, came the ringing answer:

'Slichou!' (I hear you.)

In Russian folklore, this XVIth century tale is still a symbol, and we were told never to forget that if one cannot help, one must at least bear witness.

There was so much Mamma wished to read to us, so much to tell us. Unlike other children, we were never sent to bed. And yet school homework still had to be done.

Missie would fall asleep like a dormouse, curled up in a corner of the sofa, golden hair falling over her face, and would therefore be written off temporarily as incapable of higher understanding.

I grew ever more sleepy too, but smokily sensed Mamma's solitude to which she would never own: her fight up-hill.

It seemed a small thing to humour her.

5

Much later, when we were almost grown up, Mamma told us about the murder of Uncle Boris Wiazemsky, her eldest brother. When she first heard of his death, his mother cried: 'There was enough in him to fill three lives, and they cut him down at 33!'

He was one of the most widely cultivated men of his generation, spoke and wrote beautifully (often in verse) and was Gold Medal Laureate of both the Faculties of Science and of History. He was a close friend of Stolypine's.

Elected Marshall of the Nobility during the war, the unenviable duty of being Chairman of the local mobilisation board inevitably made Boris unpopular in spite of all he had done at home to improve the condition of the people.

On the 1st of March 1917, Uncle Dimitri, Mamma's second brother, was killed in St Petersburg by a bomb thrown into the car he was driving in the company of the Minister of War, Gouchkoff.

A peasant delegation from the village of Korobovka (next to the family estate of Lotarevo) came to Uncle Boris and declared they did not wish to have him buried in the family vault.

The burial took place all the same, but it would seem that from then on, the peasants' mood changed. There followed a period of comparative quiet, punctuated by only small disturbances.

On the 6th July, the Provisional Government Forces took the Fortress of Peter and Paul in Petrograd, turning the Bolsheviks out without a shot being fired.

On the 1st August Uncle Boris wrote: 'All is calm. It is time for men of good-will to be reassured, and for evil men to tremble.'

It was not to be. Soon afterwards the 'Ochrana' soldiers stumbled across the lawn, rifles unslung, close on the heels of their lieutenant brandishing his sword. 'Spassaitis!' (Save yourselves!) they cried.

Already the alarm could be heard, and the tolling of the bells now punctuated the howl of the gathering and approaching mob.

Vanya the butler and Michailo the coachman urged them to leave in the troika, which had already been brought to the door: 'In five minutes it will be too late!'

The crowd now burst into the main courtyard: villagers from Korobovka, Podvorkov and Debrey swelled by agitators – there were none from the biggest settlement of them all (Biagora), which refused to have anything to do with these events.

Many of the peasants had known Boris since he was a baby, and with calm assurance he now went out to meet them. His wife Lili, who was 22, refused to leave his side and stood clinging to his arm.

But they had come to kill, and now a disjointed rigmarole of grievances reaching back into the days of serfdom was dug up. As he reasoned with them, Lili, suddenly jostled by a group of hostile women, found a cord slipped round her neck. But the men turned on their 'babas' in anger, and the cord disappeared again.

A village urchin had climbed into a tree, and now pulled at electric wires obstructing his view. Fearful for his safety, Boris called: 'Get down!'

As he did not obey at once, a peasant shouted: 'You heard what the Prince said? Get down, you fool!'

Here the mob seemed to pause – as if weighing this instinctive reaction on both sides.

There now emerged a wizened little man, pince-nez clamped on his nose; mocking the *moujiks*, he sneered: 'You are all serfs at heart! You will never dare touch the Prince!'

Their leader answered, 'It is true: the Prince whistles and we obey. But times have changed. We want his lands and he will not give them to us while he is still alive. Although we respect him, we will have to do away with him! But as to you', turning to the smirking agitator, 'there is nothing for you to be happy about. The day will come when we will hang you and yours – and then with no respect whatever!'

Late at night they were fetched from the village school where they had been locked up, for 'questioning', confronted this time by their hunting guns spread fanwise before a half-circle of drunken *moujiks*.

Lili broke in: 'You know these guns! Most of you have been beaters and helped at the shoots!'

Boris restrained her, saying in English: 'Don't talk, let me answer!'

The accusations became more and more absurd, until the prisoners were led back to their rooms.

When morning dawned, the guards came for Boris. They let him say good-bye to Lili in the little back bedroom, and she remembered him looking back over his shoulder at her, as they led him away.

She heard a roar from the waiting crowd when he emerged on the porch. Mutineering soldiers, whose train had by chance stopped at the local station, then took over.

Later a soldier led her to the freight car in a siding of the station, in which Boris's body was lying. All through the night Lili crouched on the straw next to him, the soldier never leaving her.

At dawn someone fetched a priest who served a 'panihida' (prayers for the dead). Children of railway workers on the line gathered nosegays of field flowers and brought them to her to lay around him.

Lili then returned to Annino, where his cousin, Maroussia Veliaminoff, who had just ridden over from Biagora, awaited her.

Pale and calm, she stretched out her blood-stained hands to her, saying tonelessly:

'They have killed Boris!'

In later years Aunt Lili told us that because of the friends who had stood by her and Boris at the peril of their lives and showed kindness, sympathy and courage; because of the butler Vanya, the charming maid Anna, the coachman Michailo, the young soldier, the railwaymen's children, the train conductor among others, she had never lost faith in the fundamental goodness in the Russian people, however deluded they may have been by all the false promises showered on them during those dreadful days.

Long afterwards Lili remarried, and I once asked her whether she often remembered my godfather. Her face became quite still as she said:

'I have been happy with Esska' (her second husband). 'He has been my lover and friend and the father of my children. Yet whenever I think "My husband before God", I think of your uncle Boris!' Smiling again, she added: '. . . but don't tell Esska.'

Just a few months later the workers of the Putilov (now Kirov) factory marched on the Petrograd Tcheka to deliver Mamma's aunt, Countess Sophie Panine, from prison. They put her on a train and escorted her to the Finnish frontier.

Far ahead of her times in social thinking, she had dedicated her large fortune to further projects improving the condition and social status of the working class. She founded the 'Narodnyi Dom', a centre for workers which included a library, night classes, a gymnasium, a theatre for cultural and musical activities and a canteen. It was staffed by liberals under the condition that this institution would not be used for political agitation. In this she was misled by one of her aides, a young lawyer by the name of Kerensky, to whom she had given his first job. It was therefore with mixed feelings that she consented to join his Cabinet in 1917 as first Russian woman Minister for Social Welfare.* After her arrest Lenin named Mrs. Kollontaï in her stead.

* From Finland, Masaryk invited her to Prague to work in the Russian archives which in 1945 were to be confiscated by the Soviets. She then proceeded to the U.S., working until her death for the Tolstoy Foundation. As always she had lived there too in monastic simplicity, with no interest whatever in material things.

6

Needless to say, Mamma's worries were not over with our settling in France. Alexander's education was one of the problems she had to face. Thanks to American generosity, a boarding-school for the education of émigré boys had been founded in Lafayette's erstwhile home of Chavagnac, in the Auvergne.

Alexander was duly sent there, but he was unhappy at first and bullied mercilessly by particularly brutal older boys. Missie and I retaliated years later at parties by refusing to dance with his puzzled ex-tormentors.

When he came home for the holidays, although only thirteen or so at the time, he was so tall for his age, we felt safe with a man in the house. Georgie followed him around like an adoring shadow, hanging on to his every word. 'Yes, Alexander. No, Alexander.'

Missie and I, who were inseparable and always in complete accord, in spite of being so different in character and looks, would listen fascinated to the tales of travel and discovery he had read. He dreamed of trips to distant lands, and was planning to become a colonial engineer, which was considered a fine profession. But there was still a long way to go, and as he grew older, we realised how unsuited he was to battle his way through life, for too tall, soon too handsome, romantic and unpractical, he seemed to belong to another age. We were his confidants and, uninhibited by experience, tried to impart Good Advice. In fact we could only sympathise, for we had no idea how to deal with his problems.

Irina, the eldest, did not waste much time on us younger ones, and far preferred the company and talk of grown-ups. Of all of us she was perhaps the most handicapped by what-might-have-been, from which we smaller ones did not suffer in the least, for we were full of curiosity and eagerness to get on our own feet, every new experience turning to delightful and thrilling adventure.

Although she seemed so much older than us, she was still only a schoolgirl, and our independence and solidarity must have been a trial to her, but when it came to running the house (and she did the cooking and the shopping) we helped her as far as possible, served at meals and cleaned up afterwards, turning it all into a game.

On Sundays the house filled with guests from Paris, and Irina would then whip up delicious lunches, frequently our favourite dish: 'bitkis' of hashed chicken, swimming in sour cream, for which she was much praised. We were included in all the gay banter and talk, in the musical sessions or long walks after lunch.

Of course Uncle Adishka would come whenever his racing engagements allowed it. He had had a passion for horses since his earliest youth, and then took over the management of the Wiazemsky racing stud in Russia. Abroad he was considered an authority and, knowing the pedigree of every horse, he always seemed able to forecast the winners. But he never betted.

Every year or so a beautiful woman whose snow-white hair did not match her young face and giggly laugh descended on us, accompanied by a lovely daughter – an ethereal creature called Elena, whom we greatly admired, and who was later to marry the American writer and critic, Edmund Wilson.

She always brought Mamma some preposterous, luxurious and useless present: a hat from 'Reboux', a dress from a great couturier, or a huge bottle of rare scent.

We thought it wonderful of her, for Mamma, who never bought anything for herself, would blush with pleasure, protesting, suddenly looking young and carefree again.

In sing-song tones, we repeated her name, which had a joyful sound: Olala Mumm, and loved her for bringing this dash of fantasy into the austerity of constant economy.

Many of Mamma's guests had become taxi drivers, or were employed in similar jobs. They joked about their work as if it had nothing at all to do with their real life.

Valerian Bibikoff, married to a Tolstoy cousin of Papa's, drove a tourists' bus, and he would describe the uneasy sensation of having thirty pairs of mistrustful eyes glued to his back. In summer he chauffeured tourists all over Europe in rented cars, which he much preferred. His latest employers had been a newly-rich South American couple. In Austria, at the end of his working day, he would leave them in their hotel, and join King Alfonso XIII of Spain (who happened to be staying nearby) for many a long chat. The King had been Honorary Commander of Valerian's Guards' Regiment.

Somehow Bibikoff's employers got wind of these meetings and were offended not to have been included in the invitation.

'They were not the sort of people he would have been interested to know', explained Valerian apologetically, as he told us about it, for they were very kind to him, and he hated hurting their feelings.

Bald-headed, with his rubbery face reflecting every change of thought and mood, his unquenchable sense of fun and human understanding seemed to work even among his Communist 'CGT' and 'Front Populaire' colleagues of the car-driving unions. He engaged in violent political discussions with them, regardless of consequences, which were often very disagreeable. But in the end they called him, 'Eh, toi, vieux Bibi', with forgiving affection.

Deprived of his once famous china collection in Odessa, Count Kapnist took to haunting the 'Marché aux Puces' (Flea Market) on his day off. Looking rather like a rotund and benevolent hedgehog with his bristling pepper-and-salt crew-cut he would go stepping lightly over the bric-à-brac spread on the sidewalk and with unerring eye picked out chipped, unmatched cups, broken or glued plates and dishes, signed by the greatest manufacturers, and within reach of his meagre income as a taxi-driver. These finds adorned the walls of his tiny flat in an unprepossessing block of a Paris 'Faubourg'.

Cooking had been another hobby, and he and his wife, with her booming voice and happily expanding girth, often invited their friends to delicious candle-lit meals. Lovingly caressing his favourite pieces, he would display the latest discovery.

Three little girls around ten years of age, in long nightgowns, we clustered, crouching, and peered through the banisters of the high gallery close to the ceiling of the house-theatre and on a level with our rooms on the first floor.

Once again, we were spending the night at the Youssoupoff house in Boulogne-sur-Seine on the outskirts of Paris, watched over by Princess Zinaïde, her devoted, buxom Russian maid, and a yapping jealous Pekinese. As friends of her beloved granddaughter, 'Baby', she was like another grandmother to Missie and me. Her son, Prince Felix Youssoupoff, and his wife, niece of the last Emperor, owning to no talent for a child's education, left 'Baby' entirely to 'Princess Bou's' loving care.

Reclining on a sofa, white hair piled high over a feathery fringe, she wore elegant high-necked, soft clothes, but always in mourning colours, for she had never recovered from her eldest son's death.

She was very frail, never raised her voice and led a very protected life owing to the loving consideration shown her by all. Yet she had great inner strength.

She was always there, always ready with a smile, always kind, always deeply understanding. Her other son, her friends, came and sat with her for hours, and left invigorated, as if they had drunk from some secret fount of life. We painted on a small table in her room and loved to play in her vicinity. Tea at her side was a special treat, allowed when she had no visitors. But soon she would have to rest, and we were careful not to make any noise, whereas we bullied and teased and tickled the dear old maid, trying to entice her to a romp and disturbing her at her work.

The Youssoupoffs had always had a theatre in their houses. It seemed the most natural thing to them. In Boulogne it had been built and decorated by their friend the painter Alexander Yakovleff. The walls were lined with cream, beige and pale green 'Art Nouveau' odalisques, frozen into contorted graceful postures. The carpeted theatre was like a wide oval drawing-room, separated from the stage by a curtain and a high curving step.

Later we heard much whispering as to the 'goings-on' in the Youssoupoff house: actors, artists, writers gravitated around Felix. Also cranks, for he was fascinated by oddity. Ill-assorted lame ducks sheltered under his protection, and never was a call for help turned down.

But as children we saw them only as a group of talented and incongruously assembled guests, inprovising music and short sketches, rehearsing amateur theatricals or sometimes only talking, which bored us, although the discussions were often passionately intense, breaking into gusts of laughter at some 'bon mot'.

We much preferred it when the cook, who was also a remarkable balalaïka player, boomed away in deep bass tones, as out of the depths of a barrel, his high white cap and badge of office laid aside on some console.

With perfect diction, in a light, pleasant voice, Felix himself sang, or rather re-told, Russian and foreign songs. He looked like an androgynous angel as he stood – one foot on a chair, softly strumming his guitar, high silk Russian shirt glinting in the soft light, great pale-blue eyes looking out from an eternally adolescent face.

Ethereally draped in tasselled slinky dresses his wife would gaze at him in rapt admiration, her face as cameo-like and ageless as his own. But, suddenly exasperated, she would shatter the spell with a dry remark in her husky, blurting Romanoff voice.

Quite unruffled, Felix would smoothly bring in the next entertainer.

We watched from above, fascinated. But presently a kindly hand drew us gently and firmly away to bed.

Everything in the house was designed by Felix in some startling and unexpected way. The bath water spurted out of the jaws of an authentic stone Roman lion, set in the wall and framed in trailing green plants and foliage. One room was a Tartar tent, another lined with strange pictures of monsters, beautifully executed down to the last hair on hideous warts. 'Baby' told us her father drew these during a short period after the death of Rasputin, when he felt 'invaded by evil spirits'. He never could draw like that again.

Huge violently-coloured parrots, presents from the ex-King of Portugal, waited to nip at us, as we ran past, prying and peeping where we certainly had no business to be, creeping in to inspect the gorgeous costume of a Persian Prince spread on the fur cover of the velvet couch in Felix's bedroom, which was carpeted in black from wall to wall. Usually his clothes were close-fitting and darkly sober, but he loved to burst into flamboyant disguise at night.

Out of doors, the mad gardener raked the gravel, attired in the remnants of a dress-suit; greenish top hat and drooping tails, like a tired swallow.

We did not question anything, as children rarely do, but as we played or painted, we discovered forgotten diamond-studded Fabergé trinkets and baubles, dropped in a box, broken and then discarded as no longer beautiful. In that house, nothing was prized for its commercial value.

But we were concerned, too, for we were beginning to understand the vulgar worth of money and the irksome debasing pinch of not having any.

The Youssoupoff fortune was in fact accelerating its downward slide. The Revolution had done away with most of it. Compared with what remained abroad, when they fled it was like transferring from an ocean liner to a raft, although to many it may have appeared a particularly luxurious one. Economy was an unknown term and as a result wild extravagance continued: strawberries in winter, flowers out of season, vast charity and open-handedness.

'Baby' unwisely asked one day: 'Where are the spoons we always use?'

'Don't ask stupid questions,' she was firmly admonished, for they had been pawned.

Meanwhile her father received his creditors downstairs, mixing them cocktails as if at a party, while he murmured blandly:

'It all belongs to you anyway, Gentlemen, so let's make this little reunion as pleasant as possible.'

Nobody we knew ever seemed to have met Rasputin.

'But what about the Empress's lady-in-waiting and friend, Anya Wyroubova?' we asked.

'She was a fool and very *exaltée*. However she meant well, and having heard of his healing powers fetched him to the Tsarevich's bedside. Otherwise only a few "wild ladies" (dikija dami) knew him and his women's third-rate friends were then inflicted on the country as Ministers, for the Emperor could not refuse his wife anything.'

Papa had glimpsed him once at a railroad station and said that his 'white' eyes gave him a startling and repulsive appearance, as if he were looking through you.

Papa was very polite with Princess Bou and her daughter-in-law, but did not approve of Felix at all, for although everybody had been yearning for Rasputin's death, Felix's involvement in his murder was viewed with mixed feelings. However he both accepted and ignored Mamma's childhood friendship with him.

It had become an established custom for 'Baby', who had a special and different relationship with each of us, to join us for the summer holidays.

'Dilka,' Felix would say to Mamma, 'you know how to bring up children, and we don't. Take her along!' Relieved.

The lease of our house was at an end, and Mamma, deciding that it was just as easy to be poor in a beautiful and interesting place as in a disagreeable one, discarded suggestions of a 'datcha' in the surroundings of Paris, and chose Brittany – so healthy for growing children.

It would be a long journey by train, and we urged her to be on time for such an important trip, for we had horrifying visions of trains steaming out of stations, the conductor oblivious of our exhortations, while Mamma rushed down the quay quite unperturbed, gaily waving her umbrella: 'Stop, stop!'

She was always late. It was a quirk of the mind, almost a mania, but she promised not to leave us stranded amongst the luggage, with an anxious eye on the 'Chef de Gare' in his red cap, meaningfully swinging his whistle, while she dashed to post a last letter or buy a paper.

With a sigh of relief as she joined us, we settled on our hard third-class seats.

In Russia spotless linen covers had lined the first-class coach hired to transport us to the Crimea, and hooked on to the long distance express. Now, in order to protect us from the dust and grime absent Nannie would not have approved of, cretonne hangings had been prepared and were rather clumsily suspended all over the compartment.

Even so there remained two empty seats which were soon occupied, the passengers staring with disbelief at the floral tent which awaited them. 'Ces étrangers! . . .'

Like a monkey on a string, the 'Contrôleur' swung along the narrow foot-rests, leading outside the coach from door to door of the non-communicating compartments. He jerked ours open and found himself in a flowering bower. Chewing his yellowed moustache in surprise, he peered over steel-rimmed spectacles and remarked,

'Ah, mais! Vous êtes bien installés!'

Irina had reached the self-conscious age: she was ashamed of us all. Still more so when, on reaching our destination in Brittany, the net containing our large india-rubber balls burst, and they bounced away merrily across the Place de la Gare like released frogs. We rather enjoyed shocking her.

Here at last we glimpsed the sea, sparkling like crumpled metal, and the peace of the expanse stretched towards the setting sun soothed us all.

In Beg-Meil we settled into the newly built 'annexe' of the 'Auberge Yvonnou', repairing in the mornings for breakfast to the main house. It was a lavish meal with crackling crisp rolls and honey, coffee and hot milk in large earthenware bowls.

Summer lessons kept us for two hours in a musty back salon, smelling of wood, sticky fly-paper and agriculture, with the sound of cows lowing from their byres close by. Here we also became expert at catching flies alive, with a rapid twist of the wrist – a technique usefully applied to clear Mamma's room of them at night.

At eleven, we dashed to the beach for an astringent swim in the foam-tipped waves. We invented all our own entertainment: and would shape fortresses or racing cars in sand, or chase each other from rock to rock, high over churning seas, agile as mountain goats in our rope-soled espadrilles. We raced the incoming tide as it crashed in, and would slip around a protruding headland just before small creeks were cut off by the next breaker.

In fine weather we lunched in the apple orchard of the 'Bon Accueil', where lobster was served once a week even to children. Afterwards we lay around Mamma's bed, spread fanwise on the creamy pine floor. In her resonant contralto voice, she read us Russian poetry. This was supposed to be good for our backs and was certainly good for our Russian.

The loosely drawn muslin curtains drifted, billowing gently in the afternoon breeze. They let in a whiff of freshly chalked espadrilles drying in the warm sunshine on the window-sill, a smell of apples mauled to cider, of seaweed and salt.

As the afternoon cooled, we set out for long walks, trailing along in Mamma's wake, as she strode on energetically, far ahead. Wherever 'Baby' went, animals and tiny children followed her. The babies were grabbed back by their mothers, but we never got rid of the dogs, who straggled along behind us in a self-deprecating procession. On one of our more distant excursions to the castle of 'Kériolet', Mamma discovered that it had once belonged to an aunt of the Youssoupoffs because the Winterhalter portrait hanging in the drawing-room was so like Baby. The estate had been left to the neighbouring town for some purpose for which it had not been used and could therefore be re-claimed by Felix, who until our visit there had had no idea of its existence. After a pro-longed lawsuit, he eventually won it back and by then it became his only source of income.

During our years as nomads we always stumbled over some Russian relatives or friends in the most unexpected places: Brittany did not fail us in this respect, for we soon found some Lopoukhine cousins on the other side of the bay of Concarneau. Wars and revolutions had passed them by and they lived in a vault-like ancient house, shrouded in its overgrown garden. It was like visiting the world of Monet and Boudin. The old gentlemen wore white suits and Panama straw hats and carried a cane, as was the custom in turn-of-the-century Bordighera, and the aunt was fat and cosy, the high collar of her lacy blouse stiffened, her hair gathered in a severe bun under floppy hats. She was quite without coquetry, as if her garments had all been assembled once and for all a long time ago.

We imagined them wading through poppy fields, or sauntering on deserted beaches at sunset. They were kind and welcoming, inviting us all, Mamma and six children, to delicious lunches composed like a song: the taste, the colour, the beginning and the end having been carefully considered in relation to each other. Our hosts never seemed to leave the house, living as if in a tethered balloon, yet with an eye open to the outside world. Mamma said they were not stultified in the least, and enjoyed their conversation.

Meanwhile Georgie, 'Baby' and I sat painting on the jetty of the port of Concarneau as the fishing-boats, furling their great red sails, came home to unload their catch of sardines, pouring them out like a churning silver river. An admiring crowd of urchins and pipe-smoking, gnarled and twisted root-like old fishermen breathed down our necks with pungent comment. It rather put us off.

Towards autumn, we ran through damp orchards, sampling apples as we chased each other among the trees. Cider time had come, the smell of fermenting apples rose like vapour from every village, which then celebrated a feast day, a 'Pardon' in honour of their patron Saint or the Virgin Mary. Peasants flocked there from far and wide arrayed in their lovely costumes, the women in starched headdresses and piped collars, the men in blue velvet-edged jackets and broad black-buckled hats. We would drive out to watch the processions winding under banners along deep, narrow lanes to converge in weather-beaten stone churches, whose twin towers rose to heaven as if the earth itself were lifting praying hands.

In Paris, the preceding Easter, on our return from midnight Mass, we had had an accident on the Place de la Concorde. Another taxi had hit us broadside. Both cars disintegrated, spilling us out like peas from a pod – bruised but intact. The insurance company reluctantly conceded a lump sum, which now usefully paid for these excursions in a rickety rented car.

Mamma's distrust of public transport having now found full justification, from then on she would declare, 'Je sors d'un accident!' to slow drivers down.

A few years later the Baccalauréat examination, without which any French child felt lop-sided, loomed ahead, and I worked harder than ever, which in fact gave me a feeling of freedom against the strain of hampering forces. As a result I got through colours flying.

Ivan Wiazemsky, cousin and close friend, chaperoned me for a few days of unrealistic and exhilarating 'quartier latin' life, for the examinations took place in the Sorbonne. The police looked away, twirling their clubs under dashing short capes in desultory fashion, while the students went giddy with the sudden relief of exams over, peppered with a dash of politics too. 'Action Francaise' and 'Jeunesses Patriotiques' tussled with the Communists. Separately. But nobody would have thought of setting fire to cars or tearing up the pavement.

8

During a journey to Kovno in Lithuania, Mamma had succeeded in obtaining permission to transfer some funds to Germany, for she was set on my studying art in Munich.

Georgie and I first accompanied her to Kissingen, where she was to undertake a cure. We travelled up the Rhine from Cologne and stopped overnight in St. Goar. Carried away by the romantic scenery, absorbed in the contemplation of cathedrals and castles, Mamma was disappointed by our infinitely greater interest in the different makes of cars passing down the road below, as we sat perched on the crumbling wall of some fortress.

We then boarded a steamer heading by slow stages for Mainz. As we rounded the bend and chugged into the widening valley towards Johannisberg, Mamma cried joyfully:

'But that is where Olala lives. We must get off the boat at once!'

Helter-skelter, we dragged our bags on to the shaky landing stage of Östrich, and Mamma phoned the Mumm house from the village. Georgie and I disconsolately visualised a fruitless search for accommodation, burdened by our trunks, but within minutes a huge car shining with chromium came to fetch us. We sank down in relief on the soft leather cushions and were soon warmly welcomed by that same charming lady who had brought Mamma such glamorous presents in St. Germain.

I asked presently, 'Who lives in the big house on the hill next door?'

'A Spanish lady. Her only son is studying in Switzerland.'

Although I was at the age when anyone over twenty appeared to me on the edge of decrepitude, I imagined a schoolboy and lost all interest – until I met and married him a few years later.

The eldest son of the house, an 'old' man of thirty or so, condescended to look after me, even attempting a game of ping-pong, at which I was hopeless. He and his sister looked so handsome and relaxed, that, in spite of their kindness, I felt overgrown, lumpy and inadequate.

After dinner we were taken to Mainz by car and moved on next day to Kissingen, where Mamma had been ordered to take a cure.

The food in our 'pension' was acutely calory-conscious: in the shortest time all surplus baby-fat melted away, and a local photographer who had seen me in the street, came to ask Mamma for permission to take some pictures. After our departure a copy must have been duly hung in his shop window, catching the eye of the proprietor of a famous garden centre near Berlin, who was in turn taking the cure.

I was then subjected to what I ungratefully considered persecution, as unwanted flowers, unanswered letters followed me sporadically for several years. He finally caught up with me, but by then I was engaged to be married and it all ended in a lovely rose being named after me and a hundred plants arriving as a wedding present. (I was shocked to hear later that this disinterested if persistent admirer had been betrayed by his secretary for disparaging Hitler; he died in a Nazi camp during the war.)

While we were in Kissingen, we were taken to visit Würzburg castle by Mamma's goddaughter, whose father had been the German military attaché in Kovno in 1914. She was accompanied by her fiancé, a handsome young officer, Count Claus von Stauffenberg, who was to make the attempt on Hitler's life in 1944.

Irina then joined me in Munich, where we would spend the winter.

We lived with several English girls in a flat in Schwabing – the more Bohemian quarter of the city, and were soon caught up in a round of private parties. We were not yet allowed to go to the public ones, although Irina was quite grown-up. She took piano lessons, while I learnt to draw at Professor Heymann's* studio in the Türkenstrasse. We worked for six to eight hours a day and I made good progress, for he was an inspired teacher and urged us on with enthusiasm. He took an optimistic view of my entry into the Academy for further tuition, which was at that time my great ambition.

I was too young and frivolous in those days to bother about the political implications of the Nazi régime, which was accepted with sympathy by many eminent foreigners. Inevitably, however, the final aims of the Party were discussed in every family, for in Germany, Hitler's advent to power in 1933 met with very divided feelings.

Most of our entourage took a critical view, in spite of the improvement of conditions in Germany since the huge number of unemployed had melted overnight. Whether this was due to the crude beginnings of Nazism in Munich, or whether stronger moral or religious polarisation

---

* Professor Heymann was soon to commit suicide to escape Nazi persecution of the Jews, but by then the blinkers were off and illusions as to their aims no longer excusable.

induced another criterion is difficult to say, but the vulgarity and excesses of Nazi doctrines, as well as their amateurish and brutal elaborations on foreign policy were openly criticised. It could all only lead to disaster, many believed, unless the Western powers did not continue to give in.

Nevertheless, life went on as before, and although Hitler's adherents were gaining ground, at no time – as far as we were concerned – were 'Nazis' synonymous with 'Germans'.

9

'Better to be a large fish in a small pond, than a sprat in the ocean,' quoted Papa. Although we could not as yet assess our own size, we found the pond too small. Ever more stringent restrictions on export of foreign currency had brought us to Kovno to join him at last, although the long deferred journey was reluctantly undertaken.

In Lithuania, Papa felt at home: the rivers were smaller, the land less open, but it still reminded him of his lost homeland, his 'rodina'. No longer capable of extreme happiness or sadness, he had retreated into a world of his own. But for us, it meant cutting off all ties with Western Europe.

At first, we stayed in the one 'good' hotel on the Laisves Aleja, the main street of Kovno, which bravely proclaimed itself the 'Versal' (Versailles). The food there was excellent: delicious pre-revolutionary Russian cooking, unrivalled by the best Parisian émigré restaurants, lavish use of cream and pastry a potential danger to one's figure.

During meals a small orchestra played soulful or three-quarter beat pot-pourris of the lighter operettas, itinerant artists contributing at times to the entertainment. Spittoons were still placed in appropriate corners, even the plumbing was pre-revolutionary – of durable quality and shattering noise. The bath water gurgled and grunted its way, W.C.s theatened flood at every pull.

We soon moved into a new two-storeyed house on the Zemaiciu street. Madame Ciurlonis, our landlady, was the widow of the only famous Lithuanian artist. He had indeed had a magical touch for light and merged translucent colours to dreamy effect. She was something of a dragon, which perhaps accounted for his early demise.

As professor of Lithuanian literature, assisted by meritorious colleagues, she also helped to invent new words, in an effort to adapt the ancient language (by now a dialect, although still based on the Sanskrit) to modern use. From the balcony above, we often heard their earnest and humourless efforts.

This new little peasant nation was violently anti-communist and proud of its independence, which it was determined to defend heroically against any odds.

Their neighbours, the Latvians, spoke a different tongue, though also remotely derived from the Sanskrit. The landowners in Lithuania had been Polish, whereas in Latvia they were Baltic Barons, descended for the most part from the colonising religious order of Teutonic Knights.

The Lithuanians were a peace-loving and honest nation, whereas the Latvians seemed of another calibre. They were tough and capable of great cruelty: even their *crimes passionels* were complicated by some gory detail, such as an outraged husband crucifying the cornered lover on a door. The Esthonians on their Eastern frontier spoke a language akin to the Finnish, but their culture was Swedish, and they had achieved a corresponding level of Scandinavian well-being in their small state. However the common language for all three nations remained Russian. It was spoken in all shops and as a result our knowledge of it improved considerably.

Originally a provincial borough of the Russian Empire, Kovno was now the 'provisional' capital of Lithuania, as long as the Poles held Vilna (Poland had grabbed the city at the end of the First World War) which would presumably be for ever. Diplomatic relations with Poland had therefore been dramatically severed: the railway line between both countries broke off in an open field, telephone and postal communication did not exist.

Throughout long years of service as Member of the Russian Imperial Parliament, the 'Douma', Papa had gone out of his way to defend the rights of the minorities in frontier States, whether Lithuanian, Polish or Jewish. They never forgot it and were always ready to help him, of which he was justly proud. The Jews of Kovno referred to him as 'one of ours', a great compliment for a non-Jew. One of his main achievements was the creation of the agricultural academy and cooperative centre of Dutnovo, which also allowed the farmers full price for their products as well as technical help, by-passing middlemen. This institution was later taken over by the Lithuanian Government who then created a number of similar 'cooperative centres' on a smaller scale.

Great Britain supported Lithuanian economy by guaranteeing import of bacon and geese. Theoretically political pressure could be applied by the threat of 'less bacon', so the British Minister, Mr. Thomas Preston and his charming Russian-born wife were important personages in Kovno. But the lack of foreign currency and surplus food produced unexpected situations, such as the young British student teaching at the University being paid in kind by a brace of fat geese. He bitterly complained he was unable to eat them because of a liver complaint and refused to walk them down the Laisves Aleja on a leash, so what was he to do?

Deciding that every occupation should either be significant or useful, Mamma had little regard for the secretarial grounding which we well realised would alone enable us to earn independence and allow us to leave Lithuania. We secretly ordered a copy of Pitman's shorthand and typing and Missie and I practised whenever possible, even at dead of night. It seemed odiously difficult, but we toiled away until I was proficient enough to take a job at the British Legation under the wing of the British Minister, Mr. Preston, who had been British Consul in Ekaterinburg at the time of Czar Nicholas II's murder. He composed ballet music, taught us to drive his car and was a versatile and pleasant friend and employer.

The shelving of my drawing study was a great disappointment for Mamma, but my heart was no longer in it for I knew I could never afford the years of study and practice.

But there were also happy sides to our life in Lithuania. As the weather improved, we rode off on bicycles into the empty country or went swimming in the great swift Niemen and its tributary the Neviaja; the diplomatic Corps organised picnics and parties, and the famous singer Chaliapine was a frequent visitor at our house. Like all Russians, he loved children and considered us no mean audience to charm. We hung on his every word as any story retold by him became fascinating, exciting and unique. An English flying officer once offered to take us up in the tiny blue plane he was demonstrating to Baltic Governments. Fired by our enthusiasm, he showed us all his tricks in turn, looping joyfully into the clouds.

Week-ends were often spent in the country at the Totlebens. Across the river from the small house on their erstwhile estate in which they lived, loomed the vast bulk of their previous castle: expropriated, condemned and abandoned.

The old Count's grandfather had been a 'hero of the Defence of Sebastopol' during the Crimean War, alongside our own great-uncle Victor Wassiltchikoff. He himself was an old friend and comrade of Papa's. They called each other 'Count' and 'Kniaz' and 'thou' – the rather archaic combination surprising us.

The Countess was once a 'Beauty', as shiny convex daguerrotype photos proved. She had been blessed with a Grecian profile and an hour-glass figure – now no longer discernible, with consequent loss of serenity.

Their daughters were sweet to us, and we loved them in return, but the Totlebens remained an awe-inspiring example for us to avoid.

There were four sisters, ten to fifteen years older than we were, whose lives drifted aimlessly on, remote from the suburban prejudice of provincial Kovno, but also in isolation from companions of their own age. Inexorably their prettiness faded to an expression of sad resignation.

And yet they were all talented and spoke several languages. At last one of them did marry and, much too late, her twin sister left for France.

Among the neighbours were several impoverished Polish ex-land-owners. Cut off from their own country since 1918, too proud to ask anything from the Lithuanians, they now looked after their once-elegant houses themselves. Any source of revenue had been nationalised, and ashamed of their destitution, they went nowhere for lack of the proper clothes, or the possibility of returning the hospitality.

As we explored the countryside on our bicycles one day, Missie and I collided with two amazingly beautiful youths, unlike anyone we had ever known. Sunburnt, tall and slim, their shirts open, their hair un-kempt, they must have been working in the fields. When they saw us, they blushed and turned to stride away, timid as deer.

We heard that they were the younger brothers of Count Zabiello, educated after a fashion by their elder sister. They only spoke Polish, and avoided everyone. But their elder brother, the slightly moth-eaten Count Czeslaw, sometimes visited his neighbours in a lop-sided vehicle put together like a puzzle. He knew a little Russian, and presently I received a proposal of marriage: white gloves, bouquet and all.

Although we laughed, we were deeply sorry for them, for they were entirely cut off from their homeland, as incongruous as if they were monsters.

Papa had got entangled – or rather inveigled – into some doubtful business, and the money remaining from the sale of his small brewery melted like snow in the spring sun. He then suffered a recurrence of the nervous breakdown which had felled him after the Revolution.

As far as possible, we all rallied round: Irina paid the household bills by giving language lessons, Missie did the same for smaller children, although she was hardly out of the schoolroom herself, while my salary filled the inevitable gaps, such as paying for Gaga's (Mamma's mother) nurse in Paris. (We were devoted to our grandmother, and shocked to hear that she had had a stroke.)

All Mamma's last treasured possessions vanished into the pawnshop, and we heard to our dismay that her chain of Fabergé Easter-eggs had been sold, only because the pawn-ticket for them had not been renewed in time.

In spite of my well-paid job, I had still hardly been able to put anything aside for my approaching departure, but this seemed a major crisis and Missie, Georgie and I set off on a crusade to retrieve them.

We ran from rag-and-bone man to 'fence', to jeweller, through the slovenly, stinking, picturesque and vastly depressing Kovno ghetto. One by one, we got them together again. Perhaps the hard-boiled dealers were touched at our efforts, for the price asked was not too exorbitant. Only one merchant refused to sell, and went on hammering the emerald out of an exquisite gold Fabergé half-almond.

There were but one or two eggs missing when – proud as peacocks – we finally presented Mamma with the reconstructed chain again.

The British Ambassador to all three Baltic States was Sir Hugh Knatchbull-Hugessen, later of sad 'Cicero' fame, for his servant in Turkey photographed all his most secret documents for the Germans under that pseudonym.

He now invited Mrs. Preston, Irina and me to Riga, to help him to entertain the British Fleet, while his wife and daughter were 'doing' the season in London.

Unspoilt as we were, it all seemed wonderful to us: the Embassy and its cars were at our disposal; party after party was given at the Ambassador's residence, or on board a warship. We would then go straight on to watch the summer sun rising from the edge of the sea, where it had been nestling in a golden mist through the twilight of a mid-summer night.

Charming, urbane and witty, Sir Hugh and our dear Mrs. Preston – chaperons out of a romantic novel – enjoyed it all as much as we did. Surrounded by handsome young naval officers, the five days passed for us in a haze of romance. Among minor souvenirs, I carried around for ages a long navy ribbon with H.M.S. *Neptune* on it in gold letters. Later in the war, after hearing that the cruiser had been sunk, I took it out again and looked at it sadly, recalling those happy days.

I returned to Kovno even more fixed in my resolution not to be caged in claustrophobic Lithuania for much longer.

Helped by Madame Fransoni, the lovely Georgian wife of the Italian Minister, who had just spent four delightfully frivolous years in Paris, we pored over *Vogue*, and gradually contrived a few pretty dresses.

Seeing that I was really in earnest about leaving, Mamma at last became reconciled to the idea, and with her usual energy, arranged for me to stay at first in London with her old friend Princess Katia Galitzine.

When I finally departed, the whole family came to the station to see me off. At the last minute Georgie thrust his most treasured possession into my hand: it was his engraved silver Russian mug.

I never forgot Kovno's white spired churches twinkling through the bars of the great green bridge crossing the Niemen, as I saw them through tears for the last time. Yet I was wildly eager to be on my way.

How could I have known then of the tragedy that was to befall the town and that violent death or deportation would crush so many people we had known. A terrible fate awaited the Jewish friends who had been so loyal to Papa, and the Lithuanian National student group, the Tauteninki, would fight the oppression of communism with hopeless and dogged determination for many decades to come.

After my departure Missie, whom I had trained, took over my job, going through exactly the same grind as I had a year before. I hoped to be able to help the family from England, and that she would soon follow me.

I stopped off in Silesia on my way: just before leaving, I had received a tempting invitation from the Birons to join them for the autumn shoots at their estate in Wartenberg, near Breslau.

We had known the Birons since our childhood in Baden-Baden, and their mother was a close friend of Mamma's. They both enjoyed their frank political, literary or historical exchanges of opinion – for they were not always in agreement.

Princess Biron was the daughter of the Huguenot Marquis de Jaucourt and inclined towards the uncompromising intolerance of a newly converted Protestant. French and now Catholic, she loathed Hitler from the very start. Nevertheless she referred to him – albeit scathingly – as 'Monsieur Hitler', as is the polite French custom towards living politicians. (Dead ones do not benefit from this courtesy and are written off as Stresemann, or Briand.)

One son, Franzi, had married a neighbour's daughter: Mädy Ballestrem. Gusti, the youngest of the three boys, was going through throes of disenchantment with the Nazis, whom he had at first ardently supported (perhaps in contradiction to his mother's pronounced views). His brothers were of a more placid temperament and preferred to avoid any political involvement, whereas Helen loathed the Nazis with passion.

It was, however, becoming even more clear that Hitler's ethics were incompatible with those of a believing Catholic, and the Birons, excepting the eldest son Carlos who had remained Protestant, were Catholic above all else. Gusti was at that time withdrawing from all his Party associations and joining the Air Force.

The few weeks passed in a flash, and unaccustomed to such carefree fun, I enjoyed it all immensely. I then travelled on via Nancy to see my older brother Alexander, who was studying at the University there.

In pre-revolutionary Russia, Alexander would have been an outstanding and romantic figure, but in émigré life all his advantages became insuperable handicaps.

He was very handsome in a Byronic way, but had grown too tall: two metres. Although he was a powerful swimmer, athletic and well-proportioned, this conspicuous height caused him nothing but embarrassment. He dressed, too, in a way which would inspire approval to-day, but at that time his appearance alone excluded him from the run-of-the-mill casual job. Excessively forthright, if he disliked someone, we often heard him say: 'I told him what I thought of him.'

He was also a passionate idealist and would not hesitate to fight for his opinions against any odds. This also meant that he fell violently and exclusively in love. Luckily, girls discerned this underlying tenderness and would rush to his aid, for he was helpless when confronted by the mechanics of living.

In Nancy he came to meet me at the station. I had not seen him for some time and was shocked at his appearance. His face was pale and drawn, he was far too thin for his height, and racked by a choking cough. I lent him a large slice of my dwindling savings, optimistically certain of a good job as soon as I got to England.

Arriving in Paris, en route, I fell violently ill with incipient blood-poisoning from a neglected scratch. I spent three days in hospital, where effective measures were taken, and the doctor ordered a week of total rest.

I then thought of Princess Bou and was welcomed with open arms, to be cared for as if I were a child again.

An orchid or an anemone – she reminded me again of the most luxuriant and fragile of flowers, or of the most humble and resistant one. Dressed as always in lacy and soft materials in grey and mauve, a wide ribbon replaced the sold or pawned dog-collar of pearls around her neck. She had never abandoned the fashions of her youth, yet she was still supremely elegant.

As we lay on our respective sofas for the next few days, gradually, as if looking back from afar, Princess Bou's tales of bygone days became confidences.

I knew she had been orphaned young, inheriting an immense fortune, even by Russian standards. She then became the ward of the Emperor, as was the custom in such cases, to ensure protection from spongeing relations or guardians. She was beautiful and enchanting too; she married for love, and now she told me again that everything she could wish for seemed to fall into her lap. First a lovely little son. She then decided that above all things she wished for a daughter: all the layette was prepared in shades of pink, but to her deep disappointment, it was another boy, Felix!

At about this time, she began to suffer from extraordinary dreams linked to her life, but with each episode ending in appalling catastrophe.

'. . . They were not really dreams at all, but like a lived-through state of what might be.'

She took it to be a warning from God not to be deluded by her good fortune. So these awful dreams, seldom as they came, reminded her to be thankful.

'... But then they began to come true: first one, then another!'

For instance, she had been staying in the Crimea with the Imperial Family, to whom she was deeply attached, and they then left to return to St. Petersburg. That night she dreamt again.

'I found myself in some closed place. There was a violent crash and the sound of glass smashing all around me in the darkness, while a voice cried: "Mon Dieu, où sont mes enfants!"'

She awoke in terror, and next morning the papers were full of the story of the attempt made on the Emperor Alexander III's life: a bomb had exploded in his coach on the train. None of them had been hurt.

She left at once for St. Petersburg and the Empress Marie Feodorovna told her all about it, adding, 'In my panic I had but one thought and cried: Dear God, where are my children!'

The Emperor, a giant of strength, had supported the roof of the coach on his broad shoulders until help came. thereby acquiring some internal kidney trouble which later caused his premature death.

'... Then again, my son's terrible duel!' ... but even after so many years, she could not go on, for her eldest son, Nikolaï, had become involved in a senseless entanglement with a married woman. According to the current code of honour, the wronged husband's regiment demanded satisfaction, and the terms were murderous. He was brought in dead on a stretcher one morning after the duel.

'She wanted him for cheap reasons, his wealth and position,' Mamma had added. 'It was never a "grande passion", not even for her. She forgot him at once. But his mother's life was broken; she never recovered from his death and their parting in anger.' It appeared that at their last meeting, she had reproached him bitterly.

I now understood why she had tried to dissuade him from ever getting into such a situation again: she had dreamt of the stretcher bringing him home on that fateful morning.

'Later,' Princess Bou added, 'these dreams became worse and worse, but I ceased to believe them, thinking my mind was sick after my son's death, and such horrors befalling my friends and my country could not come true.'

But alas, they did.

After the Revolution, the 'dreams' ceased.

'Never once again in all these years ... Only now,' she said musingly, 'just a few days ago ... I was a young girl again, walking down the gallery in the Winter Palace of St. Petersburg, towards a high, glass door, which was flung open and the Emperor Alexander II, whom I loved so much and who had been a father to me, came towards me with open arms exclaiming:

' "Ma chère, enfin! Vous voila!" '

She smiled at me and said: 'You see this time, it was a beautiful dream!'

I left next day, never to see her again, for soon after, she died.

Many years later on a visit to Soviet Russia, I made a point of visiting her house, Archangelskoye, near Moscow and the Youssoupoff Palace in Leningrad. Her portrait by Serov still hung in the Michaelovski Gallery next to Felix's. Flowing pale draperies, her head on one hand, little dogs scattered about her, she smiled out at me again.

The guide pattered on: 'Here we have the prototype of a frivolous and corrupt aristocrat.'

Over the heads of the gaping crowd I exclaimed:

'You are quite mistaken. I knew her well. She was the most charming, kind, good and unspoilt person imaginable. She was like another grandmother to me.'

The word 'Babouschka' in conjunction with the lovely ethereal vision on the picture quite floored them.

I reached England with high expectations and was at once overcome with the delightful surprise of English politeness, tolerance and common sense, added to the cosy feeling of being back in our nursery again.

The trains, the villages, the country lanes appeared on a reduced scale compared to those on the Continent. Even the mirrors and washbasins seemed to hang too low, as if for a nation of small people, which the English certainly are not. This human measure extended also to the consideration shown to others, resulting in its extreme form in a sort of aloof indifference to any outsider. But the almost watertight stratification of English society according to such unexpected criteria as the school they had gone to, or even the expressions they used, startled me at first.

I was eager to compare all I had heard with reality, from Tower Hill and Hampton Court to the taste of junket, crumpets and mince pies, dishes frequently mentioned but unknown on the Continent. (I must admit I found these specialities rather disappointing.) My fluent English met with surprise and even at times with the assumption that I had learnt it since my arrival, which would really be stretching a Russian's so-called talent for languages a little too far; but of course it made me feel at home at once. Young people my age, however, seemed unused to the easy tone between boys and girls on the Continent and they either eyed each other mistrustfully or overdid the comradeship. Older people were much easier to get on with. The small colony of Russian émigrés adopted me at once. Their welcome, open hospitality and level of talk and interests were as usual out of keeping with their modest surroundings, but one was never bored, many an evening turning to musical impromptus, tzigane songs or theatrical sketches. Yet somehow they were not cynical, even when clowning. Vexations were openly admitted but given no more importance than the equally capricious weather. As elsewhere, they accepted their reduced circumstances and blows of destiny with humility.

Grand Duchess Xenia Alexandrowna, the sister of Russia's last Emperor Nicholas II, was King George's first cousin, and personally on very warm terms of friendship with him. She lived modestly in a small house in Windsor Park, and later in a 'grace and favour' cottage. As a friend of her grandchildren, Baby Youssoupoff in particular, I was often made affectionately welcome.

Gentle, shy and unassuming, she had tremendous dignity in spite of her small size and kitten-like face. She was shy but spoke to everyone with the same diffident kindness, whether restraining Russian chauffeurs from kissing her hand, or ladies from sweeping too deep curtsies. One could not help loving her on sight.

From time to time, she went to tea with the King and Queen, and on one occasion told us that Queen Mary had shown her the latest Fabergé acquisition to her renowned collection: it was an enamelled cigarette-case, its lid embossed with the letter 'K' in diamonds.

The Grand Duchess, holding it in her hand for a moment, was swept by a flood of memories. Her husband, the Grand-Duke Alexander Michaeilovitch, had given it to her for the birth of her first child. (In Russian 'Xenia' is written 'Ksenia' with the letter 'K'.)

'How very interesting,' said the Queen, firmly restoring it to its place of honour in the cabinet.

'But Mamma!' cried her sons later. 'She didn't return it to you?'

"Of course not,' said the Grand Duchess. 'She had paid for it and had every right to it. It just happened to remind me of so many things.'

On my arrival in London the Galitzines had been particularly kind to me, and their three sons became cheerful and brotherly companions. They ran a charming antique shop in Berkeley Square. Doors were locked at lunchtime and the tiny kitchen at the back then became a favourite meeting-place for their compatriots, picnicking happily among the many beautiful objects so like those which had been part of the natural décor of their previous life.

On Sundays these reunions were resumed at their house in suburban Dulwich, often including Father Gibbs, who had been the Tsarevich Alexei's young English tutor.

In 1918, when the Imperial Family and their few attendants had been transferred to Ekaterinburg to be assassinated, Gibbs, Monsieur Gilliard (the Swiss tutor), and Baroness Buxhoeveden (the Empress's lady-in-waiting) had been left behind in Tobolsk because of their foreign passports.

(Lenin had thought it politic at the time to separate them from the group about to be murdered, for fear of reprisals from the Allies.)

Overcome with horror at the death of his pupil, and profoundly impressed by the Christian fortitude of the Imperial Family in their adversity, young Gibbs converted to the Orthodox Faith, later taking orders. In time he became Bishop of the Orthodox Church in London.

He had met the so-called Anastasia, and was convinced that she was not the youngest daughter of the Emperor, although this person having lost her previous identity, honestly seemed to believe that she was. Gilliard was of the same opinion, as was also the Baroness Buxhoeveden, who came to visit me many years later.

Mme. Pouschine, whom we had known in Baden-Baden, where she energetically organised huge picnics for émigré children, had then moved to England with her four daughters and son.

Having first assiduously learnt typing and shorthand, she sent all her children to boarding schools. As they were among the first émigrés in England, they were given scholarships. Living in a garret, she paid single-handed for all their further expenses, including college tuition. During the holidays she would rent a large flat, which became the family's temporary home, and the scene of Christmas tree parties and other happy reunions, as if they had always lived there.

When I reached London, she had almost accomplished her task, only the younger ones were still studying. None of them was to disappoint her.

To-day any young girl is expected to take a job and live on her own. At that time, even in England, this was not generally the case.

Shy, yet over-confident at times, I sometimes found myself facing embarrassing situations. For the most part supporting their families as well, the Russian girls I knew, slightly older and more experienced than I was, helped me with useful hints and half-joking advice. For them liberation from any control or constraint meant full responsibility, not licence.

Russian men (as I have even seen in Soviet Russia to-day) have a great regard for their women, whom they expect to be wife, mistress, mother, friend – and even aunt – as required. They also consider them poetic and romantic figures, which several of these girls indeed were. Having for the most part moved up from Paris they also managed to look surprisingly 'chic' and well-groomed: a twist of a scarf on a simple black dress, an individual hair-do adding that special touch. But they did not belong to any recognisable category, and there was a fascinating contrast between the extreme luxury, glimpsed at from time to time, and the hard facts of their émigré life. Quite apart from the lasting friend-ships we all made, we often met with unexpected ignorance as to anything concerning the Continent, and I was once asked:

'Are you by any chance related to Rasputin?'

'But why should you think so?'

'Oh, I understood all Russian princesses were closely connected with Rasputin.'

Or: 'How thrilling to be Russian!', while we found it nothing but a handicap.

On the other hand, public speaking at the Union Club in Oxford for instance, was on an astoundingly high level, and the wit, brilliance, lazy detachment and originality of thought with which abstruse questions were discussed would be hard to equal anywhere. British and Greek verse was quoted freely with deep appreciation, and perhaps this romantic streak explained their unrealistic attitude whenever political theories were referred to.

The Spanish Civil War was soon to end. As long as it did not base its creed on the same principles, any alternative to Communism enlisted our sympathy. In England opinions were strictly divided, although the pro-communist, so-called pro-Republican half was, as always, much more articulate. On my frequent trips to Oxford where I was often invited by cousins or friends studying there, our views on Communism, Russia or anything concerning the evil side of Soviet reality such as the purges, the camps and so on, were brushed aside with supercilious contempt. 'You're obviously prejudiced' we would hear. After a while we quite gave up trying, but wondered some years later whether this did not explain the careers of Philby, Burgess and Maclean and others.

My hopes of staying in England permanently were soon dashed by the unsurmountable obstacle of the working permit, which became im-possible to circumvent. In spite of opportunities and references, every time I embarked on some job – and I only considered an interesting one involving languages, research or drawing – (much helped by other Russians faced with the same problem), it was always to discover that I would not be allowed to keep it for the same reason. It was most discouraging.

In early spring 1938, the parents of some very good friends of mine invited me to accompany them to Tunisia. This enticing invitation was put as a favour to them: I could organise the journey and help them with my knowledge of French.

Coming just then, two weeks of sunshine and sight-seeing were a wonderful holiday, and my charming hosts spoiled me as if I had been their daughter.

On our return I was met with the shocking news that Alexander had been urgently transferred to Lausanne with acute galloping consumption. The Lithuanian Government, having confiscated our property, now compensated in some measure by allowing the cure to be paid for.

I was the only member of the family outside the country, and there was no choice but to go and join my brother in Switzerland at once. I was soon installed in Lausanne a short distance from his clinic.

The next months were so sad, I prefer not to dwell on them . . . Finally Mamma and Missie came down to replace me, and I was persuaded to go to Berlin, which was so much closer to Lithuania, and would keep me within reach of Switzerland too. Years were to pass before I returned to England again.

In Berlin I found many friends from distant Baden-Baden days, for nothing seems to cement relations like the memory of wild childhood games together. They introduced me to the intense and varied social life of the great city. To my surprise, I was immediately accepted on my own terms, regardless of present émigré circumstances; and most important of all, I was allowed the same opportunities as anyone else as far as work or study were concerned.

Meanwhile Alexander's cure proved to no avail. His condition worsened, and he died in April 1939. His death tore a great rift in our close-knit family, any other trouble seeming a minor matter in comparison; although, within a few months, these would add up to a daunting total.

Part Two

The First Years of the War

July 1939: Peace seemed once again assured and Nazi aggression placated by the Western Powers' recent concessions. The French Embassy on the Pariserplatz in Berlin, just across the street from the famous Hotel Adlon, was giving a party. Following a custom set by his predecessor, Monsieur Francois-Poncet, Monsieur Coulondre, the French Ambassador, frequently invited a few young people to enliven his formal receptions. Official cars with their stiff flags were driving up as I reached the red-carpeted stairs. The guests were diplomats (among them the Italian, British, American and Dutch Ambassadors), members of the Government and some higher échelons of the Nazi Party in their new and fanciful uniforms. At dinner I found myself sitting next to a high-ranking S.S. General.

Frivolous questions sometimes meet with surprising answers:

'Do you still believe in your "Lebensraum"?' (Life-space), I asked innocently.

'It is an essential part of our policy.'

'You will have to move thirty million Poles out of the way before you tackle 180 million Russians.'

'We have ways and means of doing so.'

'If only a dozen remain, the hatred sown will take generations to overcome.'

'We don't need to bother about that.'

My neighbour did not conform to the tall, classical-featured, cold-eyed S.S. type, for his round head prolonged his neck like a knee, with a few tortoise-like folds for articulation above his stiff collar. His rimless spectacles seemed to replace eyes in his spongy, pock-marked face. Munching the delicious food with porcine delectation, he appeared calmly convinced of what he had just said. Probably rarely emerging from his own air-tight circle where neither criticism nor contradiction penetrated, he was perhaps unaware of the enormity of this pronounce-

73

ment, since as we were soon to learn, for the Nazis theory inevitably preceded application.

It made one tremble for the future!

Dinner over, I hurried to a friend, Albert E. 'I cannot bear this a minute longer: I have been sitting next to a horrible person with mad and murderous ideas. Let's leave.'

It was a starlit night. In front of the Adlon, on the other side of the .wide square, tall S.S. men in white summer uniforms stood shoulder to shoulder in serried rows: handsome wooden faces, straight necks, heads short-cropped, flattening off over their low foreheads. They were alike as two peas out of a pod, which was why they had been selected.

Albert seized me by the elbow, 'Let's go in and see what's on!'

'We can't. They'll stop us.'

'Not in this get-up. Look cool!'

In we went, trying to look as unconcerned as possible, and sat down warily at a nearby small table. Discreetly glancing around, we saw high and highest officials of the Reich, their wives compressed into gowns plastered with embroidery. We recognised them from the papers and newsreels. Drinks were served to everyone.

A few minutes later, the doors were flung open and in marched Hitler, Goering, Goebbels and a few others: they strutted past our table in a tight group. How small they were! They looked like stuffed dolls, unreal, a caricature of the likenesses published for the edification of the people, almost as grotesque as targets at a fair, but they exuded importance and frightening power. The fascination they seemed to exercise over the hushed and reverent assembly, frozen into a servile smile, was due to the irresistible attraction of Might!

We soon slipped out after that, glad to get away into the balmy night.

'We could have shot him. No one would have stopped us!' I exclaimed.

'We didn't look like it.'

We boarded the first bus going our way, swishing past the flowering Tiergarten, down the Lützowufer towards the Keithstrasse, where we happened to live in neighbouring houses.

I never saw Hitler at close quarters again.

I was often invited by Ambassador Lipski to the Polish Embassy where I had several close friends. The Poles knew that they were next on Hitler's list of countries to be coerced or conquered, but had decided not to be intimidated.

'He doesn't mean what he proclaims', they said. 'He only intends to frighten the world into acquiescence. He cannot be so mad as to start a war.'

The horror-stricken public reaction to the very thought of war, and the explosive relief each time it had been averted, seemed reassuring to them. 'In 1914', some remembered, 'the whole country was like a blood-hound on a leash. Whereas now . . .'

Between hatred and contempt, the Poles sent home one report after another describing cardboard tanks, trumped-up manoeuvres. They were convinced that a brave stand would at last call the Nazis' bluff. But among their friends some wiser heads were shaken in doubt – for they feared these reports would prove misleading: the German Army was becoming a formidable weapon, much more so than the Poles seemed to realise. 'Read *Mein Kampf*,' they said. 'Nothing can stop Hitler now.'

The Gestapo had not yet adopted OGPU methods and efficiency: during the summer of 1939, all this was talked over most freely, and not only in the Embassies.

Many years ago, our exuberant Mamma, always ready to take some slow or even lame duck under her soaring wing, had befriended two pale and shy young German girls. They had been sent to their eminent relatives for a season in pre-war St. Petersburg.

She included them in her group of friends, and swept them along with her to all the parties and entertainments. They never forgot this happy time, and one of the two sisters, Olga, invited me to spend the last month of summer in Friedland, her remote Schloss in Silesia on the Polish border – Missie was planning to join me there from Venice, where she was staying with friends.

I was welcomed into the ramshackle old castle as if I had been a member of the family. Originally crenellated and surrounded by a moat, it had been spoilt by additions, spiced with a dash of neo-Gothic. Money had not been plentiful since 1918, and what was forthcoming had not been spent on Friedland. A sort of cosy shabbiness spread like a rambler rose gone wild over the whole place, adding greatly to its charm. But the soul of it all was of course Countess Olga herself, whose loving kindness extended to all around her.

Her figure, trim in youth, had expanded to a tea-cosy shape: narrow at the shoulders and widening downwards. With a self-deprecating sense of humour, she maintained that this had happened when she stopped riding. Crinkly, orangey hair, the tip of her nose yellowed by the cigarette forever smouldering beneath it, belied that she had once been pretty, perhaps even resembling Lori, her younger daughter. But her charm had not faded. She had a friendly word and the same tone for everybody. A cheerful mixture of naïveté and great good humour, her love of nature, happy-go-lucky naturalness and un-German inefficiency, made her a most lovable 'Aunt by choice'.

Her husband felt cheated by fate, for he had married an heiress and, after the upheavals of 1918, found himself with a wife whose delightful qualities were not of the kind he could appreciate. Under a veneer of jolliness and good cheer, he kept this unscrupulous side of his character well concealed.

The girls were charming friends: Ella gently pretty and sweet-natured and Lori with her fair hair and brilliant colouring, they set each other off with their contrasting looks and temperaments. Country bred, they were unspoilt in spite of recent personal success at parties and gatherings in Berlin, and took the days as they came, ready for any excursion, any plan.

A huge bunch of slightly squashed red roses protruded from the high doorway of the snake-like dark grey train, as it drew into the Oppeln station nearest to Friedland.

Over the clouds of steam, over the roses, slanting green eyes in a honey-brown face, framed in sun-bleached golden hair, smiled down at us. The vision would have been startling anywhere, but was quite breath-taking for remote Oppeln. Passengers and porters watched in wonder as we helped Missie down from the Venice train, collecting her bags and satchels, and the roses of course – last tribute from some ardent admirer.

We had been looking forward eagerly to her frequently postponed arrival. In a happy group, Ella, Lori and I had all gone to the station to meet her.

After a rather lop-sided teen-age period, with lank hair, gangly, unruly, coltish arms and legs, Missie had burst overnight into unexpected beauty, with a lovely trim figure, and the contrast in colouring which surprised one every time anew. As we now heard stories from Venice, we understood her delayed departure, for the weeks there must have been a slice of delightful unreality, packed tight with every romantic attention Italians tend to distribute so generously.

We could not know then that this bout of carefree fun was to cease as suddenly as it had begun. But she certainly looked all the better for it.

I had missed her sense of humour and unswerving loyal support greatly during the previous months in Berlin, for we had always got on perfectly. We seemed to attract the same friends, but never the same admirers. We also shared a sense of the ridiculous and dislike of hum-drum conformity, which in Missie became an almost dare-devil defiance of destiny. Quick, intelligent, happy-go-lucky, she was scrupulously honest but perhaps excessively uncompromising with herself and with others. I was far more diplomatic, tending to detour or soften the impact of difficulties, rather than head for them full tilt. As a result, we made a good team, and this was to help us over many a hurdle in the years to come.

We now planned visits and picnics to show Missie the neighbourhood, as we lazily enjoyed the lovely weather and helped Olga in her garden, or bicycled through the surrounding country towards evening.

Meanwhile (although we only understood this later), confident of eventual promotion, our host was busily ingratiating himself with the local Nazi Party. This was not discussed in Friedland, for Olga never questioned (or had ceased to question) anything her husband did or said. As we were with her and the girls all the time, we did not pay any attention to his doings either. Summer in the country absorbed every minute of the day, leaving little time for speculation.

There was a ripple of worry, however, when on Friday the 18th of August, a brown slip of paper enjoined our host to contact the Staff in the nearest district town. He was to be assigned to counter-espionage.

Foolishly, we did not then understand the implications of this job.

'It was the same in 1914,' said Olga, grieving, as we gazed at the planet Mars next evening. It seemed so much larger and more orange-red than we had ever remembered it. 'It is a bad omen.'

Although the 'official' tension with Poland had been heightening, according to the wireless, there was as yet no sign of strain in this remote province, close as we were to the Polish frontier. But, Olga confided in deep dismay, she thought something serious was starting.

Her husband had returned on leave for the week-end, which seemed reassuring, but early in the morning on Tuesday 22nd August, watering her flowers under our window, Olga rapped on the pane and announced with a long face: 'Troops are going to be billeted with us. They are arriving in an hour.'

She had been taking part in a course of Civil Defence Training, assisted by all the amazons of the village, clad in the same harem-like trousers, when the Mayor interrupted with the announcement that they were all to prepare for the arrival of many troops.

The house exploded in uproar: mattresses and pillows had to be collected, closed-up rooms opened and aired. We dashed down to help and met a group of officers, to whom we were introduced by a flurried Olga. Most of their vehicles were already in the Schloss courtyard. In the shortest time they installed their wireless, while the soldiers were billeted all over the village. By tea-time these had paired off with all the local beauties as if they had been there for years.

The officers were not so easily thawed. Their Colonel, though stiff in manner, seemed quite nice, with a clever, alert expression. His second in command's hair was brushed into a bristly tuft in front and closely shorn all down the vertical back of his head. When bowing, he folded up like a penknife, shedding his monocle. The two younger officers, Böcken and Schöne, were nice-looking and did not seem to conform to this other 1914 prototype.

Conversation at lunch, frequently interrupted by telephone calls, became choppy, as everything concerning their past and future movements was a dead secret. We were on tenterhooks for fear that some harmless question might lead them to think Missie and I were using our wiles on them to extract information.

In the evening, avoiding conversational pitfalls, we persuaded them to play silly games. To everybody's surprise, the Rittmeister developed a decided talent for barter at Monopoly and won. They did not seem to have much to do except for Lt. Schöne, who was often glimpsed vanishing through doors like the White Rabbit in *Alice in Wonderland*, a portfolio clasped under his arm. He joined us later, however, although drooping from lack of sleep. Every now and then he would pull himself together with a jerk to press his tiddlywink and close his eyes as soon as his superiors were not looking. It appeared he could not retire to bed before they did, and they were as fresh as daisies. We nudged each other and left all together to enable him to do so too before he fell off his chair.

Bicycling next day, we found the roads now lined with military vehicles and lorries, moving unobtrusively towards the frontier like a spreading blight.

A column of Flak (anti-aircraft) stood at the side of the road, their vehicles decked out with flowers and branches, mottoes and drawings sketched in chalk wherever there was space to spare. On one there was the rough picture of a bed with huge billowing German eiderdowns, floating among clouds – a sustaining dream for the coming campaign; on another an optimist had drawn in huge letters 'Lublin–Paris' on his lorry. For them the War was still an adventurous excursion.

The wireless announced a Pact with the Soviets: apparently the French and the English 'had pushed themselves between the Germans and the Russians, disturbing their natural leanings towards friendship'. The Colonel told Olga later, he was ashamed we should hear this – which was decent of him. What a break from the Nazis' professed ideology of anti-communism! It proved how fundamentally alike they were.

Missie and I decided not to discuss politics at all. We were not treated as undesirable aliens, but with a touch of compassion – as if dealing with a patient who must undergo a serious operation. Our impartial opinions were bound to fall out of fashion, and blind nationalism would be the only acceptable cause in the future.

From Wednesday, the 23rd August, troops began blatantly marching towards the frontier night and day, but as yet there was no mobilisation order. Olga, trembling, expected it at any moment, but the girls were calm and blasé, saying it was exactly the same the year before. We began to hope again. Anxious waiting. There was no sign of the 1914 pre-war euphoria.

At nightfall, the officers went into the garden to read some extremely secret orders. They strolled up and down for a long time, while we watched them from windows above, wishing they could tell us what was happening. But the intensifying sound of heavy traffic was evidence enough. As the night darkened, we went to watch tanks and lorries clattering over the bridge outside the gates. Only a narrow slit enabled the drivers to see their way, as they rattled past, all lights out, tearing through the night at terrific speed. Poor Poland! How could anyone withstand this steamroller of death. The thundering procession produced a terrifying impression on us all. Oppressed and silent, we went to bed on our return. The officers were hoping to make a night of it, and were very disappointed.

Next morning, Thursday, 24th August, the Franzi Birons came to pay us a visit. Their part of the country was even more infested with troops than ours. Wartenberg and Langendorf, their respective homes, were full of officers, but no civilians had been mobilised as yet.

Towards three, a neighbour, Alda Strachwitz, appeared with her daughter, another girl and a handsome Viennese Flying Officer. She had come to persuade Olga to let us go to a long-planned ball on Saturday. Olga, more than dubious, said she would think it over. The Colonel laughingly suggested placing some of his soldiers at her disposal to prevent us slipping out, but at such an uncertain time, nobody felt much like dancing. The nice Viennese officer got on the nerves of his German colleagues, for he would not take this coming war seriously and flew to Vienna to do his daily shopping. North and South Germans were very definitely not on the same wavelength.

Lt. Bücken suddenly burst into the room and called that they were leaving: they had received immediate marching orders. Within an hour, telephones taken down, everything packed, the troops lined up in the courtyard to take their orders from Lt. Schöne. The papers were then burnt on the ground in front of him, and they all leaped into their respective cars, tanks etc. and without an instant's hesitation or confusion, tore past the front gates. We stood on the steps to take leave of the officers, who were soon off too, dust and gravel spurting under their wheels.

On our return to the house, we found a young man we knew from Berlin, Theo Balthazar, waiting for Lori. Unfairly, she had no particular use for a rather floppy civilian at such a moment, and his black and white shoes and pink tie did not meet with much approval.

In the evening our host, who had just returned, had champagne served. Although nothing was said, it looked like leave-taking. One could hardly hear oneself speak for the thundering noise of heavy artillery crossing the bridge down by the gates. We four girls and Theo went out again and were overwhelmed by the sight: a dense column of enormous lorries, guns, tanks and cars packed with troops, their headlights covered except for those narrow slits, they rumbled past us at top speed like the night before, their deafening rattle over the cobblestones making the houses shake.

The soldiers waved and shouted at us and were gone next moment in clouds of choking dust. Columns of sappers followed them, their lorries laden with boards and every sort of building equipment. At one moment they had to slow down, and out of the group of tired and dirty men packed close on to a lorry, a soldier leaned down and asked us to post a card for him. It was addressed to Iéna, so they came from Thuringia.

An army on the march could only mean war. The pretence of 'manoeuvres' seemed to have been dropped for good. As also the pretence of 'negotiation'.

On Friday the 25th August, Count Haja Strachwitz, Alda's husband, came to say good-bye. In great secrecy, he told Lori that they had all received orders to attack at four o'clock the following morning. He thought it would all be over very quickly, for the German forces were infinitely stronger. (This seemed probable after what we had seen these last days.) He trusted and hoped the English would not step in; should we be bombed, which he thought improbable, we were to go out into the park or dive into any sort of cellar. On leaving he sighed: 'Poor Poles'.

The troops had stopped marching through and the whole day passed in a sort of tense silence. The evening news announced that the English had signed a military pact with Poland. World war now seemed certain, and nothing we could say could cheer Olga up.

Saturday was a terrible, beastly, waiting day. No shooting to be heard, although we were so close to the frontier. The order for general mobilisation was expected to come through at any moment.

Meanwhile unmilitary-looking men had been gathering in Friedland and the surrounding countryside. They were brought in by requisitioned vehicles and a handful of equally ill-assorted officers set to work trying to organise them into a sort of cohesion as Civil Militia. Some of these were billeted in the Schloss, but as they did not install their own telephone, they expected us to relay messages to them. Otherwise we had no contact with them, except for the smell and noise. They never greeted anyone, which irked Olga, whose dislike of living in Berlin was because 'above and below our apartment, and in the street, there are people whom one doesn't know'.

Theo and a friend came again to help in the kitchen garden, and in the evening three officers were announced: they had come for 'die Damen', and we remembered Alda's party for the first time. One of the two colleagues our Viennese friend had brought with him was wearing a Spanish order, earned in the recent Civil War in Spain. He had fought with the airborne Legion Condor on the Nationalists' side. To our surprise they seemed quite unaware of any tension. Perhaps they got their orders last.

It was impossible for us to leave Olga all alone at such a moment. Rather crestfallen, they proposed to give us another ball after the war.

The news was so non-committal, it sounded as if there were a dead-lock somewhere. We began to hope again that if nothing had happened yet, perhaps it need not happen after all.

Lori sniffed her way down a corridor and traced the source of a pleasant smell of lavender to a door marked 'Gessler'. She surmised rightly it could not proceed from any of the usual militia. Presently Olga stumbled over a small man in spectacles wandering disconsolately around the hall. He turned out to be Count Gessler, the pianist, whose name we had all seen on concert posters. He had received his mobilisation papers the day before, and between consternation and amusement described his first collision with the Army to a sympathetic audience of Olga and Ella. He was immediately bawled out by a sergeant, who had realised that even their technique of bullying would not make a soldier out of this (for him) 'contemptible intellectual'.

Whenever he could get away, Gessler played most wonderfully on Ella's piano, tinny as a saucepan, but he soon heard he must leave at four in the morning with the motley crowd which had been adorning the front doorstep for the last few days. Some of them had acquired miscellaneous bits of uniform, but nothing could be found to fit Gessler. He shied away from the sight of sailcloth underpants, and maintained that the towels presented to him by the State were even unfit for door-mats, besides rendering him incapable of ever playing a note of music again. He was in an awful state of nerves, visualising the collapse of all the values he had lived for. To add to his troubles, he had acquired a passion for Ella.

At dawn, rigged out as a scarecrow, enormous horn-rimmed spectacles under a convict's cap, he bade us farewell, his expression a living illustration of the inscription over Dante's inferno: 'Abandon hope, all ye who enter here.'

Olga and I went out on to the lawn, wet with dew. The sun was just rising on another splendid day, the roses and borders in full bloom, but we felt utterly depressed. Returning to bed shortly after, there was a scratching sound at the window and there through the bars peeped Gessler's goblin-like face. 'We are leaving for Tost!' he whispered urgently, and vanished. It was like a last message from someone dragged away to a fate worse than death by unscrupulous ruffians, and no one could come to his help. I dutifully scribbled his message on my looking-glass in lipstick, for lack of a pencil at hand, and collapsed into bed again. He probably wanted Ella to know.

Overnight the shops had emptied. They were either hoarding their stock, or sold out owing to the onslaught of customers, alarmed by news of imminent rationing.

Countess Ballestrem, another neighbour, came over with what seemed the express purpose of enumerating all the reserves of provisions, coal, soap, etc. she had stored and Olga had not. Trying to catch up, a pig was hastily slaughtered and served in various guises at every meal. Missie and I both detested pork, but personal tastes in food could no longer be considered.

Most of the horses in the region were now requisitioned at a good price. A black-out was introduced. After the first moment of panic, the people were quite resigned and eagerly obedient.

Lori and I drove the painter Dungert (who had spent a happy summer in a cottage on the estate), his wife, cat and luggage to Oppeln station. Many trains were no longer running, but he was eager to return to Berlin. Near Tillowitz we passed a dummy airport: a huge field with wooden planes planted on stands in formation, as if ready to take off. When seen from above, it might look quite convincing. The real one was somewhere near.

'Please take him. What should become of him in a war?' and a plump, pitch-black, Aberdeen terrier was dropped into my lap, as Lori, Missie and I sat painfully conspicuous in our open car, drawn in to the extreme edge of the road so as to give way to a line of Luftwaffe lorries and vehicles.

Our address scribbled hastily on a scrap of paper, the tall young Air Force officer jumped back into his official car, his driver's yellow hair fluttering like feathers under his cap, they wove their way in and out of the column, and were soon lost to view. It all happened so fast we hadn't time to consider Olga's reaction to this addition to her complicated household.

We were on our way back from Langendorf on the Polish frontier. Lieutenant Bücken had returned to visit us, his car breaking down on arrival. Count Haja Strachwitz happened to be in Friedland, his high rank enabling him to authorise Lori to drive this distraught young man back to his regiment in time for an important officers' conference, Missie and I going along for company. We re-fuelled her father's car at a military petrol station, and picked our way gingerly through dense columns of troops moving steadily towards the Polish frontier under a scorching sun – perhaps to their death and destruction.

The long avenue leading to Stubendorf near Oppeln had become a giant stable for the cavalry, the horses saddled with brand-new harnesses. Under golden autumn leaves, this scene was in contrast deceptively peaceful, and resembled an engraving of Napoleonic times.

As there were no civilians in sight, we created a minor sensation, but any ribaldry was checked at the sight of our chaperon in uniform, blushing for our sakes. We got to Langendorf in time for the conference. The other officers were amazed to see us, and beamed with joyful reminiscence of our last game of Monopoly. Lieutenant Schöne was of course invisible, but we were glad to hear his zeal had received due recognition, and he had been promoted to 'Oberleutnant'.

For our return trip, they entrusted us to the care of a motorcyclist. Armed to the teeth, his raincoat (incongruous in that weather) blowing up like a balloon, topped by his steel helmet, he piloted us back through the dense line of marching troops and vehicles. Every bridge was guarded, every man in uniform except for carts filled with workmen, wearing yellow badges on their arms marked 'Deutsche Wehrmacht': these were recently enrolled peasants who would be doing construction work.

On reaching Friedland, Lori burst into tears on hearing she had just missed a call from Athens from her unofficial fiancé, Manfred Schröder, who was attached to the Embassy there. They had been thinking of marrying in the Spring, but now a sudden urgency spurred everyone's plans: 'Who knows how long before . . .' was an unspoken thought in everybody's mind. Lori meant to leave for Athens and marry Manfred at a moment's notice if the worst came to the worst.

Olga's joy at our safe return turned to dismay at the sight of our new dog, who was immediately attacked by the grumpy old house-dog, Caesar. But our Scottie was so enchanting, she soon gave in, provided his movements were confined to our room and the garden. His name 'Sherry', and address, were engraved on his collar, adorned also with his master's Oberleutnant's star. At first he would go frantic with excitement whenever he heard a plane, and rush out to see if it was landing. But Scotties are philosophical animals: after a few days, he trotted happily at heel, unless a whiff of rabbit proved too tempting to resist, and at night slept curled up on an old sofa in my room.

His master came once on a visit. Lori, as a connoisseur of uniforms, told us he was a dive-bomber pilot. He wore Spanish orders, having also been with the Condor Legion in Spain, and said Soviet aviators were brave, but pig-headed, easy to out-manoeuvre. However they had the unpleasant habit of finishing off their enemy, even if he was parachuting from his shot-down plane.

As he played with Sherry, who bounced on all four stubby paws for joy, like a performing pony, his dark and thoughtful face lightened. But it was soon time to leave.

We never saw him again. He wrote once, and our answer returned some weeks later, with the terse remark: 'Killed in action.'

By Wednesday the 30th of August, a strange confusion of dates set everyone guessing. A neighbour had received her mobilisation papers as a nurse dated Monday 28th of August and headed 'third Day of Mobilisation.'

As we surmised, there must have been some fundamental change since Saturday 26th, when – according to Haja – the invasion of Poland was to have been unleashed at crack of dawn. Theo Balthazar's friend told us his regiment was just going to open fire, according to previous orders, when a counter order arrived by messenger. Their commanding officer nearly had him shot as a saboteur, but they induced this fire-eater to hold his hand until they heard more. Haja Strachwitz confirmed that the order *not* to shoot came in some places about ten minutes before the indicated time for the invasion.

This gave us hope again, for one would not have thought it possible to halt the advancing Army once it was on its way. Perhaps, unknown to us, some agreement had been reached? Nervous tension again piled up unbearably! Olga said in anguish, 'You are young, you do not know what it is like! All the misery, the endless dead. And no one wins in the end.'

Our rooms being on the ground floor, a revolver had been deposited in my writing-table drawer in case of prowlers, for now there was no man to be found in our part of the country. Bücken taught us how to use it, and Haja left extra bullets in case of need. They thought it would be a good idea to come and break into our window, just to see our faces as we tried to shoot. It would be worth the exceedingly small risk of being hit.

The wave of invasion had moved right up to the frontier, and now all was silent around us. The villagers stood about in little disconsolate knots. We heard that the Poles had blown up all their bridges. We never left the wireless, and in the evening the German Government's demands were announced. The Poles then mobilized.

Towards one o'clock that night, Irina telephoned from Venice, surprised not to have got through before, and ignorant of the fact that we had been cut off from post and telephone for many days now. She sounded as from another world, describing parties, people; the possibility of war no more than a ripple of anxiety. She meant to stay on in Italy, whatever happened. We had had no other news from the family for weeks, and we feared our parents in Kovno would be frantically worried about us.

The 31st August was a deadly quiet day. There was nothing to be heard, which seemed even more ominous than all the preceding clatter. A few letters and cards came through from the so-called 'Front', but this time they were really on their way! Horribly depressed, we wandered around aimlessly. In the evening the wireless proffered some detailed explanation as to the German ultimatum, which in fact had already expired!

In contrast to what we had heard about the prevailing mood on all sides in 1914, the country and even senior Army officers seemed plunged in deepest consternation at the thought of what lay ahead.

3

On Friday the 1st September, we were all up early. The chatter of the wireless, turned on at full blast, followed us around the house.

During breakfast we listened to the Reichstag speech: declaration of War against Poland! But Poland had been invaded at 4 a.m.!

So it had come at last! Somehow one had kept on hoping it would be averted. Now that it had happened, we felt stunned. It was like the telegram announcing Alexander's death. One just stared blankly at the news without assimilating its meaning. But we all realised a great crime had been committed, and there would be no limit to the price to pay.

By the next day the wireless announced that the entire Polish Air Force had been destroyed by the Germans. Otherwise no further news, except for a letter from Olga's husband, saying that they were progressing 'beyond expectations'.

On Sunday 3rd September, 11 a.m. England declared War on Germany. It was a great blow, as, unrealistically, everybody had hoped against hope they would not intervene.

We had forgotten that Hitler always made the most of the sacrosanct British week-end. His 'Blitz' moves into neighbouring countries were timed for Fridays, knowing British politicians would be away for the week-end in the country. Caught unawares, some time would elapse before any action could be taken. But his understanding of British reactions did not go much further than that.

Next day British planes were sighted over Holland: first sign of hostilities on the Western Front. They were, we were told, turned back by flak. There was as yet no sign of a French declaration of War and the Italians were also lying low. This brought us another flicker of hope: perhaps negotiations were continuing behind the scenes? But on Thursday the 5th September, the French joined in. Three days later, one week after the invasion had started, German troops were near Warsaw!

On Sunday 17th September, the Soviets broke through their Polish frontier, having first waited comfortably for the Germans to do their dirty work for them. The invasion was justified by the German wireless as being necessary for the protection of White-Russians (an ethnological group) in the Ukraine. These poor people were caught in giant pincers between Nazis and Communists.

The day after hostilities began, Manfred Schröder rang up from Athens: he wanted Lori to join him at once, and marry him. Olga was in tears, for she could not decide whether to go with her. Lori was delighted to get away from everything, excited at the prospect of marriage. The German Ambassador in Athens, Prince Erbach, and his Hungarian wife, were charming people and assured Olga they would take good care of her.

Since she was marrying a diplomat, she had to be armed with Aryan pedigrees, genealogical trees and goodness knows what else. When all was ready, she was told that according to a new rule she must acquire a special visa to leave Germany, which the local Mayor could not give her. On telephoning Berlin, she learnt that she must collect this paper between two trains in Vienna.

Finally Lori left at six in the morning on the 12th September. The leave-taking was tearful, but she was happy to be off and looked extremely sweet and pretty.

In Russia in 1918, pictures, jewels and valuables were deposited for safety in banks, later to be all the more easily confiscated by a bankrupt communist government. We therefore strongly advised Olga to take hers out of the Berlin Bank and keep them with her from now on. I offered to fetch them for her. It was to be the first of an endless series of ever more adventurous and arduous war journeys.

During the long trip to the capital, the train was shunted past goods trains loaded with battered lorries and bullet-ridden tanks, crumpled like a handful of tin-foil: the aftermath of invasion. Aeroplanes circled above the bigger towns, such as Breslau and Frankfurt-Oder, whose stations seethed with military uniforms, and red-capped train-conductors in smart new blue suits with red facings. They were waiting to be transferred to Poland, to be dropped off one by one at every station and represent the Reich and its impeccable organization.

Berlin at last. It was immediately apparent that the tone of the town had greatly changed since I had left it just a few weeks ago. Many public buildings and factories were surmounted by soldiers manning the flak guns. A greyness had fallen over the city. There was little traffic except for official or military cars and squeaking, rattling, jingling trams. People scurried about, purposefully dragging lumpy luggage. As I waited in a long queue for the rare taxi, I longed for a porter.

I was to stay at Olga's flat, but the windows were not yet blacked out, and I groped around in unlit rooms. There was still one supreme luxury: the bath water was running hot. Owing to a shortage of coal, we had been without hot baths in Friedland for weeks.

Telephone calls met with immediate response, and my short stay in town fell into a planned shape at once. Diplomatic cars were now high in demand, and their owners, conscious of a sudden state of exalted privilege, were also touchingly eager to be of help. A dinner party was soon arranged, and I was presently fetched and later driven home again through Grünewald, under a cold full moon, the roads quiet and deserted as never before.

Breakfast had to be skipped, for the last series of ration cards expired the day I left, and I could not deprive the house of any provisions. Berlin buses had been considerably reduced in numbers so it took me a good hour to reach the Hotel Bristol for lunch. I was relieved to find my hosts at once, for the place was chock-full: many acquaintances, representatives of the diplomatic and ministerial worlds, dotted with well-known actors, and some of the most dashing society women of the capital, who still seemed to go from party to party. In spite of the loud hum of conversation, the clatter of plates, and the scurrying waiters, the atmosphere seemed tense and glum, and most of the talk alarming.

The Polish campaign seemed to have passed horrifyingly unnoticed. All interest was concentrated on the coming struggle in the West. I felt out of tune with everything. This was not the case when among young people, for the men were all on the point of departure, and the girls on the verge of war work, Red Cross etc. The older generation, however, seemed only to think in numbers and units, which was numbing. Perhaps this was more noticeable in Berlin, where troubles ahead as yet appeared an academic question, and people still tried to lead the old life.

We were presently joined by my friend Renata Nostitz, recently married to Baron Waldthausen. She looked so pretty and elegant: pageboy auburn hair framing a madonna-like face with neat small features and curling, secret, Gothic smile. Married just one day before he left, she had little hope of her husband getting leave in the near future. The Chief of Protocol now loomed towering in the group around us, and proceeded to tell her that the war was going to last a long time, a few thousand losses in Poland hardly counted as there would be many more on the Western Front eventually, etc. There was so much of the Baron in height, breadth and booming affirmative, that his pronouncements carried weight and poor Renata was close to tears.

How lucky we were not to know the future! That Renata's husband would soon be killed; that the losses predicted by the Baron would amount to many millions. So much more misery and suffering on all sides, than even the worst pessimist could have foreseen.

For the next hours I was busy sending Olga's trunks to Friedland: an endless business involving taxis, fumbling along in a dark station, one bag breaking open as it was being weighed, but finally all were accepted and I was free of the bother and responsibility.

The next morning I drove to the Bank and was finally handed a large square, extremely heavy, sealed black box, containing Olga's jewels.

It was a long dull journey back again. I dared not leave my things alone for a second, not even to sleep. Slightly befuddled, I got out at the wrong end of the Oppeln station, but a kind soldier carried all my things over to the right platform, enabling me to catch the local train to Lambsdorf with about ten seconds to spare.

I was met with beaming smiles by Ella and Missie and that charming dog, Sherry. They had managed to scrounge a car from somewhere for the short trip, and all the trunks sent down from Berlin were duly collected.

In the evening, after supper, Olga unpacked her 'heirlooms', which were really wonderful. We turned them over with admiring interest, layer upon layer of beautiful pieces, many of them of Russian origin. Some were set aside for Lori, and Olga asked me to re-string her Russian Fabergé eggs before storing everything away for the time being.

Missie and I embarked on a Red Cross course in the village of Friedland, in the company of slightly bovine colleagues. The course was enriched by a dose of racial doctrine. A chart showed conclusively what dreadful things would happen when a criminal married an idiot, or an 'Asoziale' (elastic term). The deplorable result was a quantity of tiny black and striped figures marked with a cross – which meant premature death, and further figures in patchwork signifying a brood of criminals. A primitive magic lantern then projected a photograph of two fat people walking a big black poodle. This portrayed the objectionable 'birth-control' practised by the rich. The poodle certainly looked well fed – there was even a bow on his collar. The implication was that to own a poodle instead of breeding offspring was 'asozial' (anti-social). But who could prove the fat couple had not eleven children tucked away at home?

Then followed various racial types; first the Nordic prototype: stony blue stare, woodenly handsome, in keeping with the current taste in sculpture, which the Berliners nicknamed 'Popo mit Schwert' (naked heroes clutching a sword).

Latin deviations of the white race were tolerated as a concession to the Italian alliance, but then, clearly identifiable, came African and Asiatic types, followed by the sad caricature of what the Nazi paper *Der Stürmer* considered Semitic or Jewish. The last slide depicted a monster: beetle-browed, bow-legged, scowling, ears like teapot handles, high cheek bones, slanting eyes. Suggestions were proffered: 'A Mongol?' 'A murderer?' Testily, the instructor said: 'No, no. A Russian.'

They looked at us doubtfully, as we sat in the front row, head and shoulders taller, slimmer and fairer than anyone in the room, Missie's classical profile defying any qualification. Tentatively, they asked: 'You are of course of Scandinavian origin?' 'Not at all. Russian on all sides for generations.' Embarrassed silence.

But that particular slide was not shown again. It was the first time we had come up against this monstrous stupidity hatched by Rosenberg.

Lieutenant Bücken now came all the way from Berlin to see us, spending three of his eight days' leave in Friedland. We feared he would be disappointed to find Lori married and gone, but he seemed to consider this a second home and included Olga, us and the dogs in affectionate remembrance. For him the Polish campaign had been no walkover, and he spoke with compassion of the scorched country and fleeing population:

'We will pay bitterly for this, for what had we lost there?' he said sadly.

He seemed to have been through all the worst fighting and told us of the death of his two best friends during the siege of Kutno.

The delusively anonymous casualty lists, so dreadfully high for the Poles, appeared to take on their real aspect of personal tragedy as soon as they included a friend or acquaintance on any side.

The post had begun to function again, and we got disturbing news from our family in Kovno. With good reason, they were dreading the Soviet entry into Lithuania, which meant that they would have to emigrate again, and at a moment's notice. Georgie had been granted a passport, which was significant, as he had reached military age, when passports were always withheld, and meant that the Lithuanians declined all further responsibility for his safety. Mamma was considering leaving for Berlin with him, ahead of Papa.

We thought it better to dissuade her from this plan, for food rationing and bombing were likely. We could scramble along somehow, but not while having to look after Mamma and Georgie at the same time. We therefore recommended Italy, where Irina could prepare her stay, and we would help from here.

She wrote that a number of Poles had crossed over to Lithuania, hoping to escape from both the Germans and the Soviets advancing into their country from west and east. A friend and erstwhile neighbour in Lithuania, whom they had not seen for many years, owing to severed relations between both countries, Count Andrei Tyszkiewicz, reached Kovno with his mother, having fled from their Galician estates.

His brother drove through burning villages with his wife and children, a revolver in one hand, the reins in the other, and so reached the frontier safely.

The Radziwills and many others were deported to Russia. It was as if the clock had been turned back to 1918 again! Niesviez, their home, was plundered. It was famous also for its wonderful library. Although at such times material objects are of secondary importance, the wanton destruction made one sick.

(Thanks to the intervention of the Queen of Italy, and the German Ambassador, Count von der Schulenburg, in Moscow – on his own initiative – the Radziwills and all their relatives would be temporarily freed again.)

Meanwhile Soviet soldiers moved into the barracks of Vilna. They requisitioned beds from the hospital, and to free them, turned all the patients out on to the floor. They then claimed an ambulance from the Lithuanians who were eager to please and mollify their dreaded neighbours, so they complied at once, and sent it with driver and nurse. When these did not return, the anxious Lithuanians were told that the Soviets needed them too. But the driver was married and had left his wife and children at home! The answer was: he would find another wife in Soviet Russia and beget other children.

The Soviet troops were apparently still entirely controlled by Commissars, and were exceedingly suspicious of the Germans.

For our family the war could not have come at a worse moment. We were cut off from our parents and Georgie in Lithuania. Our elder sister, Irina, was in Italy and all our relations and most of our childhood friends distributed in France, England and the United States. For the first time since Alexander's death, just a few months before, we wondered whether he had not been spared from worse to come. The year before, as the same wave of panic spread over Europe, he had become frantic with impatience at the thought of being tied to the sanatorium in Lausanne.

We had not lived in Germany for any length of time since our early childhood in Baden-Baden, and the few months I had just spent in Berlin at art school. We did not even speak the language very well.

Olga begged us to stay with her, but we did not feel we could do so indefinitely, for in spite of our German and Italian studies, we were chafing under the remoteness of Friedland. It was becoming imperative for us to get jobs, as we were cut off from any financial help. Although we were not sure of getting permission to do so, this would all be easier in Berlin. On the other hand we knew we must avoid becoming involved in anything that might be compromising for us either in Germany or abroad.

Very kindly, Olga offered us her flat in Berlin, until we could get organised. She put it as if we were doing her a favour: if it stood empty, it might be requisitioned.

There could be no question of taking our dog Sherry along. After much searching, we found a kind couple who would look after him for the time being. Finally, we decided to leave after Christmas.

4

On reaching Berlin, we settled comfortably in one room of Olga's apartment on the Olivaerplatz. A few months later we moved to another tiny flat on the ground floor of an office building off the Steinplatz, which had the advantage of being solidly built, and several stone archways under which we huddled at times provided comparatively safe protection in case the house was bombed. It was to be destroyed at the end of the war, after we had all left.

The winter of 1939–1940 was bitterly cold. It was the first of a series of appalling war winters, as if the elements were in league to make men's lives even more miserable than war could achieve alone. The organisation of rationing functioned well, and whatever was promised, was distributed, if it were only the weekly egg. But the quality of the food as of everything else sank rapidly, to be replaced with ingenuity by 'Ersatz' products. The current joke was that the war would only end 'when the Allies eat rats, and we here "Rattenersatz".'

German cooking on the whole can hardly be considered a product of fantasy or even of taste at the best of times. War restrictions rapidly did away with the two or three staple national dishes of repute and soon the food offered for general consumption began to look and taste ever more dubious. Meat was frequently horse. After all the French ate horse without a qualm, perhaps the sweetish taste was just a question of habit. But presently one could not be sure it was not dog or even cat or rat. The better to disguise it, the meat would be mixed into hard greyish lumps and served with a sticky sauce, the 'Tunke', varying in colour but never in taste. Another particularly revolting item on the menu was listed as 'Fischbratklops', although it was neither fish nor 'brat' (grilled), but by all means 'Klops' – a squashy mess relieved at best by over-steamed chopped turnip: 'Kohlrabi bürgerlich'. Dessert was usually some sculptural form of pudding in cheerful botanic shades, wobbly but elastically resilient. Potatoes and greenery were soon planted every-

93

where: in garden plots, in flower pots, even in bathtubs. Salad was concocted from dandelions and hitherto unknown weeds, spinach from nettles, coffee from acorns until there was a dearth of acorns. Tobacco grew on many a balcony. Fruit seemed to have disappeared in winter, and there was not an orange to be found in spite of friendship with Italy, whereas wine remained easily available and helped one through many a soggy main dish. Italian 'trattorias', few and far between, were our main resource for they were always magically provided with excellent 'past'acuitta' and vegetables.

We heard that the occupied countries were much worse off, but at least their cooking must have been more imaginative.

Textiles, soon nicknamed 'Deutscher Wald' as cotton or wool were replaced by cellulose fibre, were also distributed according to a system of points, and one therefore hesitated between buying a blouse or the corresponding number of dish rags. Hats were exempted from points, leaving the field free for flights of imagination, so with a little black dress and some gay concoction over one eye, the future would appear less bleak for a moment.

At night, darkness fell like a shroud over the unlit streets. Equipped with a squeaking, self-charging mechanism, pocket lamps warned one of someone approaching over the muffling snow. Any attack or theft would be so severely punished, it became quite safe to walk home alone in the dark.

Germans fall into obedience as others fall into bed. Once organisation takes over, any improvisation becomes heresy, so now at the slightest infringement of stringent regulations there came the pointing finger, for every second person had overnight become an 'ersatz' policeman: if pocket lamps were flashed higher than one's knee, if the doorstep of each house was not swept free of snow by its inhabitants, if one stepped out of a queue, if this, if that . . .

Nation-wide consternation at Hitler's declaring war on such a flimsy pretext had been succeeded by a wave of euphoria at the astonishing and swift success of the Polish campaign, bolstered by the still comparatively passive attitude of the Allies. To this was added the natural relief at personal survival (or that of one's sons and brothers), for the fighting in some places, such as Kutno, had been extremely severe. All in all, some thought, it had been an exciting adventure, military objectives carried out as on a chessboard.

On the other hand, the invasion left a feeling of deep misgiving, impossible to stifle by thought of duty and discipline, however little one could do about it. Many had seen the horrifying reality of war at close hand: the smashed towns, people buried alive in cellars under houses collapsing like cards, refugees streaming through burning villages. Their one wish was for peace. When this became ever more improbable, many unreasonably considered the Allies were as much to blame as Hitler.

'Germany MUST lose this war, or we are heading for a fate infinitely worse than defeat,' said our friend Helen Biron. Her three brothers were in the Army, and although quite a few thought as she did, we were startled to hear it so emphatically expressed at that time. She was a few years older than we were and saw further for she had many friends in Poland and knew more of what was going on behind the scenes. 'The Western Powers should have stopped Hitler last year. They never understood the Nazis didn't want power because the country was well or badly off: they only wanted power. They are building up the dark face of Germany,' she added. 'The Germans tend to love false gods. Once instilled with the idea that they are fulfilling a mission, nothing can stop them. The Nazis have upset all conceptions of good and evil. They use the same weapons as the communists: first insult, then calumny, then murder. Blomberg was forced to marry his mistress, then discharged for doing so. Fritsch was accused of being a homosexual, then thrown out of the Army. Now they lie about the Jews and the Poles, to-morrow it will be the turn of the Church and then of all those in their way, especially people like us. (Goebbels already calls us the "internationales Gesindel".) It will never stop unless we lose the war.'

We believed her, but it was already too late for us to return to the West. 'Mitgefangen, mitgehangen' (caught together, hanged together) seemed to be our future.

Our status as White Russians was becoming a liability from the Nazi point of view, but the recent alliance with the Soviets was much distrusted in the country and to our surprise we found ourselves treated with kindness and understanding.

Wartime Berlin had become a centre of attraction for many young people from remote regions of the erstwhile Holy Roman Germanic Empire, which were now willy-nilly reassembled in the 'Reich'. Germanic, Slav, Italian, Hungarian, even French names were met with at every turn. Many of them were as foreign to the régime as we were, and as lost. Perhaps their friendship for us gave them the feeling of still belonging to the international civilisation which was their heritage, and one of the butts of Goebbels' venomous oratory.

As a result, we quite unexpectedly found helping hands on all sides. Within certain groups, there was a climate of discretion, allowing everything to be discussed freely, without fear of denunciation. This eased the sense of oppression. Besides, it is impossible to live with horror all the time, and life goes on whatever happens.

Our original intention was to join the Red Cross, like Helen. It seemed the most 'neutral' job one could undertake, and would enable us to be of help wherever possible, since, without distinction of country, we could only feel desperately sorry for all the unfortunate young men on all sides who were preparing to drop bombs on each other.

But this was not as simple as we had assumed, for we could not afford ourselves the luxury of unpaid work. We would soon have to support Mamma and Georgie in Rome, as they preceded Papa out of Lithuania.

To complicate matters, the Nazis had nationalised the International Red Cross, reducing their organisation to the status of an appendage of the Army. This meant mobilisation and assignment wherever they thought fit. Should war with Russia break out, as was rumoured already, this would put us on the spot. Soon every young person was going to be mobilised into the war effort anyway.

It was, however, a tremendous help for us to be together. We could chaperone each other, and as our voices were identical we took calls and dealt with difficult situations on each other's behalf.

We were not very experienced, particularly in German, but typing and shorthand and our knowledge of several foreign languages appeared to be an asset. We took it in turns to go to interviews, hating this part of it, for we were rather shy and proud too, handicapped by the fact that we did not look as demure as secretaries were still supposed to look.

Through a friend of a friend, I was presently offered a job in the Public Relations Department of the Foreign Office, and required to give an answer next day. Careful enquiry about what exactly the work would be brought only evasive answers. I then remembered a diplomat, Herr von Breisky, whom we had recently met and liked. After increasingly frantic telephoning, I managed to track him down. We met late after dinner in the foyer of the Hotel Kaiserhof, and then sat in a distant corner and talked in low voices.

He was even more inclined to extreme caution and the warnings he gave me were to prove useful. First the contract: leave Russian out as a language. The German attitude towards that country was becoming ever more ominous. I should not sign anything enabling me to see 'secret' documents, only 'confidential' ones. Everything was confidential, so that didn't mean much. He then assured me that H., who was giving me the job, was to be trusted. The head of the office, Klatten, was a beast. There were a few decent people working in the same Department, but keep away from the main office, away from Ribbentrop.

Later I realised what sound advice this was, for how could we know at that time that in every Government office a hidden fight for power was going on. The fact that we were new to Berlin life, young Russian émigrés recently arrived from France, made us a safer proposition for those already plotting against the régime, than the average secretary. The same applied to young girls of what had recently been a more privileged society, less liable to succumb to Nazi slogans.

Next morning, the contract was to be signed. H. prepared a draft. I was only to do translations, read the foreign Press and prepare general information. Then I met Klatten, the department head, for the first time. He was of medium height, with weak sloping shoulders and looked soft all through. A youngish pink face, thinning red hair, cold little pale eyes, spongy handshake: 'Heil Hitler, Heil Hitler!'

He was almost rude to H., who for his part remained elaborately, insultingly polite, drawling: 'Ja, ja. Na also . . . da wäre es . . .'

The work was easy. H. often dropped in to see how I was getting on, using some flimsy pretext such as a paper to be translated or read. One morning, he closed the door carefully behind him, warning finger lifted, and coming up to my table, showed me a small paper concealed in his right palm: 'Microphones have been fitted into your telephone this morning.' I gazed at him open-mouthed, while he tore the message into tiny fragments.

Meeting him later by chance at an Embassy lunch, he told me a small packet of coffee, slipped into the electrician's pocket, had elicited this useful information.

Coffee, even in tiny quantities, had become equal to erstwhile gold doubloons. It was an exchange medium, a narcotic, a sort of Wodehousian Buckup-O.

I cordially detested my immediate chief, Möllhausen. Levantine in aspect, olive-green, damp-looking, egg-shaped face under dark strands of receding hair. He was also flat-footed and walked without lifting his knees. Our association was not to prove too happy, but my fluent languages were apparently indispensable to secure his own job. Occasionally he would dash off abroad, and later to France. Returning with suitcases laden with smuggled goods, he would potter around with his loot behind locked doors. As the office used to be a private house, there was still a bathroom next door to his room, and one could hear him splashing around in the still functioning bathtub, coal and heating being on the State, and therefore plentiful.

Even all these distasteful ablutions did not seem to improve his greasy look. He must have sensed my dislike:

'One feels you are not interested enough in your work. You are like a bird in a golden cage.'

'Perhaps a cage, but certainly not golden,' I unwisely replied.

5

Brandishing umbrella and walking-stick (tied together for the journey), as she tried to catch our anxiously searching eye, Mamma stood on the steaming railway platform amidst an ant-hill of minor belongings. Georgie had been despatched in search of a porter or pushcart, or both. Neither was easy to discover.

Wherever she was, even after an endless, exhausting journey on hard third-class seats, Mamma brought sparkle, amusement and life with her: also friction, exasperation. But never boredom or discouragement.

As our little procession wound its way through scurrying crowds towards the waiting taxi, even the drab station became colourful. In spite of the reason for it, it was a most joyful reunion. There was so much to relate, weaving trailing threads of our past lives back into a pattern again.

As Soviet pressure tightened around Lithuania, Papa had sent Mamma and Georgie on ahead. If things became really rough, it would be easier for him to act alone.

Mamma was quite undaunted by this second emigration, as if only the first time anything happened could really count.

Sitting around the table in the large old-fashioned kitchen of our flat, with its one, easily blacked-out high window, we were all soon happily plunged in talk.

In spite of the present uneasy friendship with Soviet Russia, she still believed in Hitler's 'anti-communism', establishing the Nazis as a 'Rightist' party. We tried to persuade her how similar were the two régimes, both based on the worst instincts in men, wrapped in high-sounding slogans. We told her of the sinister Berlin rumours, which were not heard anywhere else, and how you must look over your shoulder when talking, for the Gestapo was rapidly learning from its counterpart – the OGPU. An eye-witness at the time had told us that as Ribbentrop signed the pact with Soviet Russia, Stalin – with an eloquent gesture –

had pushed the German Press photographer to take a snap of the representatives of both Secret Police Forces together, while he watched the proceedings with a sardonic grin.

Georgie had grown and thinned from recent typhoid, with the positive result – to his and our surprise – of a lion-mane of luxuriant hair. Our rations made his growing boy's appetite difficult to satisfy, for he could consume inordinate quantities of food at one sitting.

We were sad to see them both go on their way again, this time to Italy, visiting Olga in Silesia on the way.

Who could guess how long our separation would be? Although my family are inveterate letter writers, long and frequent missives were no real substitute.

Occasional references to current events were transparently and rather naïvely camouflaged by remarks on 'Uncle Joe's', 'Hermann's' or 'Aunt Martha's' respective healths (Stalin, Hitler or Mussolini), or concealed in allusions to the weather: 'We fear you are heading for a long cold spell' (in May!).

Should any trouble with the Gestapo arise, Missie and I had decided beforehand that she would go in my place, and I in hers, in order to win time. Time for what? We did not like to think further.

A girl working in the Censorship department, whom I met at a party, told me how very interesting she had found a letter from Mamma, and how many facts unknown to her had now enriched her knowledge of history. I thought this a tactless remark, and said: 'Bad enough to have one's letters read, without having to talk them over with strangers afterwards.'

But one morning the post delivered a folded slip of cheap and unpleasant-looking yellowish paper: Missie was requested to appear at the Gestapo Headquarters on the Prinz Albrechtstrasse. Although this address had not yet acquired the sinister ring attached to it after the plot of the 20th July 1944, it made us very uneasy.

I went in her stead at the hour indicated. On entering the huge, leprous, khaki-coloured building, I signed a slip stating the time, trying to appear quite unconcerned, but feeling reduced to the status of a faceless number.

Up the noisy dun-coloured stairs, down the maze of passages echoing with heavy footsteps, lined with blank doors, into a starkly empty waiting-room. Finally Missie's name was called.

Behind the table of an anonymous office sat an expressionless, bespectacled functionary. There was a pile of papers in front of him, one of which was in a folder, into which he peeped surreptitiously.

Trying to swallow a cowardly ingratiating smile, and not to feel like a rabbit faced by a boa-constrictor, I caught a fleeting glimpse of Mamma's characteristic, spiky handwriting. So that was it! Those letters, of course.

I launched into an explanation of why I had come instead of my 'bed-ridden' sister (influenza and high fever). There followed a catalogue of questions. 'Who is this? Who is that?' Even 'who is "Hermann"?' (I would have thought he would have guessed.)

I invented a close connection living abroad, who had recently been ailing, adding: 'I suppose my mother refers to him in her letter, for she always keeps us posted as to his convalescence.'

Angrily he shut the folder with a snap. 'Why should you suppose this concerns a letter from your mother?'

'She was worried because we had not heard from her for so long and I see you have one from her on your table. Perhaps I might read it?'

'It will be sent to you through the post,' he said peevishly. But that was all. What a relief!

A few weeks later, it was Missie's turn to go.

Living in Italy, it was impossible for Mamma to conceive the difference in climate between Hitler's and Mussolini's régimes. Far too confirmed individualists to accept regimentation easily, the Italians expressed their aversion to both their German allies and to the war with a freedom of speech and behaviour unknown to us living under Nazi rule.

When Spring came at last, the contrast between frequently sleepless nights and the crisp scented mornings brought new strength and hope. Bunches of lilac burst through high garden gates and children called to each other on their way to school as we ran to the office, down avenues lined with flowering chestnut trees. The Berlin organ-grinders moved from backyard to street corner, and the jingling waltz tunes wound out of their gaily painted machines were always rewarded with a shower of 'pfennigs' from every window.

I often visited my friends Luisa Welczeck and Louisette Quadt who worked a short distance away. Their office on the ground floor led into that of their immediate chief, the career diplomat Josias von Rantzau, and opened on to a charming garden. Luisa Welczeck was just back from Paris, where her father, the Ambassador, had been much at odds with the régime, never fearing to be outspoken too. The previous establishment was still functioning, although it would be gradually superseded or ousted by the new.

There was a tune of other languages in lilting Welczeck voices. Lovely, graceful, flower-like, with a kind word for everyone, Luisa had dreamlike clothes, and we would beg her to describe in detail the evening dresses she had worn to balls in Paris the preceding winter. We were quite without envy, for where would one ever see such luxurious and romantic creations again?

One day I burst out to Rantzau: 'I cannot bear Möllhausen any more!'

'One must admit that he is not everyone's cup of tea,' laughed Rantzau, and there was understanding in his smile. Before many days had passed, I found myself transferred to his department. Frequently from then on, with tact, courtesy and flashes of sardonic wit, he would quietly move in to help us.

For the first time we were becoming aware of wheels within wheels in this department. A small group of trusted friends had managed to converge. They had all known each other for many years, either studying together, or abroad at some previous diplomatic post.

Upstairs Adam von Trott zu Soltz, Alex Werth – nicknamed 'Worthy' – and Hans Richter were more friends than colleagues. Newcomers were observed with microscopic care. If undesirable, whenever possible they were shunted on elsewhere.

My room was half-way up the stairs, a central point of communication between lower and upper floors so that messages were often relayed through it. At first the head of this section was Count Adelmann, a traditional diplomat, at sea in the intricacies of Nazi policy. He was followed by Rahn, who at first seemed more of an opportunist, but soon conformed to the general tone set by the others. Much later, he would have the courage to stand up for Trott, when even to have known him was to feel a noose around your neck.

After that, the going became more rough as one party member followed another at the head of the department, from which they instinctively felt something had to be weeded. Surprisingly, until the 20th July 1944, things worked the other way, and it was fascinating to observe the civilising influence our friends achieved in concerted and often planned effort. It was rather like an oyster forming a pearl, adding layer upon layer until the intruding piece of dirt got effectively isolated.

Gradually we understood that all the work done in the 'Informationsabteilung Kurfürstenstrasse' was not quite what it appeared to be.

In this clublike atmosphere of mutual confidence, certain precautions were taken as a matter of course: all telephones when not in use were automatically stuffed among cushions into closed cupboards. Although coffee and drinks were always available for the constant stream of visitors from other Ministries (mostly the same ones), our chiefs would often go out for a stroll with the person they were talking to. They travelled frequently to neutral countries, bringing us generous bottles of French scent. Every possible liberty was allowed us, as long as it did not become too conspicuous. We did not realise then, that they felt deep concern for us, well knowing what lay ahead, and wished to spare us as much as possible.

They laughed when we were late: 'Is this really you, or an optical illusion?' not minding as long as the routine work got done, and sent us home earlier if the bombing had been particularly bad. Our age-group friends, on leave from the Front, started dropping in, glad to read the confidential international broadsheets. They were mostly cavalry officers, now motorised to tank divisions, very much in the Front line during the first campaigns and therefore exposed to the hottest fighting. Several of them already wore the highest decorations, the respected 'Ritterkreuz' for valour. Others were staff or liaison officers and therefore intimately acquainted with the mental attitude of their respective generals or marshalls.

In easy talk, a probing question slipped in every now and then, our 'chiefs' taught us how to assess the background and views of any person we were with. When we sometimes made mistakes and slipped up on a new acquaintance, they warned us at once.

On high seas, one needs a compass for navigation. To sail through troubled times, one needs thermometers by which to gauge whom to trust. Such a 'thermometer' was a tale handed round at this time:

'Mother Germania produced a son. The Good Fairy who had been invited to the christening, promised to fulfil three wishes. These were: that the child should be a staunch Nazi, clever and honest.

But the Bad Fairy, who had been omitted from the feast, now whirled in on her broomstick and announced that although she could not reverse the gift, she would ensure that only two of these three wishes would be fulfilled at the same time.

So from then on, little Germans were staunch Nazis and clever – but not honest; staunch Nazis and honest – but not clever. Or clever and honest – but not good Nazis.'

This tale was to prove extremely useful, as it would be under any totalitarian régime.

Gradually our relationship to our chiefs had become one of affectionate and trustful comradeship. Our jokes and anecdotes made them laugh and must have been a welcome break in their difficult and dangerous tasks.

The harmony in our little group made everything bearable and extended to the whole building.

On arrival in the morning, we were supposed to be clocked in by the porter. Born in Russia of German origin, he was a clown by profession. Deeply sad little eyes looked out of a brown, crumpled, rubbery face. He loved us and would always jot down the time of our arrival as it should have been, and not as it often was.

The charwoman was a friendly soul. We found her sniffling one day, which was not in character: her canary had died. Living alone, she had no other companion. Luisa procured her another at once, hoping he would warble as enthusiastically as had the dead one.

We made friends with the telephone exchange girls, sitting in their airless cubicles in the big house of which ours was an annexe. Soon underfed, never getting much sleep, miles to walk or to drive wedged into crowded trams from their distant homes, they were much to be pitied.

Friendly exchange of gifts took place – we dropped French scent, soap, stockings or nail polish on their tables, and received in return a sausage from the country, a flower stuck in a vase, and . . . all our personal calls slipped through unobtrusively, or jotted down with touching accuracy. For of course our life began the moment office hours were over, and the evenings needed careful planning to fit in all the different people we wanted to see.

They were not envious of us, for overnight we had become a classless society, an achievement of Nazism which would survive long after the war. Envy had taken another turn: the stupid now hated the clever, the ugly the beautiful. The misfits, the morally twisted, the mediocrities were now jostling and scrabbling for status, for power, for survival at any cost. They tried to reduce all to their own measure, recoiling from any form of superiority. In the name of the People, they bullied and tyrannised those same people. Like rats they surreptitiously gnawed away at the law, replacing rights by endless stifling regulations.

We learnt gradually that when courage, especially civic courage, was conspicuously lacking, all other qualities collapsed with it: there was no room left for kindness, consideration or fidelity. The exceptions, those of independent thought: the happy-go-lucky, the chivalrous, banded together in instinctive solidarity. They at first hoped to change things from within. When they realised the impossibility of doing this, the final decision to overthrow Hitler in spite of the war began to take concrete form.

At first it was important to assess the Allies' reaction to these plans, to dissuade them from the principle of unconditional surrender, and from repeating the same mistakes Hitler was to make in Russia.

This was the policy pursued by Trott whenever he travelled to Sweden and Switzerland, which he did frequently. He could not accept the fact that the Allies had embarked on a crusade against Germany without making any distinction between Nazis and non-Nazis.

Of course we did not know this at the time, but we realised that the personality of Adam Trott, quite apart from his striking looks, stood out in stark relief beside all those around him, for he was such a many-sided man, in search of a challenge and a meaning in all things.

He was always happier when speaking English, as if it brought on pleasant, lighter memories. He had studied in England and had many friends there, but although he spoke the language perfectly, the rhythm of his thought was German. He usually sat, lazily draped in easy grace over his hard office armchair, dictating at a leisurely pace. But he could suddenly switch to intense concentration, for he had an untiring capacity for work. His brows drew together, his eyes seemed shadowed, his face hardened, while incisive sentences formed in his mind.

Although perhaps at times his total unselfconsciousness could be mistaken for arrogance, wherever he was one felt at ease, but also somehow on one's mettle. Always direct (but not obvious) in his dealings with people, he would listen with great attention, feeling for the colour of their thoughts. If no headway could be made, he asked ironic questions in a gentle voice. He treated his chiefs with condescension, and was never afraid of speaking his mind.

One day Trott invited me to dinner to his house, saying: 'I particularly want you to tell me what you think of a friend of mine, who will be there.'

We were only four: his friend von Haeften, Adam, his charming young wife Clarita, and me. Adam, taking the talk in hand as usual, touched on a variety of subjects.

As he drove me home, he asked: 'Well, what did you think of him?'

'But what can it matter what I think of him? He is an old friend of yours. A charming and cultivated person. How can one say more after one meeting?'

'I would like to know what impression he makes when one doesn't know him.'

Rather exasperated at his insistence, I said: 'Well, I wouldn't like to steal horses with him: one would be caught sitting on the fence.'

To my great surprise, he was stunned: 'Why should you say that?'

'I don't know really. Unrealistic, perhaps too much theory about his views. He loses touch with the main issue.'

Only much later did I realise why Adam had minded so much what I had said quite thoughtlessly, for he was on the verge of associating Haeften closely with his plans. Quite by chance, I was not far from the truth.*

Luckily we presently managed to pull Missie out of her very stultifying job, stranded in an alien atmosphere. She was to work with Trott, and soon the association became a close friendship too.

Through the open door, during dictation, one heard his lazy amused voice, gently reminding, 'Aus, bei, mit, nach, seit, von, zu . . . nimmt Dativ!' – an elementary rule of German grammar.

Much later, a marked coolness suddenly broke out between Trott and Rantzau. They were no longer seen together.

We protested: 'You have been friends for so long, since your University days. Nothing should be important enough to break that up!'

---

* Haeften was to die heroically after the 20th July 1944 plot, and although he typified the plotters' unrealistic planning, he had no responsibility for its failure.

'Even old friends can differ on an important issue,' said Trott drily. Sadly, too.

We learned later that the conspiracy had reached the conclusion that Hitler had to be killed, and Rantzau would not agree. He hated him, but could not accept that final step.

After his marriage with Louisette Quadt, Rantzau had himself transferred to Rumania, and was therefore out of immediate reach when the plot failed. But the Soviets caught him in Bucharest, and he died miserably in an OGPU prison.

6

'Fall Gelb' they called the French campaign.

We were stunned, for that was exactly what it had been: an exercise in military manoeuvres, brilliantly carried out by the German Army, and unfortunately confirming all Hitler's claims. It had taken seven weeks: from the 10th May to the 26th June 1940. What remained of the Maginot Line, of the glorious 'bleu-horizon' French Army we had so often seen parading in St. Germain-en-Laye as children? What remained of all their proud boasts? Our loyalties were only personal, but France was for us really 'une seconde patrie', and we were profoundly distressed. The only consoling thought was that this 'Blitz' campaign meant less loss of life on all sides.

A Spanish friend later told us that he had been sent to meet the Germans at the Spanish frontier – for that was where General Franco intended to halt them. He asked a German tank officer: 'How did you manage for petrol?'

'No problem at all. We refuelled at all the petrol stations, buying food too as we went. It was like a holiday outing.'

Some years earlier, spending the summer near Pau, in the South of France, Mamma had indulged in long political discussions with our garrulous and friendly doctor, who would wind it all up by sighing nostalgically:

'Une petite guerre arrangerait bien les choses!'

Both his sons, our friends, were killed in the ensuing 'petite guerre', which seemed so bloodless to outsiders.

Spanish pilots maintained they could now easily distinguish their frontier from Biarritz to Irun thanks to the bathers: pink blobs on the German side, and olive-brown on theirs.

It became the fashion for less scrupulous Nazi officials to go on shopping sprees to Paris. In compensation the conquered country was immediately awarded the doubtful blessings of ration coupons and a military band on every village square. The rationing, as in all occupied countries, was at a lower level than in Germany until the end of the war, when this was drastically reversed.

An Austrian friend, with his unerring instinct for people, decided that we should get to know the Bismarcks. One Sunday, he, Missie and I took the rapid suburban train to Potsdam to have lunch with them.

Governor of Potsdam (Regierungspräsident), Gottfried Bismarck had joined the Nazi Party in the early 'thirties and become a high-ranking official of the S.S.

In those early days, he had thought that as a Bismarck, thoroughly trained for State service, he could – with the help of a few others – get control of the whole Party and persuade Hitler to sift out its more extreme elements and views. He had hoped that they could then, on the basis of nationalism and socialism (both valid precepts), achieve what at first Hitler had announced his aims to be.

As an effort at a sort of legitimisation of his 'Movement', Hitler proclaimed himself in direct line with the traditions and policies of Frederick the Great and of Chancellor Bismarck. In fact, he certainly meant to base his policy on actions like the invasion of Silesia and the declaration of war on France in 1870. Their injunctions as experienced statesmen (such as the Iron Chancellor's warning to Germany never to fight on two fronts at once) were, on the other hand, to be ignored.

King Frederick II was remote in history, but the name of Bismarck still carried weight in Germany. At first it seemed indeed as if Hitler were willing to learn. Foreign diplomats such as the British Ambassador, and Monsieur François-Poncet were on the friendliest of terms with him; and was not old Marshal Hindenburg treated with touching respect?

But this illusion was soon to be shattered. As far as the Bismarcks were concerned, Hanna von Bredow, their elder sister, could pinpoint the exact moment.

She was of a highly independent spirit, and certain ruthless aspects of Hitler's demagoguery were detestable to her from the start. But her brothers disagreed, 'You must meet him to judge. He has extraordinary magnetism . . . Dedicated to the nation's welfare . . .'

Hitler was still 'meetable', von Papen being the bear-leader. He had even taught him how to dress and 'behave' at social gatherings, the Austrian gesture of gallantly kissing ladies' hands, disarming criticism.

In 1933, the Bismarcks were invited to one of these receptions. Surrounded by his companions, von Papen at his side, Hitler stood shaking hands with the guests as they approached in a long queue. Meanwhile Frau Goebbels made polite conversation to the ladies as they awaited their turn.

Prince Berthold of Baden stood just in front of the Bismarcks. Although he loathed Hitler by instinct, conviction and tradition, he had come to ask permission to keep Dr. Hahn as Director of the renowned Salem school, founded by his father. His diffident manner belied the resolution behind it, for he belonged to that classless race of the 'aristocracy of the sensitive, the considerate and the plucky', strengthened by living so close to the soil, and as incomprehensible to the Nazis as they were to him.

Hating every moment, but determined nonetheless, Prince Berthold unfortunately slipped in the traditional sentence: 'He is very attached to our house,' which gave Hitler the opportunity he must have been waiting for. Everyone present was now treated to one of the first public explosions of uncontrolled (or intentional?) rage:

'Everybody seems to have his "house-Jew"!' – 'This must be stopped! There are no exceptions!'

Prince Berthold, pale with disgust, at first tried to stand his ground, but soon realising it was hopeless, turned on his heel and left. From then on he did everything in his power to get Dr. Hahn out of the country, and to establish him in Britain, where he eventually founded Gordonstoun school.

Meanwhile Frau Goebbels twittered to Hanna von Bredow, as she stood next in line: 'Gnädige Frau, where do you live?'

'In Potsdam.'

'Enchanting little town!' she gushed. 'And how many children have you got?'

'Nine.'

'How happy the Führer will be to hear it!'

'I certainly did not do it to please *him*!' said Hanna in her incisive way.

Now it was her brother, Prince Otto Bismarck's turn. Bravely disregarding what he had just heard, he launched into his prepared speech. 'Mein Führer. There is a rumour that certain extreme elements in the Party contemplate terroristic activity against a section of the population [the Jews]. Out of moral principles and also because of deep concern expressed by our neighbours, this would be highly inadvisable.' And with unwonted intrepidity, perhaps encouraged by Hanna's quizzical glance, he repeated – mopping his brow: '. . . Highly inadvisable!'

Thereupon a storm of vituperation burst over their heads: 'Everyone thinks themselves entitled to an opinion. . . !' and on it went.

The Bismarcks went home, deeply thoughtful, Otto still muttering: 'Ghastly! . . . Ghastly!'

The mask was soon to fall.

Like a warning flash before the storm, one night in 1938, 'Kristallnacht', groups of young ruffians, led on by units in S.A. uniform, 'spontaneously' smashed and plundered Jewish shops and institutions. Here and there some onlookers joined in the looting, which goes to show how fast corruption can set in.

A friend told us later, that seeing a bunch of louts hurling stones into a shop window and then rifling its contents, she had turned in indignation to the nearest policeman:
'Do something! Call for help! . . .'
'Young lady, look away as I am doing. Don't you see who they are?'

It had all started gradually. First they put yellow stars on the Jews. These were worn almost proudly. Or in mockery, pinned to their dogs' collars. Their friends sometimes wore them too, in defiance. People shook their heads when they saw it, as if brushing off a mosquito. Or unpleasant thoughts: 'Nein, so was!'
Soon 'stars' vanished off the streets. There was a rumour that lorries carried them away to an unknown destination. 'Where to?' Nobody knew. 'They were being concentrated,' one heard. Several well-known doctors and artists committed suicide.
'What happens to them?' people asked. Dark hints, which nobody at first quite believed, until it hit someone one knew.
Faced by direct questions, a high-ranking S.S. answered a foreign friend of ours:
'When all the men of the country are mobilised to fight, it is natural that political prisoners should also be mobilised for the war-effort.'
That this 'mobilisation' meant mass murder, was not even clear to neutral friends at that time.
One young Waffen S.S. officer, who had only known Front fighting until 1943, wished to find out for himself whether these rumours were true. Thinking his uniform and Ritterkreuz coverage and pass enough, he walked into Dachau, the concentration camp near Munich.
He was held up at once.
'What are you doing here?'
'I came to take a look.'
'Then you can just stay here.'
He found himself locked up until the end of the war. In spite of the hardship endured, he was lucky, for the Allied liberation in 1945 white-washed him as a victim of Nazism, and he could return to civilian life without further trouble.

Although the names Dachau, Auschwitz and Buchenwald were often mentioned, the mass of the population remained in ignorance of the planned murders, unless they happened to stumble over proof of them.

as was the case when the German Army began to retreat across Russia, colliding with the Gestapo 'at work'.

As far as the Bismarcks were concerned, they now knew that any order concerning the Jews came direct from Hitler, and hopes they may have harboured until then of restraining extreme elements in the Party, were dispelled for ever.

From then on, Gottfried used his high office in order to fight Hitler from within, and as a means to help as many individual victims of Nazism as he could.* His Government House in Potsdam was to become a centre of anti-Nazi resistance, one of the safest of them until its tragic end.

Missie and I were still innocently unaware of these undercurrents. We were warmly welcomed. Melanie Bismarck was of Austrian origin, and a cousin of her husband, to whom she was completely devoted. She had a logical if rather dry French Cartesian turn of mind – inherited perhaps from her Lois-Chandieu mother.

Gottfried seemed to possess all the qualities of his family. Tall with a slight stoop, dark and striking-looking, his pronounced features were those of his grandfather on all the painter Lenbach's portraits. He spoke in the sudden, incisive, characteristic Bismarck way, and had their ironic sense of humour. His restrained and sincere warmth was all the more winning.

His upbringing had trained him to responsibility towards the nation, and this feeling was to prove one of the strongest bonds between the members of the conspiracy planning Hitler's murder. He had an enquiring, practical, and at the same time detached mind. Perhaps to counterbalance this very earnest side of his nature, he loved the company of young people. He would listen with interest to their opinions, which he soon elicited by casual questions, first launching some apparently innocuous subject.

After that first lunch, we returned frequently. He encouraged us to bring our friends along, which we gladly did. He maintained we could not know whether they were to be trusted, and nowadays one could not risk consorting with anyone, without knowing what their 'code of honour' was – for it boiled down to that. He would talk to them, and we could then judge for ourselves.

He was right, for indeed a sentence here or there, some apparently innocent remark, and a young man we had known slightly was written off. We hardly needed Gottfried's mild reminder, 'Better stop seeing that one.'

* In the inevitable wave of retribution which followed the end of the war, the Allies tended to be more severe towards earlier Nazis, who might perhaps have reformed the party. They were much more lenient towards later members of the Party, who, unless awarded honorary membership – a pitfall difficult to evade – could not pretend ignorance of real Nazi intentions.

We were delighted when he approved of the ones we preferred, and as the months passed, we valued his protective hand over us ever more.

After the destruction of Berlin, when my parents joined us in Königswart, Melanie and Gottfried took Missie to live with them in Potsdam. The house was reassuringly solid, and perhaps Gottfried still considered his name a shield in case of trouble at the office.

With her half-French background, Melanie Bismarck tried to help several young Frenchmen recommended to her, who had been mobilised for work in Germany. From 1942 until February 1943, these workers were volunteers, but after that they were conscripted, sometimes just rounded up leaving a cinema, taken off trains, or grabbed off the street.

It was difficult even for Melanie to get in contact with them in Germany, but she claimed as many cousins as possible, for one was allowed to enquire after relatives. Missie and I sometimes took some of these young men down to Potsdam with us on Sundays.

One of them was Henri de Vendeuvre. To our question, 'What on earth are you doing here?' he answered, 'Don't laugh! I am a floor sweeper at Deutscher Verlag!'*

* He later escaped home, but his brother was tragically killed fighting in the Allied advance into Germany in 1945.

7

On a June evening in 1940, Missie and I happened to be invited to a large semi-official dinner. There were several foreign Ambassadors present. It was the sort of function where, in moments of crisis, messages are handed portentously to important guests. A few minutes after the arrival of such a communication, the rumour spread that the Soviet Union was annexing Lithuania.

When the Russo-German Pact was concluded in 1939, it was thought likely that the Baltic States would be sacrificed. Owing to the comparatively preferential treatment the Lithuanian Government had given him, Papa had been loth to leave until the take-over by the Soviets was certain.

Now he could have no further illusions: this meant deportation or worse for him. The communist steam-roller neither forgives nor forgets.

There were several influential persons from the Foreign Office at that dinner. They were approached by some friends with the request to notify the German Legation in Kovno to protect Papa, seeing that the Ambassador was a friend of his. Our friends met with the significant answer from the Protocol: 'This is not the moment for sentimentality.'

Working for the 'Abwehr' (Army Intelligence) under Admiral Canaris, another friend got in touch discreetly with his chiefs. He assured us next morning that they had warned their agents, and promised to get Papa over the frontier.

For several days we waited in growing anxiety, obsessed by visions of the Loubianka. Then came a phone call. 'Your father is well and will soon join you.'

Where had it come from? The telephone girl repeated it 'They would say no more than that. It came from a State office.'

We did not have to wait long before he walked into our tiny flat: lean, sunburnt, rejuvenated, spotlessly neat as always, relieved of all earthly possessions except for shaving tackle in one pocket, and a small parcel containing a shirt, a pair of socks and an ancient green-coloured glass he liked to hold up against the light: a typical choice.

He assured us it was a delightful feeling to travel so light, and was almost regretful to find his wardrobe rapidly replenished from all sides. All too soon for his taste, he needed a cupboard and a trunk for his belongings.

It appeared that he had been in the country for some days, and as he emerged from Kovno station, he saw the square in front was filled with Soviet tanks, blocking all the streets leading into town.

Without attempting to reach his flat, he took a small path heading for the bank of the river Nièmen, and boarded the first steamer sailing downstream. As the steamer cast off, Soviet soldiers appeared on the bank to put up controls.

But by then the boat was already chugging on its leisurely way. Sitting on deck, he evolved a plan, deciding to return to his erstwhile estates, confiscated since 1921. They were called 'Yourburg' and 'Tauroggen', and stretched along the German frontier near Tilsitt.

As they drifted along, the countryside seemed peaceful: no Soviet soldiers in sight. Towards evening he stepped off and proceeded on foot until he reached the house of one of the foresters who had been in his employ in bygone days.

He was made welcome at once and put up for the night, while his host went under cover of darkness to reconnoitre the surroundings and collect support. Some hours later he returned with two friends and together they devised a plan.

The frontier guards – as they had soon found out – were relieved at midday. They stopped patrolling just before that, until the relief guard took over. They had been given new orders to shoot at any running figure, so it would be best to walk across, as if by mistake. A good place had been found, where the range of visibility was fairly limited.

Next day, when the time came, the two helpers went on ahead and settled down, stretched in the grass, one on each side of the chosen strip of ground. They had arranged to whistle when the guards were out of sight. The forester then led him carefully to the point decided on. Holding a wide-open newspaper in front of him, into which two small holes had been torn, so as to enable him to see his way, Papa stepped out into No-man's land, watched by his companions.

The sun stood high, everything was quiet, and, still pretending to read his newspaper, he walked on steadily into Germany, towards the red-roofed village outlining the horizon.

At the nearest Police Station, they exclaimed: 'We were expecting you!' and they put him up at a hotel at State expense. At first this reaction seemed quite incomprehensible, but soon two polite gentlemen appeared, much relieved to see that he had got across. He was given a railway ticket to Berlin and assured we would be warned of his arrival. They were the agents from the Canaris organisation.

Papa was rather pleased to have managed without their help.

As we settled down together, he was at first unused to our independence and a little uncertain as to the tone to take: heavy father with lifted eyebrow, or understanding friend. He would answer phone calls with a dry: 'Not at home', cutting off before anything more could be said. We tried to explain: 'We have our private life, and it begins after work. These messages are important to us.'

From then on he tried to help in every way. He would prepare our breakfast, see to the shopping and dutifully note the innumerable calls and messages without further comment.

His Olympian calm (which our friends called his 'thousand-year Asiatic serenity') was most reassuring during the nightly bombings. When vexation piled up, he drily announced: 'When bombs fall on one out of the stratosphere, it is useless to fuss about anything.'·

Quite by chance we heard one day that he boasted proudly to his friends that he lived with his daughters on a footing of equality, as if we were students lodging together. It made him feel young again.

He soon began to give lessons in French and English. Speaking an exceptionally beautiful Russian, with sensitive and colourful shading to his thought, he was not really at ease with other languages in spite of English nurses and French governesses in bygone days.

We laughed when he told us with profound disgust about his classes.

'They sit like crows in a row, and an odious fellow keeps on asking for grammar rules. What business are they of his, since he can barely say "How do you do"?'

A lady pupil confided in him that she was in the throes of unrequited passion for a foreigner of distinguished appearance with greying temples . . . remarkable in character in spite of adversity . . .'

We added, interrupting, '. . . with a drooping eyelid! Papa she means you: she is in love with you!'

He was shocked at this embarrassing suggestion.

The sense of acute danger from all sides, quite apart from the bombing, did not much restrict our personal and social lives.

In retrospect, the constant round of parties and gatherings at this time may appear almost bizarre. Perhaps the urge to meet, to talk, to laugh, is particularly strong in difficult or dangerous times. It is certain that those who lived in the country in comparative safety suffered greatly from the lack of news and communication. No jokes were as funny as those invented in the teeth of Nazi Party oppression and repeated with the spice of danger. Besides, our diplomatic friends had more and better food than less privileged mortals; no mean consideration when one's health and resilience depended on at least one decent meal a day.

Being young, we felt immune to death or catastrophe. There was almost an added zest to living, a sort of euphoria at having survived so far. There were not many 'international' young girls in Berlin at the time, so we were much in demand. When the day's work was done, we would repair straight from the office to evenings frequently interrupted or indefinitely prolonged by the bombing. We changed in a tiny washroom in the office. It became a standing joke that the delicious scents wafting up the stairs (Luisa's 'Arpège', Louisette's 'Je reviens', and finally my 'Moment Suprême') informed our bosses that we would not be working late that night.

We were invited to lunches, dinners, picnics organised by the remaining Embassies, the Italian, Chilean, Spanish, Swedish, Hungarian and Swiss. The guests were widely varied – musicians, artists and also politicians, as far as they still associated with foreign diplomatic circles. One could therefore find oneself seated next to unexpected neighbours.

Once an aide-de-camp of Hitler's wedged in between Luisa and me. The French campaign had just ended, and we asked tricky questions with a look of wide-eyed innocence: 'How did the Führer get on with Huntziger?' (the French General who had signed the armistice).

'He had not expected him and his colleagues to be so decent,' he replied. 'In fact it induced him to alter his plans for France, which he now regrets. But in time we'll get that in order.' Ominous words.

'What did the Führer, as a connoisseur of architecture, like best in Paris?'

'The Opera. He thought it the most beautiful building he had ever seen. And then of course the Eiffel Tower.'

We avoided exchanging meaningful looks, but began to feel claustrophobic.

The diplomats we saw most were the Italians, so refreshingly and unassailably human at all times, and the semi-neutral Spaniards, negotiating every inch of the way to keep Hitler out of Spain. Many of the Italians resented the alliance Mussolini had forced upon them. They were also completely outspoken, not to say roaringly indiscreet, which made parties at the Italian Embassy as amusing as they were also disquieting. Our hosts could count on diplomatic immunity, whereas their guests could not.

One evening the Ambassador described in vivid detail a reception for about fifty guests given by Göring. The 'Reichsmarschall' came to meet them in a flowing red velvet dressing-gown, or rather 'tea-gown', with immense mink fur lapels opening over cascading lace flounces frothing down his ample bosom.

On one summer picnic seemingly like any other, on reaching the Embassy villa on the lake of Wannsee, near Berlin, we found a procession of official cars, flanked by police escort, wheeling up in a cloud of dust. Out stepped Count Ciano, Mussolini's son-in-law, followed closely by a galaxy of beribboned and bemedalled Italian officials, flashy in their fancy uniforms.

We seized the first opportunity to make our escape, but not before we had glimpsed in a darkened room Ciano and two or three of his gorgeous satellites dancing cheek to cheek with the very fastest of the beautiful ladies of Berlin.

8

'You must help me to look after Paul Metternich,' begged Luisa. 'He is here for three days' leave, and has never been to Berlin before.'

She had an important date, which could not be dropped or changed, even for a childhood friend whom she had known since the days when her father had been German Ambassador in Madrid.

We were not too eager to take on an extra man, for our own week-end was packed with engagements, but Paul Metternich joined us after lunch in the hall of Eden Hotel, our usual meeting-place. A large group of friends was setting out for a summer picnic in Kladow.

He was on a brief leave from France, where he was stationed with his cavalry regiment. As an ordinary soldier, he explained, he was supposed to wear uniform at all times, but it smelled too strongly of horse to be worn in public. In a wild moment, his sergeant had ordered them all to shear their heads to a bristly 'Hindenburg' level. In spite of liberal applications of brilliantine, Paul's hair now stood on end when he laughed, at ease among us, although he was the only newcomer.

Half-Austrian, half-Spanish, he spoke nearly as many languages as we did, excepting Russian. In the Spanish Civil War two years before, he had volunteered on the Nationalist side to fight with his cousins and friends in their struggle to avert communist dictatorship. The experience had certainly matured him far beyond his 23 years.

Paul and I made the most of the next two days, meeting for the last time for breakfast in the sunshine outside a Kurfürstendamm café before he returned to his regiment and I to the office.

From then on, I was followed by a steady stream of little notes, written on paper table-cloths, on W.C. paper, on napkins, on the back of military orders or sheets torn out of school copybooks: there must have been a shortage of paper in the German Army.

These notes contained colourful descriptions in English of Paul's life on his present assignment in the depths of France and of his trips in a motorbicycle's side-car 'scratching the road with his behind', as he organised the supplies for a number of villages.

Next time he came on leave, we knew we had fallen in love, and would marry as soon as possible, although we did not then realise that we would have to wait a whole year before doing so. As it became apparent that our minds were made up, Papa declared it was time for Paul 'to come and talk to him'.

It seemed an out-dated suggestion to us, but we did not want to hurt his feelings. I sat on the stairs outside, watch in hand, ready to interrupt if the talk became too prolonged. But there was real understanding between them. Paul said appreciatively later that he got very good advice: 'One should leave room for each to develop in their own way, and neither try and impose one's personality on the other.'

One day Paul said, 'You have only to look at the map: the war is lost already. The longer it takes, the worse it will be for everyone. However it ends, people like us will lose everything, just as your father did before.'

It was August 1940, and although the French campaign was only just over, his down-to-earth grasp of reality had inspired this sober view.

Paul's great-grandfather, the Austrian Chancellor Prince Clemens Lothar Metternich, whose portrait by Lawrence had graced our French Malet-et-Isaac history books, had succeeded in establishing a lasting European peace after the Napoleonic era at the Congress of Vienna in 1815. In recognition of his services, the Emperor of Austria had then given him the estate of Johannisberg on the Rhine.

Stemming from the nearby Moselle, as dignitaries of the Holy Roman Empire, the Metternichs had gradually gravitated towards Vienna, and later exchanged estates in Germany for that of Plass near Pilsen in Czechoslovakia. The property of Königswart, in northern Bohemia, however, had been in the family since the early XVIth century.

Once the fact that he expected to lose them all had been faced, Paul described Königswart with detachment but evident love. Plass and Johannisberg did not count for him in the same way. Although material values were as secondary to him as to Papa, as long as he owned it, he was deeply attached to his home.

Paul was thirteen years old when his father died. Three friends of the family were then asked to look after his properties until he came of age: Prince Clary for Königswart, Prince Leopold Lobkowicz for Plass (in the Czech part of Bohemia), and Count Walter Berchem for Johannisberg.

All three were men of high integrity and well-chosen for their selfless task. Although it would have been difficult to bring together three more diverse colleagues, the association apparently worked perfectly, smoothed by my future mother-in-law's proverbial charm.

On the Wiazemsky side of our family, we were remotely related to the Clarys, and when Missie and I first arrived in Germany, they had treated us as loved nieces, although in fact the cousinship went back a century or so. We became deeply attached to the whole family, and their three boys were soon our close friends. When on leave they would drop in and out of our tiny flat in Berlin, often collecting the bread and the post from the doormat in the mornings on their way.

Handsome, highly cultured, kind and worldly at the same time, Prince Alphy Clary was one of the most enchanting people not only of his generation, but of an epoch. Addicted to the study of history and genealogy, quite apart from his personal affection for both Paul and myself, he greatly approved of our approaching marriage which he considered 'an interesting historical combination'.

Now at last, after months of all-too-brief meetings, Paul had been given a short leave 'To put his affairs in order'. We feared this meant 'in view of the coming Russian campaign', but at least the date for our wedding could finally be fixed.

My future mother-in-law had returned from Spain, where she had spent some months with her family, the Santa-Cruz's, who appeared to extend from her aged mother, to numerous young cousins of Paul's age. He had arranged to take Missie and me down to Königswart to visit her.

We had already met once before. I had thought lunch alone together would be less embarrassing for both of us. We had a gay and easy talk, while Paul walked up and down the pavement opposite the restaurant – too nervous to go and lunch himself. Only then did I realise how important it was for him that we should get on. But what else could one have done!

Her own marriage to a foreigner was a break from custom, for by then the long association of Austria and Spain had faded into history.

Although Spanish from all sides, except for a remote Waldstein great-grandmother, my mother-in-law Isabel (as I was to call her) was not in the least Spanish in appearance. She was very tall, held herself well and was both shy and self-assured, her beauty lasting all her life. She was like a person out of an Edwardian book, yet modern in her views. Immensely disciplined as to minor vexations, well-groomed at all times, she was a living proof that there is no beauty more attractive than that due to transient effects of light, and the surprise of a fleeting change of expression.

She would say firmly that she had never allowed anyone to bore her. I was to learn that she also never bored.

When Countess Melanie Zichy-Ferraris, her Hungarian mother-in-law, indulged in one of her usual scenes, rolling on the floor in hysterics, hurling the family jewels at her, she had walked out of the house, leaving both mother-in-law and jewels on the floor, and never saw her again. She offered Melanie the choice of any one of the three family houses to live in on condition their paths did not cross. It must have been very galling to the poor woman to be deprived of the opportunity for making these scenes and the reconciliations that would have followed – for some people remembered her kindly.

Isabel advised me never to quarrel with anyone, because it was 'so tiresome'. She had found herself several times obliged to leave the hotel she was staying in because her mother-in-law, 'boring' as usual, had taken it into her head to turn up.

To the astonishment of young great-nephews, my still-so-youthful mother-in-law had been a friend of Winston Churchill's mother, and of the Empress Eugénie of France, born Montijo. The friendship was of ancient origin, for she had even inherited the Montijo girls' English nurse, Miss Kidd, and remembered cutting up beautiful Worth dresses sent as cast-offs from France, combining a sleeve here with a flounce there to achieve something wearable for her.

Isabel was a sensation in Vienna. The old Emperor Francis-Joseph would often sit and chat with her at official balls. 'He was such a dear!' she told us.

Everyone thought her ravishing, her willowy height an added advantage among tall people. Her jewels and clothes were as famous as her completely natural, gay and enduring charm. Also her great detachment: never go too deep or show excessive emotion. But she did not lack compassion – unless someone bored her, the cardinal sin. He would then be written off for good.

She fell deeply in love with her second husband, Ladislas Skrzynski, but she never could pronounce his name and called him 'Tchousko'. He was Polish Ambassador to the Vatican at that time, having begun his career in Austrian diplomacy, one of his first posts being St. Petersburg. Deeply interested in world politics, he had awakened the same fascination for them in Paul. He was tactful and full of warmth of heart. Paul loved him too, and I regretted having missed knowing him by a few years, for he had died on Christmas night in 1938. He had at least been spared the disaster which was so soon to overtake his beloved country.

My mother-in-law kept a Canova bust of Palmerston near the corner where she liked to sit in the big salon in Königswart, for it reminded her of 'Tchousko'.

His death increased her Spanish aversion to what she regarded as the tribal custom of Yuletide, which from then on she avoided, fleeing to

icy hotels on the Riviera, but giving me beautiful and lavish presents:
'. . . since you are the one who believes in Christmas!'

Approaching Eger in the train to Königswart with Missie and me,
Paul eagerly explained: 'Now we can see the Kaiserwald, and on the
other side of the low range of wooded hills lies Königswart, deep in the
valley.'

He then went on to explain it all to us.

The region around Königswart, the Egerland, lies in the North-
Western corner of the Bohemian rectangle, which forms the Czecho-
slovakian Northern frontier to Germany. Populated by German-speaking
Sudetes since ancient times, it was originally part of the Kingdom of
Bohemia, and of the Holy Roman Empire under Habsburg rule.

More to the South, the population became Slav and spoke Czech. In
the South-East, the Slovaks (also Slavs) spoke another variation of Czech.

The diligent and hard-working Sudetes had turned their region into
a prosperous small paradise, with beautiful towns, monuments and
flourishing forestry, agriculture and industry.

Cut off from Austria after 1918, new Czech nationalism had subjected
them to coercion and much abuse. In 1938, with Hitler's drive towards
'Home to the Motherland' ('Heim ins Reich') for all German-speaking
minority groups in neighbouring countries, great unrest had broken out
and the Nazi Party forming in the Sudetenland had at first met with
sympathy – not because they were Nazis, but because they promised
protection from Czech injustice.

Everything then went too far. The Sudetes were soon to discover that
Hitler had only used them as a tool, as a pretext for invasion.

When he marched into Czechoslovakia, they felt as ill-used as their
Czech neighbours.

An ancient square box of a car was waiting for us at the station. It had
been modified to run on wood gas and a contraption like an iron oven
smoked and puffed behind us.

We bumped along, down golden roads, past the baroque-style
'Ökonomie' which looked over a wide span of lawn, dotted with groups
of huge trees, towards the Schloss, shimmering like a white horseshoe.

Isabel, my future mother-in-law, and Marysia Borkowska her niece
by marriage, were already waving to us. What a welcome! The first
moment of shyness was soon forgotten as we were led in to lunch.

We were then taken to see my mother-in-law's little island on the lake.
It could only be reached by crossing a small bridge with a padlocked
gate. No one was allowed across except by special invitation. She would
wave gaily to guests, but that did not mean that they should join her;
it was therefore a special privilege for us to be invited there.

Before leaving, Isabel gave me an emerald ring and a diamond bracelet, saying she hoped I would feel with Paul as she had with her second husband, 'My heart smiled every time he came into the room.'

On our way back to Berlin, as the train approached the capital, sirens howled. We slowed down, then came to a hesitant stop. There was a cry of 'Tiefflieger' (low-flying planes). All the passengers got out and lay flat in the fields, hidden from each other in the ripening corn. Silly jokes were cracked: 'Cover your bald spot. It shines like a mirror.'

We felt defencelessly exposed to the sky, now dotted with tiny silver dashes and echoing to the drone of engines like a giant bee-hive. The bombers appeared and reappeared between the few woolly clouds sailing peacefully over our heads.

Soon the crack of anti-aircraft guns could be heard and we saw the flashes of shellfire exploding among the planes. Before our eyes, about twelve miles away, there rose a huge yellow-black smoke curtain, gradually shrouding the peaceful summer evening and carrying towards us a smell of smoke and burning.

We could not enter the station after the 'All clear' had sounded. Berlin had seemed so close, and now we were shunted around, reaching the town hours later, exhausted and dusty.

We were back in the war with a vengeance!

My mother-in-law and Marysia soon decided to move from Königs-wart to Johannisberg. While Marysia travelled to and fro to arrange the details, they had taken a few rooms in the Hotel Steinplatz in Berlin, as a temporary 'pied-à-terre'.

Isabel insisted this move would cement our good relations, for we would see much of one another and yet both be completely independent. She was determined not to repeat the friction she had suffered from with her own mother-in-law.

Marysia had come to live with her after her second husband's death. With no looks, no fortune, no personal happiness, she always radiated beaming good humour coupled with indefatigable energy and great common sense. Her interest and understanding for others won her untold friends wherever she went. When her uncle, Paul's stepfather, died, he left her his estate in Poland. For a very short time, from Christmas 1938 to September 1939, Marysia was comparatively well off, owned a car, and was apparently even a competent skier, which we could hardly believe, for she refused to control her ever-expanding figure, and it was difficult to imagine her speeding down the slopes of Zakopane. For me, she was to become a close and dear friend.

Between Johannisberg and Berlin the Gestapo now suddenly picked her off the train, and kept her for questioning, while my mother-in-law grew frantic with anxiety. She reappeared after forty-eight hours. She had been quite terrified at first, knowing her brother Henri, fighting in the resistance in Poland, was in grave danger with the Gestapo on his heels. But after desultory and seemingly meaningless interrogation, the major 'corpus delicti' was produced: it was a gramophone record. Expecting anything but that, Marysia heard shuffling noises, a clearing of throats, and then: 'Padre nuestro . . .' in a sing-song tune, followed by the mumbled responses: it was my mother-in-law and herself reciting the Rosary in Spanish before going to bed in the Hotel Steinplatz.

Their faces fell as she explained it all. Deeply intrigued, they really thought they had got hold of something: an important conspiracy at the very least.

Marysia seemed none the worse for her unpleasant experience, laughing it off: 'Luckily, they are extremely block-headed,' she said cheerfully.

Paul was furious and would not let them remain at the hotel.

After this fright, Paul got in touch with Admiral Canaris, Head of German Counter-Intelligence, the 'Abwehr', in an attempt to save Marysia's brother Henri. Paul's distant cousin, the Spanish Military Attaché Count Juan Luis Rocamora, served as willing intermediary.

He had known the Admiral since the Spanish Civil War. Until the S.S. under Heydrich openly launched the S.D. (secret police) into foreign affairs and started organising foreign espionage, the 'Abwehr' (Army Intelligence Service) was the only organization in Germany with the knowledge, experience and personnel able to do such work.

Like most national-minded Germans, Canaris had at first welcomed Hitler's national policy, and only turned against him on realising that he was deliberately planning a world war.

The Abwehr succeeded in warning Henri that the Gestapo was aware of his activities in the Polish Underground, but he refused to leave the country. The Gestapo then moved in.

By then Marysia was in Vienna, staying with Isabel at the Hotel Bristol. Early one morning she saw her brother come into the room through the communicating door.

'Henri, how wonderful! So Paul managed to get you out after all! But that uniform is impossible here: you must change at once!' As she spoke, he smiled at her and then was no longer there. She heard later that he had been executed at exactly that moment.

Count Rocamora and his charming wife were among our closest friends in Berlin. He was the embodiment of courage and sense of honour and looked as if he had stepped out of Greco's picture, 'the burial of Count Orgaz'. He was not tall, but with strongly marked handsome features, thick raven-black hair, his long sad face lit by a disarming smile. He had an almost innocent weakness for beautiful women, and when confronted by hard boiled and scheming females trying to add him to their bag (and there were quite a number of them in Berlin), his normally steady judgment failed him. 'Douce et féminine', he would sigh mistakenly.

Although we were so often invited to their house, we were to find out later that things were happening under our very noses of which we had no notion at the time.

His friendship with Canaris was based on comradeship dating back to the Spanish Civil War, but even that could hardly explain his trustful relationship with the Chief of German Military Intelligence, although the Admiral's hatred of the Nazis was an open secret in certain circles.

Many years later, in Madrid, Rocamora told us the reason. Shortly after the invasion of Poland Admiral Canaris came to ask him a special favour. He told Juan Luis that he was the third Military Attaché he was turning to: the others had refused to help him because they could not do so without informing their Ambassadors. Rocamora reassured him that his Ambassador, Magaz, was a friend and would understand the situation when he told him about it later.

All the military attachés, still present in Berlin, were invited to military manœuvres, which were taking place in Poland. Canaris asked Rocamora to accept. In due course he was told to go to a certain spot, at a given hour, and there he was to pick up a number of people with false papers and bring them back to Berlin with him. He was to hide them in his flat until he received further instructions.

All this he did. The Polish family were charming people – at first he did not even know their name. One of them fell gravely ill. Very discreetly, Canaris was informed, and a trustworthy doctor was sent over to look after him.

During the following weeks, we were all frequently in the house, never suspecting that all the back rooms were filled with refugees. Finally, false passports having been procured, the entire little group was moved down to the Swiss frontier and over the border.

Canaris then told Rocamora: 'Anything you want from me, I will do.'

Sprachregelung – secret 'speech directives' – circulated regularly through all ministries and government departments, like a slug's slimy trail. These papers also indicated their intentions. In the early days, as the Nazis evolved their racial theories to suit expansionist politics, Russians had already been declared barbarians, spread thinly over a vast continent, leaving plenty of 'Lebensraum'.

With the Russo–German Pact of 1939 Russian music came over the wireless and Tolstoy and Dostoyevsky were in fashion again.

Now, no more mention was to be made of Russian culture and

history. Russians were to be referred to as 'Untermenschen' (subhumans), as a menace to Western culture . . .

All this pointed to coming invasion.

Paul could hardly believe it when I told him, but rumours had already begun to spread through Berlin. They did not penetrate other towns, for there it would have been easy to find out who had leaked the dangerous news.

Although we were now quite accustomed to the rapid switch from 'Übermensch' to 'Untermensch', according to the drastic volte-faces of Nazi policy, this meant that a German soldier would soon be forbidden to marry a Russian. Rantzau therefore advised me to acquire a German passport before this rule was applied.

I had to go through a sort of racial examination in an institution called 'Rassenamt'. Out of curiosity, and for company, Missie came along too.

A Nibelungen-dwarf-like hunchback led us through this department of Rosenberg's Ministry, which seemed half classroom, half anthropological museum.

He measured our skulls, then our height, having to climb on a chair to read the result. Our hair and the colour of our eyes were then compared with desirable models. Nodding approvingly, he murmured: 'Scandinavian prototypes!'

By now we were in a state of helpless giggles. Had not the Berliners nicknamed Goebbels 'Nachgedunkelter Schrumpfgermane'? (Post-darkened-shrunk-Germaner.)

Trott and Rantzau listened to our tale in shocked consternation. Their advice was to marry soon and forget this 'evil nonsense'.

It was as yet difficult for us to conceive the criminal consequences of this farce, built up with such efficiency. But the Nazis knew that a lie, if repeated often enough, became an axiom, a lethal weapon leading to the mass murder of Jews, gipsies and soon anyone stamped as 'Untermensch', whatever he might happen to be. They only had to switch a few slides, a few labels.

A legend warned that the day Tamerlane's body was disturbed in Samarkand, a greater catastrophe than any he had caused would be let loose. The Soviet anthropologist, Professor Gerassimov, opened Tamerlane's tomb on the 22nd of June, 1941.

On that same day Hitler invaded Russia. It hardly needed Bismarck's reminder: 'Never fight on two fronts', to guess that the campaign was predestined to disaster for Germany, and would bring untold misery to Russia.

As the intervals between memorial services shortened, the sorrowing families in their dark veils became almost identical symbolic figures of mourning.

Ronnie Clary was killed early in the attack on Russia on the 28th July 1941, a month before his twenty-fourth birthday. He was hit as he stood in the turret of his advancing tank. For him as for so many, the stages of life – youth, maturity and death – had merged into one, for our generation seemed to be faced by all three at once. As death stood so close at hand for all, it appeared robbed of its injustice and fatality, which the bereaved parents felt so acutely. It gave a liberating sense of timelessness and an easier acceptance of fate, even of war, difficult to understand for those no longer exposed to this in later years, when youth, maturity and death had resumed their individual and inexorable progression.

When Ronnie died, he left a trail of exceptional grief. I went to Teplitz at once to visit his family. Like Königswart, Teplitz lay in Northern Bohemia and had been the residence of Kings and Emperors shepherded by Metternich during Congresses succeeding that of Vienna in 1815.

After the death of their eldest and so promising son, the Clarys would lose the youngest in Yugoslavia towards the end of the war. Marcus, the second boy, was to survive after long years of imprisonment in Russia.

9

On the 6th September 1941, a breezy golden autumn day, Paul and I were married in the small Catholic Church of Grunewald, on the outskirts of Berlin. There was not a house to be seen through the tall trees around us: one might have been in the depths of the country.

'I wish it were over!' I had sighed to charming Maria Pilar Oyarzabal, wife of one of the Spanish diplomats, as all the minor complications a wedding implies rose like a hedge of question marks around us.

'It is the happiest day of your life!' she said firmly. 'Let things take care of themselves.' They did. Some time after, Maria Pilar and her husband were to die when the train carrying them home to Spain blew up near Poitiers on a mine laid by the French Résistance. They had just changed places with another couple who survived.

Our families arrived in the nick of time from Madrid and Rome. Father Shahovskoï, later Archbishop John of San Francisco, our Russian priest, tactfully read the Orthodox Mass all through the Catholic ceremony. Considering Paul one of themselves, the Spanish Embassy put all their available cars at our disposal. The Rocamoras offered their house for the party, for as none of us lived in Berlin, it was preferable to hold the reception privately. Champagne and wine were sent from Johannisberg, and food from Königswart, where my poor mother-in-law had been subjected to a prolonged diet of macaroni in order to accumulate sufficient quantities of game and poultry.

Crowds of friends came, although the invitation lists compiled by Paul, Missie and me, at odd moments, were erratic. Many guests arrived straight from the Eastern Front, and would be returning there.

Paul's leave was brief, yet the war receded for a short moment, and the party became such fun even we found it difficult to tear ourselves away. In Vienna next morning, we heard our guests had suffered a severe bombing.

Lemon-yellow, green-shuttered low baroque houses, wedged in between scruffy gardens, factory chimneys or hideous workers' dwellings, had heralded the approach to the erstwhile capital of the Austrian Empire, now reduced to a Nazi province, the 'Ostmark'.

Even so, Vienna still retained a sort of dowdy nobility, with touches of operetta scenery to colour it. Low yellow houses still surrounded inner courtyards, where trellised walls and leafy bowers reminded one of Strauss and Lanner, while on the lower windows delicately wrought ironwork curved over pots of geraniums.

We walked to the beautiful Cathedral of St. Stephen, and then took a *fiaker* cab around the city.

The Wilczek town-house on the Herrengasse was a centre of Viennese life. This was not due to opulence or position, but to the exceptional charm of all the family. Apart from their good looks, they were warm-hearted, considerate and witty. Missie and I knew them well from frequent visits to Berlin, accompanying a cousin or a husband on his way to the Front. Paul of course, was considered one of them.

Our host was Count Cari, my mother-in-law's contemporary and friend. He was slim and tall, with slightly battered good looks, the family sense of fun darkened by a touch of caustic melancholy. Like many of his generation, he seemed to symbolise the shrinking of the 'K. and K.' (Royal and Imperial) Monarchy, to its present tadpole state – that of a great capital of a few impoverished agricultural provinces. He was deeply distressed to see the peaceful cohesion of the erstwhile Austrian Empire between its diverse components reduced now to a mixture of accents in the capital.

I had not been able to buy more than a few dresses before marrying, but they were at least very pretty, for fashions were charming and simple in 1941. Now if we asked for anything in the empty-looking shops, they immediately produced some hidden hoarded treasure: a silk tie or shirts for Paul, a Paris model for me, along with a touch of gossip and nostalgia. The jeweller Paltscho remembered my mother-in-law giving a pair of immense diamond earrings to her sister-in-law Aunt Titi Taxis: 'For she thought they looked like crystal drops off a chandelier!' he recounted, shocked and yet admiring such disregard for solid worth.

Wherever we went, the name Metternich seemed an 'open sesame', a reminder of happier days, and yet Paul's great-grandfather is the only outstanding statesman of his time who has never been honoured by a monument to his memory by his countrymen, as if succeeding governments could not forgive him for having kept them out of power for so long.

We went on to stay in Dellach on the Wörthersee, but we were not to have much time for a honeymoon, for a telegram announced that the great barn in Königswart had burnt down. We returned there at once for Paul to give necessary orders.

Here we found my mother-in-law, Marysia and Paul's cousin Cassy

(Casilda Santa Cruz), who was more a sister to him than a cousin. They had all come down after our wedding, and that terrifying bombing. Friends and visitors were soon to join us for the week-end, but as the last one departed, Paul, still with two days' leave, said, 'Let's go to Prague.'

'When?'

'This afternoon.'

It was my first intimation that, quite beyond necessity, we would never stop travelling!

From Prague we returned to Berlin. Here we were unexpectedly informed that Paul's long-deferred regular leave had now suddenly come through. He had even been given permission to spend it in Spain 'for family reasons', and was to set off at once. But it took me a whole month to fight through a forest of obstructions, and join him at last in Madrid.

The aeroplane touched down in front of a few sheds in the middle of an arid plain, under brilliant skies. After a bumpy ride over a moonscape of mountains, we had safely reached the Madrid Airport of Barajas.

Paul was waiting for me. As we drove into the city he pointed out everything with eager pride. He had spent many happy holidays in Spain among his numerous cousins and felt that here he was a member of a loose-knit but profoundly united tribe. His attachment to the country had become more personal and taken even deeper root, since the recent Civil War.

In 1941 the town was unpretentious and cosy, full of gardens and trees spreading luminous shade, dappled with gold. Until shortly before the war, at dawn herds of sheep and goats wandered down one of the main streets of the city, the Calle Alcala, sometimes colliding with late night revellers, for the *Via Pecuaria* (livestock roads) ran across the country from times immemorial, regardless of towns and cities sprouting up in their path.

The rickety old-fashioned car, lace curtains in the back window, communicating tube at hand to give instructions to the aged chauffeur, soon passed the burnt-out husks of the Alba Palace on the Calle Princesa, and that of the Counts of Toreno, already on San Bernardino, reminders of the war. Bumping down the uneven cobbles of the noisy little street was like entering a village seething with its own life.

A melon vendor was installed on the small square. Wrapped in his blanket he squatted next to a glowing coal stove, the brasero, for the morning air was crisp. At night he apparently slept on top of the pile, and if a scrounging hand tried to filch a melon from under his snoring form, he would be caught off balance, and came rolling down the crumbling heap in time to crash his stick on the offender's shoulders.

Half-way down the street stood the Santa Cruz Palace, a classical two-storeyed building, the stone-paved entrance framed between two doric columns, shaded by a balcony carrying the traditional dried-palm branch from last Easter.

From a small door to the right the main flight of stairs, covered with deep carpets, led up to the first floor. It was lit at every bend by the great lanterns (Farolas) of the flag ships which had taken part in the Battle of Lepanto in 1572 under the command of Don Alvaro de Bazan, first Marquess of Santa Cruz, and High Admiral of the young Don Juan of Austria, Charles V's illegitimate son.

Paul's cousin Cassy had declared: 'None of us will marry in this house, for no bridegroom will be brave enough to pass those Farolas!'

Up in the far right corner, a small window would fill with peering and whispering children of the house whenever King Alfonso XIII and the Queen came to dine. He knew they were there, and would wave to them in passing.

To reach our rooms, we climbed stairs lined with full-length portraits of Carvajal ancestors on Paul's grandmother's side. In stiff white collars, a roll of parchment in one hand, their functions were proudly enumerated: 'Principal delegate to the already discovered Indies, and to those to be discovered in future.' (Correo Mayor de las Indias descubiertas y por descubrir), a reminder that no conquistador was allowed to govern in the King's name. Royal representatives would be sent over the ocean to replace him at once.

In contrast with these severe pictures, our small drawing-room was hung with Tiepolo pastels and flooded in sunshine, for our rooms ran along an open balcony high over the central courtyard shaded by trellised vines. This wonderful southern invention of the 'patio' ensured intimacy, cool shade and silence just a few steps from screaming children, glaring sun and the clatter and noise of the surrounding city, turning the severe town palace into a cosy country home. Every detail had been attended to with loving care. A Russian icon hung over our bed.

In the drawing-room downstairs, the family waited to welcome me: my mother-in-law, her sister Mariquita, Countess del Puerto, numerous cousins, and above all Paul's grandmother, for the house was like a sub-dued beehive, firmly ruled by the gentlest of Queen-Bees.

An indomitable ivory-pale old lady, smelling faintly of lilies of the valley; transparent hands, snowy curls that no wind would ever ruffle, she was tiny but somehow awe-inspiring. Only her grandsons would nuzzle in her neck kissing her with tender sounds they used for their dogs while she waved them away with a delighted smile. She picked her way daintily past what she did not wish to hear or know as she would have stepped past a puddle in the street. Any complaint or cry would seem to her as much of an imposition on others as to keep someone waiting, fail to answer a letter, or refuse to grant a favour.

Friends had commented: 'How sad for you your favourite grandson should be marrying an Orthodox.'

Firmly she had replied, 'C'est tout à fait la même chose!'

I was touched to hear it, for it could hardly have been so for her, staunch pillar of the Catholic Church.

For more than three quarters of a century, San Bernardino 14 had been her home. When her husband died, she had taken back her own title of Duchess of San Carlos. For many years she then fulfilled the duties of Mistress of the Robes at Court.

Her four children, her widowed daughter Mariquita (Condesa del Puerto), her sons the Marquess of Santa Cruz and the Duke of Miranda, and my mother-in-law, all lived in the house with their families, comfortably tucked away in rambling wings of the old palace.

We were absorbed at once into the great rabbit-warren. Nobody ever disturbed anyone else in their private rooms, unless specifically invited, but everyone met in the main drawing-room downstairs to talk to whoever might happen to be there.

We nearly always lunched at home, rarely fewer than ten at table. When the conversation became too racy, Grand-mamma would gently intervene with an irrelevant question and the subject was dropped.

Our life was regulated by the clang of the house-bell: once for a letter or message, twice for a visitor, and three times whenever the Master of the house came home, even from going to Church or from a visit. 'Abuela', as Paul's grandmother was called, was so extremely punctual that her life even in great old age moved like clockwork, and the whole house could time itself by her.

In the afternoons old ladies came to visit, often two ageing spinster cousins from Eybar, shrouded in black, one tall, one short, with bristling moustaches, stuffed birds on their black straw hats, flat laced shoes, with turned-up square toes. Long ago they had travelled, even been to St. Petersburg when their uncle was Ambassador there. They spoke English in a Colonel-Blimpish manner, slapping their thighs at a joke.

At every new arrival, the Pekinese, after a prolonged growl breaking into ear-splitting yaps, nipped at cringing ankles, and then surreptitiously wolfed sandwiches from the lowest tier of the cake shelves. He was an asthmatic dog, whose health gave cause for concern, so he knew much would be forgiven.

Although everybody spoke other languages, they reverted to Spanish when talking to each other, so I was eager to learn the language. The cousins laughed to hear sentences Grandmamma had taught me, such as 'tener malas pulgas' (hold bad fleas) '. . . Cela se dit de quelqu'un qui a mauvais caractère.' (Said of someone of coleric disposition.)

'Where on earth did you pick that up?'

'But from Grandmamma. She said I must know some idiomatic expressions.'

In fact far cruder terms came floating up from the street and all the dwellings around us.

We and the younger cousins lived our own lives busily and unpunctually, dining out nearly every day. But before departing, we would always go and take leave, to be warmly admired: 'What a lovely dress! How nice you look!' It made a cheering start.

The house was run by Auntie Mariquita, who dealt gently with a number of old and ancient servants. They had been there as long as anyone could remember, as had their parents and relatives before them. Their calls and songs and scolding and snores rose up into the sky from an inner courtyard around which they lived. They were set in their ways, and bore with the family's idiosyncrasies, expecting and receiving equal patience in return.

The old butler, Isidoro, had been imprisoned during the Civil War with friends of the house, and for years they had all shared whatever they had. When these friends came to visit, there were great embracings as he received them at the top of the stairs. Isidoro had his own ideas of protocol and would sometimes intervene, oblivious of disapproving frowns, placing a guest where he thought best, and not at all the way his mistress had intended. It was no use expostulating with him later. He stood in stony silence.

'Why don't you answer?'

'I don't wish to perturb the peace of my soul.'

Another old retainer, Bartolomeo, would walk calmly into Cassy's bathroom, delivering some message.

'But Bartolomeo, don't you see I'm in my bath? You can't come in like that!'

'I have seen you in your bath since you were so big [measuring the size of a small loaf with his hands]. It cannot impress me,' and he retired from the room in his own good time with flat-footed dignity.

Though Cassy exploded with exasperation, nothing would change his ways. But there was a warm welcome whenever any member of the family returned from a journey, their children brought to be looked over and admired. All joys as well as troubles were shared as a matter of course.

If the weather turned really cold, icy winds blew straight down our street from the Sierra (the not-so-distant snow-capped mountain-range), and the warm old house would suddenly become an ice-box. Perhaps the windows didn't close as well as they used to, perhaps the old furnace needed overhauling?

But presently a more thorough investigation solved the mystery. The furnace was Antonio, the porter's, job. Too lazy to accept this however, he had found a man from the coal merchant's opposite, who promised to look after it for him, in return for some small remuneration.

Lazy too, or perhaps too busy, the 'carboneria' man paid a child a few pesetas to do the job for him. This 'niño' or errand boy diligently heated the house. But when the weather became too cold, his mother would not allow him out on to the streets and kept him at home.

So the house froze until his return with warmer weather.

The ancient car could only be started with a crank, and one day when Auntie Mariquita and I had been driven out to do some shopping it stalled as usual.

The elegant and handsome young chauffeur with a Shakespearian name jumped down, took off his white gloves, and red in the face while trying to ignore the jeering urchins crowding around him, he started to wind the crank. It slipped in his nervous grip and smartly and painfully banged him on the knuckles. Losing all self-control, he kicked the car and cursed out loud.

Auntie adjusted her lorgnon, leaned out of the window and gently admonished: 'Leandro, don't use obscenities.'

Auntie Mariquita loved to wait, for she said those were the free moments in her busy life: a present of time. Time to think, to plan, to pray. When harried, she became very absent-minded, and some years later produced her mother's passport at a frontier instead of her own. (She had carried it around after her death as a keepsake.) Hers was at the bottom of a trunk sent as freight. The official made her out to be therefore close on 110 years of age, which caused some commotion until the misunderstanding was cleared up.

Aunt Mariquita could never have been pretty, but she had the charm of great goodness, combined with a very subtle, self-deprecating sense of humour.

As elder sister, she had a gently protective attitude to my mother-in-law who was nine years her junior, so much more beautiful and dashing and capricious. As they grew old, they became inseparable. She told me that her married life, though short, had been so happy, and her husband on his death-bed assured her he had never been unfaithful.

'I had not liked to think about it, but it was nice to know.'

For many years she had presided over the upbringing of the two infantas, Beatrice and Crista, and they loved her like a second mother.

Both her sons were professional sailors. She was quite under their charm, and they adored her in return. Paul was the smallest, loved and spoiled by all and for her he seemed another son. The Santa Cruz children would turn to her when in trouble with almost more confidence than to their own parents. Nothing could exceed her kindness to me.

Her opinion carried great weight and when once one of her beloved boys overstepped the limits of what she thought best overlooked, she only said:

'Children of this house do not do such things,' and left the room.

The 'child' was over thirty, yet the blow landed like a sledgehammer.

The keys of Tunis, symbol of the surrender of the town to Don Alvaro de Bazan, had been kept on a velvet cushion in a glass case under his portrait and his personal 'Farola', in a gloomy red velvet drawing-room, hung with portraits of severe-looking ancestors by Carreno, Antonio el Moro, Claudio Cuello. Breaking into the house during the Civil War, the invaders were intrigued by these keys, huge and unwieldy as they were. Surely they must have been meant to open some treasure chest? But none could be found, so in disgust and rage they hurled them under the great stove in the kitchen. Then intervening walls were pulled down: it was a miracle the house had not collapsed.

Now painstakingly, room by room (for money was scarce), the old palace was put in order again.

We stumbled over women from the 'Real Fabrica', the famous Gobelins factory brought from France by Philip V, as they sat mending holes in the fine old carpets, piecing bits together with nimble, clever fingers, chatting without pause as they worked.

The chimney in the Goya damask drawing-room had always smoked, and no fire was ever lit there. The wall was finally ripped open for a thorough investigation, and disclosed the remains of a French officer of Napoleonic times in full uniform and plumed hat. The workmen did not think this at all surprising, for even after their war, Napoleon was still for them synonymous with devastation and horror, and 'walling-up' was a form of dealing with one's enemies which recurs in Spanish history.

(The Palace had been the French Embassy for a time in the days of Joseph Bonaparte, and the officer must have been left in charge when the French retired.)

In the green Salon, 18th century pastel portraits of young Waldsteins lined the walls again, between cabinets filled with gaily painted Viennese china.

The tiny maid, Casilda, would trot over from the ironing-room, our clothes held high like banners at the end of long sticks. She peeped through their folds like a cheerful sparrow out of a bush, and scolded the scrambling dogs out of her way.

'Those poor children,' she called us, although we towered above her. But she knew what war meant, and that we would soon have to return to what awaited us 'Por Alli'. ('Over there' was the term used for practically any region beyond the Spanish frontiers, from Irun to Siberia.)

She tended me lovingly when I collapsed with a bad attack of hepatitis. To cheer me up, she sang me folk songs and demonstrated Spanish dance steps, as light-footed as a young girl. She told me stories of the past, and of Paul's childhood, and how she would take him to the cinema when he was small. 'But he always insisted on carrying the money and paying himself.'

She was the third or fourth generation of her family in service in the house, and had spent all her life in San Bernardino. She had always been so happy, she said. Happy with Manolo, her husband, happy with her love for the family and her own children.

'How many?' I asked.

'Two now. But I had fourteen.'

'*Twelve* died! But how appalling. Poor Casilda!'

'God took one and gave another. There were never more than three at a time. One boy, Jesùs, he grew to nineteen and then he died. Ah, then I cried a lot! But I have two good ones left, and so I am happy again.'

When I recovered, I surprised the family by bursting into fluent Spanish ('overnight' it seemed to them). The praise should have gone to Casilda.

The proverbial clannishness of the Santa Cruz cousins was balanced by a passion, almost a mania, for personal independence. They were discreet about their own or each other's concerns, but their solidarity in moments of crisis became as unyielding as a rock.

Before going out in the evenings, either all together or each on their own, Auntie Mariquita's sons Alvaro Urzaiz (resplendent in Naval uniform), and his brother Mariano, Duke of Luna (soon to be Naval Attaché in London), would join the Santa Cruz girls Casilda and Maria Luisa, to have a drink with us.

Poetic, willowy and rather languid, Maria Luisa Santa Cruz was a few years younger than me, and we went shopping together or walked the dogs in the gardens around the burnt-out husk of the Alba Palace, talking over her love affairs. She was the beauty of the family, resembling my mother-in-law. Should she marry Pitulis Quijano? She couldn't decide. Paul said, 'As you are wearing his medals, his shirt, his cardigans, and his identity disc, you might as well marry him!'

Her sister Casilda, or Cassy, was full of ideas and plans but none for her own future. With her wit, charm and exceptional personality it seemed a pity for her to settle into humdrum domesticity. In time she was to become a notable and loved figure in diplomacy.

Returning home at night the scent of 'jara' lavender and thyme came wafting down from the Sierra as we clapped our hands for the *sereno* (night watchman), the Galician Florentino. But soon his cheerful cry 'Voy' echoed down the empty street. Swathed in blankets, swinging his keys, tapping the ground with his long stick, he came with a waddling run. As the great door swung open, harmless black beetles, *Cucarachas*, scuttled away with no undue haste.

Although the Second World War was well under way, bringing untold suffering in the wake of the German armies, I was shocked to see the destruction and misery of this already poor country. Crowds of beggars waited outside every building, and we always kept money loose in our pockets for outstretched hands. Kitchens were set up and food distributed for the most part through private initiative. Having achieved victory, resentment was now over, as if the roaring furnace of hate had been smothered with ashes no one wished to kindle again.

Without help from any side, it was to take some years before the gaping scars left by the Civil War had healed and for a new balance to be found. Above all the country needed peace. As a concession to Hitler, whom Franco considered capable of any folly, and as a demonstration of anti-communism (their only common ground), a division of volunteers would be sent presently to fight in Russia.

When the Civil War had broken out in Spain in 1936, Paul crossed over at once at Dancharinea near Irun. He joined his cousins and volunteered for any assignment. He soon found himself much in demand as messenger, courier, liaison man, chauffeur or soldier.

He was just nineteen years old.

He was now eager to show me some of the places where he had been, for whenever the fighting died down in one place, he would join another cousin or friend who happened to be in a tight spot.

Telling me about it all, Paul tersely remarked: '. . . You can't do two things at the same time. The Republican Government had given every man a gun, and they were so busy murdering their personal enemies there was no time left to fight. As a result except for the trained International Brigades, their troops were inferior.'

'Nosotros', 'Ellos': 'We' and 'They'.

Painted roughly on slivers of wood, these two words marked the zig-zag dividing line of the Madrid Front, as it ran between the 'Reds' and the 'Nacionales' (as they called themselves), or 'Government Republican troops' and 'Nationalists', as they were named abroad.

It was the final choice in a fratricide war.

For many, the division cleaving Spain in two had been a matter of chance, depending on where the risings had been successful, but for most it cut through the country, through the provinces, through layers of society – even political convictions.

But for all Paul's friends and numerous relations all over Spain, their engagement on the Nationalist side (at that time headed by General

Mola) was an automatic response through religion and background, to the fight for survival of both.

Everyone he knew joined up, the girls taking on hazardous assignments in flying Red Cross units, which at times led them up to the Front Line. They had no bandages, few medicines: everything had to be improvised.

But as the veil of rubble, grey hunger and tears spread over the land under its indifferent sun, the enthusiasm of their personal conviction was to carry them to final victory: they knew what they were fighting for.

The Caso de Campo, on the outskirts of Madrid, used to be the King's Park. As a child, Paul had played and driven there with the slightly older Royal children: the Infantas, and Don Juan (future Count of Barcelona).

Step by step, he now showed me where the Madrid Front had frozen for two years, when the Nationalist advance halted to free Toledo. Tito had then established his Headquarters in the Golf Club of the Puerta de Hierro.

The moonlike landscape was barren and scarred: torn by bombs. The University Faculties, once set among lovely gardens created by King Alfonso XIII, burnt out or gutted.

We climbed in and out of trenches and hollows, past half collapsed buildings riddled with bullet scars. The positions were still clear, intertwining at times, penetrating each other's defences. The tenuous line meandered over uneven ground, following no strategical plan, but as if bursts of individual courage had pushed it forward by impulse or chance. We stumbled over the flotsam of war: heaps of barbed wire, half-fallen-in dugouts, a twisted tin pan, broken rifle or bullet-ridden helmet under earth and dust.

On this front, everybody knew everybody else: here so and so had been killed, here the wounded were collected and tended under fire; here a push had been made at dawn, and an outpost established on the other side of the road. It was a hand to hand, house by house visceral war.

Paul had fought here under Generals Varela and Yague during the first winter, when they had nearly taken the capital, and then again under Colonel O'Duffy with the Irish Legion. He was fascinated to see the site again for the first time from the 'other' side.

One day a car had broken out of Madrid, trying to escape down the main highway which divided the two fronts.

It was driven by a girl with long, streaming hair. She was caught from both sides, killed at the wheel by murderous fire and remained there for the next two years, Among so many deaths, it had left a deep impression.

The car had been thrown down below the road, and we looked down on it lying on its side in the stony river-bed, a burnt-out husk.

As the war drew to its end, Madrid fell suddenly, like a rotten apple.

It was difficult to procure a car, but at last we were on our way to Toledo.

Except for some home-built tricycles, equipped with a motor which must have previously powered a sewing-machine, there was hardly any traffic. The road plunged bravely towards the horizon, lined on both sides by natural herbaceous borders of wild flowers, blooming in bursts of colour and fascinating variety. Goats sheltered in the shade of a mangy tree.

The country seemed flat, yet one horizon melted into another. Appearing over a ridge, sharply delineated church spires set on a pedestal of clustering red roofs pierced the sky. Emerging from nowhere, a man on a donkey or a shepherd among his flock stood out against the clouds which seemed never to obscure the sun's hot rays. For a painter, there would be no waste of time looking for a subject: they were presented one after another in stark simplification, as for beginners.

Natural fortress, ancient capital, heart of Castile, Toledo with its dramatic approach is one of the few places which can never disappoint. Surrounded by a desert landscape sparsely dotted by unmoving sheep, pressed like pale worms against the barren hills, under a blazing sun or great clouds of incandescent sunsets, there is no measure and no restraint in its setting.

It now rose before us like a fantastic crown, cushioned on the encircling bed of the river Tajo far below. Bristling spires culminated in the great cathedral and in the dramatic ruin of the Alcazar ('castle' in Arabic), whose crumbling towers seemed to pour down over surrounding buildings like lava.

We tried to drive all round the opposite bank of the river, without entering the town. The bridge crossing a deep cleft, where far below torrential waters rushed, had been blown up in the war. A few planks roughly nailed together, without railings, were supposed to provide a makeshift crossing. A road-worker urged us on. Impossible to hesitate, so on we went, trying to look neither right nor left, feeling like an ant on a grass stalk. The slender improvised bridge swayed and creaked beneath us, but we got across in one piece under the interested and sardonic gaze of the single onlooker, honour saved.

We then entered the town from the southern side.

In 1936, Paul had joined the troops advancing towards Toledo to deliver the town, and now, five years later, as we wandered among the rubble roughly swept into heaps, he described that epic siege. The corpses, which he had seen floating in the swimming-pool, were still walled into the recesses around it, where the youngsters had hung their clothes. Otherwise, not much had changed since then. Piles of débris blocked a number of rooms in a half-standing wing of the vast building. The doors could only be pushed open a few inches. Under a cross sketched in chalk were the names of those still lying under the heaps of rubble and dust just beyond.

All the dead would later be gathered and laid to rest in a votive chapel in the reconstructed Alcazar.

To supplement her family's income, Marysia, my mother-in-law's Polish niece by marriage, had started a small shop in partnership with another woman, who lent her flat for the purpose, glad of the extra money.

One day she noticed an unshaven, gaunt, rather frightening-looking individual in the private sitting-room. He would return at frequent intervals.

'Who is he?' she asked her landlady.

'The man who murdered my three sons.'

During the Civil War the troops of the garrison of Madrid, reinforced by cadets of the officers' school, attempted to resist the 'Reds'. They were shortly besieged in their barracks, the 'Cuartel de la Montana', perched on the Western edge of the city. The rising was put down almost immediately and the defenders, for the most part young recruits from Madrid and many barely eighteen years of age, were systematically and cruelly murdered. The relatives of the butchered boys were then rounded up and brought to the scene of the massacre to see for themselves what sort of death they had suffered.

Marysia's landlady was among those dragged to the Cuartel de la Montana.

Now, five years later, the same man knocked on her door once more. He had come to say he could not live with what he had done. Perhaps she could forgive him?

'Out of the question!'

'But if you get used to me, perhaps you would?'

She thought it over; doubtfully at first.

'Perhaps . . . Come when you like.'

He would drop in now and again and sit in her drawing-room, reading the papers, silent; a cup of tea at his elbow.

One day she said:

'You were right. I have got used to you and can now forgive you. Go (Vaya Ud. con Dios.), and do not come again.'

'Gracias Senora,' he said as he went away.

'It is true I feel better now,' she told Marysia. 'One cannot live with hate.'

Paul's cousin, Alvaro Urzaiz, Aunt Mariquita's eldest son, was stationed in Algeciras as Spanish Naval representative. He commanded a small flotilla of torpedo boats there.

He invited us to come down and visit him, and knowing our time in Spain was soon ending, we were glad to do so and see something of the country on the way.

The road to Andalucia passed the 'Hill of the Angels' near Madrid. It was a pilgrimage centre to which many a survivor of the Civil War had repaired on foot as a votive offering for deliverance. Paul too had walked there, while I drove the 13 miles or so in slow stages, reading a book until he caught up with me again.

A series of hazards lay in wait for us on our way south. Apart from the unreliability of our engine, the roads seemed to be strewn with nails and punctures were frequent. Much damaged through neglect and war, the roads were slowly being repaired and little men armed with pickaxes hacked away at granite blocks. It seemed like excavating with a toothpick, and yet imposing slices were cut off mountains and tunnels hewn out of solid rock.

The sun shone into our laps as we headed for the next church spire. There did not seem to be any driving rules, as some travellers had discovered to their sorrow, for the few accidents we saw on our way seemed total: the cars crumpled and tossed away like used tissue-paper. The road would suddenly stop without warning and we then had to follow a detour leading across a dried-up river bed or a stony field. If by chance a piece of wood nailed to a stick announced 'Peligro', it meant impending catastrophe.

As we continued south the accent changed. The tone of Spanish is so different to lilting Italian: deep and sonorous in Madrid, the words drop like pebbles falling on a tin roof. In rural Cataluna it becomes a duck's cackle or a nasal drawl, and in the south a husky burr, with different intonations in Cordoba, Granada, Sevilla or Jerez, ending in the soft and slurred pronunciation of South America. The names of places now began to sound like the trumpet call of Islam: Guadalquivir, Alhambra del Monte, Almuñecar.

Approaching our destination towards evening, the flocks of sheep were outlined against the setting sun on the mountain ridges like silver-lined, small puffs of cloud above the darkness gathering beneath them.

I remembered hearing that further south, the Marquesa de L. and her mother were recently travelling on a bus to their nearest town. Owing to frequent hold-ups, two guards always went along to protect the passengers. In case of attack, the young and lovely Marquesa would be presumably exposed to worse than mere robbery. One of the guards, pointing to his pistol, thought to reassure her:

'Descuide (Do not worry) Señora Marquesa. I will not let you fall into their hands alive.'

She tried to remonstrate: '. . . Virtue was all very well, but . . .'

'Descuide,' he insisted. 'I have never missed.'

In Sevilla we stayed with the Medinacelis in their house built to the same plan as Pontius Pilate's summer residence near Jerusalem. After visiting the lovely city untouched by the war and unspoilt by modernisation, they took us to sample caviar on the Guadalquivir. A pre-Revolutionary Russian, ex-Minister of Fisheries under the last Tzar, was successfully extracting it from local sturgeon.

One evening we drove to the country to watch young heifers being tested for their courage, bulls apparently inheriting their moral qualities from the mother's side. Under a flamingo sky, the cloud of dust approaching us over dark stubble gradually dissolved into a herd of cattle pursued by riders in their picturesque dress, prodding the animals with their long sticks. The small black cows would turn and attack, or roll in the dust, or flee – as unpredictably as a human would react under pressure.

Early in 1942 our time in Spain was over. Paul was to return to Bad-Cannstatt, the base of his Cavalry Regiment 'Reiter 18', and join an officers' training course. He would then be posted to the Russian front. We left with heavy hearts.

In Paris he would not let me leave the station. 'I want to return here one day when the war is over,' he said. I telephoned my cousins during our long wait there, and we then walked up and down the platform with them.

Our few days in Berlin passed in a flash. All the talk centred on the Russian campaign and – 'sotto voce' – on the Nazis' incredible incomprehension of the situation.

When my parents had heard that Leningrad – their Petrograd – was besieged, they were heart-broken. Paul told them he did not think the German Army would succeed in taking the city, for the Front Line was stretching endlessly from north to south; and towards the East, on the Ladoga Lake side, the town remained open, which might enable the Russians to evacuate civilians. But Tsarkoje Selo was directly in the Front Line, and shells were apparently crashing into the Palace. Even though they would never return there, Papa and Mamma could not bear to think of the devastation of their country and their hometown. Every place mentioned in communiqués revived old memories.

For White Russians such as my parents, the Soviet Government and the OGPU were 'bolshevik', whereas the Russian Army and the country were 'Russian'. They were much surprised when this clear distinction was misunderstood.

'Frozen meat winter' was what the German Army called the Russian campaign of 1941–1942. Officially, it went by the code word 'Operation Barbarossa'. The German Ambassador in Moscow, Count von der

Schulenburg, told us that Stalin had hoped to stay the blow until the last moment, 'keeping to all agreements with painful correctness'. Having just done away with all his High Command and well knowing that wars tend to bring Generals to the fore, Stalin was neither ready nor eager to go to war.

Hitler had thought to re-enact the Blitz campaign against Poland. Being self-taught himself, he would listen to no expert advice, for he deeply distrusted professionals, specialists, and even any form of academic learning. He was 'inspired' and that was enough. His incredible ignorance of both the history and geography of Russia, supported by half-baked party theories, was to lead instead to a prolonged repetition of Napoleon's 1812 invasion of Russia.

Intending to instal the invincible *Wehrmacht* in winter quarters in Moscow, he personally cut down all orders for winter clothing, leaving the army lamentably unprepared to meet Russia's eternal ally, 'Grandfather Frost'.

In 1812 Napoleon had expected a 'Nation of Slaves' to welcome him as Liberator, for was he not the bearer of Revolutionary slogans, all decked out in Imperial trappings? Yet the entire population remained loyal to their Emperor and their country: there was no treason.

Now, 130 years later, even Nazi rule seemed preferable to communism, and at first the German Army met with comparatively weak resistance. Hitler refused to admit the implications of this initial collapse, when thousands of Soviet soldiers surrendered, or were even at first prepared to fight on the German side. He wilfully ignored all political possibilities and the opportunity of turning the war against Russia into a war against communism. It would jeopardize his plans for the East as 'living space' for densely populated Germany.

To the despair of many high-ranking officers in the German Army, the Party let the Soviet prisoners die of hunger in camps. Stories of cannibalism spread gradually, in spite of the hermetic secrecy imposed. The inhuman application of Rosenberg's inhuman racist and 'Untermensch' theories played into Stalin's hand.

(More than any other insanity of Nazi thought, my parents considered Rosenberg's vile institution – occupying 30 buildings in Berlin alone – the cancer which would finally destroy the Nazi régime.)

Laying Comintern interests aside for the time being, Stalin now declared the defence of Russia to be a patriotic war in the great tradition of 1812. The Soviet High Command then dared to tell him that the rank and file soldier would not fight without the support of their priests. Stalin had thought the Church to be practically eliminated, and that the new peace which he now concluded with the Patriarchate of Moscow would be but a minor concession until the war was over. In this he was mistaken.

Surprisingly little attention has been paid to the amazing fact, that after a quarter of a century of religious persecution, Russia was still a Christian country.

Meanwhile the onslaught of the motorized German Army was halted within sight of Moscow. They bogged down in sleet and snow, froze in hastily contrived shelters. Belatedly, furs, any furs – mink coats, woollen blankets and rugs were collected and bundled off, often lost on the way and inadequate on arrival. The soldiers froze, and were then court-martialled for freezing.

It seemed already the beginning of the end.

We were all the more grateful for the short respite ahead of us in Stuttgart.

We were installed soon after in the Station Hotel there, which had the advantage of being within a few minutes distance of the train Paul had to catch every morning. Trains rumbled away under our feet night and day, and later it was to prove a favourite bombing target.

In the Spanish Civil War, Paul had been a volunteer. Never a spectator by nature, he was used to having things his way, setting up his own challenges. But when World War II broke out, and on the 1st October 1939 he received his mobilisation papers, there was no question of his not complying.

In international European families, owing to long experience of changing fortunes from one generation to another, events are treated as a climatic condition: to be dealt with when possible, borne with when not. Wherever one lived (even if one happened to live in several places), when things went wrong, you stayed to face the consequences.

Paul's Catholic upbringing and down to earth sense of proportion induced a natural aversion to the Nazis' vulgarity and bullying. He distrusted all they propounded, although the excesses they were already planning at that time only became blatantly evident with the war.

During the recent Sudeten-Czech crisis of 1938, the Western Powers had condoned Hitler's action and acceded to his demands all down the line. Therefore, at first, Paul took his mobilisation philosophically. The Spanish war and physical training had inured him to the hardships of military life, and his unselfconsciousness of manner made him a popular figure.

Although gradually the coercion of German Army life would become ever more irksome, at first he was content to remain in the ranks.

The alarm clock would ring at 5 a.m. precisely. With one leap, Paul was in the middle of the room, rapidly pulling on his rough uniform, eyes still half-closed. A dash down the stairs of the hotel, straight out on to the platform of the station and into the waiting train which left for

Bad-Cannstatt at 5.09. There he began another arduous day, more brow-beating than training, as a private soldier of the Cavalry Regiment No 18, known as the 'Cannstätter Riders'.

By contrast, my life was for the present quiet and uneventful. As the town simmered in the summer heat I could escape to some swimming pool, avoiding the ones the regiment occasionally used, or, following the advice of Princess Margarita Hohenlohe, the regimental Commander's wife, born a Greek Princess, take a tram out of the city and then walk around exploring the attractive countryside.

Prince Hohenlohe, and his wife, were to become close friends. He always referred to Paul as 'my favourite Corporal', but at that time it was more tactful to keep some distance between the soldiers and the Com-mander, and Margarita and I could only snatch moments to chat, seated on boxes in the cellar of the Bahnhofshotel when the air-raid sirens had sounded. Unfortunately, she and her husband would not be staying in Stuttgart for long.

Having only recently recovered from hepatitis, which every now and then brought on shattering colics, I rested a lot and read all the time. Shopping was not on the programme as there was nothing to buy.

Bringing with him a strong smell of the stables, Paul returned at five in the afternoon and life began again. First a hot, scented bath (pine extract was still to be had), followed by a siesta of an hour or so.

Meanwhile, snatching odd moments, I amplified and neatly tran-scribed into a copybook the notes he had taken during the pre-officer course. His superiors would have no opportunity to see his handwriting, so for the final examination the copybook passed the test. This greatly amused his comrades in the know, who considered that I deserved simultaneous promotion to the rank of ('N.C.O.') 'Unteroffizier' (shortened to 'Uffz' when used officially).

Then, after a final shower, we were off to dinner, sometimes taking a friend or two along. There were still charming, rather French-looking, 'guinguettes' all around Stuttgart, where the cheery host proudly produced asparagus and ham, a local speciality, bretzels and delicious wine to improve the taste of everything. We sat in green bowers, lanterns swinging among the leaves, and then Paul would recount the happenings of the day: the odious chores, the oppressive badgering of the sergeant, the systematic conditioning to unquestioning obedience, turned to hilarious anecdote.

'Wieder so Einer!' (another one of those), they had sighed when he rejoined them. The previous ones were an Ingelheim and three Wittgenstein cousins who had graced the regiment in rapid succession. Witty, independent, country-bred – therefore physically tough and quite inured to smells and dirt – also at home with horses – they were, worst of all, impervious to the sergeant's flow of outrage. Instead they registered every colourful simile for future mimicry while trying at the same time not to grin.

They were finally on the best of terms with their would-be tormentors. Udi Wittgenstein later maintained that an enlarged photograph depicting him wielding a rake on the manure heap still hung in a place of honour over his sergeant's bed next to the coloured lithograph of Jesus wandering among His lambs.

Once Paul was ordered forward to be yelled at by a diminutive sergeant; invective followed insult in the expressive jargon of the Swabian peasant. Paul, gazing fish-eyed over his head, tried not to laugh but finally exploded into a loud and contagious guffaw. Grins spread over the faces of the company behind him.

Hastily the sergeant broke off the session and called him into his office.

'How could you laugh?'

'. . . but imagine the scene! I am so tall and my sleeves and trousers are too short. You are small and your sleeves and trousers are too long. You stand and shout into the third button of my jacket. We must have looked quite ridiculous.'

Disarmed the sergeant said, 'You shouldn't have laughed in front of all the others!'

He left Paul alone after that and much later, in Russia, they became friends.

Although a tremendous amount of pointless exercising took place in the vast courtyard, the horses were always the main concern. They had to be groomed, fed and walked. They were rarely ridden, but that was no great loss as they were so hard-mouthed.

For the French campaign, Paul had been given a horse called Metternich, for they understandably enjoyed hearing the answer to the roll-call: 'Metternich on Metternich'.

Metternich was an obstinate brute addicted to every nasty trick an ill-used horse can think up in self-defence against recruits: sudden kicks, crowding hapless scrubbers against the wall, rearing when his saddle was buckled on, so that when on parade his rider soon found himself slipping sideways, spread-eagled.

But the next day they were going to war so Paul tried to placate and cajole him in every way. After all, they depended on each other for whatever was to come.

He fed him the juiciest oats, watered him, scrubbed and stroked him and finally, for good measure, kissed him on the nose.

Years of profound distrust had warped the horse's character. He misunderstood the gesture and retaliated by biting him full in the face.

Blinded by pain and shock, Paul seized a rake and, remembering to use the blunt end, whacked him hard on the rump. Metternich kicked back with the mastery of a circus horse, so the punishment was short. After that, armed neutrality was the only basis for understanding.

Some evenings were called *Kameradschaftsabende*, or friendly reunions. The wives helped in the kitchen, but they would not allow me to lend a hand which was very embarrassing as I did not want to appear to them as a useless flower.

As long as Paul was not yet one of them, we avoided seeing the officers, except when some of them sometimes came to our hotel to dine with us. To the soldiers they seemed like beings from another world.

They had expected Paul to join their ranks long ago. One of them watching him trundling a wheelbarrow on the manure heap exclaimed in despair: 'Have you no ambition?'

But Paul wanted no responsibility in a cause for which he felt no sympathy. Inevitably he would be pushed into the officers' school after more than two years of war, but at that time his army life gravitated between drudgery and grotesque.

Bombing attacks on Stuttgart were gathering momentum. One night, arriving there after frequent alarms all the way down, we stepped out into destruction. The station, and incidentally our hotel, had both been practically blown sky-high. As we climbed over one obstacle after another, to our astonishment we were met in the remains of the lobby by our hotel director, kind Herr Loeble, who then led us to a half-standing wing:

'Luckily your room is quite untouched!' he announced cheerfully.

It had been cleaned and dusted and on the table, conjured out of limbo, stood a bottle of iced champagne and a huge dish of oysters: an undeserved tribute to what he considered our heroic return!

Every day in Stuttgart now, meant twenty-four hours more won from the inevitable moment when Paul would be thrown into the seething cauldron of war in Russia. We could count on our fingers how soon this would be, for he was finishing the preliminary course and was soon to join the officers' school in Krampnitz for a final polish.

But as long as we were still stationed in Stuttgart a longer week-end now and again allowed us to reach Johannisberg.

Overlooking the Rhine valley is a vast sweep from Mainz to Bingen including countless villages nestling in the folds of gentle hills. Johannisberg is the centre of vineyards of world repute. Tradition says that wine grew on its hills since the Roman occupation, for the northern frontier of the Roman Empire, the 'limes', ran along the ridge of the 'Taunus', just beyond our woods. Around 800 Charlemagne established his summer residence in Ingelheim, opposite Johannisberg. As the snow melted first on that hill, he ordered wine to be plantedt here again.

Cut off from the North, yet open to Western civilisation, 'freemen' since centuries under mild Church rule, the inhabitants of the Rheingau province developed their own specific mentality, which made them singularly independent and impervious to slogans and false promises even during Nazi times.

More recently, Johannisberg had for a short period belonged to Napoleon's Marshal Kellermann, the victor of Valmy. After 1815 it reverted to the Austrian Crown and Emperor Francis I then gave it to his trusted counsellor and friend, Metternich, in compensation for destroyed property during the recent wars and as a token of gratitude for the peace achieved at the Congress of Vienna.

Parsimonious in his habits, and by nature averse to granting gifts, the Emperor usually retained what the Austrians call 'ein Zipferl', meaning the corner of the tablecloth. In this case it was a tithe (the tenth part of the harvest) to be delivered in wine for the Imperial table. All the Courts of Europe then ordered the same wine, confirming its great reputation.

It seemed a small obligation then, for Johannisberg was just a delightful place to own, no source of important revenue. When the Habsburgs were evicted from Austria in 1918, Paul's father maintained the tithe. His family owed so much to the dynasty he would not deprive them of this last right.

After annexing Austria, the Nazis tried to usurp the tithe as well – were they not heirs to all Habsburg property? Paul insisted this was a personal obligation, from family to family. The Nazis also wished to eject the Franciscan monks from the convent of Marienthal on Paul's land. A popular centre of pilgrimage, people coming from far and wide to Mass, held out of doors under shady chestnut trees, it was also a provocation to the régime, which was surreptitiously developing an anti-religious campaign.

They could not get at the monks or at the tithe without first dealing with private property, in this case Paul.

It seemed a little too soon for that, however, as extreme measures were always distasteful to the Rhineland, and Paul was, after all, fighting for his country. So after an initial attack, the authorities decided to bide their time.

In Johannisberg, Paul was ably and courageously supported by the Administrator, Labonte, who now came to meet us, hand in hand with his small pig-tailed daughter, shyly clutching a bunch of flowers for me.

His ancestors had been falconers, brought from Provence by the Prince Elector, Bishop of Trier. This may have accounted for his fortunate combination of French lucidity of mind and sense of measure, with German trustworthiness.

Our rooms were in the east wing and we were awaited by beaming, apple-cheeked Babette, the maid, who was also apparently a passionate devotee of Rhenish carnivals.

All down the Rhine valley, on either side of the lazily coiling silver river, the low hills, downy pink and white with blossoming fruit trees, seemed to melt into the pale spring sky like earth-bound clouds.

The upstairs drawing-room was extended by a balcony on which we had breakfast, feeling part of a panoramic engraving of the early XIXth century, perched as we were over the immense view. Living so high in the sky made one weather-conscious, and I longed for the day when I would have time to try and paint the ever-changing pearly light, turning from golden in the early morning, to shrimp pink as the sun sank beyond the Rat-Tower of Bingen.

A plush-padded winding staircase, lined with English hunting-prints, led straight from our rooms down to a small drawing-room, where Paul and his young friends used to dance, for the floor was as slippery as a mirror. Two further steps took one into the bamboo-lined hall, which opened out on to the terrace. Before lunch we sat there in high fan-backed exotic wicker chairs, tasting delicious vintages, such as 1933 and Blue-Seal 1937.

There was no garden. It had been replaced by vines planted during Paul's minority as a measure of economy. Beyond the gates the small park ran wild. Magnificent cedars spread welcome shade, framing wide views between their wing-like branches. The grass was mown for hay, the hedges cut, but not much more could be done in wartime.

The house, however, still stood in perfect order, the Chancellor's taste for lovely 18th century and early Empire furniture supplemented by contributions from Pauline Metternich, when her husband was Ambassador in Paris during the late eighteen-sixties. Buttoned chairs of every shape, *causeuses* with a flowerpot in the middle, were covered in striped Indian silks, now much faded, but still full of charm, once superfluous tassels and ornamentation were removed.

In the afternoon, Wendolin the coachman, inordinately proud of his impeccable horses, would drive us into the woods. In the village he was nicknamed 'Der Lord' for his grand manner and distinguished appearance.

All too soon, it was time for him to take us to the station of Rüdesheim, the horses' hooves echoing along the empty roads.

As the train passed along the base of our hill up the Rhine again, we could see Babette brandishing a huge sheet from the main balcony to wish us good-bye.

The passengers, gazing up, said, 'Imagine living there!'

We did indeed consider ourselves lucky, but now we stood in the over-crowded train. There was not even anything to lean against, so we leant against each other, like our horses in the stables, and slept in turns fitfully all night through.

Paul's final officers' training began at Krampnitz, just outside Berlin, in the summer of 1942. On reaching Berlin we settled again in our 'pied à terre' under the eaves of the Gersdorff house in the Woyrsch-strasse. Missie was still living there too, and after the quiet months in Stuttgart, we found ourselves drawn into a busy social life again. This also meant that we were soon up to date as to what was really going on.

Since the Reichstag speech of the 26th April 1942, in which Hitler arrogated himself the power to decide everything alone, without being bound by any legal regulations, the rule of law had ended and the climate of moral sickness in the capital grew steadily worse.

'Divide et impera', the dictator's motto, was but a preliminary to a total police state. It resulted in the Army, several Ministries and the all-pervading Party each disposing of their own Press, Secret Police, foreign contacts and policy and even Finance departments, all at odds with their 'colleagues' who were in fact competing rivals, doing the same jobs in other institutions. Goebbels fought Göring, Rosenberg, Ribbentrop and Himmler, while Canaris of the Army Intelligence fought them all. Vehicles and arms for the Front for instance, were diverted on the way by the S.S. or by Göring for his Air Force. The result was a shambles of parallel authorities and total lack of coordination. This may have suited Hitler's one man rule, but it was the gradual end of common sense and drove reasonable men to despair.

Surprisingly it did not result in paralysing the war effort, for in Germany relentless efficiency and minute attention to detail seemed to lead a life of their own.

Meanwhile 'men of good will' were foregathering in spite of tight Nazi control. This was easier in the capital where parties, picnics, and a wider range of social life offered excellent cover for less innocent meetings and discussions, resulting in elaborate (*too* elaborate!) planning, which was to lead to the plot of the 20th July 1944.

TOP: *My mother in mourning, 1917.*

BELOW: *Mamma and her family with Irina and Alexander.*

TOP: *My father with Irina and Alexander, 1917.*

BELOW: *Leaving Russia on board the* Princess Ena. *Some Aunts, Papa, Commodore Unwin, V.C., Irina, Alexander and small cousins. I am on the right.*

Irina, me, Missie and Alexander in France, 1920.

ABOVE LEFT: *My mother-in-law at the time of her marriage. She was Isabel Silva y Carvajal, daughter of the Marquess of Santa Cruz.*

ABOVE RIGHT: *Paul in 1940.*

OPPOSITE PAGE
TOP: *My father, Prince Ilarion Sergueevitch Wassiltchikoff, 1942.*

BELOW: *Missie in 1944.*

ABOVE LEFT: *Paul and me at Königswart in 1942.*

ABOVE RIGHT: *Tatiana Metternich, a portrait by Molly Bishop.*

OPPOSITE PAGE
TOP: *Johannisberg, as it looked until it was destroyed by bombing in 1942.*

BELOW: *Königswart.*

TREK ab 10 Ⅴ 45 (600 Km) v. Königswart n. Johannisberg
i. Begleitung v. Eltern m. franz. be- schaufieren

Tatiana Metternich

One of my water colour sketches of us on our 600 km. trek from Königswart to
Johannisberg in an open cart, May 1945.

Even in the officers' school these contrasts were apparent, for many units of the Army had become a refuge from political persecution. If one was faced with Party suspicion, badgering, or even with a 'distasteful' job, there always remained the choice of volunteering for the Front. Even in our office there had been several instances of this last recourse. When our friend Hansi Welczeck, the Ambassador's son, returned from Madrid where he had been attaché at the German Embassy, the head of Personnel in the Foreign Office, a Party man, advised him to 'dive below the surface' by joining the Army as soon as possible, for the Party was otherwise 'going to attend' to him.

The tradition-bound cavalry regiments recruited their officers and men mostly from rural regions, where the relationship between the different levels of society was based on centuries of familiarity resulting from living side by side. The officers came frequently from circles bred to a tradition of integrity based on strong Christian ethics. This enabled them to retain longest a sense of direction and to discern more easily between right and wrong. Patriotism meant responsibility to the nation as a whole and not primitive loyalty to Hitler, now so often claimed as moral justification for immoral actions.

The cavalry regiments were fertile ground for anti-Nazi planning, for young officers would be sent as aides-de-camp to Generals, to key Army liaison posts, where they could sound out the temper of their chiefs and of the troops.

They would become the flying messengers of the conspirators.

For the Party, the Army was only an instrument of power, to be treated as cannon-fodder. When the High Command protested against the ever more extended Front, causing particularly high losses among young officers due to ill-considered strategy, Hitler coolly replied: 'That is what they are there for.'

To replace them ever more rapidly, the officers' training course was reduced from six to two months. Draconian rules locked young men into their barracks at Krampnitz. Free Sundays were cancelled.

Nevertheless a number of cadets slipped out in the evening to return at dawn. If the exercise of their duties did not suffer, their immediate superiors tended to ignore this infringement. They were well aware that their fledglings were heading for the Front to refill the thinning ranks. Life expectancy was very short, and punishment meant transfer to a 'special' company, which in most cases was equal to a death sentence.

As often as possible, Paul would escape to nearby Berlin: out of a window, on to a hidden bicycle, from there to the nearest station taking him straight to the capital. At dawn, we breakfasted in haste, and off he went again. This was repeated so often as a matter of course that we forgot the risk, until a close friend, young Hatzfeldt, nailed at last for consecutive nightly escapes, was transferred to a 'Strafbataillon', and killed in action a few weeks later.

'Enough of these ostentatious deaths,' Goebbels vituperated.

The eldest son of the Kronprinz and grandson of Emperor William, killed in action, had been given a spontaneous state funeral by the population of Potsdam.

The traditional cavalry regiments had nearly all been motorised and converted to tank units. Inevitably in the front line, bearing all the brunt of attack, their officers and men acquired many decorations for valour. The losses were also high and the obituaries in the *Adelsblatt* impressive. A growing number of eldest sons of great families, killed in action, were brought home to be buried in the family vaults of their castles. This gave rise to local manifestations of sympathy on a scale which could be interpreted as anti-Nazi demonstrations.

Hitler planned to dispossess and eliminate such people from any influence in the country after the war, which would certainly be more difficult if they were among those considered as heroes.

A decree was therefore issued discharging 'undependable elements' from the Army, specifying sons of ex-reigning families, and mediatised princes, especially if they had foreign mothers or wives, as was often the case. It was nicknamed the 'Princes' decree'. This order came too late to save many, but in the end achieved exactly the opposite of what the Party hoped. Those who survived returned at a crucial moment to fill influential positions in their homes. They were, however, indignant at the discrimination at the time, and for the most part much preferred to be with the Army rather than badgered at home by the Party.

Returning from Krampnitz one evening, in the dead sort of voice which announces disaster, Paul told me that he was transferred to Russia with a bicycle company.

In view of the tremendous losses sustained in the infantry, they were transferring cavalry officers into newly formed regiments. Life expectancy was not much longer than three weeks, as neither the troops nor the officers were trained for this sort of warfare.

For some obscure reason, Paul had to repair to Bad-Cannstatt first. That morning, without saying anything to him, I ran to Rantzau's office and asked for advice. He walked up and down his room thinking, and then gave me a note to a friend of his in the 'Personnel' department of the Army Headquarters in the Bendlerstrasse.

This was considered a security Holy of Holies, and my courage sank to a low ebb as I signed the paper noting the exact moment I had entered the building. As I waited, I realised the enormity of this 'démarche', but there was no going back now.

I was presently received with great politeness by a good-looking young man, lean as a greyhound. This cheered me up considerably, for he would not be the type to feel envy and lack of sympathy for someone like Paul, as was for instance the case with our local Marienbad Kreisleiter.

'What can I do for you?' he asked.

Hesitantly I explained that my husband was heading for an assignment which gave me a pretty good chance of being a widow before the year was out – and we had only just married. The job besides did not correspond in the least with his training and capacities. Couldn't something be done about it?

At first he looked severe and said: 'I do not know if you realise that you are the first wife who has come here to ask for a transfer for her husband?'

'I hardly expected to be even listened to, but wanted at least to have tried!' I said sadly, and added that my husband obviously knew nothing about this visit.

He smiled then, and said he would take a look at Paul's papers. Could I give him the particulars, and he would let me know the result?

We left for Bad-Canstatt that afternoon. A few days passed, and there came a long-distance call, a personal one for me: 'Your husband has been transferred as Liaison Officer to the Spanish Division. It is, I am sorry to say, no life insurance. Do you agree with this?'

'It is so much more what he would like!' I said gratefully, deciding never to tamper with destiny again.

I never knew later what happened to my friend and could only hope he was not caught in the holocaust after the 20th July 1944, when so many others had died. There was no one left I could ask.

But nothing could now alter the fact that Paul was leaving for the Russian front. Our few months of respite were over and there seemed no end to this terrible war!

The last days rushed by. A quick trip to Königswart, and from there I returned to Berlin with Paul to see him off. On my way back to rejoin Missie, I lost my way hopelessly, only realising much later that I had not seen where I was going, people and streets dissolving as in a creeping fog. Night had fallen when I finally reached her flat.

I returned to Bohemia alone this time. Officially I was now supposed to replace Paul on his estates, which would entail much travelling and free me from mobilization into a munitions factory or some similar assignment.

Sitting or standing for long hours in dark crowded trains often led to strange conversations, even intimate confidences from strangers one would never see again. Reference to politics was of course carefully avoided.

As I sat in the train heading south, a young soldier sitting opposite offered me chocolate and cigarettes, while I shared my sandwiches with him. He was soon telling me of his war experiences, and described his horror of the French retreat: from Paris to Bordeaux the roads had been choked with columns of fleeing refugees inextricably mixed with the retreating French Army. The pursuing tanks ground down everything in their path.

His unit had passed a stranded cart, piled high with hay, carrying three little children, their fair hair waving in the breeze. As they overtook it, they realised they were all three dead, silhouetted against the blue sky. He could not get over it: 'Three tiny children, quite alone in all that mess! I will never forget it.' Now he was in Poland.

Full of sympathy, I said: '. . . but that must be even worse?'

'Oh no,' he answered. 'The French are like us, but the Poles after all, are quite another sort of people.' (He meant 'Untermenschen – subhumans.) He was no longer capable of independent thought – mesmerised by Hitlerian propaganda.

12

Remembering the war years, it seems always to have been winter. Or dark. Slush and dirt and cold wherever one turned.

Endless journeys were repeatedly undertaken from stations looming like gaping tunnels, their iron-trellised roofs riddled with shattered glass panes. Under stopped or broken clocks there were no porters, no trundle carts selling their wares, no bookstalls. Even the posters warning against a goblin-like figure carrying a huge sack: the 'Kohlenklau '(coal pilferer), hung torn and flapping, no longer renewed.

The sad uprooted crowds thronging the quays became faceless faces turned to paler patches in the dark human stream, as they shuffled past slogans painted in large uneven letters dripping like blood: 'Wheels run for Victory!' 'Führer command: we will follow!' ('Räder rollen für den Sieg!' 'Führer befiehl: wir folgen!') Then came the sudden desperate struggle to board the train and sit crammed in darkened compartments, barely allowing a glimpse into the navy-blue night.

Their stomachs rumbling from hunger and gnawing oppression, people had become puddles of insensibility, except for an occasional burst of aggression, like an air-bubble reaching the surface.

How could they face the fact that it was all for nothing?

But whenever I think of Königswart at this time, the house gleams in sunshine. Even in winter, when the country outside, the trees and distant forests were blurred with snow, it was penetrated by an irradiating white light, like another state of being.

As the months passed and I waited for Paul or for news of Paul, long hours stretching ahead, the house, at first silent and waiting, gradually became companionable. As if one only needed to perceive its muted tune to find it warm and welcoming.

There was also a great deal to do. Indoors all was meticulously cared for by Kurt Taubert, the butler, and his wife Lisette, daughter of a Marienbad chemist, assisted by whatever help was available.

Kurt had been valet to Paul's father, who had died in his arms. Lisette as Paul's Aunt's (Countess Maria Puerto's) maid, had travelled far and wide with her, whenever she accompanied the Spanish Royal Family.

To run a place like Königswart was like directing a combination of palace, museum and hotel, and Lisette was an eminently capable housekeeper, with the qualities of a Staff-Officer. She ruled with a rod of iron, not always velvet-gloved, but as we worked together we became allies and friends.

In spite of a skeleton staff, everything was still carefully maintained, and the rooms we lived in kept up as well as the times allowed. My mother-in-law's new apartment was now installed with all the furniture she had used for so many years, in order that she would feel at home when she visited us. Inventories had to be revised, pictures re-hung, and adjusting to changing conditions, we planned ahead to meet every new upheaval: first an invasion of refugees from bombed towns to be installed overnight in the ground floor; then stores of hospital supplies to be stacked in what used to be servants' dining-rooms.

I was officially Paul's representative on all three estates, which meant frequent trips from one to the other, and constant consultation with their respective administrators as we dealt with succeeding crises, and tried to advise and help all those around us. This brought me not only into close contact with the wives and children of our employees, but also with those living in neighbouring villages, for soon, except in Czechoslovakia. all the adult men would be mobilised.

All so-called 'charity' or social work was dealt with by the authorities, who strove to curtail our influence wherever possible. So even in this respect one had to proceed warily, keeping to personal contacts alone.

As Kurt hovered over me, serving lunch, he would gossip away about current events on the estate, the family, the past, and above all about Paul, whom he loved more than if he had been his own son. He told me stories of Paul's scrapes as a child, how every whim was at once met, whether he wished for a pony-carriage or a car, for his doting father refused him nothing. His mother then sent him to a boarding-school in Switzerland, although he was only eight at the time. She feared he would get spoilt, but Kurt said staunchly: 'He could never be so, by nature.'

He now spent more time than they could possibly require attending lovingly to Paul's things, sighing as he did so: 'If only nothing happens to him!'

Paul's great cupboard opened to a woody whiff of leather and tweed and eau de Cologne. School photographs showed smiling groups surrounding a football, or an ice-hockey puck, or earnestly clutching tennisrackets. Shelves were stacked with trophies, medals and cups. A tasselled cap from the recent Spanish Civil War hung next to only a few antlers, for shooting was for Paul no more than a concession to custom.

His father's and grandfather's belongings were still geometrically laid out on the wide dressing-table, their seals and soft leather folders on the writing-desk, their brocade smoking and shooting jackets quite naturally worn again by the next generation.

Although he had been surrounded by beautiful things all his life, there was a spartan simplicity in Paul's personal requirements. The dark-green narrow couch was hard and well-worn. In a corner stood a heavy oak prie-Dieu, and on its shelf a childhood prayer-book began with the sentence: 'Give me strength to accept whatever death is sent to me.' A strange prayer for a small boy, but how significant to-day.

It all brought him closer, as if I now met another side of him, in this house which was his home.

Kurt gathered up a pile of girls' photographs. 'Shouldn't 'we' put them in an album?' he suggested tactfully.

The long line of guest-rooms were furnished in the French-Consulate style after the Chancellor had been Ambassador in Paris in the early XIXth century. English cottons, ticking clocks, pastel portraits or engravings on the walls, added to their charm. Past a line of corresponding bathrooms, the long corridor led finally to a large sunny corner-room in the south-east tower, the 'King's room'.

King Alfonso XIII of Spain, childhood friend of my mother-in-law's, came to Königswart every summer after his departure from Spain in 1931. He was loved and respected by the whole household, and not averse to boyish pranks with the young, such as painting the Canova statues with lipstick one night. My mother-in-law did not appreciate the joke in the least, and when the King said: 'Isabel, do not be angry,' she tartly answered, 'You are old enough to know better.'

But such moments of playful relaxation were few and far between for him. I met him once in Lausanne just before the war and was won over immediately by his kind enquiry after my brother's health. Born a King, for his father had died before his birth, he had that winning simplicity of manner which distinguishes all his family. Apart from his dignity and consideration for others, he had proved his personal courage and resourcefulness on many occasions. It seemed an irony of destiny that a man so suitable to be King should have felt obliged to abdicate.

He followed events in Spain with passionate interest, and of course a flow of Spanish and foreign visitors appeared in his wake to Königswart.

After the accidental death of her husband, Don Carlos, the Duchess of Madrid had arrived to announce the news in person. The King went down to meet her, and great embracings took place in the courtyard, for

Don Carlos handed all his titles back to the main line of the dynasty, and this meeting seemed an end to Carlist separation and strife.

But the most dramatic visit occurred during the first days of August 1936, just after the Civil War had broken out in Spain. General Mola had sent Luca de Tena on an urgent mission in search of planes. King Alfonso seemed to be the only person who could ensure their delivery from Italy. Hearing that he was staying in Königswart, Luca de Tena and Victor Urrutia made a forced landing near Pilsen in the latter's private plane. They were promptly arrested and much negotiation was required to get them out of prison. When they at last reached Königswart, they talked all night to the King, for they were the first Spaniards he had met since the war had started. They urged him to return with them. He feared the moment ill-chosen and sadly refused. But he telephoned Rome at once, and the planes left for Spain the next day.

Earlier still, a steady stream of celebrities, many taking the cure in Marienbad, would find their way to Königswart, which was only an hour's drive by carriage.

Now when we had guests, Kurt and Lisette would shake their heads at the austerities with which they were handicapped, but would exert themselves to conceal them as far as possible.

In this they were assisted by a time-honoured institution, which my mother-in-law called 'the Weibs', in other words willing cleaners from the village, of nondescript age and Brueghel-like appearance. In those hard days they were glad of the extra pay and many other amenities: free milk and wood for their fires, also help when required in dealing with the authorities, who were given to bullying the underdog mercilessly unless they were active members of the Nazi Party.

Kurt, in his slow and careful way, tended his beehives and small kitchen garden, in which he grew his own tobacco, and watched over his side of the house. His underground tussle with the Secretary Thanhofer, concealed by politeness, was never resolved. Secretly, they each thought it their duty to protect us from the thieving practices of the other, but in fact they were both scrupulously and almost painfully honest: everything was jotted down, classified, pigeonholed.

Thanhofer rarely came upstairs, so the landing delineated the invisible frontier of their activities.

This was also the case between Kurt and Lisette, who lived in perfect harmony, only quarrelling when packing for us, as to which trunk or pillowcase was mine or Paul's. They glared at each other, muttering angry words. It was better to look away.

Thanhofer lived buried in huge ledgers, jealous guardian of what he termed 'Usus' (custom), at which he hinted – very politely – whenever I came up with any new ideas.

The Secretary's devotion to the family was beyond question and for him a source of dignity and deep pride. He watched over the museum and its collections, and composed stilted answers in curly calligraphic script to similar documents announcing births, marriages or deaths in other 'princely' houses. Probably no one concerned ever saw these archaic documents.

When writing to Paul, Thanhofer would pen his letters laboriously in the same voluted writing – as a sign of high regard – and finished them off with a sentence reminiscent of: 'Ich wälze mich in dem von Euer Durchlaucht hinterlassenen Staube' (I roll in the dust left in Your Highness's wake). Paul joked that one would find him one day, hanged on a tree in the park, with a piece of cardboard around his neck inscribed: 'Für die Herrschaft' (for the family). Alas, how close we came to this actually happening!

Even in earlier days, when the Metternichs were still established near the Rhine, Königswart had been in close contact with their landlords, but in time it became their favourite country seat.

Paul's great-grandfather, the Chancellor Prince Clemens Lothar Metternich, had rebuilt the earlier Gothic building to suit his taste, which was unerring. He turned it into a charming, turn-of-the-18th-century country-seat. In time it had all grown into a cohesive whole: the house set in the park seemed to melt into the landscape. It was all meticulously planned, yet with a dash of random unexpectedness, as if it had happened by chance. The balance was so perfect that to cut down a tree or move a picture became a major decision.

The horse-shoe shaped house embraced a wide courtyard, surrounding a three-tiered fountain and lined with flowering shrubs. On the other side of the house, a wide lawn sloped down to the lake. The Southern wing contained all the guest-rooms and overlooked the garden leading to the tennis-court. All the so-called 'Paradezimmer' led across the first floor from one wing to the other, through the central 'Saal', or hall, with wide balconies to the front and back of the house. It was most cosily arranged and therefore much in use, in spite of its size, which reduced Canova statues to the proportion of decorative ornaments. Huge bunches of flowers gave it life through the changing seasons.

The panelled dining-room next door led to the Chapel and to the Museum with Metternich's vast library and fascinating collections. His son had added Alexandre Dumas' writing-table, and an unpublished novel rolled on a cane, later varnished: a game of patience even in that leisurely century, in which the horse had hardly been superseded by trains.

Succeeding generations would relegate objects they did not care for to the Museum, replacing furniture or ornaments according to changing taste.

In the 'loge' of the Chapel hung three fine 15th century Bernhard Strigel paintings. I was on the verge of sending them away later, when

Papa most inconveniently remarked that it brought bad luck to remove things dedicated to a church. Not daring to tempt fate, I regretfully hung them up again.

On feast days, the good old priest donned vestments made from the Chancellor's gala uniform which he had worn for the Lawrence portrait.

The room we lived in most was the south-west corner drawing-room, called the red salon. The lovely full-length portrait of Antoinette Leykam, the Chancellor's second wife, hung over the mantelpiece. My mother-in-law had made me a present of the embroidered vermilion shawl, and of the brooches in the golden belt she wore in the picture. All the drawing-rooms led away from this room in one direction and all the bedrooms, after my little writing-room, in the other, so the house could be opened up according to the number of people present, and one never felt overwhelmed by its size.

In 1911, when the Vienna Palace was sold, the entire library, panelling, inlaid floor and all other fittings were moved to Königswart, and built in next to the corner salon. It was an enchanting room, not too large, and when Paul and I were alone, we would have dinner there, eating at small tables in front of a cheerful fire, for it was often chilly in the evenings. A secret catch on one side of the mantelpiece opened an entire bookcase and let one out on to the landing beyond.

My French education had instilled me with a very jaundiced view of Metternich. Living among his personal belongings, collections and papers, this now underwent a radical change.

Metternich's personality must have been completely incomprehensible to narrow-minded historians prejudiced by the upsurge of nationalism and liberalism. He did not lay much store by their opinion either.

Like so many statesmen of his time, he dealt with serious affairs with seeming levity and appeared to treat frivolous matters, such as the organisation of a ball, with exaggerated attention. He was profoundly distrustful of abstract political theories and attached supreme importance to organic growth – in statesmanship too. He also maintained that two elementary realities were all too frequently overlooked by politicians: History and Geography. His family came from the Moselle region, but generations of service to the Church and to the Emperor of the Holy Roman Empire induced an infinitely wider outlook than that typical of subjects of smaller principalities. He had a profound aversion to the ever-recurring German passion for 'clear situations' leading to catastrophic 'final solutions', brutality when in power and disastrous subservience when not. His persuasive talent doubtless aroused resentment at times, for he would proudly say that he never gave up until he 'heard his own words repeated by his adversary'.

Although his far-reaching views of 1815 were no longer applicable in 1848, Metternich was always consistent, never losing sight of his aim, which was to replace Habsburg power by Austrian influence, as opposed to that of Prussia. He considered this to be the keystone of European peace.

Unlike some of his contemporaries who find far more understanding with modern historians, he never changed allegiances or took a bribe.

His patience and capacity for work must have been as overwhelming as the wide range of his interests. The Museum contained a library of 30,000 beautifully-bound volumes, covering every possible subject including natural history, science and archaeology, often annotated in his hand. It also housed his collections of engravings, medals, coins and arms, as well as curiosities of every sort – from Queen Marie-Antoinette's ring and prayer-book, to the longest female hair, or Madame Tallien's tiny shoe. The Empress Marie-Louise, Napoleon's second wife, had sent several personal souvenirs of their son the Duke of Reichstadt after his death: his cane, his washbasin, a ring.

Metternich must have seized any available moment to write, and liking lovely things around him, the writing-tables in every room of his houses were as different as they were beautiful. They seemed to suit every mood – from spindly ladies' 'sécretaires', to the double-desk in his smaller library, where he and his secretary spent long hours over despatches.

He wished all around him to be happy, for there were a number of slips of paper and memoranda in the archives referring to the most minute detail of the management of his estates, the planting of trees, the labelling of wine-bottles, but also directing the distribution of rooms for his children and their programme for the day. In drawers and cupboards I found forgotten souvenirs, diaries, and letters. There was for instance a note to his wife posted from Dijon in March 1814 on his way to Paris on defeated Napoleon's heels, describing a little dress 'with matching pantalettes' for his three-year-old daughter Léontine, which he had just had copied and sent home by courier. In a secret drawer of my own writing-table, I discovered two leather-bound copybooks in a flowing schoolgirlish hand by that same Léontine, now a teen-age girl. Here the 'Arbiter of Europe' appeared as a loving father, often in the company of his children, even at crucial moments of European history. His first wife had died some years before and when his rather lonely little daughter was saddened by the departure of her best friend, he found time to give her an outing and buy her a present.

The writer Varnhagen once said of Metternich:

'One felt at ease in his company.'

A hundred years later we felt it still.

As I lay reading on the leather-buttoned sofa in the library, the warm silence was hardly disturbed by the ticking of old clocks, from time to time breaking into a sigh and a whirr of chimes, or by the Scottie slithering on polished floors as he snapped at a buzzing fly caught in a beam of sunshine. The slow, quiet hours were like a soothing balm.

In the world outside, as in Goya's picture 'El Coloso', the Giant of Panic was waiting to scoop up everything into a spiralling dark cloud, but here, for a while, all was serene, and time stood still. There was the delight of room to think, room to move in the vast old house, sniffing its musty smell – a mixture of waxed floors, old leather-bound books and dust, with a dash of lavender and fresh roses.

Through all the loving care spent on it, I felt accepted as part of what it had been and of what was to come.

Never far from corroding anxiety, I experienced an explosion of relief when the telegram announcing that after months of absence, Paul was coming on leave, finally arrived.

As often as not he would have no time to reach Königswart, and I then dashed for the first train to Berlin.

There followed long hours of standing, wedged in packed train corridors, or perched on the edge of an up-turned suitcase; hungry and anxious lest some air-raid should prevent the train from arriving on time and steal moments of this brief holiday; dreading the desperate frustration – as in a bad dream – when it arrived at the outskirts hours late and then could not enter the city and I would have to trudge to the nearest tram station only to find on arrival that Paul had disappeared while looking for me, wasting golden hours.

But many happy meetings ended those arduous journeys. Paul would laugh as he seized me, saying he had found me in the dark station after catching a whiff of Moment-Supréme scent above the damp smell of soot and steam and people.

After a quick wash in the tiny flat of the Gersdorff house, we would go out to dine. Late at night, came the walk home through the dark and empty streets, Paul singing like a bird for he remembered a number of songs from the Spanish Civil War, and many Austrian ones from Vienna. His subdued baritone rang clear, carrying a promise of sunshine, of a land at peace at last, where people sang as easily as they breathed.

All too soon it was time for him to leave again for his assignment as a liaison officer between the German High Command and the Spanish 'Blue Division' entrenched before besieged Leningrad, where the fighting was still very severe. He had known many of the officers in the Spanish Civil War, and as I left him with some of them on their way to Russia, it was like leaving him with his family, heading for high adventure. They laughed and joked, with the detached indifference of those already on their way.

But we all knew that the endless front line was impossible to hold, and a Soviet breakthrough many months overdue.

Mamma then came to stay with me in Bohemia. The bombing was intensifying, and it had also become imperative for her to be further away from the Gestapo Central office in Berlin.

'One must learn to choose one's friends,' Rantzau reminded Missie one morning as he produced a copy of a denunciation of Mamma signed by the husband of her life-long friend, Olga, with whom we had stayed in Silesia at the beginning of the war: 'Her pro-Russian views', it ran, 'were not in accordance with the Führer's principles . . .' (true enough as far as that went!) 'He therefore considered it his duty to mention this to the Party.' Rantzau added: 'One copy we shall destroy, but the other is in the Gestapo's hands. Should your mother ever ask for a visa or come to their notice, it will be fished out at once.'

It was a great shock to her, for besides the horrid feeling of betrayal, she had hoped to join Georgie in Paris soon. When we stayed with her in Silesia in September 1939, Olga's husband had been just a comfortable materialist with no polarised values. How cunning the Nazis were at getting people of his kind to associate in crime, and then they were committed beyond return. He was too clever not to know it, and for that he was to be pitied.

Chafing at the enforced inactivity of her life in Königswart, Mamma threw herself into a world-wide correspondence, using friends in neutral countries to forward her letters. Her first purpose was to get in touch with prominent Russians abroad in an effort to procure food for starving Soviet prisoners, who received no Red Cross parcels.

She succeeded in contacting the Russian-born aeronautical engineer, Igor Sikorsky, among others, and finally collected an entire ship's cargo which would be despatched from Buenos Aires. General von Hase, Military Governor of Berlin (later a victim of the purge after the 20th July plot), tried to help her forward this shipment to its intended destination. But the Party got wind of the project and hastened to oppose it.

Not to be outdone, Mamma then turned to her old friend Marshal Mannerheim, the President of Finland, who had been a regimental comrade of her brother's. He always owned to Russian, if not Soviet friendship. Owing to their attack, he now found himself involuntarily fighting on the German side. He immediately accepted the shipment, and sent Mamma a charming and treasured letter, guaranteeing that all the parcels would be handed to Soviet prisoners of war in Finland. Their safe arrival was later confirmed.

Arriving empty-handed on a short leave from the north-eastern Leningrad front, Paul told us:

'Emiliano is bringing my luggage.'

Sure enough, some days later our life in Königswart was enriched by the presence of Emiliano Zarate Zamorano. Half-soldier, half-tramp, tousled hair standing on end, he trudged up the drive dragging the remains of Paul's suitcase, tied crosswise with his shirt to keep it together.

As the Civil War ended in Spain, he had been arrested for lugging a time-bomb with which he was supposed to blow up some vulnerable objective. Since he could neither read nor write and was incapable of co-ordinated thought, he was probably expected to go up with his bomb. He was then given the awkward choice of facing a firing squad or 'volunteering' for the Spanish Blue Division in Russia. However his compatriots there could find no use for him: strangely enough the vocation of 'hired assassin' finds surprisingly little scope in wartime and Emiliano could not conform to any sort of discipline.

For some obscure reason, he attached himself with dog-like devotion to Paul and would take orders from no one else, so when Paul left for home, his Spanish colleagues said:

'Take him along with you: he is no use to us.'

Brandishing a crumpled scrap of paper inscribed with the address of his final destination, Zarate boxed his way from lorry to crowded trains declaring:

'Make way! I am a courier of the Spanish Embassy.'

Surprisingly, everyone believed him.

For Paul he became a sort of 'King's Jester'. He sent him off for twenty-four hours' holiday in Berlin, and on his return Zarate proudly exhibited an S.S. ring and watch, both marked with the infamous skull-head, which he assured us was a parting gift from a girl-friend. He had got in touch with a flourishing black market, of whose existence we had been blissfully unaware, and boasted he could procure us anything from a wireless-set to firearms: he was quite crestfallen when we did not make the most of his suggestion.

When we drove in the woods, he perched next to the coachman. Paul once asked him:

'Emiliano, if the Reds come back in Spain, would you kill me?'

'Señor, never!!'

'And my wife?'

A slight hesitation: 'Neither!'

'And the coachman?'

'No lo sé . . .' (I'm not so sure.)

When Paul left for Russia again, Zarate lay all day sprawled on his back on the front lawn and at night he tried to rape the maid. So we sent him back to Spain where Paul persuaded the Army to accept him again. For some years all went well, then he was discharged as 'unemployable'.

In later years whenever Paul returned to Madrid, as if prompted by some telepathic instinct, Emiliano stood at the great front door waiting for the clap on the shoulder, the clothes and the tip he was sure to receive. But he never wanted a job.

13

As the war continued, every able-bodied German was mobilised, but the fields still had to be tilled, the harvests brought in, the animals fed and the woods felled. To replace the missing hands, groups of French and Russian prisoners of war were assigned by the authorities. At Königswart we had our quota.

By strict order, the Russians were locked up at night, and guarded by an elderly soldier. We insisted however, that they be allowed to name a spokesman, who could come to us and discuss their problems, or ask for anything they might require. We were horrified to hear later from the French prisoners, that the man they named was the only political Commissar among them, and that he was a brutal bully. The German soldier was an unpleasant fellow, indifferent to whatever went on, once he had locked the door on them for the night.

Officially, we were not allowed to speak to them alone, so my parents or I would wait until the guard was out of sight and then go and talk to them as they worked on the farm or in the fields. At first they seemed browbeaten and cowed. We succeeded in having the soldier replaced by a kind old dodderer, who helped us to ensure fairly normal conditions. Gaining confidence, as they realised our genuine concern and the difficulties we met with wherever the authorities were involved (were they not conditioned to a police state themselves?), we were soon on a friendly footing. One of them had passed through those terrible hunger camps when first taken prisoner by the German Army. He told us he had held his dead brother high over his head all through an endless night, so that he should not be eaten by his famished comrades.

The cow-man Ivan would hang around the kitchen-door on the pretext of bringing in the milk. He had discovered that Paul was very free with Schnapps as a remedy against colds or anything else. He would clear his throat ostentatiously whenever he saw us, a broad grin lighting up his round face with the potato nose, so characteristic of many

166

Russian peasants. Sure enough, Schnapps was immediately forthcoming.

I asked one of them one day again, 'What can we do for you?'

'Conditions are decent, but there is nothing to be done. It is a sad lot to be prisoners, and the rest is not important.' But another added sadly, 'I worry about my wife and children. Who will feed them now that I am gone?'

'How many have you got?'

'Four, and all small. If they also take the wife away, the kids cannot fare for themselves.' ('They' always meant the Soviet Régime.)

It seemed incredible that Stalin allowed them no letters. All the other prisoners of war could at least get some news from home.

'When did you leave?' they asked. 'Ah! . . . then you understand,' they would sigh, regarding us without resentment, resigned. We were earlier victims of a Revolution for which they felt no responsibility.

'Will "they" allow us to go home after the war?' (again meaning Stalin).

'Of course. It is not your fault that you are prisoners.'

They sighed doubtfully, although with reason, as it turned out, for who could have known at the time that once the war was over, they would be treated as traitors and sent by the hundred thousand to the dreaded slave labour camps?

It was heartbreaking for us to realise how little we could do for them, although in time, and against great Party opposition, the Army succeeded in achieving decent treatment for Soviet prisoners. In some divisions, they were said to form almost 15% of the personnel behind the Front. There were units of Armenians, Azerbaijanians, Georgians, North Caucasians, Turkestanis and Volga Tatars, apart from the Cossacks fighting under General von Pannwitz in Yugoslavia from anti-communist convictions.

The insignia on their uniforms were so varied and exotic that an English officer in full battle-dress, escaping from his camp, was able to travel peacefully and unmolested all across Germany in a first-class coach before his appearance attracted any attention.

But although conditions in the country, where so many prisoners of war worked as farm hands, were on the whole fairly normal, in factories or State enterprises, and particularly in the organisation later headed by Speer, they still suffered abominably.

The French were treated as if they were local labourers. They were not allowed to travel any distance, or to return to their own country, but were free to move around in the vicinity and meet each other in the evenings. They were always extremely well-informed through grape-vine news and clandestine wireless sets. They feared the Russians, who resented their difference in status, and in fact one often met Frenchmen leading Russians to their work, whistling as they swung a little twig in one hand, their caps set jauntily over one ear.

They often replaced the absent men on farms in every sense. Faced with similar problems, they were becoming our allies against the ever-growing encroachment of the authorities.

One of 'our' Frenchmen turned out to be 'tapissier de son état' – an upholsterer – who worked for the best Paris shops. Covering a chair, he would lovingly stroke the shining wood, saying: 'Ça fait plaisir de voir de belles choses!'

'P'tit Louis' was from Béziers. Before being dragged from France he had married a flashy, over-painted, over-everything local beauty (or so she appeared on the snapshot he showed me). She would have been a handful for any husband, even were he at her side. Handicapped by absence, poor P'tit Louis was consumed with jealousy and despair. He brought me his letters for her, which I passed on as soon as possible. He was longing to escape, but penalties were severe should he be caught. One of his comrades filched a funeral wreath from a cemetery, and wearing a top hat, bicycled all the way home – some 1500 miles – un-molested. The controls on the way thought he was heading for a nearby burial service. But this remarkable achievement could hardly be repeated.

My cousin Jim Wiazemsky had been filled with pride when he became a French cavalry officer. It meant also final acceptance in the country he had come to as a small boy, and which he was enthusiastically ready to defend.

But there was no opportunity for heroism. He was taken prisoner, rounded up with his entire regiment near Beauvais during the seven weeks' campaign through France.

Some time elapsed before information reached us that he was in an officers' camp near Dresden.

General von Hase soon procured all the necessary papers and per-missions and Mamma and I would set out in turn to visit him. It was a long and arduous journey from Königswart, for the camp lay off the main line.

Rounding the final bend, the compound came in sight. It formed two squares bordered by low wooden houses, surrounded by garden plots, all clustering in the shade of a small hill. Smoke curled out of the chimneys. A man in shirt-sleeves, wearing military boots, wandered around with a pail, while others weeded vegetable plots: a deceptively peaceful picture.

Coming closer one saw that their discoloured caps were French or Russian, and that the whole camp was surrounded by a double line of barbed wire.

I produced my pass at the entrance. The bar lifted, and I entered a neat little office.

Promoted in rank by the pressure of time, a pince-nez balanced on his nose, the Camp Commander turned out to be a country doctor.

While Jim was being fetched, he asked me confidentially to persuade him that the mild régime he was still able to maintain was only due to the fact that none had as yet escaped. Should this happen, he would be held responsible and removed, while the re-captured men escaped the jurisdiction of the Army (we all knew what that meant), and conditions would change radically for all. Jim had influence and served as interpreter for the Russians also: 'And they would be worst off,' he added with a sigh. Horror visions of starvation camps rose, unmentioned, between us.

Here was Jim at last! His anxious, thin face with slightly jug-handled ears lit up in radiant surprise as he saw me. The kind little doctor left his office at our disposal for the picnic I had brought with me, and said we could go for a walk outside the camp if we wished to do so.

Poor Jim was frantic for news. I told him all I knew and found him as informed as I was, for they had put an entire wireless set together, bit by bit, which they re-assembled every night.

He was amazed I should be allowed to see him, and would be able to do so again. He was still more surprised to hear Paul approved of my visit and sent him the champagne and all the cigarettes available. This was his first inkling of the very different undercurrents at play in Germany just then. He was of course obsessed with escape plans, but I tried to hand on the doctor's hint. He understood this differently, however, thinking he would compromise us, and for that reason promised to wait a while.

He held me at arm's length to look at my pretty dress and hair-snood. 'Is that what women wear now? Let me see you from all sides!' His question shocked me deeply. How unnatural that I should be free to come and go, and he locked up here while the years went sliding by.

We picnicked in the tiny office and he talked as if there would never be enough time to say everything. His frayed and discoloured uniform was spotless and patched, the épaulettes re-made, his jaunty French officer's cap impeccable. This was due to the care of the Russians, with whom he was on the best of terms. They called him 'Comrade Prince' (Tovarisch Kniaz), and soon 'Ivan Wladimirovitch', unexpectedly proud of the historical implications of his names 'Wiazemsky' and 'Worontzoff'. His great-grandfather had been the famous viceroy of the Caucasus, whose palace Aloupka in previous times would have been part of Jim's inheritance.

We talked gaily as we walked down the country road after our meal, surprised at the complete indifference of a detachment of the German Army, as they marched past us in a steady crunch of thick boots to the rhythm of a blaring song.

Before leaving, I begged him to protect the kind doctor when the tide turned.

Had he known how long the wait was still to be, his cheerful spirit might have wilted. He thought these years wasted, his youth rusting away, but his assistance to his French and Russian colleagues was invaluable – even more so than after the war when he worked for international relief organisations. Perhaps this time was not as lost as it seemed to him then.

Meanwhile in another P.O.W. camp, Baron Elie de Rothschild, member of the French branch of this illustrious financial dynasty (interned as a French officer but always threatened with transfer to an extermination camp), learnt Russian from his co-prisoner Jascha Stalin.

Hitler offered to negotiate the latter's release – not for humanitarian reasons, needless to say. However Stalin refused to have anything to do with his son. Having lost interest for the Nazis, they then did away with him.

Luckily Rothschild survived the war.

14

Whenever Paul was home on leave, we would drive over to Plass. It was the largest of the three estates, quite close to Pilsen in Czechoslovakia, and had been bought by the Chancellor early in the last century. The drive there took about three hours. The wood-alcohol powered car bumped along, coughing and spluttering with but little effect, for it never achieved more than 30 kilometers an hour.

Plass nestled in a wide valley. The rambling complex of baroque buildings, originally designed to house Cistercian monks, was later extended and cluttered up by smaller additions, clinging to its wide spreading wings like barnacles to a ship.

Paul's Aunt Titi (his father's sister) lived here in retirement in her own apartments. In her youth she had been the best woman four-hand driver and shot of her generation; photographs showed her skating in an elegant ankle-length outfit, peeping coyly over a lifted muff at her cavalier. She must have indulged in many a caprice in her day, but now she had abandoned all thought of a waistline and turned to the pleasures of the table. This was much to our benefit, for every dish was planned, tried out, improved on, after having in fact grown under her vigilant eye, since everything from a radish to the finest goose liver was produced on the farms of Plass.

Apart from eating, she read new publications in German and French, with a leaning towards racy novels and Indian love lore (where the titillating bits were frustratingly in Greek). She also gaily played ping-pong with the local dentist, bouncing light-footed around the table, her bright blue eyes darting under a fringe of hair dyed to a botanical hue.

She still had the cajoling manner of an 'Art Nouveau' woman who had been certain of her charm – lips pursed, head on one side, fluttering eyelashes, toying with an endless rope of pearls.

Aunt Titi was not a stickler for morality, but she believed in moral

171

rules (especially for others), perhaps because diversions from them would not have been such fun otherwise. Referring to ex-admirers, she would sigh nostalgically, her tone full of 'sous entendres'.

I had the feeling she thought we did not make the most of our opportunities. Life in the country was monotonous: a dash of exciting (if restrained) scandal would have added a touch of spice. Paul was obviously restricted by the war, but as for me, she was at a loss. I suppose she must have finally decided I was still too much in love to indulge in any flights of fancy.

She was, in fact, great fun, though Paul rather dreaded her asking for more and more favours, well knowing he could not be so churlish as to refuse.

My mother-in-law warned me never to allow myself to be 'locked-up' in Plass, as had been her lot. She had spent several years there, cut off from the world in the days of horse-drawn carriages, loathing every minute of it. Eventually the main administration of the estates was transferred to Königswart, so one only went to Plass occasionally, for shoots and short inspections.

Königswart and Johannisberg were so outstandingly beautiful, each in its own very different way, that Plass fell rather short in comparison. But it had its own charm, like that of burrowing into a cosy warren from which one was remote from trouble. Or so one hoped, until the end of the war when all hell broke loose.

On Sundays, here as on the other estates, Paul would join the local football team in their matches against the neighbouring villages. He donned their apricot and plum-coloured jersey, and a chair was brought out for me to watch the proceedings, balancing precariously in the mud.

The Nazi régime, faceless and omni-present in the towns, was reduced in power in varying degrees in our three estates, where our relationship to the people around us differed in the same way.

In Johannisberg we were slightly larger landowners among many small ones and we met on an equal footing of common interests, quite naturally shouldering a larger portion of responsibility.

There was never any subservience or misplaced humility. Many years later we were touched to hear the Mayor say, in an address to Paul, that when citizens of Johannisberg travel, we were their visiting card. In Nazi days this relationship did not change in any way.

In Königswart the village and farm people were more 'untertänig' (humble). They appeared ostensibly attached to the family, weeping copiously at every departure. Much more had been done for them individually: children sent to the best doctors to be cured, houses built, help proffered when they were in trouble, etc. But when the Nazis gained power their affection seemed to dissolve into an over-eagerness to accept the new masters and one could trust only very few people, even among the old retainers.

In Plass they regarded the Nazis as our common enemy. Their first loyalty was to us. Never for a moment did we think that our Plass people would suffer at the end of the war since they had no contact whatever with the régime. They were all Czech and had been with the family for generations. Yet in the end they fared worst of all.

The responsibility of ensuring that the Archives were preserved weighed on us heavily. In the huge hall of the 'Konvent' in Plass, under the soaring frescoed ceiling, piles and piles of numbered and neatly ordered wooden chests lined the walls. They contained all the family papers, and a quantity of state papers too, as was usual in those days.

Richard Metternich, the Chancellor's son, had laboured to achieve complete order and classification. I glanced wistfully at the piles of boxes of private letters, hoping to be able to go through them one day. There were Metternich's letters to and from Napoleon, his correspondence with Wilhelmine Sagan, with all his ambassadors and all the important men of the day as well as every family paper including ours.

In Chancellor Metternich's will his wish was clearly stated that his great-grandson was to be the first of his descendants to publish any private papers. Paul intended to do this after the war.

It was still possible, although difficult, to have them transported. Preparations for the transfer began in Plass, the chests were reinforced and more firmly sealed.

But presently an ominous letter arrived from the Government of the 'Protektorat' in Prague, threatening 'extreme measures' should we not comply with the accompanying order not to move the papers, for 'the archives were part of the cultural heritage of the Protektorat', which was untrue.

Much later we heard that a Nazi official in the Vienna archives denounced us, without rhyme or reason, as these papers were most certainly part of the Austrian cultural heritage. This man hanged himself at the end of the war, but the harm had been done. By then the frontiers had been hermetically closed and the papers were lost perhaps for ever.

After much thought we resorted to another plan. A cellar under the Brewery was sealed off, cleaned and prepared to receive the chests. They were then gradually transferred one by one, with great stealth, and piled in correct order. Ventilation and constant temperature were ensured, so the entrance could be sealed off and, we hoped, forgotten!

From Plass one naturally gravitated to Prague, where one could do some shopping, see the doctor and dentist, have a dress or coat made, and visit friends. Prague was comparatively peaceful, resigned to await the outcome of the war. It was a meeting place for country neighbours, and the Gestapo, although active, not as conspicuous as everywhere else.

We gathered round barrels of salt cucumbers in the tiny shop on the Hradschin, run by a Jew someone had declared to be his illegitimate son in order to save him from Nazi persecution.

Quite undaunted by his narrow escape, he ran a flourishing black market for the minor necessities of life. He could procure anything from a hunting suit made by an excellent Czech tailor (and they were renowned throughout the Austro-Hungarian Empire) to a chunk of lard or a bottle of Tokayer.

Another meeting place was the studio of the painter Kossuth, where I never got beyond two sittings.*

* To our surprise, during the short Dubcek era in 1968 nearly a quarter of a century later, this unfinished portrait was sent to us. We just had time to pay the kind sender before the frontier closed down again.

15

Our frequent journeys became ever more dangerous as wave upon wave of bombers now rolled over the towns, dropping their lethal loads at precisely the same moment over entire sections, previously allotted to each formation. Bombs were often linked together for added effect, and slowed down by parachutes to prevent them sinking into the earth. They fell with a yawling-barking sort of noise, which was terrifyingly discernible. Cornered rats as we were, there was nothing one could do about it, except resist a strong urge to cringe away from the low ceiling, or crawl under a bench – as if that could help – especially if the hot water pipes exploded over our heads.

'Carpet-bombing' they called it on the Allied wireless.

Finally, after many bad, very bad and worse bombardments, the time came for what seemed like the total destruction of Berlin. It was the 22nd of November 1943.

It began as usual, but the warning voices were more insistent: 'Huge formations, hundreds of bombers approaching the capital.' Like a tide of death, they swept on their way: carpet upon carpet, whistling direct hits, chained bombs, every anti-aircraft gun busily barking, fighters wheeling over the city. The crash and thunder of the guns was accompanied by dull ominous thuds and thumps shaking the walls of houses and blowing up clouds of dust in the cellars.

As the lights fused in the all-pervading noise, people felt as if their heads were in a pail and a giant stick was banging on it.

Papa and Missie had spent that apocalyptic night in Berlin, after which it ceased to exist as a capital. As the city flamed, the wind aroused by the heat reached hurricane proportions – howling louder than the din of explosions and Flak. A rain of sparks and cinders whirled from house to house. When the wave of bombers retreated, helped by two students who had been taking their evening lessons of Russian with Papa, they had rushed to the roof and watered the house, while pails were strung up to them. Everyone was doing the same, oblivious of danger, blackened by soot, charred, exhausted, but feeling also that this struggle was at last worth while. The serpents in the nearby Berlin Zoo had been previously destroyed, but that night the elephants died, a crocodile waddled over broken barriers into the cool Spree river and a lion crept into the first shelter he could find near the Eden Hotel on the flaming Budapesterstrasse. There he came face to face with a friend of ours.

Next morning as the sun filtered dimly through the clouds of dust thrown up by still crashing houses, people searched for each other, scarves tied over their faces to breathe. There was a smell of smoke, escaping gas and death. In one of these muffled figures Missie suddenly recognised Irene Albert, whose house on the Tiergarten we had often visited. Her mother was an indomitable gently fading American, married to a German industrialist – owner of the Albertwerke near Wiesbaden. Their home had just been obliterated. They had found a lorry leaving for the country but had no idea where to go. Missie wisely proposed Königswart, for we would certainly have to make room for evacuated Berliners and friends were all the more welcome.

Some days later, with no more luggage than the clothes they stood in, Mrs. Albert, Irene, Papa and Missie piled into the overloaded lorry and drove out of town. But before they had reached the outskirts of what was now a sea of rubble, the warning sirens howled again. They barely had time to squeeze into the nearest shelter before the same hell was on once more. During a lull, as the attacking waves reformed, Mrs. Albert called across the crowded cellar (in English) to her daughter: 'Lovey, we have witnessed the greatest disaster of modern times. I wouldn't have missed it for anything!'

Missie and Papa prepared mentally to be lynched, but the planes were back at work, and for once that was a welcome diversion.

The wave of refugees overlapped far-distant provinces. Piling into any available accommodation, grey crowds surged here and there, dragging their loads, like ants disturbed by a giant's kick. There was no time for dismay or reproach. To survive became an obsession, spurred by the instinct of a hare on the run.

Over three hundred astonishingly fragile towns were to crumble and sink like melting candles, from gilded spires to a chaotic mass of hollow protruding teeth, the all-pervading dust failing to veil their hideous nakedness, whereas trains and communications were re-established in record time.

The worst thunderstorms became soothing in comparison. One slept on then, deeply reassured, while crash upon crash of thunder shook the skies, lightning flashes seeming like the brush of a feather.

No planes could come: how safe one felt.

In Königswart we filled the ground floor and tower-rooms with families of women and children, trying to help them as much as possible. Even so it was impossible to establish normal conditions for such a number, although we at least ensured that they were given fresh vegetables, milk and eggs. The children were easily absorbed into the charming 'Kindergarten', and village school life. They blossomed in the country and the tough and healthy climate of Bohemia. Swimming and berry-picking in summer, tobogganing and skating in winter, they were as happy as their mothers were to be pitied.

These uprooted, destitute women, separated from their husbands for many months and even years, their nerves still jagged after so many sleepless nights spent in cellars, often quarrelled bitterly over trifles. My main role soon became to reduce friction between them.

It seemed to me Solomon must have faced an easier task.

With unswerving tenacity of evil will, the *Kreisleiter* of the Marienbad region continued to do all in his power to prevent Paul from coming home on leave, tried to mobilise everyone within reach, and in general to make life as uncomfortable as possible not only for us, but for all those within his jurisdiction. As representative of the Party, he wielded supreme power over civil authorities.

One morning our *Forstmeister* Herr Dobner came to tell me there had been a tragic accident. A plane had crashed into our woods, leaving a trail of fire and destruction. Both airmen were killed as they ground through the trees. They were from a neighbouring village, and had wanted to drop a birthday parcel on the house of the pilot's mother. They must have come down too low, or miscalculated as they swept up again . . .

Herr Dobner had brought the parents to see me. They asked me to intervene with the *Kreisleiter*, for, using any pretext to make himself unpleasant, he had refused them Christian burial. Should the family insist on it, he would blame the crash on the pilot and forbid all military honours.

I was glad to ask for something which did not concern us personally, and went to see him in Marienbad at once. Glowering with rage that they should have requested me to be their spokesman, he refused to give in. I then said:

'Why do you do these things? They do not bring one luck.'

At that, he suddenly seemed to go mad, eyes popping in a distorted face, as if seeing a ghost, or perhaps suddenly confronted with himself:

'Go, go, go!' he cried.

But we could still appeal to higher levels in the Army, and the Christian burial was promptly allowed so as 'Not to cause unrest among the population', as they put it, for in that respect even the Nazis still stepped warily.

If our pathetic refugees symbolised a ravaged future, our life increasingly resembled the ways of the past. During the long periods of waiting between Paul's rare leaves we reverted again to living as if the calendar had been put back. Unable to travel abroad, the changing seasons became our journeys. Spring brought squelching mud, swollen streams racing past patches of lilies of the valley, and a burst of activity: building and repairing, sowing and planting with frequent visits to the farm houses to count hatched chickens, piglets and calves.

And then at last the summer, the harvest to be brought in before the oncoming rain, the dark red mountain-ash berries announcing another punishing winter.

Just before Christmas, the sluice gates of the lakes would be raised, and we became part of a Brueghel landscape as the carp and the trout were collected in huge nets for distribution and sale. The smaller fish were then poured back again like molten silver into the rapidly filling pools.

The snow blurred outlines and muffled sounds, while all the children in bright jerseys and caps skated on the lakes, and snowballs flew in the pale sunshine.

This rhythm through the seasons was like a streak of sanity, running steadily in spite of the rising madness all around.

The use of even the gasoil-car was severely restricted, and our main means of transport became our old carriages, dug out from lofts or sheds, and now repaired for everyday use.

The coachman Christ (a name frequently encountered in our region, the Egerland), his black coat and old bowler hat now a mossy hue, took up his duties again proudly. But, however diligently he polished the original harnesses and vacuum-cleaned the faded buttoned seats, they still smelt of mould and dust. The springs however had softened with time, and we swayed as comfortably as in a cradle.

When driving out alone, I used a lighter vehicle, high-perched on spindly wheels as out of an engraving. It was harnessed to a pair of horses whose growth had been stunted for lack of fodder. But they were healthy and strong nevertheless and cantered along at a brisk pace.

Leaving the carriage high on the rising sandy road, we slithered down through the bushes to a secret place, to which Paul's father used to lead him when he was a little boy. It was a small pool, bubbling hidden under a thicket, but the water in it had a strange consistence: the mice and small animals which crept down to drink in it, died on the rim of the spring. It had been analysed and found to contain radium, and this Paul intended to investigate further one day.

In winter the black sleigh was brought out. It was upholstered in dark green, and in spite of its venerable age, the beautiful lines of its curved runners made it an elegant conveyance. Snuggling into deep warm, sheepskin-lined, slightly moth-eaten sacks, bells jingling merrily as the horses tossed their heads in the crisp air, we swished rapidly over creamy snow.

Miraculously, Paul was granted a longer period of leave to 'bring in the harvest' and attend to his and incidentally the State's interests, for agriculture was now high on the priority list. With his arrival the whole place was infused with new life.

Missie and Sigi Welczeck had come down to keep me company as so often before. Finding us pale, thin, and depressed, Paul now energetically took us in hand: morning swims before breakfast, then he lined us up in a row and made us do gymnastics: we broke down in gales of laughter, which was by far the most effective cure.

We laughed again to see him in the evening, relaxing in an armchair after a bath, arms and feet outstretched, Kurt hovering over him, fussing, dressing him like a doll, while he imparted all the local news. It was such a contrast to the Paul we knew, impervious to hardship after years of war and every sort of sport before that. But it was a restful moment, and they did not like their chat to be disturbed.

Paul had found a private photo album lying in a corner of the gutted Palace of Pavlovsk during the siege of Leningrad. He brought it back to my parents in case they knew its owner. As if it were flotsam from some shipwreck, they pored over it, recognising many people, for it was full of regimental photos. They decided that it must have belonged to one of Grand Duke Constantine's murdered sons, Igor, who had been a close friend of theirs. He had died with the Empress's sister and many other members of his family in 1918, thrown down a disused mine shaft in Alapaievsk in Siberia.

They later managed to send it on to Paris to his brother, Prince Gabriel.

It was the only 'loot' Paul ever brought back from his eight years of war, certain that my parents would know whom it belonged to.

Hearing Paul was home, friends came down in groups for week-ends, often travelling all the way from Berlin or Vienna to do so. At a time of darkness, worry and increasing state pressure to obliterate individuality, people would seize any opportunity for fun and laughter – even if it was for the last time.

In the country the food was entirely home-grown, and though restricted in variety, infinitely better than in town. For Missie, mushroom-picking in early September was a passion. She and Kurt, enveloped in rainproof clothing, would creep through the damp undergrowth, their faces shining with a fanatic gleam. They were overcome with rapture at their finds, and we were glad to consume their booty for dinner, trustfully confiding in Kurt's expert knowledge.

We followed Papa's advice never to leave alcohol on the premises at the end of a war, for it would always be an encouragement to plunder. We therefore proceeded to empty the Königswart cellar, which was comparatively small though stocked with excellent wines. It was a fascinating experience to sample outstanding vintages, which would otherwise only have been consumed for special occasions. We learnt as we went that Johannisberg 1901 was about as far back as one could go unless it could be filtered and recorked. Red wine lasted longer, and champagne could not be kept for more than 25 years.

In the evenings we listened to music, played cards or billiards in the painted room leading to the hall, or childish round games.

The presence in the house of Irene Albert and her mother proved a blessing. They were pleasant, discreet and independent guests, keeping my parents company during long winters and our frequent absences.

When still a boy, as son of the house Paul was expected to prepare shoots for the numerous guests under the Head Forester's able guidance. This often meant missing a lively game of football with the village boys. He never really acquired any particular taste for shooting, even less so since his experience of war.

But he did not have the heart to disappoint Herr Dobner, whom he trusted and respected, and it was therefore more to please him than himself, that when on leave, he would go out in the evenings to shoot roebucks in July and stags in October.

In quiet voices the two men could then discuss future plans and inspect the new plantations of small mixed clumps around one tall tree, widening to meet the next island of young green. Where the trees had been cut their stumps were hollowed out to provide saltcellars for the deer, who would lick them bone-dry. But to prevent them from nipping delicate young shoots these were painted with some white bitter mixture.

On one of the last days of his leave, Paul and I went out one evening with Dobner. In the depths of the forest, havens of peace awaited us: the fenced-in 'tree-schools', meticulously weeded. At one end of the enclosure, there was always a shed of rough-hewn tree trunks, with a bench to rest on under a small crooked porch. A pair of antlers was nailed over the door, and from the roof protruded a chimney improvised out of two bottomless pails, as in Rackham's illustrations to Grimm's Fairy Tales. These refuges offered warm cover against a sudden downpour or snowstorm.

We fell silent as we approached our destination. Gusts of wind brought down a whirling copper rain of leaves, floating like weightless coins. Sparked with the red gash of single Canadian oaks, the larches were turned as by a magic wand to giant amber feathers, etched against dark firs. At times the wood seemed to float in a sheaf of autumn sun-rays, forming a shifting pyramid which streamed like a veil through the tree-trunks.

Careful to avoid crackling twigs, we picked our way gingerly towards the steep ladder of the chosen 'Hochstand' – a pine-thatched cabin, perched on high stilts, ingeniously contrived.

There was always a long wait, and we listened keenly. In a haze of purple foxgloves, vast views stretched away through the trees growing down the slopes. They framed the golden light of the setting sun over the bluish layers of distant horizons. The acrid smoke from the dying embers of the wood-cutters' fire mixed with a nutty smell of freshly chopped pine and moulding leaves.

The woods grew silent and still after the windy day. A dog barked in the distance. Every rustle startled us, but it was, more often than not, just a bird or two hopping around in the bushes. A cat slunk by stealthily.

Then at last our 'Sechzehnender' (16-point stag) came slowly through the trees. He was so beautiful that Paul hesitated a moment too long before he fired. The stag bounded away, crashing through the under-growth.

Cursing under his breath, Paul aimed carefully as he appeared again for a fleeting instant. The second shot felled him.

'That brings bad luck,' he said sadly, and did not cheer up when proud Dobner presented the bloodied twig of fir for his hat with the customary 'Weidmann's Heil'.

Two days later Paul left us, destined for the suffering and misery of the retreat from Russia.

Part Three

The Defeat of Germany

When my parents were overcome with grief at the destruction in Russia and the abysmal distress of the population following in the wake of the German conquest, Paul sought to reassure them: the sheer physical resistance of the Russian soldier was amazing, he said: a prisoner had been taken as he ran towards the German lines. He had been shot in the stomach and held his intestines back with both hands as he stumbled towards them. The surgeon sewed everything back into place again, hardly expecting his patient to survive, yet a few weeks later he was chopping wood lustily, as fit as a fiddle.

The birch-tree seemed to many a symbol of Russian resilience: it would be cut down, sawn into logs, built into huts and furniture. But when Spring returned, green shoots sprouted again unexpectedly from walls, seats and rafters: nothing could destroy the sap of life!

In spite of rigid censorship, everyone now knew about the plight of the 6th Army besieging Stalingrad. No martial music blared over the wireless, no triumphant defiance in Hitler's rasping speeches, no shout of victory could drown the agony of an intact army condemned to annihilation because the Führer allowed no retreat.

Our friend Lieutenant 'Teddy' Behr, one of the very last men to leave Stalingrad, told us the following story:

Shortly before they were completely surrounded Behr was despatched by General Paulus, the G.O.C. of the trapped army in Stalingrad, to the High Command in East Prussia.

He left on one of the last planes to take off from 'Gumrak' air-strip. All his fellow passengers in the converted HE111 bomber were critically wounded and Behr was ashamed of his comparatively safe assignment as a staff officer. His resolution grew ever stronger to do all in his power to inform and then convince and persuade Hitler to allow the longed-for retreat.

The landing on the short airstrip was almost as hazardous as the take-off had been, and they all expected to be killed as the plane crashed through a low wooden structure at the end of the strip. Behr was taken straight to Hitler, who received him surrounded by his staff.

The 'Führer' with the support and approval of his Generals, then launched into a long speech about the situation in Stalingrad, while Behr waited in growing exasperation.

He was on the verge of being dismissed without having uttered a word, so he hastily blurted: 'I have been sent here to report: may I do so now?'

Hitler looked astonished and Behr delivered his detailed report, frequently interrupted by the Generals who attempted to contradict him. Not one would listen, or accept the facts laid before them.

Realising that he had made no impression and losing all hope, Behr left possessed by the one driving wish to get back to Stalingrad and die there with his friends.

However as he tried one available air-strip after another, he discovered that they were all blocked for Oberleutnant B. 'by order of General Schmund, A.d.C. of the Führer'. They did not want the Stalingrad Army to know that Hitler had already written them off.

This took place on the 12th of January, and the 6th Army finally capitulated on the 3rd of February, 1943.

A wave of horror and despair rolled back over Germany. Hitler found a palliative: all women were to be mobilised for priority war-work. It took people's minds off distant Stalingrad. Some months later, sacks of letters from Stalingrad prisoners reached Berlin and were then deposited at Army Headquarters in General Olbricht's office of the Bendlerstrasse. But Hitler, vying with Stalin who had declared that Soviet soldiers would be treated as traitors if they surrendered, now ordered that no details of the defeat should penetrate to the homeland: the letters were to be destroyed.

Loremarie Schönburg, trying to get news of one of her brothers lost in Stalingrad, begged Olbricht to allow her to look through them. But, as she was to understand later, he was one of the conspirators and used his job as a cover: he could not permit himself any added risk. The sacks were then removed and incinerated 'by order of the Führer'.

Anonymous letters even came trickling in from Soviet Russia: they announced imprisonment or death of German soldiers to their families.

Just before the attack on Russia, the Soviet Red Cross had tried to get in touch with the German Red Cross via Sweden to discuss what would happen to prisoners in case of war. The contact was promptly forbidden by Hitler and both institutions, which had hoped to achieve some humanity in their dealings in spite of two such similar forms of Government, were rendered powerless.

On an ice-cold winter night of 1943, we found ourselves in what remained of Berlin, and once again Paul and I faced one of those dreaded partings.

We had had supper and now walked the short distance to the Nollendorfplatz underground station. It awaited us like a black mouth yawning in the dark shadow of the broad avenue running between gutted houses. The trees stood out in disorderly bunches against the pale sky, brandishing their lopsided shapes, sliced off from repeated bombings as by a giant scythe.

In the dark, I clung to Paul's rough military coat, feeling the hard buttons, the buckled belt, the dagger, the hip-flask. Shaky giggles . . . it was like embracing an iron-monger's shop, pots and pans everywhere. But in the dim light his anxious eyes no longer smiled. The northern front line he was heading for had broken, and he was travelling into no-man's-land, not even knowing where to look for his unit.

It was a dreadful feeling of good-bye for ever without even the moral justification of fighting in a worthy cause, which at least the Allies could claim.

One always knew that the war had to be lost, but now that the end was in sight, it was as if the tears shed in so many countries, mixed with the dust of crumbling houses, were seeping into people's hearts.

There followed the long journey back to Königswart, the grey faces of my fellow passengers barely discernible under the single mauve, soot-streaked bulb. We looked as if we were all drifting under water. Through a slit in the blacked-out window one glimpsed puddles shimmering like lost coins in the intermittent moonlight. Towards dawn, the dew turned the fields grey-white, as under a suspended sheet of muslin over which houses and trees floated, the crows perching like strange black fruit on the bare branches of poplars lining leaden ponds.

There came a spell of terribly cold and windy weather in Königswart. I thought of Paul out in the open, exposed to murderous Siberian winds and frost. He told me he had watched Russian soldiers leaping out into the snow behind the German lines from low-flying aircraft without parachutes. Some died, some were wounded; the survivors joined the partisans fighting in the woods. Regiments of Russian women, tightly buttoned into the same uniforms as the men, were hurled into the battle and then fought desperately. Young boys and old men were killed in tens of thousands as they attacked with practically no arms – one gun for every fourth man. It certainly demoralised the Germans, but at what cost!

If they were so ruthless with their own people, what treatment would they mete out to the enemy, especially guilty of invasion followed by such atrocities as the Nazis then perpetrated in Russia!

There was still no news from Paul and my anxiety was like an ever-present shadow in the room. I put through a telephone call to a friend, a liaison officer from the Foreign Office to the 'Führerhauptquartier' (High Command) in East Prussia. First I had to get the code names of the intermediate stations: 'Erica . . . Berta . . . Anita . . .' All night it went on like this but by morning I reached him and a kind, reassuring voice said:

'Yes, I understand your concern . . .'

That struck cold, for it meant the Front was rolling back as feared. He would keep in touch with me, he said.

Missie, too, tried to get news. A high-ranking officer of the Abwehr asked to see her and told her they had grave tidings: Paul was danger-ously ill or wounded. They did not know for sure, although there were as yet no losses in the liaison group. The Front was breaking up everywhere.

The Foreign Office had been partly evacuated to Krummhübel, a small mountain village, south of Dresden. From then on I only thought of joining her; it would be easier to get news through the Foreign Office channels, than by myself, at night, so far from any centre.

There followed another of those terrible train journeys, dragging a small suitcase which always seemed to weigh a ton.

The train stopped fitfully, avoiding bomb attacks whenever possible, and chugging along again as the 'All clear' sounded in the distance. There were endless waits in remote stations, sustained by a cup of hot and dark liquid, labelled 'coffee', but by now Ersatz of an Ersatz, and commonly called 'Muggefug'.

I found myself wedged next to an undersized boy with an old and wrinkled face lit by a cheerful, toothy grin.

He was from Cologne, sent down here for a few weeks' rest. He had not been to school for years and was one of a group of boys of the same age who were set to dig people out of bombed cellars and retrieve whatever belongings could be salvaged. Although on principle they returned what they found, he told me they were never short of cigarettes or hidden food – especially chocolate.

He offered me both and chatted freely in the delightful sing-song dialect of Cologne.

'But how old are you?'

'Fifteen.'

'And Cologne, what does it look like to-day?'

'Nothing much left. We say in Köln: "Next time they come, they must bring the houses with them . . . to bomb!"'

'What would you like to do after the war?'

'I'll travel over the whole world!' – a typical German dream.

Hitler understood this well, when – as compensation for the searing misery of war, he offered his soldiers the world to travel in – a heady combination of adventure and assuaged 'Wanderlust', based on slogans. Tourism and conquest at State expense, or so it seemed at first, when the going was easy. They did not foresee then the price they would have to pay.

Missie came to fetch me from the station of Krummhübel. Remote atmosphere of a minor ski-resort, bustling with Foreign Office officials, as if with incongruous grey mushrooms from another climate. They felt on holiday – away from the bombs and from the probing Gestapo eye, so omnipresent in Berlin. I soon discovered that our dear old friend, Count von der Schulenburg, the last German Ambassador in Moscow, had procured a Laissez-Passer to Riga for me, should Paul, whose condition was said to be serious, ever reach that huge hospital.

'Is he wounded?'

'Difficult to know. They say unfit for combat. The Army is in full retreat,' added Schulenberg.

Some days passed and we heard that Paul would be transferred to Riga as soon as possible. However, the Front was collapsing so fast that Schulenburg warned me against trying to join him. All the wounded would be moved back and civilians left to fend for themselves: I would inevitably get stranded.

The next news was that he had reached Riga and that he was not expected to live. Schulenberg tried to console me, saying no doctor would say this if it were true. But it could mean they were giving him first priority for further evacuation as a serious case.

Then came the message: 'Out of danger. Will be moved as soon as he can travel.'

I was still on tenterhooks to join him, but received so much advice against doing so, that it made me hesitate.

And then, slowly, little notes began to arrive in a very shaky scrawl. The days turned to weeks and at last I learnt that Paul was on his way.

Against all rules – for we were only allowed to use it in the vicinity and for trips to Plass – I took the old gas motor-car to Carlsbad, driven slowly by Ignaz in a cloud of fumes and loud noises.

Leaning on a stick, ashen-faced, bluish veins standing out, unrecognisably thin and fragile-looking, there was Paul at last. Where was the striding, straight-backed, sunburnt athlete I had seen off just a few months before? But nothing mattered at this moment, With a sigh of the most profound relief we settled on the hard seat of the ramshackle old car as if it were the downiest cushion. Home to lovely Königswart, untouched as yet.

For Paul it seemed quite incomprehensible that I could have known what was happening to him. He had thought not only he but the entire

Army was lost, having been cut off from any communication for many weeks past.

As the night of his departure from Berlin seemed warm and rainy, he had travelled in his military raincoat, but approaching Russia, owing to frequent train changes, his luggage got mislaid, and finally, still in the inadequate raincoat, he stopped off at Army Corps H.Q. where an officer called Helldorf told him that, since he was on his way to the front line, he could tell Colonel X. to prepare for retreat as the orders to do so were imminent.

Paul reached the front to find a scene of pandemonium: the German lines had been pierced at several points and the harassed Colonel X. had not slept for several nights.

On hearing Paul's message, he flew into a rage, and yelled:

'You'll be shot for this sabotage. Undermining morale at a time like this!' At last Paul persuaded him to telephone Headquarters. As luck would have it, there was another officer by the name of Helldorf there, who said he knew nothing of this order.

The rampaging Colonel told Paul to sit down just as he was, and as soon as he could find a moment to court-martial him, he would be shot.

The night dragged on. Already frozen and exhausted from the journey, Paul really thought this madman would do as he threatened.

At dawn the order to retreat came through.

'Entschuldigen Sie,' (Sorry) said the Colonel.

Still in search of his own liaison group, Paul then found himself fighting night and day in driving sleet and icy winds wherever he happened to be, until he at last located the Spanish Division on the Wolchov River, where it was still holding its ground.

By then he was running a high fever. A doctor was found to give him a sulphonamide injection: he diagnosed inflammation of both lungs.

Firing could be heard from both sides as the Russians broke into the village. His friends then carried him – still fully dressed – into an open military car, wrapped him in blankets and told the driver to risk anything and try and break through the surrounding enemy towards the German lines.

Glad enough to get out himself, bumping over sticks and stones, under a hail of fire, the driver got them through to Luga. Here another doctor gave Paul some more shots of sulphonamide. By now inflammation of both lungs had become double pleurisy and the pain almost unbearable, so a shot of morphia was added.

Unconscious for most of the time, he lay on straw among rows and rows of wounded men, a certain number of whom were selected for transportation westwards. The choice seemed arbitrary – this one yes, another no. Perhaps they took those who seemed capable of surviving?

Yet so many more died on the way, as they lay side by side on the slow-moving floor of railway waggons.

One train followed closely upon the tail-light of another, so that partisans could not blow up the tracks. But four armed guards for each train were inadequate, and at night these saboteurs would creep up and lay bombs between the rails, shattering the cotton wool silence.

The track then had to be repaired, and survivors transferred to another waggon and on they jogged for a short while. So the chainlike procession moved in fits and starts, interrupted by long hours of waiting, until far, far away – in Pskow perhaps – a train moved, and they could proceed again.

Those shot in the head or stomach suffered worst. They nearly all had pneumonia as well. In the morning, the men who had died during the night were wrapped in their Army blanket, and laid in the snow by the side of the track, for no one dared move any distance from the train.

There was nothing to eat. For drink, one of the less seriously wounded would melt some snow in a tin kettle and hand it to those who could not fend for themselves.

After many days they reached Riga.

The doctors in the huge military hospital found that Paul had a large abscess in one lung, but decided he was far too weak to operate. At last, finding that he was beyond help, he was left alone in a small room to die.

Meanwhile the officers of the Spanish Division, now in full retreat, had heard that Paul was in Riga, and as they were being pulled back from the Front to return to Spain, one of them, Mariano Calviño, went out of his way to pay him a visit.

Although used to many terrible sights, his friend's sunken bearded face, and the fact that the doctor said there was no hope, quite knocked him out. So he took the hip flask of Spanish cognac he carried with him and filling the tooth glass, lifted Paul with one arm and poured the contents of the glass down his throat. Then he drank the rest himself – 'to console him for dying so young, and myself for losing a good friend,' as he told me later.

They talked for a while, then Mariano left, never thinking he would see him again. But, after all that Cognac, Paul began to choke and then to cough. As a nurse rushed to help him, he spat the whole abscess out – a glass full. His temperature dropped from over 40, where it had stuck for days, to under 36. Doctors crowded around his bed, for he was now a medical wonder.

They fed him with everything that could be procured, and slowly the climb back towards health began. On his first outing, he was, however, still so weak that he fell off a tram and had to have an anti-tetanus injection, which set him back considerably.

Now, together at last, we left for Vienna to see a good doctor. He thought Paul would inevitably catch T.B. on his weakened lung, and recommended mountain air whenever possible 'after the war'. But at least he would not be fit for combat for months. That at least was an unmitigated blessing!

But then our local Nazi Kreisleiter stepped in and tried to prevent Paul from coming home, even if someone else had to be freed from military service to do his job. Fortunately, he was still an invalid, and several months elapsed before he could be assigned anywhere.

We heard presently that the Spanish Division had been repatriated, returning for the most part by train directly from Tallinn in Esthonia to Spain.

A few days before their departure from that city, it was heavily bombed and next morning a lovely girl in tears came to beg the Spanish liaison officers to take her with them, for her parents had been killed that night, and her last hope was to rejoin her 'fiancé', a Spanish officer who had gone home some time before.

Dubious as to the relationship ('novia' is not a binding term in Spanish), they were, however, loth to leave her. After some consultation, they regretfully cut off her long fair hair, and disguised her in a soldier's uniform, with the 'requete's' red cap as finishing touch. They then decided that from then on she would share sleeping accommodation with the 'Padre': '. . . Up to him to observe his vows and resist temptation. They could not vouch for themselves . . .'

When they reached Irun on the Spanish frontier, proud of their achievement, they discovered that the rank and file had successfully smuggled at least twenty girls along with them!

The 'fiancé' was found, and wedding bells soon pealed, the entire liaison staff acting as 'padrinos' at the ceremony.

2

(Before I mention the tragic plot of the 20th July 1944 against Hitler, I would like to emphasize that this is an entirely personal account of this event as far as it affected us, and does not pretend to cover the ground many more competent contemporaries have dealt with.)

'Should I tell you? . . I can't make up my mind . . .' said Missie, uneasily pacing my room in Königswart on an autumn day in 1943.

'Sit down and speak up: what is it?'

'They are planning a coup d'état against Hitler. It is apparently important for them to know the mood of the higher échelons of the Army should it take place. To sound this out, the conspirators are moving staff officers they can trust into key positions. There are rumours that Paul's name has been mentioned, and that he is going to be approached. If things go wrong, it means the end for all those involved: I think you should know about it.'

Within a widening circle of friends these plans seemed to be under close discussion.

'Who are they in contact with?' I asked.

'There seem to be many different groups, but it is essential to get the Army on their side. Of course it is all hearsay: a word there, a hint here . . .'

When Paul came in, and after some hesitation, we had told him about it, he burst out laughing:

'Don't look as if you've seen a ghost. This has been talked about for many months.'

'You know about it too?'

'But of course. We don't know the details, but they are trying to work them out.'

'Are you joining them?' we asked him.

'For the moment, they need information about the morale of the High Command. It's about all we can do for them at the Front.'

While military success still continued there could be no question of the country's support for the conspirators and yet we heard later that one attempt after another was made. They were all doomed to fail.*

As the long months went by, the journeys from Berlin to Königswart became ever more hazardous. On one week-end Missie arrived looking as if she had been pulled through a sack of coal: the train was bombed on the way and the passengers had crawled under the coaches for cover. Hers happened to be close to the engine and her fair hair was grey with soot, her face smeared: she was on the verge of tears from shock. A hot bath, shampoo and forty hours' sleep put her on her feet again. Before she left, as we drove once more in the woods over mossy roads, she told Paul and me:

'It may happen at any time. But they no longer think they can succeed in getting the country to back them. The Allies have refused anything but unconditional surrender and that forces many wavering Army Commanders into loyalty to Hitler. "They" have reached such a point of despair that it now seems as if they intend to go ahead whatever the consequences, if only to prove that there are some at least who cannot accept what is going on.'

We were aghast!

Heinrich Wittgenstein, the ace night-fighter and one of our closest friends, was shot down in early 1944, after around a hundred victories.

During 1943, he was ordered in to Hitler's presence to be awarded one more distinguished addition to his *Ritterkreuz*. Beforehand, he asked some of us whether he should take advantage of this opportunity to shoot the Führer. We gasped in horror, but he replied quite seriously, 'I am not married, I have no children – I am expendable. He will receive me personally. Who else amongst us can ever get as near to him?'

On his safe return, he told us, however, that he had been relieved of his pistol before the interview, and, rather illogically, was outraged at the indignity.

Hitler seemed to have an animal intuition for personal danger, for the police had never discovered any clue to previous abortive attempts.

Therefore, once again, it did not seem possible that they would manage to kill him. Yet, owing to the importance the Army attached to the 'oath of loyalty', there appeared to be no other way of overthrowing the régime.

* Looking back now on the conspirators' efforts to build a shadow Government so that a future Germany would have a basis of discussion with the Allies, and knowing as we do today, the enormous influence Philby wielded at that time, this may well have been the cause of all the difficulties the German resistance met with, as they negotiated for peace conditions abroad.

This tremendous emphasis on the personal oath to the Führer, taken by every soldier, seemed incongruous at a moment when all beliefs and allegiances were discarded so easily. It did not seem to have quite the same importance for practising Christians, who put their loyalty to God above that to Hitler, yet for them too it was a stumbling block and paralysed direct action when it came to betrayal or assassination.

Did we imagine it or, as the days passed, was there a feeling of unbearable tension in the air? In fact we were quite ill with it. We walked up and down in the park, and in the evenings Paul paced the room incessantly, too uneasy to sit still.

'They don't know how to make revolutions,' he ruminated. '. . . Much too decent people. They plan and plan. They take notes of everything but they can't improvise. At the last moment they will have thought of every detail including lists of future Ministers, and overlook the one important thing, which is to do away with Hitler!'

On Thursday, 20th July 1944, the blow fell with the news announcement: '. . . There has been a plot to kill our Führer . . . A handful of "conscienceless" officers . . .'

The attempt had taken place at last and it was a failure! The news added that the Führer was to speak himself that evening, which extinguished any spark of hope that they might be trying to conceal the fact that Hitler had been killed.

The world stood still around us for a while. We talked in low voices. It was almost as if someone was lying in the next room awaiting burial.

The weather continued serenely lovely, the sun shining hot in complete contrast with the black cloud over our minds. For it was easy to imagine what would follow: the tidal wave of retribution, reaching the friends, and the friends of the friends, of those more flagrantly compromised: the moral élite of Germany.

My parents' shocked surprise at the news was magnified by their horror when they realised how deeply people we knew seemed involved, and above all by their indignation at Missie having been aware of the planning. This was the inevitable consequence of the solidarity which had protected us from the beginning of the war, but it seemed to them a high price to pay. She was still in Berlin, and it was impossible to get direct news as yet.

A few days later we got a postcard. We could hardly believe our eyes as we read in English, in Albert Eltz's familiar hand (no signature of course): 'How awful to have missed this unique opportunity! But they were sure to bungle it.' He then continued in German, for the edification of the censor: '. . . Our destinies are now in the hands of Heinrich Himmler, as we stride towards final Victory . . .'

In fact, the message appeared to have slipped past vigilant eyes, but I now hastily hid or destroyed quantities of letters, papers, diaries and address books.

After the failure of the plot, it became quite unbearable to remain in ignorance of what had happened, so when Paul told me he must leave for Prague, I had grave misgivings that he would go on from there to Berlin. His departure added to my anxiety. Instead of his pistol, he took along an ivory-handled cane. It might appear a frivolous appendage to his uniform, but beneath the plaited wicker it was made of solid iron and could fell an ox. It helped him to feel less defenceless.

On arriving in Berlin (which was of course his destination), he went straight to the Hotel Adlon, in the hope of finding some acquaintance there. He did not dare go to anyone's private address until he knew more.

All the carpets had been removed from the stone-flagged hall. Small round tables were distributed around an empty space. At one of them sat Giorgio Cini. Alone.

Some months earlier Giorgio had come to Germany to try and buy his father out of Dachau concentration camp, the millionaire industrialist having been arrested by the S.S. in Italy, shortly after the Allies landed there.

Handsome, charming and spoilt as he was, nevertheless Giorgio left everything to come to his father's help, retiring at first into seclusion so as to cudgel a working knowledge of German into his brain. On reaching Berlin and fearing for his father's health, he had at first offered to replace him in Dachau as hostage, but this brave gesture was rejected.

Meanwhile he had acquired an intimate knowledge of the inner workings of Nazi corruption. He had good reason to hope for success, but with the failure of the plot, his plans were also now in jeopardy.*

Paul slipped into an empty chair beside him, as if they had arranged to meet beforehand. They ordered breakfast – not a very sustaining meal – while whispering one name after another. The answer was monotonous:

'Arrested!'

'. . . Gottfried Bismarck?'

'Arrested!'

Even though he was expecting it, Paul was so startled he dropped his

* Several years later, in Rome, he told us that he finally achieved his father's liberation by pushing diamond bracelets and other jewellery across the table during negotiations: 'Not even *under* the table!' he told us. 'They shamelessly pocketed the lot. As I was leaving the country, they thought I wouldn't tell on them.'

Not long afterwards, Giorgio was killed in an aeroplane accident, and in his memory his father established the fantastic 'San Giorgio Foundation' in Venice, on the island of that name.

cane, which crashed and bounced on the stone flags, causing other guests to jump in their seats. As the hotel lobby was always full of Gestapo agents, to attract attention was the last thing he wanted to do. But two young men breakfasting together did not appear sufficient to arouse suspicion.

Presently Otto Bismarck came in, looking harassed and fussed. He joined Paul and Giorgio, and told them in a low voice, that he was considering visiting Himmler to intercede for his brother.

'If you don't go now, it will be too late to go at all,' said Giorgio drily.

'Yes, yes, of course. *Grässlich!*' said poor Otto. But, to give him credit, he went. At that moment, it was not easy to reveal an interest in any of the suspects, even if he happened to be a member of your family.

'If you are not back in an hour, we will know that you have been arrested too,' were Giorgio's not too encouraging parting words. But there was a faint hope that we knew more about his brother's activities than the Gestapo did. Himmler might not welcome investigation into the affairs of the S.S., in which Gottfried had originally served, and the eventual discovery that – all unknown to him – a number of his collaborators were also involved in the plot, or had been holding back information until they could assess which side came out on top. Besides 'Bismarck' was still a revered name in the land.

Just as they were leaving, a friend came in and irresponsibly shouted, 'Paul! You are still alive?'

He was so angry, he could have boxed her ears!

He then went to find Missie. The office was like a graveyard, the arrests had engulfed Trott and Haeften, whose brother had already died at the side of Colonel Claus Count Stauffenberg, and so many others besides. She had been to the prisons several times to try and get news. Shocked at how involved Missie had become, Paul persuaded her to come back with him to recuperate. Wasting no time, they decided to pick up her things in Potsdam, as she had left everything in Gottfried's Government House, the Regierung.

They had to get out at the first station of the inter-urban express, and Paul held her head while she was violently sick.

'Courage, young lady,' said a friendly soldier who no doubt thought they were recently married and she was unwell for natural reasons.

Everything had become so unreal and improbable that the element of horror actually began to recede. Besides, they were so busy dealing with the practicalities that there was hardly time to realise the dangers as they arose and were circumvented.

At last they got away from the whole infected Berlin area, and I greeted them with indescribable relief at Königswart. Now I heard for the first time all the details of the plot and its tragic failure.

Apparently, Trott and Stauffenberg had only met comparatively recently: their agreement on every issue was cemented by immediate and deep friendship. Stauffenberg's sense of responsibility to the nation as a whole had driven him to the decision that nothing could be solved without killing Hitler, and this must have been a difficult conclusion for a devout Catholic. He was by all accounts that rare combination: an intellectual and man of action, and his outstanding personality and talent for persuasion had enabled him to become the link between all the different groups and opinions of the conspiracy.

Unfortunately, at that time he was also the only person with the will and means to carry out the assassination, for as a brilliant soldier and Chief of Staff of the Reserve Army, he alone of the conspirators had direct access to Hitler. Twice before he had been on the point of killing him, but there had always been some hitch.

On the 20th July Missie was in her office when Gottfried von Bismarck came by and told her and his relative Loremarie Schönburg, Missie's friend and room-mate, to join him and Mélanie in Potsdam as soon as possible. He refused to say more, but seemed strangely excited.

Shortly afterwards they heard that the attempt on Hitler's life had taken place, and that he was dead. At this news, they danced a jig for joy, and dashed out, calling to the porter on the way that they had left 'on business'.

In Potsdam they heard that Colonel von Stauffenberg had placed the bomb in an attaché case under Hitler's feet during a conference at his Headquarters in East Prussia. (Having lost his right hand and several fingers of the left in the African campaign, he could not shoot.) He had then waited outside long enough to hear the explosion, and see the 'Führer' carried out on a stretcher covered with blood.

As leading spirit of the conspiracy, his presence was essential in Berlin. On reaching the 'OKH' – High Command of the Army – in the Bendlerstrasse, he found Gottfried, Trott and many others awaiting him. At six that evening an announcement was to be made that a new Government had been formed: Gördeler, ex-Mayor of Leipzig (an economist of socialist background) as Chancellor, Ambassador von Hassel as Foreign Minister, Trott to be Under-Secretary of State.

By some incomprehensible omission, the conspirators had failed to sever communications around Hitler's Headquarters, or to take over the main wireless station in Berlin.

Meanwhile, however, the entire officers' school at Krampnitz and their tanks had advanced on Berlin, where they faced irresolute S.S. detachments. Not a shot had yet been fired.

But now the tide of events turned against the conspirators, although Gottfried still believed the uprising could succeed. Our friend, General von Hase, Commander of Berlin, although a member of the conspiracy, was so naïve and unimaginative that he put full trust in his subordinate, Major Remer, commanding the Berlin Guard Battalion, and he never considered for one moment the possibility of his dashing off to Goebbels for confirmation of Hase's orders to cordon off the Government offices – which he did! Goebbels thereupon phoned Hitler in Remer's presence and at once transferred all military responsibility in Berlin from von Hase to the Major.

Goebbels himself remained for a while uncertain of the outcome, and we heard later, had pocketed two pills of cyanide before leaving his office.

Then came the fatal announcement that Hitler was after all alive, and would now deal with the conspirators. Everyone knew what that meant.

In the Bendlerstrasse, that arch opportunist General Fromm, Commander of the Reserve Army, had betrayed his friends and associates. Count Stauffenberg was first wounded as he ran out of his office, then shot with his ADC von Haeften (the younger brother of Missie's chief), General Olbricht and Colonel Mertz von Quirnheim. General Beck, who had been Chief-of-Staff of the Army and who had resigned after the Czech–Sudeten crisis of 1938, when he became convinced Hitler was heading for war, committed suicide.

That night Hitler spoke on the wireless with paralysing effect. At dawn the Krampnitz tanks returned to their barracks without firing a shot.

But in France and in Vienna, the take-over by the Army from the Party continued as planned. General von Stülpnagel, Commander-in-Chief in France, was ready to commit himself against Hitler. General von Kluge, Commander-in-Chief of all German forces in the West, consented to do so if things went well. This prudence was not dictated by cowardice, but by a sense of responsibility towards his subordinates. He did not realise that for Hitler even hesitation ranked as betrayal. Kluge then committed suicide when they came to arrest him.

General Rommel, the 'Desert Fox' who had finally joined the conspiracy, died mysteriously the day of his arrest. He was so popular, he was given a State burial all the same.

As in a Greek tragedy, each character in turn had played his part.

To take the country's mind off this major crisis, totalisation of the war effort was then announced. By mobilising the entire population, the Nazis still hoped to strangle any initiative in the rear.

Gottfried Bismarck was arrested on his country estate near Stettin at two in the morning. The order came from Berlin, but the local police, considerate and still polite, allowed him to take leave of his family. This also gave him the opportunity to whisper last instructions to Loremarie, to remove and hide the two boxes containing the bombs, only two of which had been used for the attempt. (Stauffenberg had been disturbed as he was trying to fuse the second one by someone coming into the lavatory of the Wolfschanze, and therefore only one of them could explode.)

Gottfried was then led away, but at first no other member of the family was molested. Loremarie dashed off through the back door to catch the first train from the tiny station of Reinfeld which would take her to Berlin and Potsdam.

She reached the Regierung around 6.30 a.m. and was let in by the startled cook. She found the boxes hidden in the cellar. They were the size of shoe-boxes, and the remaining bombs nestled in compartments 'like Christmas-tree decorations', as she described them later. They were also as heavy as blocks of lead.

The bicycles she and Missie used were still downstairs. She piled one box into the small basket fastened to the handlebars and pedalled away towards the park of Sans Souci, with a vague idea of dropping it into deep water. In her haste and breathless anxiety, she overlooked a crossing and collided at full tilt with a baker's boy on a tricycle. As she fell, she flung herself upon the box, expecting it to explode, and preferring to go up with it.

They disentangled themselves, the boy kindly trying to lift the box for her. Panic-stricken, she wrested it out of his hands: 'Thank you, I can manage!', pretending it was light as a feather. Muscles straining, she heaved it back into the basket. Many apologies on both sides, and she was on her way.

Losing heart and hard-pressed for time, she rode on to the *pièce d'eau*, at the foot of the steps leading up to the terrace of the Palace of Sans Souci. Dismounting, she hurled the box into the shallow pond. Unfortunately, it fell too close to the edge, and a corner of the box remained protruding from the water, ominous as a shark's fin.

Finding a long branch, she pushed and prodded until at last it disappeared. But, looking up, her heart froze, for on the opposite side of the pond stood a man, watching.

How long had he been there? It was impossible to tell. She leapt back on to her bicycle, zig-zagging wildly through all the small streets of Potsdam to throw off any pursuers, and regained the Regierung.

Now for the second box. But she no longer had the courage to carry it out again. There was a tiny patch of garden in the courtyard below. She tried to dig a hole with a very inadequate coal shovel. It was July, there was no water to spare, and the earth was as hard as stone.

In despair, she called the cook and together they chopped and hoed and dug under a small tree. In went the box, all traces smoothed down. Then she left, enjoining the cook to silence.

Half an hour later, the Gestapo arrived and sealed off all Gottfried's papers and his safe. They then searched the house. Had they found the boxes nothing could have saved him.

Perhaps they are still where Loremarie hid them.

We were determined to keep Missie out of Berlin for good. Meanwhile there were several projects afoot to save some of the prisoners.

It became urgently necessary to find out when the conspirators were coming up for trial, this being theoretically the only possible moment for a rescue, as they would then be transferred from one place to another.

Peter Bielenberg, Adam von Trott's friend, had evolved a plan for freeing the prisoners, but soon he too was arrested. Count Helldorf's son had gone to Goebbels to ask for a reprieve for his father, who had been the Chief of the Berlin Police. Goebbels refused to see him, and did not even trouble to tell the young man that his father was already hanged.

Braving imminent arrest themselves, some friends succeeded in attending the trials, but the ranks of those who could help were thinning rapidly.

Gottfried Bismarck's wife, Melanie Hoyos, and her brother and sister were arrested and questioned for hours on end by the Gestapo. Melanie suffered a miscarriage and was afterwards so weak, she fainted and, falling, broke her jaw.

They told us later that in their case the stupidity of the police had been a great help. You just kept on and on talking, dwelling on pointless detail by the hour, so that by the time the crucial questions were reached, days had passed, and their interrogators had become quite confused.

We were full of admiration for their courage and resource, besides the ability of reeling off endless convincing yarns.

Loremarie had made the acquaintance of a high-ranking S.S. officer, and now she visited him frequently in his office.

Between badinage and playful flirtation, she managed to extract information as to when and where the trials would take place. Also who would be accused.

Suddenly, quite unexpectedly, Gottfried's name was mentioned. Caught by surprise, Loremarie jumped from her chair, dropping the rosary she had always clutched during these difficult meetings.

'You have dropped something!' The S.S. officer had been quicker than she in retrieving it.

White-faced, he looked at her, understanding in a flash that it was not affection for him that had brought her here. On the contrary, for her it must have been like facing the devils in hell. Hence the rosary.

Incapable of further thought or speech, she took it from his hands and ran out of the room, never to return. She expected denunciation any day, but surprisingly, he took no revenge.

Avid for news, friends and neighbours came to see us frequently. Among them were some fellow-officers of Paul's recovering from wounds or illness in the nearby spas of Marienbad or Carlsbad. As I gathered up their raincoats to put them on a table, I felt revolvers in their pockets and my heart missed a beat, for as a rule, they never carried arms.

I asked Kurt to be sure to tell any visitor coming by car, that we were not at home, and then to warn me. Just to gain a little time. Any car now would be a Gestapo car.

The men talked and talked anxiously about their threatened friends as they paced restlessly up and down, fretting that they could do nothing to help.

I remained upstairs. From here I could see the wide courtyard and any approaching vehicle. One afternoon, I gasped with horror as a huge black car rolled through the main gates. It was obviously petrol-driven too.

The front door opened below, and I could see Kurt's worried face as he said politely: 'Nobody at home!'

But out stepped a gaily dressed girl, fair hair streaming down her back – Reni, Sigi Welczeck's sister, and she was alone.

I ran downstairs to meet her. 'How could you give us such a fright!'

She was blissfully oblivious of what had happened, had never heard of the plot and only meant to visit her sister and brother-in-law, who were staying with us. A Croatian friend had lent her his official car.

Her visit eased the tension, and for a time distracted the men from their worries.

Incomprehensibly the British wireless named possible suspects who had not yet been implicated, just as if they wished to precipitate the downfall of Hitler's enemies.

Over the German wireless a million marks were offered as a reward for information as to the whereabouts of Gördeler, one of the conspiracy's ringleaders. At first we were reassured to hear that he had succeeded in evading his pursuers, but soon some horrible woman turned up to claim this blood money.

We tried to plan what we should do if a friend came in search of refuge. We could always say it was a relation of mine fleeing from the advancing Soviet Army in the East. But after that . . .?

Missie declared that for the first time since the beginning of the war, she was no longer afraid of air raids. Before the 20th July she had been getting more panic-stricken every time. One cannot apparently be terrified of two things at once.

One of the most astonishing things about the 20th July assassination plot was that so many people – not all of them discreet – knew about it, and yet the police had never had an inkling. They seemed only to poke around in the dark. But during the next months – practically until the end of the war – the Gestapo rounded up everyone they could lay their hands on, on the flimsiest evidence. An interrogation mark in someone's notebook was often enough; an exclamation mark was equivalent to a death sentence. Some of the most compromised conspirators had not even tried to escape, as if the scale of the calamity had deprived them of any initiative. Many had felt that their gesture would carry greater meaning and influence if they died for it: as if losing hope they had also lost all fear, or perhaps all wish to live.

The ones to escape were for the most part officers at the Front, and those lucky enough not to be included on any list. In some cases the Gestapo bungled, in others they proceeded with the keenness of bloodhounds, as in the case of one fugitive.

After the most exhausting investigation, they discovered that his nurse had married a Bavarian farmer many years before. They went to this solitary farm, high on a mountain, but could find no one, even after the most thorough investigation. Just as one of the searchers was leaving the loft under the great roof of the spreading farmhouse, he turned round for a last look: a thin swirl of vapour arose from the hay in the cold winter air. There, forewarned of the approaching police, their quarry had hidden. His breath betrayed him.

Hearing that Goerdeler had been drugged and had then spoken too much, Count Hardenberg of Neuhardenberg, with whom Stauffenberg and Haeften had spent their last week-end, attempted to commit suicide before his arrest, quite against his convictions as a Christian and a brave man, but he was afraid of betraying others. Gravely wounded, he was then taken to the concentration camp of Sachsenhausen, but miraculously survived the war.

All the accused, even the Ambassadors Count von der Schulenburg, our old friend, and von Hassel, who had been consulted on the formation of a future Government in Germany, then suffered a fate no longer meted out to common criminals in civilised countries: to be hanged from a butcher's hook in a cellar.

'There has been an attempt on our Führer's life,' announced the Gestapo agents in Vienna, standing in the office doorway of Count Walter Berchem, once one of Paul's guardians.

Unkind wags had it that he had answered, characteristically, 'I already knew.'

To which they had countered: 'Then come along with us.'

The fact was that he had known nothing about the plot, and was arrested in the wake of his highly compromised chief, Colonel Marogna-Redwitz. They locked him up in the same Hotel Metropole, Gestapo

Headquarters in Vienna, where Schuschnigg had been kept for some time.

Home on leave, Paul decided to visit him, thinking it would cheer him up and give him courage, for Berchem had shown him unfailing kindness.

He set out jauntily in full uniform, hoping that he would not be arrested and trying to look as if it was the most natural thing in the world to visit a friend charged with high treason at Gestapo Headquarters.

After some preliminary discussion, a surprisingly polite policeman from the regular police, which often to their disgust was now amalgamated with the Gestapo, took him up to the second floor, and there in a small bare room, he found Berchem.

They were left alone together, but Walter made frantic signs not to talk, and then loudly proclaimed that they could speak quite freely – all for the benefit of hidden microphones. Paul tried to discover what he could really do for him, but he was too petrified to specify. He admitted, however, that the air raids were quite terrifying, for they were locked up in their rooms and not allowed to take cover in a shelter.

He was extremely touched by Paul's visit, so it had been worthwhile. He was to be one of those saved by the ending of the war.*

In a desperate effort to help the escape of incarcerated officers compromised by the 20th July plot, Ursula von H. dragged two sacks of food and civilian clothing to the fortress of Küstrin. She had previously found out that one of the S.S. officers in charge was a decent man and had been given a description of his appearance. Leaving the sacks at a nearby inn, she hid within sight of the main entrance until she saw him come on duty. She then accosted him and told him she was engaged to be married to one of the prisoners and begged for a 'last' interview. He said he himself preferred to ignore her démarche, but that by a lucky chance that same night a soldier on guard at the side entrance could be 'persuaded' to let her in.

She waited until nightfall and then found the soldier, who indeed allowed himself to be 'persuaded' by a generous offer of coffee and cigarettes. He even helped to fetch the sacks. Her friend could not believe his eyes when he saw her.

After they had exchanged all their news, the other prisoners asked whether she would allow them to 'take a look at her', for they had not seen a woman – and a pretty one at that – in months. It might be the last chance they would have of doing so.

* In later years, every autumn brought Walter to his beloved Johannisberg for the harvest, and one would see his purposeful figure in turn-of-the-century tweeds and Phineas Fogg cap, striding through the vineyards, or stopping to chat with the grape-pickers.

She then sat on a chair in front of the open door of one of the cells and all the prisoners passed down the corridor, stopping one after the other to smile and bow to her. She felt rather foolish, but was glad to do so if it made them any happier.

She stayed in the fortress until the same soldier was on duty three nights later, when in great stealth, he led her out to safety.

For some reason the judgment of most of these officers was deferred, and thanks to the civilian clothes she had brought, they escaped to the West as the war ended.

Politically, the ideal of the conspirators was a democracy based on Christian principles, but their profound motivation was to take a stand against Nazi amorality and its fundamental denial of individual human dignity and rights whenever this was in conflict with the interests of the Party.

Many of the 'new' high-ranking Generals owed their careers to Hitler and therefore often sailed with the wind. The main nucleus of the plot was therefore to be found among the officers of the traditional regiments, especially in the motorized cavalry, whose opposition to the régime was based on Christian ethics and the code of honour of the landed gentry. But as the arrests continued, it transpired that the plot involved Germans in every walk of life and of all political views, including renegades from the Party. Only the military, however, had access to Hitler and could organize a coup, although their passion for detail bogged them down when improvisation might have saved the day.

In critical times of moral crisis one reaches a point where finally nothing remains but the metaphysical question of choice. After the 20th July it was indeed very strange to see how conflicting ethical outlooks polarized under Nazi pressure. Free-thinking consciences lost their last hope of compromise. Many were now ready to die rather than add one more lie to the stifling heap.

During the trials when the Nazi President of the Peoples' Court, Freisler, screamed at Count Schwerin: 'How could you lift your hand against our Führer?', the poor young man still found the strength to say: 'Those countless murders alone . . .', before he was silenced.

Between the benighted or unscrupulous leaders and those ready to oppose them at any cost, marched the great majority incapable of choice, led on by Hitler in a sort of 'Pied-Piper' trance towards the 'thousand year Reich'. It saved them from personal responsibilities, from the trouble to think and draw conclusions. In time a crescendo had been reached when any demand could be made of the country, for their essential preoccupation remained to try and save their earthly possessions (their 'Hab und Gut'), to survive against overwhelming odds and to believe that all this misery was not for nothing.

'The Führer knows best,' was all they said.

But now this solid conviction had become quicksand under their feet. Who was to blame? Any name called loud enough:

'Reactionary officers' clique!' 'Bishop Galen!' 'Jews!' 'Traitors' of any denomination.

Never themselves.

During those first weeks after the 20th July plot, public opinion was difficult to assess. We were amazed to realise how uninformed the country as a whole continued to be. Yet there was little sympathy with the Government: the attempt on Hitler's life seemed hardly to concern the people. Only in Berlin was the reaction of the pale, poorly-fed, exhausted inhabitants, 'It is enough to make one sick!'

In the Armed Forces the same resigned indifference seems to have predominated too, but Paul's cousin, Count Clemens Kageneck, who commanded a decimated regiment of tanks, told us that disappointment at the failure of the plot was intense, not only among his officers (who were nearly all ex-cavalry men), but also among the rank and file, who had to pay the price for Hitler's 'genius' as Commander-in-Chief. 'Better an end with terror, than terror without end,' they said.

As the fighting Army retreated step by step across Russia, the troops often collided with the S.S. who set up Courts Martial to try them for cowardice. The Army's distrust and hatred of the Party and finally of Hitler himself had reached a point where they knew that only his assassination would bring an end to their suffering.

This view was often shared by the Luftwaffe, who felt cheated by Göring's false promises. Besides, stationed close to home, they were better informed as to conditions inside the country, and this was not conducive to Party loyalty.

On the other hand the Navy, and especially the submarine crews, lived and fought as if inside an egg, cut off from any outside influence or distressing news. They were therefore still surprisingly loyal to the régime.

It will probably never be possible to say for sure whether Hitler's death had been as essential as the conspirators thought, or whether his régime would have collapsed like a house of cards if Remer, the Commander of the Berlin Guard Battalion had been on their side or neutralised.

The executions after the plot numbered thousands. Two hundred men were hanged alone in the cellar of the Berlin Plötzensee prison on those butcher's hooks, and untold suffering inflicted on their wives and children who had been distributed in homes under false names.

Was it worth the price?

More people died on all fronts, including civilians on all sides, during the months following the 20th July 1944 than in all the preceding five years of war. And yet, in later years, it was this individual stand against the fundamental evil of Nazi oppression and their institutionalised murder which stood out memorably in stark relief, while the death of millions receded into the haze of history.

Travelling in Poland many years after the war, I visited old Prince Janusz Radziwill in the tiny workers' flat in Warsaw which had been allotted to him.

He had been a highly respected figure both in Russia and in Germany before World War I, and was often referred to as 'the uncrowned King of Poland.' Thanks to the intervention of Ambassador Count von der Schulenburg he was let out of the Lubianka prison in Moscow, where he had been incarcerated after the Soviet occupation of Poland. Returning to his country, he was promptly arrested again by the Gestapo and presently found himself in the Prinz Albrecht prison in Berlin, in the company of a number of people involved in the 20th July plot. Telling me about it, he added:

'I had been an officer of the Royal Prussian Army before 1914. After what happened to my country, I thought I could never shake the hand of a German again. But in that prison I found a group of people from every walk of life of such a high level, both morally and intellectually as even in my days I had rarely met. I believe very few of them were to survive, but they reconciled me with Germany.'

Until then Missie had managed to escape the glare of the Gestapo's searchlight. It was, however, essential for her to leave Berlin for good. Finally, thanks to a medical certificate, official permission to do so was obtained and she went to collect her papers in Krummhübel in Silesia, where part of the Foreign Office had been evacuated. Von Blankenhorn, one of Trott's friends, arranged to meet her on a seat in the public park, for the attempt had taken place since they had last seen each other. For a while they sat back to back, reading newspapers. Only then could they venture to exchange their news.

It had seemed to us that in a large city such as Vienna, it would be easier for her to escape notice. Besides one somehow still expected preferential treatment for Austria after the war, which was perhaps an unjust assumption when one remembered that Hitler was after all an Austrian. We well knew that Missie would never be allowed to stay in Königswart, and whatever dangers the advancing Soviet Army might presently bring, hospital work in Vienna seemed therefore the best solution for the moment. One could also expect hospitals to be on the priority list for evacuation.

Sita Wrede, to whose parties we had frequently gone at the beginning of the war, was working as a nurse in a large military hospital there, and she now did her best to get Missie on to the staff. But her name must, after all, have been on some Party list, for the moment it was mentioned, an order arrived: she was to leave at once for the Eastern Front as an ambulance nurse. But the Front was disintegrating, there was not even a precise indication of where she had to go, and the order as peremptory as if she was condemned to a punitive battalion.

In desperation Sita rushed to the head doctor and produced a photo of Missie, demanding, 'What do you think of this girl?'

'Lovely,' said the head doctor appreciatively.

'She is as charming as she is beautiful! And to think that *she* should fall into Soviet hands! Herr Doktor, you must do something.'

'But we have not got a single vacancy.'

'She can type perfectly. Put her in the reception office, and we'll find something later.'

He must have had a sense of humour, for he took a pen and scribbled across the order: 'Working here until further notice.'

Sita proclaimed jubilantly that this saved Missie's life, and she was probably right. The job was no sinecure, for air raids over Vienna were to intensify dramatically during the next months.

We still managed to visit her once and see how she was getting on. At first she had taken a flat with a friend, Antoinette Croy, whose husband was fighting in Yugoslavia.

As the air raids worsened, Antoinette left for the country, and Missie then transferred to the Hotel Bristol. Life still continued somehow, friends still managed to get together for meals, or sat together in cellars, the companionship and solidarity making it all more bearable.

On the 3rd of March 1945, the Opera House was burnt to a cinder, and the Jockey Club in the centre of the city destroyed. Around three hundred people were killed in its cellars, which had been considered solid enough to weather any attack, and were therefore packed. As they dug down to the victims during the next few days, the stench became so overpowering, people would make a wide detour to avoid it.

The feeling of the Viennese for their city was intensely intimate and personal, and they were as offended as if someone had walked into their bedroom uninvited.

At Missie's hospital there was an air-raid shelter in a tunnel nearby to which most of the staff and the less serious cases repaired. By some fluke, Missie had remained in the main building the night the tunnel received a direct hit. The wounded who had walked there were killed, or carried back on stretchers in an appalling condition. In the centre of Vienna one collided with lorries transporting sacks containing the corpses collected out of bombed shelters.

Meanwhile the Soviet Army was getting closer to the city every day. Rumours of the murdering, looting and raping in Budapest were confirmed by refugees streaming over the frontier into the rat-trap Vienna had now become: still the order for evacuation did not come. It made us all frantic with worry about Missie, especially as communications were being severed as if scissors were clipping wires and cables on all sides.

Inexorably the end was approaching.

3

From Königswart we could hear the booming and barking of anti-aircraft guns over Nürnberg, followed by the dull thud of bombs. Flares, like summer lightning, illuminated the sky.

Paul had suddenly been transferred to nearby Bamberg to rejoin Cavalry Regiment No. 17, the famous Bamberg Riders. It had been Stauffenberg's regiment and a centre of anti-Nazi resistance. That did not sound too bad, although an uneasy spirit would prevail after the execution of Stauffenberg and many of his brother officers.

Baron Erne von Cramm, awarded the Ritterkreuz, was the new Commander. (Cut off in the depths of Russia with all his men, Cramm was given orders to retreat over the telephone. He announced tersely that someone would have to repeat the order from where he stood. After a ferocious battle he managed to break out with most of his men. Between a court-martial or a reward for courage they decided on the Ritterkreuz.)

The Barons von Cramm were staunch Hanoverians, anti-Prussian and monarchist. Eight brothers were brought up in the country in a vast castle by a galaxy of tutors, tennis and riding being part of the curriculum. They had also grown up remote from any alien influence. They incorporated just about everything the Nazis hated most. Erne was a law unto himself, with a lordly disregard for such regulations as might threaten his own rigid code. The seeming aggressiveness of his jutting chin was belied by kind, appraising, trustful eyes. He was always impeccably turned out, as generally seemed to be the case with those who had survived filth and privation.

His brother, Gottfried, the tennis champion, had been a go-between of the plotters to neutral countries, whereas Erne was one of the volunteers who offered to kill Hitler. He never could get close enough to do so.

Recovering from wounds, he was, like Paul, his entire staff and most of his men, unfit for combat, so since Paul was not going to be allowed home, at this cheerless moment, the new assignment was a comparatively pleasant one. It consisted in training recruits for the Front and, the war drawing to its inevitable end, even this job seemed unrealistic.

Paul left, and soon after I prepared to follow him. For once, I could rejoin him easily, so I left without misgivings. Winter 1944 was setting in. Caught like swirls of smoke in the hollows, the morning mists drifted up from the meadows, veiling the gentle landscape as the carriage jogged me to Eger.

The train was very late, but far down the line I contrived to find a seat. A pretty young girl in country 'Lodens' slowly edged her way towards me through the packed corridor in a movement of solidarity, expecting as I did, the imminent rudeness of the crowd. By this stage of the war, people could no longer bear anyone to look as if they had had a less hard time than themselves and were ready to spit venom on the smallest pretext.

It was prolonged misery that brought about this state of mind rather than suffering and danger which seemed to make people remote and kind. One only felt safe from vicious remarks if there was someone in uniform in the vicinity.

As we approached Nürnberg, the sirens began to howl. Everybody piled out and rushed to the nearest shelter, which – rather unsuitably – happened to be just underneath the station. It was tightly packed with nowhere to sit, so many stood leaning against one another while crash upon crash resounded over our heads, clouds of dust rising like choking smoke as a bomb fell close by. Children cried, but the grown-ups for the most part sat frozen-faced through it all, wincing a little when the crashes were near.

Then there was a long silence and the 'All clear' sounded. Out we trooped at a run, a tidal wave of people breaking with a roar towards the train, which was already full as it drew in.

They stormed it, climbing through the windows. Limping on crutches, a tall young officer accompanied by an orderly carrying his bag, nearly got pushed under the step.

I was looking for Paul, who meant to meet me in Nürnberg, so at first did not try to push with all the rest. He was nowhere to be seen, and I gave up, hoping to get on to the next train and reach Bamberg on my own. But again the sirens sounded and down to the shelters we went. It was worse this time; wave upon wave.

This devil's dance went on all night: up into the ever more battered station, impossible to board the crowded train pulling in, then back to the shelter! There was no sign of Paul in the struggling crowds.

Finally towards five in the morning, I managed to find the office of the Station Master. His red cap was dusty, his face grey, but he was still polite. 'Is there a coach anywhere in the station which will eventually go to Bamberg?'

He ordered an official to accompany me. We climbed over debris and rubble, across packed platforms. Standing on a distant siding the coach was intact. He unlocked one of the doors.

'You will have to stay here now if there is another attack,' he warned me.

By then I could not care. In the empty, ice-cold compartment, curled up in a corner on the hard bench, I went to sleep at once, barely conscious of other passengers following my example and creeping into the lonely car.

Some hours later, with a jerk and a bump, we began to move. We were shunted on to one of the main lines and with a final jerk, shackled to a train. Wonderful feeling: we really seemed to be on our way to Bamberg.

I left my bag at the station and walked to the hotel: Paul had only just got back, after having spent the whole night looking for me in the same station in Nürnberg, through all the same bombing attacks. Finally he gave up, hoping I would find my way to Bamberg too.

He had to leave for his regiment almost at once. Just time for a bath, blissfully hot. For a moment we lay exhausted on the hard bed, recovering.

I slept all day, and joined Paul and Erne and his other A.d.C., Herr von Braun, in the evening.

Then began an unreal sort of life. The atmosphere in Bamberg was incredibly oppressive. Everyone we met was related to or had been friends of the Stauffenberg group. Their hatred of the Nazis was like a festering sore, partly concealed only by the despair of defeat since the failure of the plot. Day by day victims were still being rounded up on the strength of some hint, some denunciation.

An 'NSFO' had been sent down to spy on Erne and the highly suspicious Bamberg Cavalry officers. He was the equivalent of the Soviet Commissar, and openly called 'Politruk' by the soldiers. Coming straight from the Gestapo, he was unused to horses. Erne indulged in baiting him, as was his right, for riding after all remained essential in a cavalry regiment. He would stand flicking his boots with a switch, rasping out orders, and barely restraining the broad grin which spread over his face as the hated 'NSFO' fell over one hurdle after another. Erne was always scrupulously correct and coldly insulting.

The 'NSFO' bided his time, but we hoped the war would end before he could strike.

Every morning I took long walks in the biting cold through the charming little untouched town and its surroundings. Small chapels filled with baroque statues stood at all the crossroads, but the famous Reiter in the Cathedral was shrouded in sacks and invisible.

We all met again in the evenings. First a drink together in our hotel, then we drove out to dine in some small Gasthaus, using an antediluvian carriage at Erne's disposal.

The news was terrifying and anxiety for our friends filled our talk and thoughts.

At this time, I received a message by hand from Mélanie Bismarck, Gottfried's wife, smuggled out of prison, for the wives and often the children of suspects were also incarcerated. (They called it 'Sippenhaft' – tribal arrest.) She asked me to enquire through Obergruppenführer M. in Nürnberg for news of Gottfried in Flossenburg Camp, No. . . Baracke . . .

I realised this was probably a way to inform M. of Gottfried's whereabouts, for the Hoyos family had shown remarkable *sang-froid* until now, and always had a good reason for anything they did.

So I telephoned Nürnberg, and asked for Obergruppenführer M. He was not there, but would be informed I had called.

Two days later, towards evening, while Paul and I were resting, the worried voice of the hotel porter said on the phone:

'I am warning you. You are going to receive a visit. They cannot be stopped and are on their way up.'

It sounded ominous, but before we had time to think it out, there was a knock on the door.

'Open the door. Secret Police.'

Paul and I whipped on our dressing-gowns, and in he came: a fat middle-aged man with small eyes, under an inimitable pot-shaped felt hat. (All Secret State police, whether Nazi or Communist, were and are immediately recognisable by their distinctively hideous headgear.)

As if we could doubt his profession, he turned down the lapel of his coat to show us his badge. He seemed to be alone.

'You phoned Obergruppenführer M?' (It was more a statement than a question.)

'I did. It was to transmit a message from my friend Countess Melanie Bismarck.'

'Does your husband know of this?'

'He does, but he has nothing to do with it.'

'I am here at the wish of Obergruppenführer M., who is at Hitler's Headquarters. He wanted to know whether it was urgent. In which case he would return.'

'What do you mean by urgent?'

'If your need was urgent,' he repeated.

What a relief! So Obergruppenführer M. was indeed a friend as we had hoped. I told him that the message did not concern us, and handed it on, just as I had received it from Melanie. He promised to return with the answer.

This he did shortly after. The answer was that Gottfried was well and that one could send him parcels. I passed on the message to his wife.

After many months in concentration camps, Gottfried Bismarck miraculously survived. So did his family, with whom he was reunited soon after the end of the war. Paul and I met him and Melanie once only. I longed to ask him who M. really was, but somehow none of us wanted to talk about that harrowing time.*

It was difficult to assess what the hotel thought of all this, but so many had been arrested here before we came . . . Perhaps they sympathised with us? Anyway, they were as friendly and nice as ever, even when the clouds gathering over Erne's head broke, and that was a little too soon for all of us.

The Nazis had initiated a series of feast days, planned to replace the Christian ones. These had a Walhalla-like sound to them, and as yet had made little impact on the population, especially in Catholic provinces and towns such as Bamberg.

Erne, as Commander of the resident regiment, was supposed to hold a speech in honour of the 'Feast of the changing sun' (*Sonnenwendfeier*), which was intended to supersede Christmas. He, Paul and Braun, chuckling with suppressed and sardonic delight, had composed a juicy peroration.

When the great day came, all the local Nazi *Bonzen* (big-wigs) collected on tribunes and stands, the entire regiment lined up, surrounded by a respectable number of onlookers and townspeople. Erne stood within a semi-circle of waving flags, and in his rasping voice, which carried further than any loud-speaker, and in clipped accents, delivered his speech.

'. . . I myself have only known front-line fighting.' He twiddled his *Ritterkreuz* significantly, looked around him, casting an appraising eye on his regiment, and added, 'I observe here an imposing number of front line troops.' This was a dig at the bemedalled Nazi officials in the front row, who had spent most of the war in their offices. '. . . We have all gathered here to celebrate the *Sonnenwendfeier* but I must own that neither I nor any soldier present has ever heard of this fine feast until

---

* Melanie, one of the most generous and forgiving people I ever knew, typically tried to help S.S. officers in their prison camps immediately after the war, saying in justification that no one else was bothering about them and that it was time to put an end to the horrors and cruelties we had all known for too long.

A few years later they were on their way to visit us. Shortly after they were due to arrive, we learned that they had crashed in their car on the way. Both were killed instantly.

now. At the Front we only knew and reverently acknowledged the Christian Feast of Christmas, eternal symbol of Peace and Hope to any Christian, and both inspiration and solace for the soldier . . .' and so on . . .

There was petrified silence among the Nazi officials. Slow-minded as these Party *Bonzen* were, it did not need the thunder of applause from the military and civilian audience to tell them that things here were not going according to plan.

The State steamroller took time to get into motion, and we were beginning to think this speech would be overlooked or forgotten under the pressure of world events. Meanwhile the officers' staff had been ordered to send a delegate to a three-day intensified course of political indoctrination in a Nazi *Ordensburg* as they were called. These were training centres in Nazi-doctrine, usually housed in a mediaeval castle to emphasize their Wotanesque trend of thought.

Erne told Paul: 'As Commander, I can refuse the invitation. Braun has been, so it is for you to go.'

As they sat in rows in the classroom, Paul made the most of the opportunity to read *Mein Kampf* for the first time – 'Better remember what Hitler had said, than listen to what those fools repeated,' he thought.

Meanwhile the instructor bleated that Germany's three worst enemies to-day were Bishop Count Galen (whose fulminating pastoral letters were still passed from hand to hand all over the country), Austrian Chancellor Metternich, representing hated traditional Government under Habsburg leadership; and finally of course the Jews, thereby justifying their oppression of defenceless minorities.

With the book open on his desk at the page warning against war on two fronts, Paul marked the Russian and Allied advance on the map spread out in front of him in thick red ink.

'Your name!' shouted the harried instructor.

'Metternich,' (regretting he could not truthfully add: 'Half Galen and Jew').

We still had time to return to Königswart and share our 1944 Christmas dinner with Erne, Papa and Mamma in the kitchen. The table was laid behind a red velvet screen, for the dining-room could no longer be heated.

It was an occasion of mixed feelings but nothing could quite destroy the joy of the celebration and of our being safely together again.

Paul and Erne then returned to Bamberg without me. A sudden attack of toothache sent me to Prague, only four hours away, and about the only place left where one could find a good dentist. At the same time I would visit a doctor, so I headed in one direction and they in another.

As I lay on a sofa in the hospital awaiting my turn, there was a simultaneous siren-howl and crash, and both window and door of the room met in the middle of the floor and collapsed all around me. I dashed out in stockings, shoes in one hand, my handbag in the other, to find the corridor a shambles, full of dust and splinters and glass.

The nurses were already carrying recently operated-on cases out of their rooms. I rushed to help, supporting a poor groaning bandaged patient down to the cellar, with my feet feeling like running ahead of me. The shelter was filling rapidly with wounded and sick patients. The hospital had taken a direct hit.

It was all over as fast as it had come, and I believe – in spite of frequent alerts – that this was practically the only air-attack on Prague.

My three nights at the Hotel Alcron were spent in the cellar, and every night I found myself on a biscuit box next to the well-known Viennese actor Neugebauer. He told me that he was now acting the part of a police inspector in a detective play, and had thought it psychologically right to treat the suspected criminal in a paternal and understanding way.

To his disgust, a high official of the Gestapo came to see him and said approvingly, 'That was a good trick of yours (eine gute Masche), to wheedle information out of the man in that way. I intend to apply it myself.'

'Can you imagine,' said Neugebauer bitterly, 'everything is grist to their mill. I will not play that part again.'

4

On my return to Königswart a phone call from Paul came through. The whole staff in Bamberg had been broken up after a sort of court-martial. He was on his way to Ludwigslust to the north-west of Berlin with Braun, while Erne had been sent to Yugoslavia.

Just as they were leaving Bamberg, the most appalling air raid took place. He crawled under a stone table, and when he looked up again, the station had gone, all the houses around were blown up, while a muni-tions' train caught on a siding, continued to explode like a murderous firework display.

Rising to his feet, Paul and the surviving soldiers rushed to dig people out of the rubble of their houses. Paul slung one little unconscious figure over his shoulder, but he had not even stepped clear before small hands pummelled him on the back:

'Herr Leutnant, Herr Leutnant, were they big bombers?'

'The biggest,' he answered, putting the boy down and brushing the dust off him.

'My brother is still there!' he chirped.

Sure enough, a little lower down, wedged between huge blocks of stone as in a coffin, lay the brother. They got him out at once, and off they ran, hand in hand, to find their mother who had gone shopping.

But now Paul was heading for Ludwigslust, and that was a heavy blow: so far north, with the war certain to end soon, as the Soviets advanced much faster than the incomprehensibly slow Allies. Should he be taken prisoner as the vice closed in from both sides, to help Paul it would be essential to know which Army captured him. I decided to join him.

Papa and Mamma came down to see me off. Theirs had been a difficult and nerve-racking time, waiting passively in the background while we plunged into danger wherever we went.

Papa's hands trembled as he gave me his little guardian-angel icon he always carried with him, but both he and Mamma kept their feelings to themselves as always.

'. . . Are you warm enough? . . . Give Paul our love! . . .'

We pretended it was just another trip, like so many taken before. But in early 1945 time was running out: it seemed doubtful that either Paul or I would ever get back again.

One thousand five hundred and seventy-one minutes late, materialising out of the fog, the train from Nürnberg to Berlin via Leipzig rumbled puffing into the station. '*Achtung, achtung!* Step back from the line!'

Milling crowds: soldiers, children, women wearing every warm piece of clothing they still possessed. Amid clouds of steam, they fought for a place, pushing with boxes or battered trunks tied with string. They were unkempt, dirty, rude – and desperate. This was the sixth year of the war. There was no one in these crowds who had not lost a brother, or a son, or a fiancé, often a child and nearly always practically all they owned except for the bundles they still dragged around.

It was the third, or the fourth, or the sixth train they had tried to board . . . any train going north, for urgent reasons – fetching a child from a bombed town, meeting a soldier on leave, trying to retrieve or collect what might still be saved before the final crash came. Perhaps just trying to get home: *Ich will zu Hause sein!* – as if that offered some cover.

And for all, gnawing worry day and night: no news from the Front for weeks or months. At home at least the returning soldier would know where to find one. Few still had time for thought beyond the fighting instinct of self-preservation.

'Stand back! *Zurück!*' Churning of steam, a loud whistle. A sort of sigh went over the crowd on the platform as it drew to a halt. The train, as usual, was full already, and there were hundreds waiting to board it.

'Here, take her trunk. Come with us. We'll manage. Not the passenger coaches. To the back, into the *Viehwagon* (freight car for cattle).'

I was swept along by a pushing, jostling group of young boys wearing some unrecognisable uniform. Crisp orders came from a subaltern hardly older than themselves: 'Five in front, five behind; take her in the middle.' In a rush, they hoisted me up. We were in, and the train was moving.

Gradually we all found some sort of space. I sat on my little trunk, propped up on its narrow end. My small group of friends stretched out on the straw with their bags.

'The *Viehwagon* is safer against air attacks. It's made of steel – no windows, just a sliding door.'

'Any good against bombs?'

'No, against machine-guns. For them it's a sport.'

'Where are you all going?' I asked.

The sergeant told me his party was made up of boys who had been punished for some misdemeanour – usually absent without leave – and would be sent into the most desperate fighting. 'So I've been given an order: take these kids to Berlin, stick an anti-tank gun in their hands, and throw them against the Russian Army in front of Berlin. They've never seen the enemy. No training. Child murder, that's what it is.'

Having spoken so openly, we were friends.

Hours later, there was the sudden grinding of brakes. Everyone fell over everybody else. We opened the sliding door and saw fields all around us. There was the sound of sirens and firing, and the thud of bombs not so far away.

Some passengers got out, but most stayed inside for fear of losing their place which they were too tired to fight for again.

Later, we moved slowly towards the town of Hof. 'Everybody out!' The station was waist high, smoking, smouldering in the grey way things burn in waning daylight.

After a short consultation with the dusty official, still wearing his red cap, my subaltern friend took over: 'Fall in, all of you. You carry her trunk. *Kehrt. Marsch!*'

I trotted along behind them. We headed for the remains of an inn some distance away. A wing was still standing. They helped to clean the place up and found water and a shallow enamel bowl. They all washed and shaved – although there was not much beard to shave. A few tables were put together, and food produced out of their bags, their girl-friends' photos propped up in front of their tin plates. I contributed ham and precious lard. Nobody spoke, there was only the sound of munching.

Then four chairs were put together behind a table for me to lie on. They all spread out on the floor, alarm clocks set, and soon broke into loud snores.

By this time we had all learnt to sleep at once, in any position, at any time.

Tinny clocks clanged and we all got up to face the grey morning. They hardly complained beyond a grunt or two. The rails had been repaired during the night. Back we climbed into our *Viehwagon* and on we went for three days and three nights on a journey which used to take six to eight hours. At last we reached Berlin, Anhalter Bahnhof.

How the town had changed! Last time I had seen it, whole areas had been destroyed. But now it was all air and light and seemed to have shrunk, for the square miles of standing skeleton walls had been torn down, turned to great piles of rubble and ashes, as if spilled out of giant garbage cans. A 'lunar landscape' they called it. But there was no time to think of things like houses or towns. Only of people.

Out we piled from the train into the waiting crowds. Where would my friends go from here? We parted knowing we would never meet again. All around people were saying good-bye as they left from one desolate ruin to reach another.

Waves of discouragement swept over me, as I sat on my suitcase on the station platform, trying to plan what to do next.

'What are you doing there?'

Standing over me, grey-haired, still elegant in his Staff uniform, eyeglass cocked, stood Baron Uxküll: an acquaintance from diplomatic cocktails in another Berlin.

'I don't know myself.'

'Come, I will help you.'

His driver (he still had a driver!) took my suitcase and we drove off to the Hotel Adlon. Only one floor was left, encased in a sort of cummerbund of masonry. The imposing doorman was still in uniform, torn and sooty here and there. He seemed to have stood there, through all the bombardments, as if he would only go down with the final destruction of the hotel.

Firm and competent, Baron Uxküll said, 'While you wash and have breakfast, I will see that Paul is warned of your arrival in Ludwigslust, so that he can meet you. Then I will put you on the train.'

A trickle of water dripped into a cracked bowl. The soap was gritty, yellowish-grey. What could it be made of? There had been rumours of human fat. Unbelievable, but they were capable of anything! The mirror was splintered across. I tried to comb my hair, and seeing myself so pale and grey forced me to make a real effort. Back in the darkened hall watery tea was brought by the porter. He had warmed it up himself in a kettle. It was not really tea and not very warm, but he had tried to be helpful and even produced a rusk, which crumbled drily on the plate.

As I sat waiting, in my mind's eye I saw the place again in what now seemed another age, instead of six years ago; shining with gilded marble, tastelessly opulent, as when Albert Eltz and I had crossed over from the French Embassy dinner that night in July 1939, and watched the *Bonzen* of the ever-more powerful Party strut past us – Hitler, Goering, Goebbels and the rest. And those ranks of tall, identical S.S. soldiers – how many of them were already dead in the Russian snow?

From that time in 1939, the great hall of the Adlon had bustled with self-important officials caught up in the intoxication of running the millennial Empire. But, in spite of them, and of the ever-present Gestapo, it had remained a convenient meeting place, and it was here that Paul and Giorgio Cini had sat after the failure of the plot in July 1944 – only eight months before – and even that seemed years ago! It had deteriorated, even since then: the windows were boarded up, dust seeping through the chinks, as it headed inexorably towards obliteration.

The Hotel Bristol used to stand some way further down the street. Destroyed long before, the débris had only recently been sorted out: a routine procedure in the fight against waste. Combing through the charred mass, separating iron from wood, they came, quite by chance, on the safe which had been imbedded in the wall of the room Goerdeler (Mayor of Leipzig, and one of the heads of the conspiracy) had occupied. They prised it open, and found many papers only slightly singed. Among them were lists and lists of names!

There was no end to the roll of victims executed after the plot. It seemed a dream just to imagine living under a Government which would accept the ten commandments as the basis of law. Hitler had the death-throes of his victims filmed, so as to enjoy the sight. They said some officers had the courage to walk out.

Baron Uxküll soon returned. He had done all that was possible: he had telephoned Paul's regiment, and was now escorting me to the Lehrter Bahnhof to catch any train going north. The myth, still maintained by the Government, that only a handful of officers were involved in the plot, still seemed to enable those in high positions to move fairly freely, so long as they were not under suspicion.

A drive through empty streets, round mountains of rubble and ruins like grey stalactites, took us to the Lehrter Bahnhof. There was a tremendous bustle. The train I was supposed to take had come in riddled all down one side by machine-gunning aeroplanes. They were carrying the wounded out on stretchers; bleeding and still not even bandaged. Ambulances, sirens screaming, drew up at the station one after the other. Frightened faces and scurrying figures. Already pails of water were being sloshed through the worst compartments.

'You cannot take this train!' said Uxküll, horrified.

But I thought: 'Even the Allies will find it too expensive to machine-gun the same line twice running within a few hours, so it is probably safer than any other.'

We found a comparatively intact compartment at the very end. I climbed in and we started almost immediately. For the first time in the whole war, I was practically alone on a train.

Ludwigslust. Here, too, the station was like a collapsed card-house still smoking here and there – it seemed to have happened that night. Among the débris, slim, unconcerned, a yellow silk scarf printed with horses' heads adding a civilian touch to his tight-fitting cavalry uniform, stood Paul, as if from another planet. What a joyful sight. Everything forgotten, for a while we felt invulnerable again.

The officers were quartered in a rickety, chicken-pox-afflicted hotel in the centre of the battered little town. It looked as groggy as a defeated boxer in the last round, but by some chance it was still standing, although of flimsiest construction. Through the thin partitions, one could hear everything going on in all the rooms at the same time.

In the evenings, we sat in the smoky back room and played cards with some of Paul's fellow officers.

A sort of sifting had taken place. A word here, a comment there, and one knew at once whom to distrust. The difference between silence or disparaging reference to the 20th July was already enough.

The news flew like winging birds. The refugees brought it or it was handed on, jumping like electric sparks of shock from person to person. No censorship could stop it. We heard that there had been terrible fighting around Danzig, where the Army retreating from Russia was trying to defend the evacuation of civilians. The unusual weather added to the scale of suffering, for solid ice formed, then melted overnight and thousands of people and makeshift vehicles, fleeing from the Soviet Army across rivers and bays along the Baltic coast, fell into the water and were swallowed up.

Recently a ship (perhaps a holiday liner), transporting refugees, was sunk just outside Danzig by a Soviet submarine. They said over four thousand people, mostly women and children were drowned.

The Soviet Army advanced by rapid stages, for now Stettin was almost surrounded, and thereupon awarded the proud name of 'Fortress', which in no way meant that the town was defendable.

Allied planes flew nightly by the hundred over Ludwigslust, heading for Berlin. We were warned by the sirens, but the shelters were overfull, and unsafe too.

Then came the cataclysmic news that Paul was suddenly posted to Stettin, on the verge of encirclement. That meant he would fall into Soviet hands, if he was still alive when they took the besieged town.

After so many separations, each one tearing us apart as if for ever, this was the worst. 'I will never see him again!' – the words kept repeating in my mind.

The Commanding General of Stettin was called Hörnlein, a Nazi I heard to my horror. I begged Paul to be sure *not* to get on with him, so that he would not be tempted to appoint him to his staff.

Paul left at dawn, and I stood at the window watching him walk away down the street.

Shattered, cold and hungry, I slept the hours away. At night, Paul's officer colleagues put little parcels of sausage and bread on the mat in front of my bedroom door, knowing we had no food cards, for we were graded 'self-rationers' because of our farm – no matter that it was hundreds of miles away. This meant no butter, meat, egg or bread cards. There was not much left to eat, except the obnoxious 'grütze' – a sort of pig or chicken food. But people hissed if one left it on one's plate and I met with enough rude remarks anyway even though I wore no make-up, no nail polish, nothing 'irritating to the masses', as Goebbels called it – another of those Nazi turns-of-phrase.

Despair engulfed me like a stifling fog, paralysing all initiative. For the next few days I hardly had the strength to pull on my clothes, before falling back on to the bed again.

Then one day there was a knock on the door. I was lying fully-dressed, huddled under the eiderdown for warmth, when in walked three unknown young women. They were Thyra Mecklenburg, her sister and sister-in-law. Someone had telephoned from nowhere to tell them we were here, and would they please look after us. They took me back to live with them in the large Mecklenburg town Schloss on the out-skirts of Ludwigslust. What strong, thick walls, and, outside, such lovely woods to walk in!

In the unlikely event of Paul's return, we left messages everywhere: with the regiment, his friends, and at the frail, mangey hotel.

I decided to await the end of the war here, in the north, and the kindness and hospitality of my new friends made the waiting easier, in spite of the underlying desperate worry.

The cruel winter was losing its bite. We often lay on the roof in the warm spring sunshine, sheltered by great chimney-pots, and watched the Allied planes erupt in the sky overhead as they headed for their now almost daily visitations on Berlin.

I went for long walks with the old Grand Duke, whose Russian mother, Grand-Duchess Anastasia Michaelovna, had been a childhood friend of my grandmother Wiazemsky. He told me stories of Russia in bygone days, but seemed oblivious of the implications of the present.

The Grand Duchess was born Princess of Hanover, and spoke like all her family in starts and gulps. She had been brought up in Gmunden in Austria, and loved to talk of the hills there, which she had climbed so often. She still walked like a duck, both toes pointing out – one to the right, one to the left – in the fifth ballet position and old-fashioned climbing style.

At dawn, detachments of foreign recruits marched past the castle. In lusty, cheery voices, to czardas-like rhythms, they sang strangely exciting, unmilitary-sounding march-songs from their distant countries: Hungary, Roumania: '*Huszan ezred, Huszan ezred, jaj de sok van . . .*'

They had been recruited, like many others, to defend an alien cause, so very far from home! Would they ever find their way back again?

As the days dragged by, I gradually lost all hope for Paul. Ill with worry, I began to plan in my mind whom to turn to if Paul survived the siege of Stettin and became a Soviet prisoner. Perhaps in the first euphoria of Allied friendship something could be achieved – as Schulenburg had succeeded in doing for Radziwills? I well knew, however, how thin the hope of reaching Paul alive would be by then.

But one morning early, leaning out of my high window, I saw an astonishing sight: a horse was being calmly tethered to the post next to the sentry box at the great entrance portal just below me, as if it were a stable. A slim figure in officer's uniform leaned over to adjust the noose. He straightened, flung the stirrups over the saddle, and looked up.

For a second I could not believe my eyes, and thought I was dreaming. My voice failed me, and I could only croak: 'Paul?'

He smiled and waved his hand, as if it was the most natural thing in the world to be there, and he had just returned from morning exercise in time for breakfast.

I flew down the stairs, feeling suddenly dizzy with lightheadedness. All the Grand-Ducal family was already gathering on their way to the dining-room. Paul had to be introduced, and we then sat at opposite ends of the table.

They were glad for me, of course, but the fact that he was back from Stettin was just another incident in all the comings and goings within the general collapse of the Eastern Front. For them the world had not changed colour.

Paul, as I had feared, had got on marvellously well with his Nazi Commander in Stettin.

'You are the owner of Schloss Johannisberg? Let's see if we can find some bottles of your wine in this town!'

And so they drank together one night, and finally discussed the lost war quite openly.

'Why do you go on?' Paul asked him, too disengaged from himself to consider dissimulation.

'It is too late for me to turn back,' said General Hörnlein simply. 'I owe my career to the Führer. For you it is different. Why should you die here now? I will send you back. Anyway,' he added wryly, 'I can hardly allow myself the luxury of having a Prince Metternich here,' – referring to the wave of purges still in full swing since the 20th July the previous year.

We were happy to hear later that this decent man succeeded in fighting his way back to the West.

Paul was installed in the castle, too, and reported to his regiment every morning at dawn.

Easter came, and the Grand Duke gave me a lovely Russian Easter egg which had belonged to his mother, the Russian Imperial emblem in enamel on gold. 'To remember me by in happier days.'

The Schloss stood on the edge of the battered little town, protected on one side by great trees now bursting into leaf. On the other side there was an open space, the Schlossplatz, where miniature military reviews were probably held in days gone by. Now in their stead endless streams of bedraggled fugitives from Pomerania and East Prussia plodded their way across it: farm carts pulled by thin scraggy little horses, piled high with a jumble of belongings, old people and children driven by women, for the men were still at the Front, or dead, or missing.

It seemed unbelievable to the local inhabitants, as they watched the sad procession pass their doors, that in a few days or weeks, they might also have to walk out of their houses and into an unknown future. We tried to convince our hosts to start moving their more precious treasures towards the West while there was still time.

'But Berlin is obviously going to fall into the hands of the Allies!' they protested in whispers, for even now one dared not loudly doubt the 'Endsieg' (final Victory).

After all, ran their thinking, Hitler had only replaced the Kaiser after a series of governments, the country was now in deep trouble, and we must all stick together. They were so remote, so well-meaning. News of concentration camps had not filtered past the empty sentry boxes.

We took hope again, as columns of white cars from the Swedish Red Cross, nicknamed the 'Angels' column', or 'White mice', crossed the Schlossplatz.

They were at first only helping Scandinavians in concentration camps, but we consoled ourselves with the thought that 'Soon they will be able to help others too', for this was the first sign of an outstretched hand.

Annemari Bismarck, Otto's Swedish wife, arrived with the Red Cross one day, driving right up to the great door. She was like a daffodil, and her accent attractively sing-song. She subsided in a graceful court curtsey on meeting our hosts, and then spoke freely of the conditions in the camps.

The horror on the faces around her, and this sudden confrontation with reality, would, we hoped, at last induce some decision, for did they not feel on what tenterhooks we were, poised for flight?

But one morning we both awoke with violent fever and swollen throats. Called in haste, the doctor diagnosed diphtheria and gave us a most unpleasant vaccine. Paul struggled up to get sick leave from his regiment.

Within an hour he was back, brandishing quite another document: his discharge from the Army by order of the Führer.

From then on, in spite of raging fever and physical weakness, we never paid our illness a thought.

Intended as a disgrace, this order came as a godsend. It was the tail-end of Hitler's 'Princes' decree' against what Goebbels called 'Rekla-mesterben' ('advertisement dying'). It had not come in time to save Paul from Russia, but by returning him to civilian status, it freed him from becoming a prisoner of war. For the order to be valid, it had to be confirmed in his *Wehrkreis* (Military District Army Corps), which was at Eger, the next town to Königswart.

Time was running short, for the Soviets were approaching on one side and the Allies on the other, and we had to cross the whole of Germany from north to south to get home.

Fever forgotten, I leaped out of bed and packed our small bags in an instant. We dared not hug our hosts for fear of infecting them, but we waved most affectionate good-byes and thank-yous, calling last – alas unheeded – injunctions to leave.*

We were gone in a cloud of dust as the little carriage taking us to the station wheeled out of the wide square, leaving a startled and disconsolate group in the archway of Ludwigslust Castle.

Regardless of timetables, we climbed on to the first train passing through Ludwigslust to Berlin. As usual, there was the hum of incoming planes over our heads, but we hardly listened: we were heading for home.

In Berlin, a posse of Army Police combed the train for deserters. They could find nothing wrong with the order to get to Eger, but told us that civilians were not allowed to travel with the Army, and we must therefore separate. It was no use arguing, they would not listen to reason.

Last instruction from Paul: 'Wait for me in Prague: I'll follow on the night train.'

So I went on alone again, deeply anxious, as usual wedged in among crowds of passengers. Hour after hour passed as we hesitantly travelled south. Stopping. Starting again. Picking our way. Sirens howling in the distance.

Suddenly there was a hushed silence: we were moving into Dresden.

We all knew that Dresden had been terribly bombed a short time before. At a snail's pace, the overloaded train crept through the stricken city, whose plan with its streets and squares seemed to have disappeared as under an avalanche. Everyone crowded to the windows and stood in silence. Faces gleamed suddenly wet with unheeded tears, as they gazed and gazed. There was not a house left standing, nothing but shapeless mounds in a sea of rubble, with the occasional nightmarish twist of steel, jagged against the leaden sky: remains of what had once been a beautiful church spire.

Thousands of refugees from the East had been caught on their way

* Our warnings were in vain. When the Soviet Army moved in they plundered the castle, and the second son of the house, who had stayed to meet them, disappeared into a labour camp for three years.

through the town. Now there was not a living being to be seen. Everywhere piled suspicious-looking heaps: carts, horses, people? They said 200,000 died here in that one night!

It must have taken us about half an hour to chug slowly past this vision of apocalyptic destruction. Nothing seemed to have remained intact, except the elevated railway-line which carried us, and were not air raids intended to hamper communications? The war was over anyway: what use could this have been, since it had not even stopped the trains.

No laughter, no talk was to be heard as we moved on to Prague. A sort of desperate leaden exhaustion weighed on us all. At Prague I managed to get to the Hotel Alcron where we had always stayed – it seemed to be one of the last places left where one could still have a hot bath. Peeling off only my jacket and skirt, I stepped in fully dressed, not feeling able to bear anything I had on one minute longer. Then to bed, but I had reached such a pitch of fatigue that I was beyond sleep and continued to be conscious all night of the comfort of cool smooth sheets.

At the crack of dawn, I tried to phone Missie in Vienna, worrying whether she would manage to leave the city before the Soviets marched in. According to rumours, the air raids there sounded appalling, and although she was brave, the earlier Berlin raids had made her even more nervous of them.

I again wished she had left Vienna earlier. But although we all had no greater desire than for the war to end, there was a sort of strange attraction about being on the edge of extreme danger, which made the idea of being locked away in safety at such a time almost unbearable. This was perhaps what prisoners of war suffered from most.

'Calls to Vienna don't get through . . .' said the operator indifferently.

I gave up and ran to the station again. Trains were coming in from the north, but there was no sign of Paul. I tried again and again for hours. The railway line was soon going to be severed by the approaching Soviet Army. There was a last train still going through to Vienna. I tried to send a message to Missie, handing a note to a passenger.

At last, it was truly Paul! He pushed his way through the crowd, too tired to speak. But presently the hot bath and delusively peaceful aspect of the completely intact city, cheered us up again.

And yet in the restaurants, on the trams, in the streets, everybody was reading Russian primers. An ominous sign, for in the West they were reading English ones. But there was no sign of hostility, although Paul still wore his cavalry officer's uniform. They would look up and then look away again: their road to salvation was not ours, but that was all.

One dreaded to think of their rude awakening.

We headed straight for Plass, to give our people there last-minute instructions: they should try, we told them, to move to Königswart and protect their colleagues on the Sudeten side, whom they all knew well. We thought these would be in trouble, whereas our Czech employees, who from father to son had been with the family for over a hundred years, could be expected to intervene convincingly on their behalf.

How wrong we were!

Then we went on to Königswart and found that my parents had not left for Baden-Baden as we had hoped. Although they would have been safe there, they could not decide to go and risk losing touch with us.

Paul's first concern was to fetch his demobilisation papers from Eger, and become a civilian again.

We found the house occupied by a detachment of S.S., dragging with them incredible piles of luggage (or loot), their girls, numerous requisitioned cars and a few large pieces of artillery. Rather to our surprise, our rooms were still free, but they had set up an immense field gun on the lawn, in front of the house.

I tried to remonstrate with their commanding officer: 'The house is full of refugee women and children. It is impossible to defend, but it will most certainly be destroyed if you leave that gun there.'

All I got now for a reply was, 'Others have lost their houses. Your turn now!'

It was better for Paul not to argue with them, for they were in an ugly frame of mind. At night they broke into the chapel, stealing candles. During the day, they went around the villages summarily shooting anyone who had prepared a white flag. They behaved as if in enemy territory, swaggering around, armed to the teeth.

Patton's Army had not yet reached Eger. We could hear the thud of guns, and at night the horizon turned orange from the explosions. Paul and I would slip out to see if they were advancing. But no. They always appeared to be the same distance away. And yet we could see no sign of any opposition to the Americans.

Meanwhile, the Soviets were advancing rapidly, taking town after town. There was no resistance left to offer, nor had any ever been planned. We heard Carlsbad had become a scene of horror, with women raped and houses plundered. We had sent Mamma to stay with the Alberts in Marienbad, thinking a town would be safer, but now we considered fetching her back again.

Following Papa's advice, we deposited the last bottles of wine at the station warehouse in Marienbad. If things went well, we could always fetch them back later. If any still in use were left at the last moment, we would smash them.

Russian Easter came, much later that year than the Catholic one. The small church in Marienbad was like a gilded toy, icons lining the walls. I was indeed lucky to find a Russian church in the vicinity wherever I lived. The choir filled the church and was composed of wounded Wlassow* soldiers from a Marienbad hospital. Except for us, they were the only congregation.

It seemed unbelievable, seeing them there in disciplined neatness, their heads bowed reverently, that at the same time their compatriots were advancing on a wave of rape and murder in addition to the destruction inevitable in any war.

They seemed so young, and were often terribly wounded, with one or more limbs amputated, and supported for the most part by crutches. They stood and sang like angels, even the very complicated Easter hymns. After thirty years of anti-religious communism, they still knew the services perfectly.

The priest was old and bearded, thin and shaky, veiled in a cloud of incense.

Confession: It was a relief to say it out loud just once: 'I am absolutely terrified of what awaits us! Despair is a sin, but I have no confidence in the thought that all may be for the best. I am frightened all the time, and it has got worse every day since the 20th July . . . Especially for others, for those I love and for all around us . . .'

He did not contradict, just patted me on the head as I knelt and said: 'We will pray together . . .'

At every moment we had to live with and accept the thought: 'Now we must be ready to die.' Or perhaps even much worse than death, helpless acceptance of horrors inflicted on those dearest to us. If we got through this, we felt each year of life would be a gift to be appreciated anew.

---

* Wlassow was the Soviet Army General who agreed to build up a division of Soviet prisoners, if they were under his command and not used against Russia. Perhaps he thought to save them from death by hunger in the terrible camps.

But the sonorous roll of orthodox prayers re-charged me with energy and hope.

We were all conscious of a lull as the Americans approached from one direction, the Soviets from the other. There seemed to be no escape for us. Königswart was caught between these armies, and we could only pray the Americans reached us first while wishing they were not so desperately slow!

Outside our circle of friends, we felt we could trust no one. The only one of our employees Paul spoke to openly was Labonte. Taking all precautions against being overheard, even by Kurt, we listened at night to the foreign news.

At last, at last, Hitler's death was announced on the 30th April.

We had reached the 'Glorreicher Untergang', and how inglorious it was: the great leader and his mistress swallowing pills or shooting themselves, their corpses then deluged with petrol to escape the consequences of all these endless wilful crimes.

Then Goebbels had murdered all his defenceless children and followed Hitler's cowardly example. Having set the world on fire they now stepped out of it leaving Germany on its back, under a hail of destruction.

Meanwhile the Soviet Army was pounding Berlin as with an iron fist. We heard that the desperate inhabitants, hunted like rats, sought refuge in the ruins or in the Underground stations. But then bombs burst the water-mains, flooding the tunnels and thousands perished. The raping and murdering had reached an apocalyptic scale.

This was incomprehensible to my parents. After all, the Russian Armies had reached Paris in 1815, and camped on the Champs Elysées, while all the inhabitants would wander around among them, open-mouthed. There may have been individual abuses, but never had there been any question of such behaviour in previous campaigns, on such a scale, and with such impunity.

We were also desperately worried about the fate of Vienna, which had fallen into Soviet hands on the 13th April. So many friends of ours must have been caught in the town, and above all Missie. We were frantic to know what was happening there.

The Americans crossed the Rhine at Remagen on the 7th March, which meant that Johannisberg was in a pocket, and the people there better off than if the main drive had come over Mainz as expected. Once the Americans had broken through, conditions would not be so bad for the population, so Paul's advice to Labonte to resist evacuation from Johannisberg had been justified.

We were deeply concerned about Königswart's unique collections in the museum, and what could be saved, what put away in case the storm blew over. Liquidating the past was indeed a thankless task. As custodians we felt assailed by a paralysing feeling of inadequacy, well aware that every decision would probably be the wrong one. As an afterthought, we hid our guest book, which was generations old and carried too many compromising names, such as the plot participants, of whom no one would want to be reminded.

Now that our way of life was jeopardised, we realised what a source of inner strength it had been to maintain it, whatever the circumstances, trying to preserve, against all the pressures of our times, what was worth preserving, and ensure a continuity in a cultural tradition.

A few weeks earlier, one of the refugee women, whose house and small shop in Hamburg had been destroyed, had confided her troubles to me. She was the mother of two small children, and had had no news from her soldier husband in Russia for many months. Her fifteen-year-old daughter had been sent to a children's camp in East Prussia. 'She is happy there, and there is no bombing, but I have not heard from her for some time . . . It is a long journey, and perhaps they would not allow her to leave. I will write and ask . . .'

I had tried again to persuade her to drop everything and go and fetch her child. I could not tell her: 'The war is lost and time is running short . . .' She was incapable of decision, used to meek obedience to orders, paralysed when 'order' collapsed.

Now it was too late. She was desperate with anxiety . . . Why had she not listened to me then?

Doubting it myself, I tried to console her: 'Perhaps the children's camp would have been evacuated before the advancing Soviet Army . . .'

Two little Ukrainian girls trudged in one morning. Hearing I was Russian, they had walked a long way to find me. They were very young, and had been swept back by the German Army – set to work as they went. They came from the same village: plump and round-faced, blue eyes, flaxen pigtails, they gazed at me trustingly.

'What can I do for you?' I asked.

'We only wanted to talk,' they said simply.

I piled food into their hands and gave them money, adding: '. . . We too may be leaving soon.' They looked around the lovely room, unbelieving.

I could not keep them while the local authorities still functioned and the house was occupied by the S.S.

(Afterwards I bitterly regretted not to have done more. Had I found some way of hiding them, perhaps they could have got out with us, for I dared not think what may have happened when their countrymen caught up with them.

Working for the Red Cross in later years, the memory of those two poor girls spurred me on to help refugees and defenceless fugitives wherever possible.)

The S.S. left without warning one night, moving rapidly south. We awoke in the morning to find them gone. They had taken the huge field-gun with them and our strongest farm-horses to pull it.

An expectant silence descended on Königswart. But not for long. Suddenly there was a shattering roar. Kurt dashed in, shaken out of his usual calm. 'It's the gun,' he cried. 'The S.S. are firing on us!'

The Russian prisoners of war who were working on the farm, and the French too, ran panic-stricken towards the park, where there was a cave under the hill, used for storing ice in bygone days.

The Schloss had no cellar, so we went downstairs and stood under the arches of the vaulted corridor, remembering that when houses collapse, archways tend to crash last.

Another smashing thud, this time to the left. Kurt, a veteran of the 1914 war, said reassuringly, 'Just one more: they only had three shells left!'

In Paul's copybook for the 'Uffz.' examination, it had clearly stated: 'One shot to the right, one shot to the left, and the last a bulls eye,' which was what we were now.

Here it came, a whizzing hiss. But they were just a little too high, and only the main chimney was carried away like a comet, bricks hailing down in its wake.

Shortly after, one of our Frenchmen galloped back with the horses, full of excitement at having recaptured them. 'I couldn't let them have my beasts.'

Towards evening a bedraggled detachment of the Luftwaffe marched up the avenue. With great politeness, they asked for shelter, and took the place of the S.S. up at the farm and in the house. But what a difference!

After seeing that their men were all right, the officers cleaned up as best they could and came over to visit us. They were all highly decorated Air aces, wearing the Ritterkreuz and more, what one called 'Spinach with cutlery', including the oak leaves and crossed swords, the highest award of all. They were on foot, without any fuel for their aircraft 'for weeks' they told us. They were now supposed to defend the rear of the retreating S.S.

We shared whatever we had to eat with them, also Napoleon brandy, and ended by having a cheerful evening. They would be on their way next day, as the Americans were on the move at last!

'Auf Wiedersehen, we'll meet again at the Chicago Fair,' waved Captain Count Schweinitz as they left, for they had joked about what they would do when the war was over, and the only profession they were trained for was acrobatic flying.

They left us two small tractors hidden in the hay of the big barn, in case we had to leave in a hurry, as the S.S. had stolen the Spanish Embassy car we had hidden all these years.

A freight-car full of new-born babies, identified only by numbers round their wrists, closely packed in tiny cots, arrived at Marienbad station. The accompanying coach, which must have contained the people looking after them, was either inadvertently hooked on to another train, or bombed. No one would ever know. The babies were transferred to one of the military hospitals, but their names were never discovered, and many died before help could reach them. Poor, poor parents!

We ran around, giving last directions.

An ominous silence settled over the countryside, as if all waited with baited breath.

Exhausted, we went to bed at last.

6

At sunrise, there was a knock on our bedroom door. It was Kurt. 'The Americans are in the park!' he said as if he were announcing a guest. We leapt out of bed and rushed out, throwing on some clothes.

'Which side of the house?' Paul called out.

'In the courtyard, now!'

We ran into the corridor and peeped through the closed shutter of the first window in the wing we lived in.

It was a balmy scented spring morning, and the first rays of the sun were drying the dew. The world looked washed and shining. With loving care, the courtyard had been lined with particularly hardy and vigorous rhododendrons, leaving a passage behind them all around the house. We were exactly in the corner, where the paths met at an angle.

Just below us, to the right, crouching one behind the other, a long line of American soldiers, armed to the teeth, guns cocked, disguised as bushes, leaves stuck into netting over their helmets, were creeping with bouncing rhythmic tread down the wing path.

We had warned the refugees installed in the ground floor rooms not to open a window or a door until all was over, but curiosity was too much for them.

A large double door, just opposite our window, led into the museum wing. Inch by inch it now opened slowly, and through the widening crack peered children piling one behind the other: the smaller thumb-sucking toddlers below, and craning over their heads – curly hair, blue eyes, smudgy pinafores, leather knickers (leder hosen), pigtails. Through the pressure, the door opened wider and wider.

As the stalking soldiers, step by elastic step, reached the corner and wheeled round it with practised jerk, there, crammed in a doorway at the other end of the façade, at least twenty wide-eyed children faced them. What an anti-climax!

There was loud hammering on our great front door. Kurt opened it politely while we waited at the top of the stairs. In they marched, still disguised as vegetation, led by an officer. They brushed Kurt aside, and us too.

Within seconds, the house was no longer ours.

We walked along beside them, answering calmly when questions were put to us, opening doors and explaining the topography.

Soon we were on quite friendly terms and discussed possible quarters. They took the remaining upstairs guest rooms, so recently evacuated by our Luftwaffe friends, leaving us ours, and even consenting to have the latrines dug behind the tennis court – out of sight and smell.

Their tone was very decent and polite. They were also as busy as bees and extremely surprised at the relief shown by all the inhabitants at their presence. They still seemed to think of the Soviets as their dear Allies and friends and could not comprehend the waves of terror caused by the news of rape and murder in Carlsbad and elsewhere. Nor would they believe the stories until they were later confronted by the facts.

As the structure of the Nazi state collapsed around us, we resumed our role of mediator between all those around us and the new authorities.

The Americans were surprised at our friendly relations with both the French and Russian prisoners working on the farm.

'Slave labour you've been having around here!'

'They have asked me to be their spokesman,' I countered coolly.

Since none of the Americans spoke any other language they had no choice but to accept this. The French and the Russians surrounded me anxiously and trustfully. I told the Russians they must obey American orders implicitly, and I would convey all their requests to the commanding officer. (We feared the Soviet prisoners might go on a rampage if not restrained.) The French had only one wish, and that was to leave for home at once and not via Russia. To their consternation they now heard that there was no question of their doing so. There were no orders concerning them, nor any transport. They stood around in worried little groups.

I asked for permission to go to Marienbad and fetch Mamma back. Papa had been walking the ten kilometres there every other day. A pass was promptly made out. It was our first glimpse of the magical slip of paper headed: 'To Whom It May Concern', from now on the 'Open Sesame' on which our lives would depend.

In the afternoon the coachman in his frayed livery drove up to collect me. He had taken the larger open carriage, and we wheeled off in comparative state.

The entire American Army present around the house and grounds had produced cameras, and now lined up on both sides of the courtyard to photograph this sortie. They lay on the ground, knelt, stood on the edge of the fountain balancing precariously, busily clicking:

'It's like Hollywood!' they exclaimed.

Taking this rather shabby vehicle for granted, we had never considered it a luxury. My Scottie had come along for company, warm and cuddly, ears twitching with excitement.

It was the first moment of relaxation, a pause in which to sort things out. Perhaps the worst was over with the Americans here and the Soviet Army halted, even though they were so close. We had saved the house and no one had been hurt. 'V.E. Day' the Americans called it. Like after a grievous illness, I felt slightly stunned and a bit light-headed.

But it was also the moment when women have to take over, and that was so bad for the men. Any German was suspect for the Allies: all the struggles with the occupying bureaucracy, the smoothing of difficulties, could only be done by the women. The men had to step back, upsetting an essential balance of rôles.

Since the 20th July all our friends were caught or on the run. It would have been our turn soon. We had been surrounded by enemies wherever we turned.

In the open carriage, behind the coachman's back, from sorrow and relief, and perhaps physical weakness too, a wave of defeat rolled over me. It was all just a little more than one could handle.

Spring had come. Feathery larches powdered the woods with a green haze, sticky chestnut buds burst into miniature green fingers gloved in down, while the birds bounced chirping from twig to twig. The dreadful last war winter was shaken off for good, and I recovered as the creaking carriage climbed in and out of the deep ruts it had left like scars in the road.

We ran over springy cushions of damp moss and pine needles, to emerge from the woods between fields turning green under clumps of clotted dry grass, and at a clip, cantered down into Marienbad.

The town was seething with American soldiers, and they stared open-mouthed, dropping whatever they were doing, as we passed them on our way to Headquarters. We did not have to ask, for gay posters as for a village feast clearly pointed the way. The Commanding Officer was a Captain Mullin. Politely and firmly, I asked to see him, and then waited – uneasily – until he could receive me.

It was the same office in which I had confronted that terrible Kreisleiter a year before, when the two Luftwaffe airmen were killed as their plane crashed on to our hill.

Just a few days before, he had hanged himself in our woods . . .

The door opened. 'Captain Mullin will receive you.'

He seemed to be a nice, friendly young man.

'You are Russian? Do you by any chance know Dolly Obolensky?'

She and I had indeed been great friends when we were twelve years old, but then the ocean and a war came between us. Half-forgotten, it was as if she now reached out a hand to help me.

The official interview turned into a long and friendly talk on a variety of subjects: the 'whys' and 'wherefores' of course, so puzzling to any American, and the specific problems of this disputed region. Our situation too. He gave me a free pass to come and go between Königswart and Marienbad. Not for Paul. No man of military age was allowed to move. They called it: 'Frozen where they stand.'

'For how long?'

He then betrayed a secret: he was meeting a Soviet Russian delegation near Marienbad that same afternoon to discuss the final boundary line between their zones.

'How close to us are they now?'

'Ten kilometres.'

I reeled with shock.

'Come again to-morrow,' he told me, 'and I will tell you everything I know quite frankly. I have Russian émigré friends, so I know what this means to you. I am not a soldier by profession. I am a lawyer. I've done so many things off my own bat – just as well be hanged for an ox as for a sheep.'

I went to pick up Mamma at her hotel. She was very talkative and excited, while I remained silent and preoccupied. Indomitably courageous, although deeply concerned for us all, she had become materially detached after all the catastrophes she had met with.

Königswart lay spread out on its frame of lawns and trees, and paddocks full of grazing cattle, now an incongruous setting for the occupying American Army.

'Off Limits' signs were pasted everywhere. Sentries had been posted at all the corners. They squatted on their upturned helmets, as if they were chamber-pots, surrounded by children sucking sweets or chewing gum. Other soldiers carried piles of incredibly white bread, smells of cooking wafting in their wake. The officers wore startlingly crisp freshly ironed 'pink' shirts and moss-green uniforms: Patton's Army was in fine shape after crossing Europe. If only they had come a little faster against such weak opposition, and taken Berlin and Prague! They must have been held back by some incomprehensible agreement. It seemed such a let-down.

And now came these ominous hints from Captain Mullin!

I only told Paul, so as not to make everybody nervous, for everyone in Königswart had begun to smile and live again.

Overnight we had become a tourist centre, and found ourselves besieged by officers and soldiers asking to be taken round the house and museum.

We had no time to think or sit down. Irene Albert, who had also moved to Marienbad with her mother, returned to visit us, happy to be among those she called 'our boys'. Her loyalties were obviously clear, and she now proposed to participate in their 'V.E. Day' festivities. They kindly invited us, too, but Paul declined politely, sending them some champagne instead.

I went down to warn all the refugee mothers to lock their doors as the soldiers were going to drink and some might get out of hand.

After our dinner American officers kept dropping in by twos and threes. They just wanted to talk, and try to understand. Why this bitter fighting, then such a welcome? Why this, why that? How could the population have remained in ignorance of the concentration camps? Questions, questions, questions.

Much later in the evening, after they had left us, yells and shrieks rang up the stairs, followed by the sound of running steps.

Kurt rushed in. 'They have broken into the women's quarters!' he exclaimed.

I dashed downstairs. There was a small communicating door, which only we could use. I unlocked it and ran towards the noise. Another door at the end of the corridor stood slightly ajar. In the room a whimpering woman was pressed against the wall by a towering U.S. soldier in an unequivocal state of undress, purple with drink. Howling children and crying women filled the room. Frightened, but even more angry, I grabbed him by the shoulder and pulled, shouting, 'How dare you come in here! Get out at once.'

Bleary-eyed, he lurched around. 'O.K. Ma'am, I'm goin' . . . I meant no harm. I'm goin' . . .' And he did.

We were all very surprised at this sudden surrender. It was helpful to know that, even when completely sozzled, an American still reacts to the tone of a woman's sharp orders. No other nation would, I fear.

'Who opened the door?' I asked.

It was, of course, the same woman who had got into trouble.

Next day I returned to Marienbad. Captain Mullin told me that the Russians were taking over in three days. The Czechs would man the frontiers.

Stunned, I said: 'And you?'

'We move out. My advice to you is to get going while the going's good. And not in that buggy. Too conspicuous by far. I'll give you passes for everyone except your husband. I don't need to know he is there, but he's got to go. The Russians are going to treat as criminals all officers of the North Army for the siege of Leningrad, and of the 6th for Stalingrad. His discharge papers, however valid for us, probably won't mean a thing to them.'

Was there no alternative? Captain Mullin thought again and came up with another suggestion. 'I could get him across the frontier to Nürnberg in uniform. They are going to hold trials against war criminals there. He'll be arrested but he'll easily prove he is innocent. I can guarantee him safe conduct across the frontier.'

While I was considering these proposals I asked him if he would allow the 'Wlassow' soldiers to leave too.

'How do I identify them?'

'I'll send you the priest. He knows them.'

He also intended to move the wounded in Marienbad military hospitals out with him, especially the officers, who would be in greatest danger.

Mullin kept all his promises, but he could not know that the 'Wlassow' soldiers would be rounded up later anyway and returned to the Soviets via Lienz, with thousands of others, as well as the Cossack divisions, to be indiscriminately butchered; nor that soon all returning Soviet prisoners of war would meet with the same treatment as German officers and condemned to five, ten or twenty and more years hard labour.

My return met with consternation in Königswart. Pale and haggard, Papa helped me by saying: 'There can be two opinions about everything, but now there is no time to argue. So just tell me where I can help, and I will do it.'

Paul, marvellous in a crisis, gave short, clear orders. He was not certain yet whether he should accompany us or take up Mullin's second 'safer' alternative, which would ensure him not falling into Soviet hands.

The French heard we were preparing to leave, and came to say they would like to accompany us, as it was too dangerous to go alone. Several Frenchmen on their way home had already been robbed and murdered by groups of marauders returning East.

I went down to talk to the Tauberts and organize their departure, but met with raging hysterics. They showed me cyanide pills, probably procured by their deplorable chemist son-in-law, and announced that they were preparing to take them. I lost my head completely and tore upstairs to fetch Paul, who flew into a towering rage, as only happened a few times in his life. I heard him shouting, 'If I can leave, *you* can! I have no time to bury you now. You will pack and leave to-morrow with horse and cart at seven. I shan't speak to you again until we all meet at Johannisberg.'

Like lambs, they did as they were told. And never was this untimely melodrama referred to again.

There were only a few hours left before we had to leave and there was still much to be done. Last instructions had to be given. The group of seven Frenchmen would take the two strongest farm horses, leaving all the others at the disposal of our employees, and drive a cart out to a point in the woods where we would join them shortly after seven in the morning, the curfew prohibiting an earlier start. We added bread and a hunk of lard, plenty of fodder for the horses, and as a last touch, four or five remaining bottles of Napoleon brandy thrust into a pail. After various sums had been given to everybody, we took the remaining money from the safe – a sum of a few thousand marks. How much luggage could we still carry? I asked Paul. 'One suitcase each,' he replied firmly. I sadly abandoned all thought of the second one I had packed with a few particularly lovely things, but there was no time to extract them again.

Paul and Papa pocketed pistols. I slipped all my jewels into a small leather shoe-bag, and tied them under my khaki blouse, taken from a shelf of things used for safaris long ago. Big-game hunting in Africa! How remote all that seemed just now. This time we were the prey.

What was one to wear? A grey flannel skirt and Paul's top boots re-made to my size the year before, and a dark blue wool trouser suit out of the Red Cross stores piled in the ballroom. That might be useful at night, I thought.

All my evening dresses were left without regret, for when would I ever need them again? But I felt a pang as I glanced at my neatly stacked books, all special favourites. As he lay dying, the Russian poet Pushkin, I remembered, had gestured towards his library and murmured: 'Good-bye my friends . . .' I took only the manuscript diaries of the Chancellor's small daughter Léontine which I was reading, and an English novel to while away the long hours ahead of us.

How do you choose what to save from a house like Königswart, as full of rare and valuable treasures as many a museum? Especially if you are on foot! And with no certainty of getting safely across the frontier! How well I understood my parents' dilemma when they were forced to flee from Russia. Food came first, then clothing, and last of all beautiful things, for these mean nothing in a chaotic world, to be regretted later in reverse order.

The Museum itself in the northern wing was intact. Perhaps if we left it that way, it would be respected? I hesitated over the beautiful walking sticks with jewelled knobs. They had belonged to Napoleon, to the Duke of Reichstadt – the ill-fated 'Aiglon', to Alexandre Dumas, to Metternich.

'Only what we can carry,' said Paul. So we left the collection of coins, and the wonderful cameos (it seemed barbarous to remove one or two), and took Marie Antoinette's ring, and the Chancellor's watch. Paul slipped an 18th-century black-enamelled ring on to my finger. Perhaps the inscription in diamonds 'Je te bénis' would bring us luck?

With an inward prayer that the two magnificent libraries in the house would not be ransacked and destroyed, I pushed the pearl of the collection, Arioste's *Orlando furioso,* into my satchel. It was illustrated with hand-painted miniatures. Inside the cover there was a letter in the Chancellor's easy, flowing hand. He described the vicissitudes this precious volume had been through during the Napoleonic wars, when it had been transported from burning Koblenz on the Rhine to Mainz, and then carried with other valuables in open carts under gunfire, until it finally reached Königswart. Now if we were lucky, it would complete the circle and return to the Rhine again – sewn in old oilcloth, hidden under the straw on our cart.

It was at least consoling to feel that Metternich would have understood our troubles, for they were the same evils he had fought against himself.

Towards evening several American Generals came to visit us. They were comparatively young, and not unlike their German adversaries: polite, specialists in their profession, and yet oddly naïve too.

We did not have much time to destroy the illusions they had picked up about 'Uncle Joe' Stalin, although the news already coming in from behind the Soviet advance was enough to make them think again. The Czech Red Guards (who could they be?) had issued a proclamation entitled 'Death to all Germans' on the 5th May, just a few days before, after having remained as quiet as mice until then.

We were well aware how easily anything we said to these Americans could be misinterpreted. And yet it was terribly important to get them to realise what an abyss of human suffering was opening under their innocent feet without appearing to overstate our case or suffer from undue prejudice. Our conversation, therefore, had to be pleasant, easy, seemingly unconcerned, while in fact we were seething with the need to impart the truth. On top of all this we had our last-minute responsibilities, and all the anxieties connected with our imminent departure.

For these officers, as for their soldiers, we were a tourist attraction at the end of a long trip, whereas for us it might well be the beginning of the end. We were at cross purposes.

Nevertheless, as we now spent precious hours taking them through the house, we achieved certain useful ends. The refugee women and children who still thronged the ground floor would be evacuated at once to what remained of their home towns in Western Germany. As to Königswart, the entire place would be treated as a Museum, marked 'Off Limits', and (bypassing the Czechs) kept in American hands for as long as possible. Perhaps even the Soviets would respect the place when they came, although we had grave doubts about this.

Night had fallen and Paul was still undecided which of the two alternative courses he should follow. In case he chose the closed van to Nürnberg he decided to dig out his uniform, although he loathed the idea of putting it on once more.

The lights had been fused for days. Armed with a candle and matches, we went through the house to the cupboard where he had hidden it far away at the other end of the house. A small concealed door opened into Kurt's realm. On shelves reaching high up to the ceiling, in padded cupboards lining the whole length of the dining-room on the inside, the silver had been kept for many generations. The Gala 'décors', never used in recent years – huge mirrors surrounded by bronze gates and figures from the 'Thomire' banquet service, presented to the Chancellor by the city of Paris in 1815 – stood on tables along the wall.

We had pushed Paul's Cavalry-Lieutenant's uniform on to the highest shelf. As we now tugged and pulled in the wavering candlelight, it fell out in a pile, the belt with its heavy buckle and attached dagger crashing on to one of the great bronze-framed mirrors, which broke into a thousand pieces, like a star exploding. The candle went out.

Fate had made the decision for us. Only bad luck could come of it. We fumbled for the matches. Back went the uniform, up as high as we could reach. No time to clear the jagged pieces of glass away, but at least we had the answer to the dilemma. Now Paul was coming with us!

At each step we took back through the sleeping house, we felt, 'This is the last time. Dark friendly house with its delicious smells, its secrets unfolding like a flower, its intimacy and enriching warmth . . . We will never come back again!'

We felt drained, exhausted, and yet there was still so much to do, so much to think of. First of all, we had to help our people to leave too.

Holding a lighted candle over my typewriter, Paul then dictated instructions for each in turn: for Dobner, the head forester, for Pfreimer the chauffeur, for the Tauberts and for the administrator Hübner, for . . . there were so many. We then added a personal recommendation to help them on their way, inspired by the slips of paper given me to go up and down to Marienbad past all check points. We typed them carefully on the same copybook paper the U.S. Army used.

'TO WHOM IT MAY CONCERN

So and so . . . has been in my employ for . . . years. I herewith vouch for him and his family, and request them to be allowed to proceed on their way from Königswart to my property Johannisberg on the Rhine.

(Signed)   Prince Metternich.'

And here we carefully pressed an imprint of the big seal of the Congress of Vienna, so often used by the Chancellor.

In spite of the sadness of it all, it made us laugh, for we thought he would have appreciated the use we had found for it.

At last we got to bed. There were only a few hours left for sleep, but I tossed restlessly, tormented by the horror of Paul or Papa falling into Soviet hands. Were we doing the right thing? It was such a responsibility to abandon the house and the people. But they would not be in such danger, whereas Paul and Papa . . . I could not forget the assassinations after the Russian Revolution right up to the present day.

In those days in Russia they had however clearly seen that by defending allegiances and values that they and generations before them treasured more than life, they had justified their own 'raison d'être'.

Mamma felt all this strongly, too, all the more so because it was the second time. But the situation was not the same. We were now just pebbles, pushed here and there by the tide. If we were caught, it would only be due to our love for the house; to things, not to principles. We owed no allegiance to the forces crashing over our heads.

At last I drowsed off fitfully, and dreamt of an impenetrable tangle around us. We would never get across the frontier! And then, as we searched for a place to slip through, a wide opening appeared in the thick hedge, cut away neatly, the brambles stacked like wheat after a harvest, and a long sandy golden road stretched ahead, lined with lances pointing upwards, with no one behind the lances.

So I awoke refreshed and ready to face whatever awaited us, and went to wake Mamma and get everybody started.

Papa had spent the night on guard, as, unknown to us, an order to register all adult males had just been issued and he feared they might come for Paul. He had not wanted to trouble us with the news before morning.

Mamma's room was flooded in early morning sunshine, streaming in from the open balcony window.

It was the best guest-room, the one I had lived in the first time I came to Königswart with Missie and Paul. Pink cotton curtains with a pattern of white bows, pink armchairs and sofa, darker shade of pink carpet stained by misbehaving dogs. Big white-tiled stove, brass bed.

'Look, a picture has fallen!'

One of the portraits of early 19th-century British statesmen had crashed to the floor, glass splinters scattered over the floor.

Lisette had told me a picture always fell when someone died in the family, even when this occurred in a far-distant country. A manifestation of sympathy. I had had them re-hung, room by room. New cords, new rings on the pictures. The thin iron bar, painted white, which ran along the cornice from which all the pictures hung, was unbreakable. At that time, with Paul in Russia and Missie in Berlin, I wanted no premonitory signs.

But the new cord for this picture had slipped through the shining new ring, its double knot undone. My heart gave a jolt. But perhaps it was the old house mourning the departure of the family after hundreds of years.

Mamma, still in bed, said, 'You must go without me. I have thought it over, and am staying to save the house.'

I ran back to Paul. 'Mamma does not want to leave.'

Paul sat down on the edge of the bed, taking off the satchel he had slung over his shoulder. 'Then I don't go either. I will not leave my mother-in-law behind alone for the sake of any house.'

Pale, icy with despair, I tried to convince her, understanding her motives too for she meant so well. But there was no choice. 'Mamma, you *must* be ready in half an hour. No house is worth Paul and Papa being strung up over the front door, and they will not leave without you . . .'

Then she began to dress and I went to collect a few last things.

Before leaving our room, we made our bed neatly, so as not to be the first to disrupt Königswart.

Let others break it up. Not us.

7

We left through the little door in the left corner of the courtyard. The clock struck seven – signalling the end of the curfew – as we locked it behind us. I kept the key for a long time, until it lost all significance and became just another key.

We walked out separately, heading for the park, and arranged to meet near the statue of Diana-Huntress. When I got there, Paul was waiting on the path half hidden by the lilac thicket. We gave a last glance towards the house shimmering white beyond the drooping willow branches over our heads.

We kept to the left of the lake framed by a thin line of misty blue: irises were flowering early this summer. My mother-in-law's summer house on the island – our refuge from importunate tourists – stood untouched and welcoming, ducks swimming peacefully near the shore. Now came the steep climb to the ridge, towards the open-woodwork St. Anthony Chapel, and its naïve and touching 'ex-voto' paintings, hanging slightly askew over the entrance, depicting a child saved from drowning or fire, a rider from a severe fall, a cart from collision, a farmer from a thunderbolt: natural catastrophes, not man-made ones. What should *we* put if we returned here one day?

The path led downhill again towards the lake we always swam in, for a brook ran through it, keeping the water crystal clear.

As we reached the sandy road, Papa and Mamma joined us. They had taken another way so as not to attract attention. A little further on, under a spreading tree, our Frenchmen awaited us, clustered around the cart. They peered anxiously in our direction. We had not been sure of finding them at the rendezvous, for whom could one trust nowadays? But there they were, our allies in distress, a small, stocky and reassuring group. They had hoisted a French flag above the cart: red, white and blue rags roughly tacked together. All was ready.

245

They touched their caps, unsmiling; respectfully aware of what this must mean to us.

'Bonjour, Monsieur le Prince. Bonjour, Madame la Princesse' (indicating nothing had changed in our relationship).

'Bonjour Louis. Bonjour René . . .'

Off we went. We all walked at first, partly to relieve the tension. In silence. The morning was lovely, crisply cool, the bright sun rapidly drying the fields and bushes, steaming with dew. As we trudged along, I suddenly realised all my fear had died down, as if it had been an attack of fever. Now that the dreaded moment of fright was on us, it had turned to adventure. At least we were no longer cornered, initiative was in our hands once more, and above all we were together.

I remembered that our flight from the Crimea had also meant the choice between living in a free world or under communist oppression. At times like these possessions lose all value. The pain of leaving and the finality of defeat at having to do so would return later.

For Paul it would all be so much worse, although the element of fear simply did not exist for him. I knew that he would not refer to Königswart again for a long time.

For the moment I felt numbed, my mind concentrating on trivial things: a hare sitting in the field, gathered for instant flight, lilies of the valley flowering near the brook, anemones spreading like snow in the woods we were entering.

Nobody in sight anywhere. We were to keep to our own forests for as long as possible. Paul knew every path in them since the days when he had camped in the woods with his people during the Sudeten-Czech troubles of 1938.

The cart creaked slowly up-hill, the horses pulling bravely. As the road dipped downwards again, René hastily loosened the iron brake, shaped like a flattened question mark, and the good horses even lumbered into a semblance of a trot. He talked to them in the 'Egerland' dialect. In France, he explained, they used other words. I had thought they would react to the tone of voice, but no:

'It is the language itself they understand,' he said. 'Mes bêtes,' he added lovingly.

Wood, ready for sale, was stacked in neatly numbered piles at the side of the road. Dobner would have murmured: 'The larch logs must be disposed of first, before their favourite beetle gets at them.'

Suddenly, Sherry the Scottie gave a violent tug at his leash and we all started. There was a rustle and cracking of twigs under galloping feet, and deer bounded away through the trees. False alarm. We breathed again.

Towards midday, we approached the frontier. As a child, Paul would stand with one foot on each side, proudly crowing:

'I am in two countries at once!' (Czechoslovakia and Germany.) He now went on ahead to reconnoitre with Louis at his side. We stood and waited for his signal, the great horses' honey-coloured tails swishing off the flies.

No guards yet. All was well. We crossed into Bavaria without mishap. (We were soon to hear that a few hours later armed Czech soldiers marched up to block off all the roads and lined the frontier within rifle range of each other.)

Louis had climbed a small hill, and stood shading his eyes as he gazed towards the horizon. His friends chaffed him: 'Do you see Beziers Cathedral?' It was his home town, far in the south of distant France.

They were relaxed and easy now. The worst seemed to be over, but we had six hundred kilometres to go before we reached Johannisberg.

Paul now planned our route with the help of a pre-war motoring atlas, proudly titled 'Europe Touring'. It seemed wiser to avoid any towns, as they would be picketed with U.S. check-points.

Captain Mullin had told me that either Thuringia or Franconia would still be handed over to the Russians in exchange for Soviet permission for the Allies to enter Berlin. (As if they could not have got there on their own!) Of course there would be no previous warning to the inhabitants. And this in spite of the slaughter of the civilian population which had taken place in East Prussia and Silesia, where women and little girls were raped and tortured to death, tiny children killed as mercilessly as if they had been rabbits, the men shot or marched off to Russia.

Mullin had not been certain which of the two regions had been conceded, but at our restricted pace, we had better be on the alert for as long as possible, ready to cross over to one province or the other at short notice.

Whatever he had told us had turned out to be true, so although this new measure seemed inconceivable folly to us, we believed him implicitly and decided to keep within reach of the dotted dividing line on the map.

In our atlas, a footnote mentioned:

'. . . When driving through Albania alone, it is recommended to take a guide.'

Happy days, only seven years ago. Where could one go alone or with a guide to-day and still be safe?

Our long flat farm cart ran on rubber-tyred wheels, as thick as those of a lorry. It was piled high with hay for the horses, covering our modest luggage. René had spread the old carriage blanket ingeniously, contriving a sort of bench on which we sat quite comfortably, when the horses were not climbing a hill. A water-pail for them was concealed beneath our feet; it contained, for the moment, the last bottles of Napoleon

Cognac, rattling cheerfully as we jogged downhill. The cart was boarded high at the back, like an outsized bed, the planks roughly nailed together, and with our escort's bags and satchels hanging from nails and hooks.

Mamma's fair complexion could never stand the sun, so in open country she used her plum-coloured umbrella as a sunshade. We were beginning to look like a family picnic.

Between disjointed snatches of song, René told me they were getting very uneasy about their Russian fellow-prisoners in Königswart. When the war ended, the Soviet prisoners on the farm had again named the same man as their spokesman and representative. He had then threatened our friends that when the time came, he would know how to deal with them.

The fact that the French were never locked up at night and were free to move around within a certain radius had caused much jealousy. I asked them why they had not told us all this before. Perhaps we could have done something about it.

'One can't trust them: they're too frightened,' they said.

We carefully avoided main roads, for the American Army was on the move, and we were bound to be held up, or pushed off the road if we ran into them.

Woods again, the dappled sunshine streaming through the trees. It all seemed so deceptively peaceful that our vigilance relaxed, and even cracking branches nearby failed to disturb us. Were we not, besides, already in the American Zone?

But suddenly leaping out of the undergrowth on all sides at once, we were surrounded by menacing figures. They were in striped clothing and armed. Paul and Papa felt for their pistols, and we all pressed a little closer together.

In broken German, pointing with their short-barrel rifles, they asked: 'Wer? . . .'

'Tous Français!'

'Er? . . .' pointing at Paul, so much taller and fairer than the others.

'Français,' they repeated anxiously. 'Tous Français! France. Nous retournons en France. Nous n'avons rien.' They slapped their empty pockets with a significant gesture.

'Vive la France!' called one of the striped ones, lowering his gun. The others followed suit, reluctantly making way for the cart to proceed. They stood and stared after us for a while as if in two minds.

Our friends kept on repeating, amazed: 'He said "long live France". Ah ça, mais alors . . . They were even quite nice . . .'

As we crunched and creaked along the sandy paths, we now glanced more warily to the right and left, and again saw figures with shorn heads crouching behind bushes, or running from thicket to thicket, the young leaves providing poor cover. They were probably concentration camp inmates returning East, many only trying to get home . . . But political prisoners and common law criminals were mixed up together in the camps, and our Frenchmen now told us again some of their comrades had been waylaid a few days ago, their wedding rings twisted off their fingers, stripped of their poor clothing. Two of them had tried to resist, and were murdered out of hand.

'They have seen nothing else . . . *alors* (meaning the cruelty in the camps). It is better not to walk alone in times like this.'

We now emerged into open country, the road heading straight for a large village far ahead, clustering around its church, which sat like a brooding hen among the red-tiled houses. Just before the road turned in to it, we could clearly discern military vehicles and uniforms glinting in the sun.

It was our first U.S. check-point. Paul climbed on to the cart, so as to appear less tall next to his squat little companions. Leaning against the straw, he pretended to go to sleep.

The gum-chewing sentries inspected our paper nonchalantly. It only mentioned Papa, Mamma and me. They turned it up and down. An officer emerged from the little hut at the side of the road. He pointed at Paul, and our escort, who also had no such document, loudly repeated: 'Tous Français!'

We had not asked them to do so, but it was not for us to contradict them!

'Where are you heading?'

I named the next village, and he appeared to accept this. We could hardly believe ourselves that our intention was to cross Germany. The officer went back into the hut with our pass. While we stood there, Paul opened one eye and said: (In English!)

'What are we waiting for?'

A warning prod from me, but the gum-chewing soldier standing within hand's reach paid no attention. As far as he was concerned, we were part of the landscape. Here came our paper again, duly stamped, and we were waved on with a curt reminder to observe the curfew. We were still only allowed to move between seven in the morning and seven in the evening.

As the afternoon cooled, it was time to look out for quarters for the night.

Paul's Polish stepfather, when Ambassador in Rome, used to say that of all International Organisations, the Catholic Church was the one which functioned best. So now, as we approached another village and the sun began to slide towards the horizon, we headed straight for the church and asked for the priest.

Paul then went to his house for a friendly chat, and soon he directed us to the richest farm of the village. He went himself to ask the farmer's wife to take us in and cook us a hot soup, Paul promising to pay for everything. There was even a small room at the back for Mamma.

René stabled and fed his horses. We had been too uneasy to eat all day and now felt ravenous, as we presently collected around the wooden table with the farmer's wife and young children. The soup was delicious: fresh butter, cheese and brown peasant bread completed the meal. There was even beer.

Our hostess was a pleasant square, direct woman. Her capable hands rough with toil, she seemed to be carrying on the work alone, except for the older girl and an old woman who presently came limping in with pails full of foaming fresh milk. Her husband had been reported missing many months ago. 'Her' Frenchmen, who had helped her, had also left for home. 'Gute, zuverlässige Leute', she said. (Good dependable people.)

She was full of sympathy for us:

'You walked out? Just like that? And there was a farm, too, and cows of course. How many? . . . You had to leave them behind too? *Nein, so was!*'

It shocked her more than anything else. In every walk of life, there seems to be an ultimate gold currency. For her it was cows. I remembered someone saying that his wife could only evaluate expense in relation to Elisabeth Arden cream-pots. (The marriage didn't last.) To count riches in livestock seemed a most logical reckoning, and as she shook her head at this enormity, we began to readjust our values:

'If a man owned three cows, how rich he must be!'

After our copious meal, we all crossed over to a large barn standing some distance from the farm. It was filled with dry scented hay. Paul, I, Papa and the dog settled in one corner, all our escort in another. We spread our carriage rugs and built a fairly comfortable couch. A blanket over my shoulders, I pulled on the two-piece gym suit from the Red Cross stores. It closed hermetically at wrists and ankles, thereby (I hoped) checking the progress of creepy-crawly things as we slept. I hung my khaki blouse and flannel skirt on a splinter of wood in the planking. It was like undressing discreetly on a crowded beach. The men just loosened their ties, and dropped down as they were.

Too tired to think any more, the dog wedged against us for warmth, we all curled up and slept.

Next morning at a bucolic hour, cocks crowed and we scrambled to our feet, our escort yawning and scratching . . . They were soon joking, too. They were used to rising with the sun.

The day promised to be lovely and cloudless again, though cool as yet; damp grass brushed our knees as we crossed the field on our way to the farmhouse. How lucky we were to be over the long winter, which had proved so cruel to thousands of refugees in the East, dying of cold as they fled, often too late to escape the oncoming Soviet Army.

Taking things in the most sporting way, Mamma had procured a small basin of hot water, and she and I washed in a draughty shed as best we could, evolving a sort of progressive technique, from face to feet. It was most refreshing.

The men were all doing the same at the icy pump in the farmyard, splashing and joking.

The farmer's wife had prepared breakfast for us: a huge pot of acorn 'coffee' and steaming milk. Fresh bread, butter, even honey. A feast. In town one had not seen anything like this for years.

Paul then had a long consultation with René:

'How far can we go every day?'

'About forty kilometres for a few days. Then the horses must rest.'

Seven o'clock was striking as we got on our way.

Paul walked well ahead, a Frenchman high as his shoulder on either side, Sherry trotting happily at his heels. 'P'tit Louis' was worrying again about his wife of a few weeks in distant Béziers. She was the rather blowsy colourful girl whose photo he had shown us.

'Never mind if she's gone, you'll find another. Men are scarce these days,' they consoled him.

Albert came from Roquefort, near Albi. It was the home of the world-famous cheeses, and he and Paul embarked on long technical discussions as to their relative quality and method of production. They were stored in cellars, like wine, and every stage of the process described in special terms, a cheese jargon.

My friend the Parisian upholsterer sighed in sympathy with us as he walked next to the cart. 'Those beautiful things in the "château"! Will they smash them all?' he asked, shaking his head at the wanton destruction. Of his work too.

Papa was wax-pale from all the strain, in spite of the night's rest. His heart was not too good, and our present predicament had brought back those earlier sudden flights from Russia and Lithuania. To lighten his mood, we joked about it:

'This way of travelling is becoming an addiction rather than a habit.'

But in truth we were still oppressed and sad, and it would take many days before we could shake it off.

On the crest of a rising road, we were suddenly confronted with a tractor piled high with men and women in nondescript clothing, some striped, with those ominous numbers on their backs. They sat on a heap of bags and luggage, a sewing-machine and a lamp protruding from the jumble. They swung across the road and stopped, blocking our progress, greeting us with lifted fist, communist style.

But as we drew near, they saw the French flag, and moved off to the side of the road again, without molesting us. It was a blood-freezing moment, but perhaps we were too many for them.

They were but the vanguard of the returning wave East. Many of them were probably Eastern Europeans returning to their homes, but the Russians among them would meet with no mercy, we knew, although for the most part they had been brought out to work in Germany against their will. The so-called 'Capos' who had helped to instigate the reign of terror in the camps had good reason to flee too.

As we continued on our way again, we met these returning groups with increasing frequency. Some were roaring drunk, even at such a comparatively early hour, waving bottles of schnaps over their heads. But on seeing the French flag, they all left us alone. Our Frenchmen were much cheered by this, feeling respected citizens again. But in the woods we became aware of lone figures darting from clump to bush, as if stalking us. It was very alarming, and we kept close together, only halting when out in the open again.

There could be no question of hurrying, though sometimes we felt as if we would have liked to urge the cart along and reach some safe place to rest. The sun became ever more hot, and at last we found a group of trees in the middle of a wide field, and took the winding path leading to its welcome shade. Here we all spread out for a prolonged siesta.

In the evening, thanks again to the priest in the village we had reached, we were again quite comfortably distributed: Papa and Mamma in a clean room; Paul, I and our Frenchmen in a hayloft this time. An open skylight gave us a view of the fields around us, and let in light and air.

We were touched at our companions' discretion and courtesy. Not for an instant had their tone of friendly respect changed since our reversal of fortune. Every morning, they would come to Paul for directions, and retire to some distance when we ate or slept. As their spirits lifted with the passing days – for now they felt well on their way home – their stories became more pithy, but with a warning nudge, and a glance in my direction '. . . Madame! . . .' they restrained themselves; while I, appreciating both their tact and the joke, pretended I had not heard.

Suddenly, after a few days, a wave of refugees streaming westwards rejoined us on the empty country roads. At first a cart laden high, here or there, then a stream of pedestrians: young women pushing prams with babies, tiny children balancing on the handle bars, pushcarts, bicycles pulling small carts piled with luggage. Among them were groups of bandaged or limping young soldiers, many of them on crutches, as if shaken like dice out of hospitals. They would rest for a moment on our cart as we plodded alongside. One young boy looked so pale under his bloody bandage he seemed about to faint. A dash of Cognac revived him, and he told us the Soviet Army had entered Thuringia. Thousands of people, caught by surprise, had been overrun. The ones we saw here lived close to the frontier, and had for the most part walked out with nothing but the clothes they were wearing. Anyone who could still walk, even if badly wounded, got up and left. 'Somehow one always manages,' he added hopefully. But they had also heard of the murder wave in East Prussia and Silesia, and he said that corpses floated down the rivers there like driftwood.

At this news of the Soviet advance, we turned south immediately, increasing our plodding progress: no time for picnics to-day. Captain Mullin had been proved right again.

I remembered with regret the shining bicycle left hidden in Paul's cupboard for fear it might arouse envy on the way. As we walked and walked, it seemed the greatest loss: wings shorn from our feet. But Paul reminded me: 'What would we have done with *one* bicycle?'

'I would also like to have a camera, a box of paints and a typewriter,' I sighed.

'You will have them all soon again,' said Paul reassuringly.

Next day the pace became more leisurely. Hundreds of twisted or abandoned vehicles now lined the roads as we went along. Even the most remote country roads were strewn with what seemed the carcasses of giant beetles after some nightmarish insect battle.

The country had suffered sporadically here and there, then came a trail of devastation, mostly caused by bombing or shelling.

We crossed a railway-line threading its way through a dense pine-wood. There was a train standing on it, silent and still. As we approached we saw it had been derailed in places. Spread all down the length of broken waggons lay a huge rocket, such as we had never seen before. Although dislocated and broken in several pieces, it still shone in polished newness under the midday sun, resting on its myriad wheels like a dragon broken in combat. Could this be the so-long promised 'Wunder-waffe'? (wonder-weapon)

Nearing the next village, strange shapes dangled from the trees. Scarecrows? Hanged men? If they had found a white flag, the S.S. would not have hesitated to do so.

We did not go close enough to investigate, for the hamlet was utterly destroyed and empty, just a few chimneys standing in the rubble, accusing fingers pointing to the sky.

We were entering the Protestant part of Franconia. The villages seemed to lose character without their church like an exclamation mark in their midst. We were at a loss where to turn, and for the first time a rude and aggressive farmer refused to let us buy anything or stop over for the night. Paul said coldly: 'These men are no longer prisoners, and can now take whatever they want without permission. Consider yourself lucky to be asked, and to be paid.'

In fact he had asked our French friends never to 'take' anything, but one day, what did we see? Louis was carrying a fat strangled goose. Paul lifted a questioning eyebrow. '. . . Mais, Monsieur le Prince, on l'a seulement un peu poussé dans le fossé. Il n'a pas souffert!'

What a happy time they had, roasting it over a camp fire in the next coppice! . . .

As we approached Pommersfelden, Count Schönborn's fantastic baroque Palace, we heard that General Patton was in residence, and therefore altered our original plan of dropping in and visiting the owners: there would be too many controls. A wide détour took us around it, and we turned south again. Spring was much more advanced here and flowering trees and bushes softened the jagged gashes torn by bombs in the unevenly battered countryside, for some small towns and villages seemed to have been bypassed by the war. Mamma would have liked to indulge in sight-seeing:

'What lovely fountains; beautiful churches! If only we could stop and visit them!'

'Mamma, Paul will explode if you so much as suggest it!'

We no longer avoided the main roads, but had to pull up frequently to let columns of American troops rattle past: armoured divisions with monster tanks, jeep after jeep and lorries full of soldiers. They never appeared to move on foot, even crossing the roads in a jeep. Their young faces were smooth, unlined. Arrayed in unbelievably impeccable uniforms, mounted on these processions of new-looking vehicles, they seemed to have crossed Europe as on a parade, in search of an absent enemy, proud missionaries of liberty.

But the German Army had been fighting for four endless Russian winters and at the end was worn out, shattered and demoralised. The country waited almost gratefully – even humbly – to be overrun from the West at last!

The victors passed us unseeing, but if there was a halt, human contact sprouted once more. Cartons of cigarettes were grinningly offered in exchange for our Scottie, who was indeed quite irresistible, as with black square face, ears pointing, nose twitching, he sat up on his hind legs, one paw suspiciously lifted, like an untimely imitation of the Hitler salute.

The sun beat down on us, hour by hour, and without warning, I fell off the cart all at once in a dead faint: it was violent sunstroke. They carried me into a neighbouring field, the cart following, and everybody waited patiently in the shade of a flowering hawthorn hedge while I slept it off.

Mamma then produced a last 'Pyramidon' from the depths of her bag, and we turned in to the nearest manor along the road, for curfew time was on us. The owners stared dumbfounded, at a loss to know what to do with us. But mattresses were procured, and somehow or other we got a night's sleep. As we left in the morning, I gratefully accepted an old straw hat to protect my still buzzing head.

In more densely populated regions, it was becoming much more of a problem to find food and a roof over our heads, for all available accommodation was filled already with refugees from the bombed towns. Our journey, therefore, now took on the aspect of chain-visiting, for we carefully chose one friend's home after another, as long as it was within reach of our road westwards. The fact that we would be welcome, compensated for the inevitable détour.

It was, however, with some trepidation that we approached Langenburg in the hope that it would be neither occupied by the U.S. Army, nor bombed.

'That damned barn! . . . although we haven't got them in America . . .' as a G.I. termed it, blind with drink, waving a fist when evicted from the courtyard of the towering pile, into which he had lurched past the OFF LIMITS sign.

In fact Langenburg was one of the few German Schlosses really deserving the name, for any gentleman's home, even the size of a manor can be called a Schloss. But Langenburg is a wholly intact mediaeval fortress; moat, battlements and all, which has lorded it over the surrounding province for many centuries. Even to-day, the whole region is called 'Hohenlohe-Land'. Perched on the spur of a hill, it could only be reached over a bridge at the end of a rambling, picturesque and unscathed village seething with American troops.

We were given a warm welcome, for the owner, Prince Friedel Hohenlohe, was Paul's Commander in Cannstatt. His charming wife, Margarita, faced all the ups and downs of our recent and present destiny with detachment and earthy humour. Our host had been discharged from the Army several months earlier for the same reason as Paul, one brother-in-law killed in action, the other Prince Berthold of Baden, grievously wounded. Margarita's brother, Prince Philip, was serving in the British Royal Navy, and relations from abroad were beginning to get in touch again.

A room was found for Papa and Mamma, Paul and I crammed into Friedel's dressing-room, while our escort was distributed in comfortable quarters on the farm. We could at last halt for some days and allow the horses to recover.

I was still rather fragile, and the comfort and rest, the first warm bath and clean sheets since we had left Königswart, and above all such cheerful and congenial company, soon put me on my feet again.

We could also plan at last how to send my parents on to Baden-Baden, for a year earlier I had reserved them rooms in the neighbourhood. By a lucky chance, the future inventor and manufacturer of UHU glue and 'Badedas', later of world fame and consequent prosperity, was wending his way through Langenburg on a lorry, on his way south to Baden. He offered to take them rapidly to their destination. It was a difficult parting, uncertainty taking the place of dangers overcome, but I reassured them it would not be for long. Once we had taken stock of the situation in Johannisberg, I would visit them, and we could then plan further.

As I walked her twins with her one morning, Margarita suddenly let go of the wide pram, and flew into the arms of an American officer driving a jeep. It was a childhood friend: Paul Chavchavadze, come to see how she and Friedel were faring, but the spontaneousness of her welcome left both Langenburgers and surrounding G.I.s agape.

Half Russian, half Georgian, with all the effervescence of a Southern Caucasian, he became the entertainer of the evening with stories of his war experiences, witty imitations and tzigane songs. Suddenly he would switch to the profoundly earnest mood Russians pick up and put away again at a moment's notice, the lightning change from happy child to ancient sage disconcerting his audience.

For me, it was like meeting a brother.

Only the occupying forces had any means of communication. For us, for many months to come, there would be no telephone, no trains, no post. News flew as before from person to person, and everyone had some improbable adventure to relate. We brought the latest tidings from our parts, but were eager to know how events had proceeded in the West. We were therefore in no particular hurry to move on, according to the Spanish adage: 'Better bad things known, than good ones to come.'

But our Frenchmen sat in a row on the wall of the draw-bridge like rooks, and kept on asking:

'Quand ça qu'on part?' (When are we off?)

Prodded by this 'vox populi', we could delay no longer. Friedel gave us a letter for the custodian of his other Schloss of Weikersheim, an imposing XVIth century castle on the edge of a small, partly mediaeval town of the same name.

We reached it by seven, our Cinderella hour.

The vast building was really more of a Museum than a gentleman's residence. In pre-war days (and soon again), tourists shuffled around in felt slippers, peeping into open doorways, cordoned off by a thick red rope. The Schloss housed an imposing collection of armours, weapons, china and furniture all of the same period. The ballroom, or 'Rittersaal', was a fantastic composition of frescoes and stucco, life-size stags re-clined on the pinnacle of fake-marble columns – it was like a child's monumental birthday cake, in the gayest colours.

In the State bedroom on the first floor, the rope was removed, and the four-poster bed prepared for us: silky smooth sheets and pillows piled high, all edged with wide lace flounces. But the window had been blown out by a chance artillery hit, leaving a huge gaping hole. All the dust and débris were neatly cleared away, the weather was warm, and as we lay in the great bed, under its Lyon-velvet, scalloped canopy, we gazed past faded crimson hangings, straight out into moonlit fields.

The Frenchmen slept on mattresses in the armoury. Deeply impressed by their surroundings, they spoke in whispers, as if fearing to disturb ancestral ghosts.

Next morning, we moved on towards Bronnbach, the West-German home of our erstwhile neighbours of Haid, in Bohemia, the Löwensteins.

Princess Carolina Löwenstein was Italian by birth. Glad of a happy chat and a dash of frivolous gossip in such serious times, she had often visited me in Königswart. Last time I had looked her up in Bronnbach in return, social life being at a standstill, we had gone on a tour of remote and often most surprised neighbours with the beer van. Perched high on the driver's seat, we also delivered cases of beer at roadside inns as we went.

Her husband, Karl, was rather shocked to hear of it. Our fortunes certainly did not seem to have improved much since then.

Carolina now came running out to welcome us, surrounded by her six lovely children. She was in a terrible state, for there was no news of her husband, last heard of in Königsberg in East Prussia, and that was a very nasty place to be in at the time.

Nothing else mattered to her but this frantic wait for news! It made me realise all the more how lucky I was to have Paul with me, and how miraculous it was to survive this witches' cauldron.

Bronnbach is an Abbey, with many outlying buildings around it. Like everywhere else, it was packed with refugees, mostly from the bombed Western towns. It was therefore not easy to make room for us, but somehow it was achieved, and after evening soup (for there was not much else), the charming children sang and played their harmonicas for us, the only boy pushing his way to the fore through a forest of five little sisters, one more pretty than the other.

We left with a letter of recommendation for the next stop, and were happy to hear that, shortly afterwards, Karl returned home quite unexpectedly.

On our way down the river Main, we passed another Löwenstein castle, Kleinheubach, and were sad to see the state of total dilapidation it had been reduced to: makeshift chimneys protruded from the windows all over the beautiful baroque façade, the smoke curling up from them like black worms. Carolina told us that the refugees filled their stoves with the parquet flooring. With the greatest difficulty, bearding Nazi officials who would not let her enter her own house, she had at last succeeded in extracting some pieces of the best furniture before they met with the same fate.

A violent downpour now broke over our heads as we clumped along the river side. It was the first rain since our departure. We all scrambled under the rough awning, water running down our backs, everything mushy and sodden. We were really a very bedraggled group when we halted that evening, all the more thankful for Carolina's letter introducing us.

As we jumped off the cart, Paul caught his single pair of flannel trousers on a nail – with disastrous results. Our hostess's husband had been recently killed in action. Although it must have been quite a wrench for her, she gave Paul one of his pairs instead.

From then on, there were no more castles, no more barns. The inhabitants of these more populated regions were tired out with bombing and worry about their mostly missing menfolk; exasperated by the never-ending demands made on them by the refugees from bombed towns; discouraged by the state of their homes, if they were still standing, and hungry besides.

We were no longer welcome. They had hoped to be rid of their refugees with the end of the war, whereas our arrival presaged the beginning of an immeasurably greater wave of them from the East. Although a steady stream had already begun to trickle through even before the war was over, they could not know yet that the entire ex-Austrian Sudeten population of Northern Bohemia would soon be thrown out onto the roads. The fact that it was but another fateful consequence of Hitler's re-shuffling of peoples in the name of germanic supremacy would not lighten this additional burden.

There was, however, no ill-feeling as far as the French were concerned: so many Frenchmen had replaced the absent men in German homes, often in more ways than one, that any national prejudice had disappeared on both sides. The term 'Boche' for our friends, referred to a type of person, but no longer to Germans as a whole. As they worked on the farms on a footing of comparative freedom, the French prisoners had become the Allies of the population (mostly women), against the encroaching Nazis, and in the Eastern provinces they had protected them, and often driven them and their children on tractors over hundreds of miles to escape the Soviet Army. One could really hope that this new understanding would do away with age-old rivalry and hatred between the two countries.

In the evenings we would now stand around disconsolately, while Paul tried to find some shelter for the night. Our quarters became ever more disagreeable, until Paul and I finally landed in a very doubtful bed in a scruffy village some distance from our destination near Langen. I so much preferred the open fields, or straw in a barn. We felt cramped, sticky and unrested as we set out again next morning.

The day grew excessively hot, no shade to be found in the open country, no river or fountain to drink from. But as we walked down a long sandy road, we realised that it was lined with cherry trees. There was no one to buy them from, so Paul, standing on the cart, held up Jean-Marie 'le Breton', and ripe squashy cherries poured down on us, like manna from heaven, quenching our thirst.

On the last stretch of straight flat highway, we were passed by a small hand-luggage truck, never used before off the platform of a railway station. It was piled high with handbags, and on the small platform in front stood a man, his foot on the pedal. Cheerful grins were exchanged:

'He comes from far, that one!' commented our French friends.

Turning to the left, as we followed Margarita Hohenlohe's directions, we entered a dense wood. The trees parted with the welcome sign of: 'SCHLOSS WOLFSGARTEN. OFF LIMITS!'

With a sigh of hopeful relief, we turned up the winding drive, leading through a fringe of trees towards the walled farmyard.

8

Wolfsgarten, at a convenient distance from Darmstadt, their main residence, was the summer retreat and shooting lodge of the reigning Grand Dukes of Hesse. The present owner, Prince Ludwig, second son of the last Grand Duke, who had been deposed in 1918, had married an Englishwoman: Margaret Geddes. Hitler's 'Princes' decree' which had thrown him out of the German Army, had also probably saved his life.

Darmstadt and the Hesse palace in its centre, with all its contents, were obliterated by bombing shortly before the end of the war, and from then on the family lived in Wolfsgarten, safely tucked away in thick woods.

Conceived on a human and cosy scale, this country residence breathes harmony and elegance. The low buildings over the ex-coachhouse (now garages) lead into a square garden, framed by a low palace at one end, two rows of single-storeyed, tile-roofed, red sandstone houses on either side, and a high clock tower opposite the main building.

A flowering rose-arbour stands domelike over the fountain in the centre of the lawn, cut into dishlike shapes and edged by neatly pruned trees. Fan-tailed bushy white pigeons strut under their shade.

As we wearily walked the last steps we were met with the smell of fresh grass, of roses – and of peace.

Henry of Hesse, Prince Ludwig's nephew, painted a picture of Wolfsgarten at that time: a flowering green island, haven of refuge in a desolate landscape, floated down an icy river, its shores lined by flaming towns and smoking ruins.

We seemed a symbol of this destruction; of migrating populations, invasion and ashes, messengers from another world which began just beyond the gates, bringing first news from the East.

We produced a minor sensation, to be remembered long after our departure, as 'like in a film'.

We must have looked startling: lean and tanned, hair bleached by weeks of sun, dressed as for an African safari, our solid phalanx of Frenchmen surrounding the cart on its rubber wheels, straw and hay piled high around the bucket with the last bottle of Napoleon Cognac. Our two chestnut-brown farm horses were well-tended and sleek, thick, creamy tails swishing gently – René's pride!

We were immediately made welcome and absorbed into the charmed circle of our hostess Peg's loving and energetic care.

But there was underlying sadness to Wolfgarten's serene beauty. In November 1938, when the plane in which they were travelling struck a factory chimney near fog-ridden Ostend, Prince Ludwig (Lu) had lost all his family, as well as his best friend, Baron Riedesel. They were on their way to his own wedding in London: his mother, his loved and admired elder brother Don, with his beautiful wife Cécile, Princess of Greece, and their two little boys.

After their appalling home-coming, Lu and Peg adopted his brother's third baby, little Johanna, but two years later she died of meningitis, as if her family were calling her to join them.

The war had been a tragedy for Peg, as for all of us. But in spite of her English nationality (or perhaps even because of it), she had met with kindness and sympathy not only from her husband's frequently half-foreign relations, but also from his friends and fellow officers. Her natural resilience unimpaired, no one was now to call on her help in vain.

Paul, man of action, with his mixture of humour, fantasy and intuition, reminded Lu of his brother Don, his other opposite and yet complementary self. They would wander off into the park together, talking and talking, for there was so much to be discussed and digested.

Wolfsgarten had been the childhood home of the last Empress of Russia, Alexandra Feodorovna, and of her sister Elisabeth, Grandduchess Serge, both murdered during the Russian Revolution.

But although the more distant past pervaded Wolfsgarten, and gave it unique and poignant charm, the present had to be dealt with at every turn.

For the first time for years, we felt in touch with the West at last. Messages and visitors were a daily occurrence, especially from England, from Peg's brothers and Lu's royal cousins. They flowed in in rapid succession, chequered by unexpected shocks from the haphazard wave of 'denazification'.

Calls for help came from Kronberg, where overnight the castle had been requisitioned by the U.S. Army, in a much more drastic way than was usually the case. The entire family: the old Landgräfin (sister of the last Kaiser and Queen Victoria's grand-daughter), her daughter-in-law Tiny (Princess Sophia of Greece) with her five children and four nephews, had been thrown out without previous warning, forced to find quarters for the first night as best they could in the overcrowded little town.

Finally Tiny, having found room for them all, had to take refuge herself in the summer-house in the Park, where there was a small sofa. She barricaded the door with wicker chairs wedged under the latch. In the middle of the night she was startled by the sound of running steps and a sobbing figure hurled itself against the door. It was her nephew, sixteen-year-old Heinrich, who had just heard on the wireless that his mother, Princess Mafalda of Italy, had died in tragic circumstances in Buchenwald. (They had lost all trace of her for many months.)

She kept him with her then for the rest of the night, trying to console him.

Next morning, with all nine children, she moved to Wolfsgarten. She then took her eldest nephew Moritz (18) to visit the U.S. senior officer and find out more about her sister-in-law's death. The misguided man shouted at Moritz: 'You damn' Nazis!'

Tiny intervened: 'How dare you! Don't you understand, it is the boy's mother who has died in a Nazi camp?'

In a quandary what to do with Moritz, Lu decided to send him to work on the farm of Kranichstein near Darmstadt, in the hope that tough exercise and more substantial food would help him to recover from the shock of his mother's tragic death.

The next addition to Wolfsgarten was a small boy with tousled hair, his camouflage uniform disguising him ineffectively as a bilious land-scape, who came trudging up the drive, dragging his knapsack. He was the son of Lu's commander, killed in action. He had lost all his family in the East, and only hazily remembered his father mentioning a Prince of Hesse. Sent to throw grenades at Russian tanks with other children of his age, he witnessed every sort of horror, and had finally managed to escape towards the West. He must have been about fifteen, but seemed much younger, except for the unsmiling stricken look in his eyes. A bed was found for him at once, and he soon became a part of Wolfsgarten, as we all already felt ourselves to be.

There was some uncertainty as to whether he should take his meals with the children or with us, and finally Solomon's verdict was lunch with the children and supper with the grown-ups, hoping this would help him to find his footing in both worlds again.

He sat silent among us, but gradually the shell-shocked look began to wear off, and at last we heard him laughing and running with the others.

(Much later, part of his family reached the West, and he was able to rejoin them.)

A few days passed, and up the drive trundled a tractor, driven by a purposeful-looking woman in overalls. Two carts were attached to it, piled high with a jumble of belongings. Dogs, several horses and a number of children walked alongside. Her husband lost in Russia, she had driven her family all the way from East Prussia.

Nobody was ever turned away, although there did not seem to be any particular reason why they should have come to this part of the country. But they explained they were all set for emigration, and thought this would be easier to achieve through the U.S. zone, and that the Prince would help them. Which of course, in time, he did.

The eldest boy was barely fifteen, completely silent, incredibly hard-working and totally obtuse. He had a strange name: Malte. We wondered had he been shell-shocked, or was he incapable of thought? His mother was so deserving and indomitably humourless, we felt like wilting violets in contrast. Even Peg.

As one new arrival followed another, Peg conjured order out of chaos with great cheerfulness and a firm hand. She was bent on a judicious distribution of labour, and tried to keep us potato-peeling, jam-preparing, weeding or hay-making – that is to say when she found us, for we would often slip through her fingers. Her impatience with our inefficiency was however quickly tempered by loving forgiveness and her bubbling sense of fun.

Someone sighed, 'If only the harvest is good!' and from Paul there came the heartfelt cry:

'Oh for fields and fields of delicious Châteaubriands!'

Tiny was the heart and soul of our party. Brought up in France, she had – like me – absorbed the incredible quantity of miscellaneous information pumped into any pupil heading for the French Baccalauréat.

We decided it had been a humus, from which much was supposed to grow, but that it had not prepared us for all the situations we had had to face. It remained, however, a cryptic common language, and this we greatly enjoyed.

Her keen sense of humour and talent for relating the most grotesque (though never unkind) stories, went with total unselfishness, and smooth peace-making whenever called for: she was to get on beautifully with two proverbially difficult mothers-in-law. This sweetness to all and sundry, coupled with charming looks, gave her a sort of radiant grace, and carried her unchanged over and through rapid switches from the lowest pedestrian status, to that of 'Super VIP', when she became the sister-in-law of the Queen of England.

The Hesse family now found that any source of income had melted to almost nothing, while their obligations seemed to have multiplied in reverse proportion. At this time two representatives of a renowned picture gallery in the United States came to offer them what seemed an astronomical amount for the world-famous Holbein Madonna, which had been in the family for generations.

The picture was removed from their estate in Silesia in the teeth of Soviet invasion and had escaped the bombing in Dresden by a mere chance. The train transporting it westwards was then hit by artillery. Finally it reached Wolfsgarten and was shoved under Peg's bed, from which safe refuge it would be frequently pulled out and admired. One night, just before the war ended, bombs began to fall nearby. In the consequent rush for shelter, Peg stumbled in the darkness over the Holbein, lying in the middle of the floor of her bedroom, and for a moment thought she had trodden on it. When the lights went on again, she found she had stepped through one of the cardboard wrappings, but to her immense relief, the Madonna was intact.

Here came the tempters offering a huge sum in foreign currency: 'Think of all you could do with the money!' they coaxed.

Lu had become ever more depressed as the offer mounted, but at this he suddenly brightened and exclaimed:

'I know what I would do with it!' (Eager expectation appeared on the faces of the visitors) '. . . I would buy the Holbein.'

Later the picture was lent for some years to a Swiss Gallery in exchange for free holidays in Switzerland for Berlin children. It then became the pride of the private Hesse Museum in the rebuilt Castle of Darmstadt.

It was time something was done about clothes, for ours were reduced to an almost inconceivable minimum.

We managed to borrow two bicycles in fairly good condition and set off for Frankfurt (about 30 kms away). Tiny remembered a little dressmaker there. We felt very optimistic about it all.

Even though we were used to much destruction, Frankfurt was a most depressing sight: hardly a house higher than one storey, beside gaping empty-eyed façades. The hot wind blew rubble, dust and loose paper into our eyes. No dressmaker to be found anywhere, her old house a shapeless pile of stones and bricks. There was nowhere to eat, and when a summer thunderstorm broke over our heads, there was not even anywhere to take cover. There was nothing for it but to return, sadly pedalling down the Autobahn in driving rain.

Columns of lorries full of coloured troops passed us. They shouted and waved, brandishing offerings. One beaming driver produced a leather bag and a pair of shoes to tempt us.

Slowly the storm passed, and soaking wet, we at last reached the final stretch of road leading to Wolfsgarten, where we could pedal side by side.

Tiny remarked with profound disgust:

'We have been living in a Fools' Purgatory!' – which rather summed things up.

(Years later, Paul and I drove down that same road in his smart Porsche, people stood crowded on both sides of the road, which was lined with extremely polite police officials. On seeing our special pass we were waved on, with a salute and a smile, as we turned into the familiar drive of Wolfsgarten.

A private dinner for ten people had been arranged for the Queen of England, who was visiting Germany officially with her husband. All protocol stopped at the gate, and we assembled, as so many times before, in the beautiful big 'Saal', to dine then in the red Spanish leather drawing-room, the table a sea of lilies of the valley around the candles. Our host had the elegance to feel that however beautiful his china and silver were, nothing could impress the Queen, therefore masses of spring flowers replaced them as the most suitable homage to a charming woman.

What a contrast, Tiny and I thought then, to our dripping bicycle ride in 1945!)

From Tiny's home came the news that the castle safe had been broken open, and all the family jewels of the Landgrafs of Hesse stolen. The carpets, which had seemed too large to the occupants, had thereupon been cut up into smaller squares for distribution among the bedrooms.

Peg's brother, an English officer, was one day absentminded enough to shove his army pistol into Lu's chest of drawers, between two layers of shirts. He had wanted it out of reach of the numerous children of all ages drifting in and out of the house. He then left, forgetting all about it.

But next day, without previous warning, a jeep drew up to arrest Lu mistakenly, as had happened several times before. Peg rushed to get him a change of linen for the night, and was horror-struck on finding the pistol, for it was a heinous crime to be found in possession of firearms, especially Allied ones. She shut the drawer hastily, breathing a sigh of relief when they left without searching the house.

We had had such hopes of the Allied occupation delivering us from Nazi lawlessness, that it was quite a surprise to be exposed to such arbitrary dealing. The overwhelming quantities of prisoners in Allied hands certainly made the problem of selection difficult to deal with. So much then depended on the goodwill of the local civilian or military authorities, as had been the case with our Captain Mullin in Marienbad.

The few days of rest in Wolfsgarten had flown by, and although we still felt far from well, our French escort was getting restive again: it was time to set off on our last lap to Johannisberg.

We wound our slow way out through the park and turned down the long straight road to Mörfelden.

Leaving the intact beauty of Wolfsgarten behind us reminded us inevitably that our own belongings had fallen away like leaves in autumn, ending in a vertiginous loss of houses, trunks, clothes and precious objects, as unimportant at the moment as they would have been on the verge of death. So beyond a small sigh, no use repining. All our real worries were still on another plane, for we were desperately anxious about Missie and so many of our friends, and faced a more than uncertain future.

Nevertheless, as we strode along on the cool and lovely June morning, we realised how comparatively lucky we were to be alive and together, trekking in fine weather, and finding welcoming friends along the latter part of the way.

We presently glimpsed a carton marked CARE in the bushes and stopped to inspect it. It was the first time we had seen one. It must have fallen off some truck, for it was still intact and seemed like a Christmas parcel: powdered eggs, peanut butter, instant coffee, chocolate, cheese, biscuits – a rainfall of unbelievably delicious delicacies. We nibbled at this and that, sharing it all with our friends.

(We heard later that these CARE parcels would be sent by U.S. citizens to the hungry in Europe – a generous gesture at the time!)

All the bridges had been blown up, and the crossing of the river Main to Mainz-Castell had to be undertaken on a rickety sort of barge, functioning as makeshift ferry. The horses and cart could hardly find room on it. Paul held their heads firmly, standing on the extreme edge of the boat with his back to the water, while all the Frenchmen hung on to the edges of the cart as counterweight.

Slowly we pushed off, but in the middle of the river the current became very strong and the barge, gathering momentum, swirled around, tipping slightly to one side. The horses, thrown out of balance, took one step forward and Paul leant over backwards. From all sides the little Frenchmen pulled and heaved, trying not to frighten the animals, and slowly he recovered a vertical position.

We all breathed again as our barge swung gradually towards the other shore. Then came the tricky moment of getting horses and cart over an improvised jetty. The loose planks sank into the water under our weight, but at last we hauled our way up the steep embankment.

The empty road leading to Biebrich was scarred and deeply dented, as if trodden by some dinosaur. Black dust and soot had settled like a film over the ruins and vegetation along the way. The sun was burning and there was no shade to be found, the broken tarmac hot under our feet.

Towards midday, we decided to picnic under a scruffy lilac bush, blossoming bravely between the burnt-out factories of 'Kalle' and 'Albert'.

But as we moved on towards the Rhine, thankful to leave the devastation of Biebrich behind us, a cool breeze came to meet us, and the small towns stretching like a rosary along the great river were shabby, scarred but intact.

Here came Winkel at last and the road winding up towards Johannisberg.

We climbed the darkening hill into the setting sun. Its last rays shone through the gutted ruin of the castle, now a jagged line against the blazing sky. The hollow windows were lit to red and gold, as if a ghostly party were taking place inside, obliterating the ugliness of destruction for a moment.

We rounded the bend and reached Villa Mumm. It was packed with American soldiers. They seemed a wild lot and had spread all over the place, their vehicles crowding in front of the porch, smashed crockery strewing the road.

Here came the turning to the left. As we finally plodded down the elm avenue which led to our house, the last blaze of light had died down and Johannisberg loomed dark, and still, and lifeless.

9

Johannisberg had been bombed out of existence on the night of 13th August 1942. I was alone in Königswart when a telegram was delivered. It was just two lines long:

'Castle and farm buildings totally destroyed by air-attack, nobody killed.'

It was followed by another from my mother-in-law:

'Unhurt staying at Mumm's.'

Then came a call from Paul. He had been given one day's leave to inspect the damage. No one could fetch him from the station when he arrived, so he walked up through the vineyards, still thick with the dust and the smoke of the raid, bits of fur from the fox-fur rugs floating down to meet him.

Although air-raid sirens had warned of an attack on Mainz, nobody had expected any trouble in Johannisberg. But when 'Christmas trees' came floating down over the hill, the house-keeper, Fräulein Allinger, rushed to wake my mother-in-law, who lived with Marysia in the garden-wing: these brilliant flares always meant imminent attack.

Isabel had time to grab her jewels and her dog. Joining Marysia, they dashed through the upstairs ballroom, bombs crashing just behind them as they ran, down the stairs and out on to the terrace, where they crouched in the little summerhouse, which used to stand at the right hand end. Already Allinger, the 'Kellermeister', was beckoning from the open cellar door. Holding up their dressing gowns, for incendiary phosphorus sticks were raining down on them, they ran on to the cellar.

From all sides figures rushed to join them and soon the entire set of buildings overhead was a roaring sea of flames.

The lights went out in the huge vaulted cellar, and clouds of dust billowed up from the explosions overhead. The noise was like being under a tunnel with trains thundering overhead.

Hours seemed to pass before they could creep out again. As the lower floor burst into flames, fire engines drove in from every surrounding village, for Johannisberg is a treasured landmark, the pride of the province.

There was a stampede to salvage whatever was possible. Pictures were torn off the walls, objects handed out of the windows: the silver, the china, the linen. There was hardly time for the furniture, as it was impossible to quench the fire.

When it was all over, there was nothing left but the thick walls, still smoking. Luckily, the few prisoners who had been working on the farm and were locked up for the night by their guards, had been let out immediately by our people, who broke down the door. All the cows were dead, the machines burnt. Wendolin drove his beloved horses at a mad gallop down the tall elm avenue, shot at by a low-flying plane as he went. But he got them out into the fields unhurt.

In the hospital of Rüdesheim, some six kilometres away, a Johannisberg girl was called to the window by the doctor:

'If you want to see your home for the last time, come and look!'

To her horror, she saw what appeared to be the entire hill-top of Johannisberg, blazing like a torch, huge columns of smoke rising in the clear night sky.

Across the Rhine, in Bingen, the inhabitants ran down to the river's edge and stood watching the distant hill in flames, illuminating the whole region. They wept at the sight.

Indeed at that moment, the Schloss again justified its nickname of 'Symbol of the Rheingau'. As so often before, in the course of its turbulent history, Johannisberg's destiny was again associated with that of the town of Mainz, whose total destruction the night before had turned the Eastern sky into a sunset on the wrong side of the compass.

The family found shelter at the Mumms, the famous champagne owners, whose white-columned country-house stood just beyond our park. Next morning the village shoemaker faithfully delivered a pair of shoes he had been mending for my mother-in-law. She missed her photographs most of all and we tried to get as many as possible together again. She and Marysia then left for Spain, not to return to Germany until after the war.

In time I collected a few dented gold and silver objects out of the rubble and some of them could be mended for her again; a china dog survived the blaze.

I felt like an inhabitant of Pompeii, returned to poke among the excavations.

Shortly after the raid I happened to be in Vienna; I then visited Professor Srbik, the eminent biographer of the Chancellor, to enquire

whether he knew what archives had perished in the burnt-out house.
(The diaries of Metternich's third wife had unfortunately not been sent
to me in time because of the frequent bombings in the West.)

'Johannisberg destroyed? What frivolity!' he exclaimed.

A historian's view.

As we drew up in our battered courtyard after we had left Königswart,
people rushed to meet us from every corner:

'Unsere Herrschaften sind da!' (Our masters are back!) they cried in
joyful relief.

They had been waiting with increasing anxiety ever since Kurt,
Lisette and Thanhofer came trudging in behind the black horse, Irma,
pulling another cart all the way from Königswart. The Tauberts'
daughter, Ilse, had pushed her baby in its pram all the 600 kilometres in
spite of her limp.

The 'To Whom It May Concern' laissez-passers, which we had typed
for them the night before leaving, seemed to have worked like a charm,
getting them – and even all those who travelled with them – past every
U.S. check-point without delay.

'The Chancellor's seal produced a great impression,' they said. (Der
Kanzlersiegel imponierte sehr.)

Owing to the destruction, we had been spared the billeting of troops
in the few buildings left standing. Thanks to the administrator Labonte's
energetic intervention, the population of the Rheingau was not thrown
out on to the roads just before the German front broke at the bridge of
Remagen. On the other side of the Rhine the Mayor of Ingelheim was
hanged by an S.S. unit for trying to halt the senseless order of evacuation,
so this courageous stand was not without risk.

We soon arranged to have our small group of Frenchmen sent home
on lorries. They were happy to leave, but we parted sadly, not expecting
to see them again.

Some years later a friend of ours, taking the cure at Bobet's Thalasso-
thérapie' institute in Brittany was asked by his 'masseur' as he kneaded
away: 'Do you happen to know Prince Metternich?'

He turned out to be one of our Frenchmen and still remembered our
trek with almost nostalgic affection.

Meanwhile we had all been crammed into rather tight quarters in the
small houses on either side of the gates, which had been rebuilt.

Strangely exhausted, for the next weeks we seemed to do nothing but
sleep, remembering at one point that we had had diphtheria and never
paid it the slightest attention after that one hasty vaccination in Ludwigslust, in spite of many days of fever. In fact healthwise we were both

in very poor shape and Paul's damaged lung hurt him at the slightest effort: it would take some years before we regained normal weight and strength again.

As if flung up on some beach, shipwrecked after a great storm, we had landed on this ravaged piece of land which was at least ours. From then on there would be so much to do on this smashed and impoverished estate, so many people to look after, that we soon began to feel that Johannisberg was also 'Home'.

10

It was to take many weeks before we heard what had happened
to Missie. We had somehow assumed that her hospital would be
evacuated in time, however slow they were about it. But this was
not to be: indeed nothing could exceed the suicidal folly of those
last months! The Viennese catacombs formed a vast underground
labyrinth which had been put to good use during the Turkish siege
in the 17th century. They had been re-opened as air-raid shelters,
enabling people to escape from one burning house to another. But
it appeared that on entering the town, the Soviet Army broke
through the flimsy partitions dividing these cellars and stormed up
into the houses from the basement, rifling stores of wine and
scooping up the women on the way. It was impossible to ward
them off.

Luckily however, Missie and a few friends managed to escape
from Vienna on one of the last trains leaving the beleaguered city
and had then worked in the hospital of Gmunden on the Traunsee.
We therefore planned to go down to Austria and join her as soon as
we had got ourselves organised and found means of transportation.

We at last got news from Irina in Rome and were much relieved
to hear soon after, that Georgie had spent the last months of the
war in Paris where however the take-over had not been without
risk but where a siege had been avoided thanks to the surrender of
the city by the German Commanding General against Hitler's
orders. I presently succeeded in visiting my parents in Eberstein-
burg near Baden-Baden. They were fairly comfortably installed
but very short of food, which I tried to remedy by contributions of
vegetables and wine.

One by one, or in small groups, our Königswart people joined
us. Some could be employed on the estate; for others outside jobs
were found. The last to arrive was our Forester Dobner with his
Czech wife and eighteen-year-old son. Their younger boy had

disappeared in the siege of Königsberg and poor Frau Dobner wept whenever she mentioned him, this great sorrow adding to the pain of her exile. Although destitute, Dobner himself was happy to be with us again, and with his usual calm diligence, set about putting the tiny Johannisberg wood in order. Armed with a pail of white paint with which to mark the trees, I re-planned the park with him, cutting out views down to the Rhine. Still cluttered with broken vehicles, it had become part jungle, part dump-heap.

Dobner told us that we had not left Königswart a minute too soon, for shady-looking Czech officials came asking for us that very same morning. The disciplined and considerate U.S. troops who were at first in charge of the place had been replaced by others, who treated the house as a recreation centre. Girls from the village put on Missie's and my clothes for their parties and went home dragging bulging suitcases.

'It was a shame to see how they "sinned against" the lovely Schloss!' he said.

A mass evacuation of the entire province was taking place. Over four million Sudeten-Germans would be ejected from Bohemia with four pounds of luggage per head, abandoning houses, villages and towns they had built and inhabited for centuries. Sorry as their lot had become, they were finally almost glad to leave.

Their contribution to the future prosperity of Western Germany was to be immense.

We had thought that our people in Plass, on the Czech side, would be able to help the Königswarters, but it all turned out quite differently. Expected as liberators, the Soviet Army had indulged in an orgy of plundering there: all the furniture, papers and books were hurled out of the windows. But they did not find the archives.

Some years later however, a young man remembered hearing in his childhood that a cellar under the Brewery had been rebuilt to house some treasure. On breaking in, the Archives were found stacked just as we had left them. They were then transferred to Prague and after a less happy period, put in the care of conscientious custodians. We can only hope that this is still the case today.

In the wake of the Soviet Army 'Red Guards' from nearby Pilsen, who had prudently remained unknown until then, murdered the administrator and good honest Prohaska, the brewer, although both were Czechs and had never had anything to do with the Nazis. Their families were subjected to every indignity before they were allowed to cross into Germany, a country they had never considered their home.

One of Loremarie Schönburg's last surviving brothers (five

others had been killed during the war) was in a military hospital in Prague, recovering from a severe wound. He and his companions were murdered in their beds some weeks after the war was over by those same 'red guards'.

'Eichkatzelschweif' (squirrel's tail) and 'Spinnradlspuhle' (spindle): two harmless words scribbled on a piece of paper were to be the key to life or death for thousands of prisoners of war rounded up by the Soviet Army in Czechoslovakia.

Flanked by cold-eyed OGPU officers, two ex-convicts from the Ottakring district of Vienna lolled behind a rickety table set up on the edge of the makeshift camp. As they filed past the prisoners were supposed to repeat these words in the suburban vernacular. The Austrian rank and file were then allowed home, whereas their officers would be condemned to three years in Soviet labour camps. But no German could pronounce them right. Swilling beer, the two improvised judges slapped their thighs in merriment as they detected even the slightest Bavarian accent. Hungarians and other nationals were equally at a loss and would be turned back to a lingering death in Soviet camps with all the rest.

As a result of some obscure agreement between the Western Allies and Stalin, the wounded Russian Wlassow soldiers whom our U.S. friend Captain Mullin had evacuated from Marienbad were then handed back to the Soviets with all their comrades one could lay hands on in the western zones.

Entire Cosszck 'stanitzas' (clans), violently anti-communist since 1918, had agreed to fight in Yugoslavia. With their wives, children and priests and any chance white Russian émigré at hand (even if resident there since the Revolution), they were rounded up by the thousand by the Allies and forcibly repatriated to Russia. Many committed suicide rather than consent to do so, for they rightly suspected that they would be systematically murdered or sent to the labour camps on arrival.

It was a tremendous disillusion to see that proverbial Anglo-Saxon respect for individual life and human dignity could go by the board when in conflict with national policy.

Prince Josef Liechtenstein, independent ruler of the tiny principality on the Austro-Swiss border, alone refused to do so, although his foreign policy was usually identical with that of Switzerland, and he was personally much exposed to retaliation, owing to his possessions within the Soviet zone and Vienna: no Russian would be evicted from his territory. Several hundred then departed for South America; a small number expressed the wish to return home, and these then disappeared for ever.

After their expulsion from Teplitz in north-eastern Czechoslovakia some weeks after our departure, Paul's erstwhile guardian Prince Alfons Clary and his wife, born Countess Eltz from neighbouring Eltville on the Rhine, had finally take refuge with their cousins in Bronnbach, the Löwensteins.

They presently managed to visit us in Johannisberg. Knowing that they also had left their home on foot, I tried to procure some clothes, but slim tall Alphy was impeccably turned out from well-cut coat to beautifully polished English shoes: there could be no question of producing any cast-offs, even if what he wore was all he possessed.

Apart from the joy of seeing them again, we were eager for further first-hand news from Bohemia. We had heard that many neighbours had been overrun before they could leave, that a Count Preysing had been shot out of hand by a plundering Soviet soldier, his wife and small son escaping out of a first-floor window.

The Clarys now told us that just as they were being marched off by the Russians, they had entrusted their family jewels to an unknown French prisoner of war who happened to be standing nearby. They did not even have time to ask his name before their arrest, but thrust a chamois bag with an address in Belgium into his hands.

'Can you imagine, he has already delivered it to my sister (Countess Baillet-Latour), and never even stopped to say who he was!'

'And then?'

'Well of course at first, when the Russians broke in, it was not so pleasant. Very rough, especially after our arrest as they were dragging a girl away and Lidi interfered. A drunken soldier hit her and blood spurted all over her face. She turned on him however before I could intervene.'

'. . . I got extremely angry and it worked!' said Lidi firmly. With her aquiline profile, steel-grey hair swept back over a high forehead and deeply-set large blue eyes, Lidi certainly had all the staunchness of her indomitable race, advancing through the centuries from feuding barons entrenched in their fairy-tale 'burg' near the Moselle, to enlightened magnates of the Holy Roman Empire.

'But then,' added Alphy, 'something almost miraculous happened: she and the girl jumped out of the little window, like Nijinsky in the "Spectre de la Rose". As if spirited away. Suddenly they were gone! The soldiers stood staring at the empty square, quite bemused, and in the far distance there were two small figures running.'

'And afterwards?'

'They made us walk for days on end. Nice weather, though perhaps a little hot. Then we were forced to work in the fields, which in fact Lidi didn't mind at all, as they left one alone. But I was never endowed with green fingers and was inclined to pull out the wrong grasses. No food to speak of, so one really got very hungry. But then in the evening we poked around in garbage cans.'

'Oh Alphy, how dreadful! What could you possibly find!' I cried, remembering sadly the small silver-bound notebook next to his plate in Teplitz Castle, close at hands for hints for the cook, unobtrusively jotted down.

His still so handsome face crinkling with laughter, he quickly said:

'Oh no, my dear. It wasn't so bad. One often found delicious little bits of cabbage.'

Lidi, listening with keen enjoyment and appreciation, added:

'I never felt so well in my life!'

We were rather proud of them.

The steady stream of visitors became ever more colourful as relatives of mine in every conceivable Allied uniform came by to see how we were faring.

The first to drop in was my cousin Jim Wiazemsky, straight from his prisoner-of-war camp near Dresden where Mamma and I had so often visited him. He had saved the friendly German Camp Commander from the Soviet Army by the simple expedient of taking him along with them to the West.

Surrounded by friends, spick and span in his new French officer's uniform, disposing of jeeps and the sort of props of war Paul had been so eager to lay aside – although still thin and pale – he was beaming with happiness at his new role after five years on ice.

He married Claire Mauriac, the writer's daughter, shortly afterwards, and at the special request of some high-ranking Russian officers who had been interned with him, was named French Liaison Officer to the Soviet Army in Berlin. His ex-colleagues from the prison camp would often come to visit him and his young wife. Soon after, one by one, they began to disappear without warning and to his shocked surprise, he presently heard that the victims of Stalin's horror rule included his own war heroes.

Some days later Kurt whispered discreetly in my ear:

'There are several American admirals downstairs: they say they are uncles!' (By now nothing could surprise him.)

The visitors turned out to be Gherghi Scherbatoff, my father's brother-in-law, now an American Naval officer, accompanied by two American admirals.

He had come to find out if I was alive and was bursting to tell me about the Yalta Conference in February, just four months before.

At one point he found himself in the same Worontzoff Palace of Aloupka, where we had all played as tiny children. He was in those days a young boy and well remembered holding us for the ritual photograph, as we small fluffy bundles sat astride the lions flanking the terraces which lead down the sea. A quarter of a century later, he was there again, looking across the table at Stalin, as he stood behind the U.S. Navy representative's chair.

Furniture had been hastily re-assembled and the whole place put into a semblance of order for the occasion. It seemed quite lived-in, almost as he remembered it, and made him feel as if he were his own ghost.

'How did Roosevelt deal with Stalin?'

'He was mesmerised. He thought he would win him over by agreeing to everything. Europe was written off as easily as slicing a cake. They moved matches around on the map! It made one shiver. ('Joutko bilo.') The Russians were amazed at what they achieved, for they had been prepared for arduous bargaining and they got it all for nothing!'

'But why didn't Patton take Berlin?'

'Because in Yalta it was agreed that the Soviets should get there first.'

'But then why hand them Thuringia?'

'So that the Allies would be permitted to enter Berlin.'

It sounded like ignorant children playing with bricks. And every time millions of people were handed over to Soviet Communism, hands tied, just to placate 'Uncle Joe'.

'But what of Churchill? Surely he knew what it meant?'

'He was not in a position to carry much weight. Besides the climate of the whole meeting had been prepared and conditioned by "influences" in key positions long beforehand. The fate of Poland and of Eastern Europe were to be the price to pay. I simply had to tell someone about it who would understand!' he confided ruefully.

It seemed as if the last months of the war had brought more losses to all sides than ever before. The list of casualties and of those missing never seemed to end. The news of Paul's former Commander Erne Cramm's safe return was all the more cheering.

After the commanding staff had been dissolved in Bamberg and Paul sent to Ludwigslust, Cramm had been transferred to a Cavalry Corps of about 50,000 men stationed in Hugary. Every Company Commander had been assigned there as a punishment (strafversetzt). There was not much fighting. As the war ended they turned around to surrender to the British Army, which had reached the Austrian frontier behind them. They were referred back to the Russians. Thereupon Erne persuaded his Commander to threaten to attack the Allies in full force unless they were let in. The British yielded and they marched in, in battle formation, handing over their heavy equipment as they passed through the lines. They finally got back to the regiment's home town of Pforzheim some weeks later, and marched in behind their regimental band as if on parade. The town went mad, having given them up for lost: they were showered with flowers, while the Americans rushed out crying: 'Who won the war!'

But presently demobilisation proceeded as arranged so far away, and Erne returned home in his own car with several of his fellow-officers from Eastern Germany who had nowhere to go. He got jobs for them all.

Paul never wanted to dwell on the loss of Königswart again. From then on, however, he would contrive to have a foot in several countries, instinctively keeping his roots from growing too deep in any place: the departure from his home had left a more searing scar than he would acknowledge. But in my dreams I still haunted the house, the doors opening with their specific creak as I searched for some forgotten object, or planned again desperately, with the oppressive feeling that it was all for nothing. Lisette would come and cry on my shoulder now and again. She and Kurt mourned their lost property, particularly bewailing their feather-beds – made up through the years from the down of their own geese: they felt adrift without them, like a snail without its shell. But most of all they minded the waste of all their effort.

With loving care they now ironed and brushed and mended Paul's single pair of flannels, his tie and my skirt and safari blouse. Soon a neighbour gave me an old chintz curtain and I became the proud owner of a summer dress: the summer was so hot, one did not really need anything more.

To procure food had now become the main preoccupation. Potatoes and vegetables were planted in all ex-flower beds and the horses and carts from Königswart put to work in the fields and vineyards. Wheeling their babies in prams, the villagers walked up and down the terrace with its broken vases, past the ruined husk of the castle.

'It used to be Paradise!' sighed the old gardener nostalgically, referring to Paul's grandmother's time.

'It will be that again.' I told him firmly: he shook his head, unconvinced.

But first of all help had to be organised for the destitute population. Central kitchens sprouted in every village and we tried to produce sufficient quantities of milk and vegetables for ours. But in church on Sundays, dull thumps every now and then meant that someone had keeled over, weak from hunger. They would then be carried out to recover in the fresh air as if it were a natural occurrence.

Plans to re-build the castle had to be shelved for the time being: first of all our employees had to be housed and the farm and office buildings reconstructed.

Once again we found ourselves the intermediaries between the authorities and the village, once again we were in a position to advise and help them and to become in time their 'visiting card' as they would call us. In their turn the villagers took a personal and active interest in all our plans.

The village of Johannisberg was blessed with a priest of quite exceptional character. Fortunately he came in the name of God, for he might otherwise have made an impressive Nazi 'Gauleiter'.

He was fired with the admirable ambition of re-building the bombed-out village church, which is a part of the 'Schloss'. But his methods were high-handed and wishing to re-erect the ancient Basilika on its previous ground level, he began by ejecting all the monks' skeletons interred beneath the stone flags of the main nave. Stumbling over piles of skulls and bones, Paul exclaimed:

'What will the Americans think if you make the place look like Buchenwald! I insist on their immediate burial. And a Christian burial too!'

'If they are not in heaven already, they won't get there now,' was the airy reply.

But for once he complied. With commendable ingenuity he then acquired long lists of Catholic churches in England and the United States and proceeded to bombard them with postcards begging each for five marks. It was implied that should they feel so inclined, they could of course contribute a larger sum.

'After all, "their" people destroyed it. I don't rub it in, but it is mentioned.'

Should the five marks not be forthcoming, he would send them the same amount himself by return of post, adding that: 'he was sad to know they were so poor as to be unable to help.'

'I hope that shakes them up!' he told us gleefully.

We helped as far as possible too of course, but on his own he gradually collected substantial sums of money, building as they trickled in, and within a few years the ancient church stood again.

A dust-rag framed in gold would hang one day between a Picasso and a Mondrian in the neo-Baroque home of a textile millionaire. He told me later that it was the foundation-stone of his new fortune.

Returning on foot from Russia past unfathomable piles of rubble and dust, it occurred to him that what the German Hausfrau would be most in need of was something with which to 'mop up the mess'. Starting with a half-broken machine in a shed of their smashed factory, he and his family toiled night and day to produce a steady stream of dust-rags, and the 'Hausfraus' went to work with heroic zest.

Betrayed in their faith in Hitler, their menfolk often gone never to return, forced to face decisions and disasters alone, they now, duster in hand, tackled the collapse of all they had mistakenly believed in with the primeval urge of creating a home wherever they happened to stand. Instead of the sound of motors and horns, the villages resounded with sloshing pails and scratching brushes. But the orgy of cleaning was also as if to scrub away the aftertaste of a shameful love affair.

Everybody felt the tremendous drive towards simple earthbound roots and problems: to feed the hungry and cure the sick; to plant; to build. Whatever could be repaired was stuck together again, odd pieces exchanged, missing furniture made up in the village: it became as fascinating as composing a jigsaw puzzle.

Some months before the end of the war, we had succeeded in despatching a consignment of things from Königswart to Baden-Baden. The Allied wireless had mentioned that this resort was going to harbour the French High Command after the war, which meant that it would be spared from bombing. I had then remembered that after the Russian Revolution the firm of 'Devant' there had kept some trunks in storage for us for years, even when payment was in arrears – which could easily be the case again. This first transport reached Baden-Baden safely, but as soon as the Marienbad Kreisleiter got wind of it, he forbade us to send anything else away.

The French occupation authorities now ruled that anything of French origin had to be returned to France until it was proved to be private property. In our case this was virtually impossible to do, as all our archives and records had remained in Czechoslovakia. Most of our things were indeed French, either bought in Paris when Metternich was Ambassador to Napoleon, or else gifts from the cities of Paris and Brussels after the Peace of Vienna: a degree and scale of origin quite out of proportion with our present low ebb of fortune and bound to be incomprehensible to any minor official dealing with our destinies with a stroke of his pen.

As always when there is an economic and administrative void, a crop of black marketeers of every description had blossomed. Bribed by wine, a couple of them consented to smuggle our belongings back over the zone frontier under cover of a moonless night. They then absconded with the lot.

Many weeks later we traced them again through an Austrian associate of theirs who came to tell Paul that one of them had landed in prison in Frankfurt. I then went to see him there and talking through bars, told him that if he did not hand over everything as agreed and for the same payment, he would be in worse trouble than he was at present. Hampered by his situation, he had little choice but to give in and presently the consignment returned safely to Johannisberg.

Irma, the black horse from Königswart, harnessed to a refurbished carriage found in pieces in a shed on the estate, now became our means of transportation. But Irma could never get used to the shattering rattle of armoured U.S. divisions, and Paul would leap down to catch her above the bit while I held the reins until these steel monsters had passed. In spite of the absence of any civilian traffic, German 'authorities', delegated by the Allies, tentatively tried to assert themselves. One day we were stopped at a crossing and one of these voluntary law-enforcers declared:

'You must at once . . .' he got no further.

'I "must" do absolutely nothing any more!' cried Paul, flinging years of repression to the winds like a handful of dust and on we drove, leaving him quite at a loss by the roadside.

There was a rumour that the occupation powers not only wished to discourage Wagnerian operas and music, but were even seriously considering reducing Germany to a series of agrarian provinces – which would have been like expecting fish to walk.

Wiser counsel soon prevailed however, and these ideas were dropped along with other 'Morgenthau'-type suggestions. In his day, whether battles were won or lost, Metternich had made the resurrection and maintenance of France after the Napoleonic wars the hinge of his entire policy. Beyond his personal love for that country, he insisted that without France Europe could never achieve a viable balance of power. There appeared to be a certain symmetry in history, for now, confronted with the appalling reality of total destruction, the Americans were the first to consider a complete reversal of policy towards Germany.

Meanwhile as the months passed, the Rhine flowed on, crystal-clear again and empty of all traffic, past its destroyed bridges, burnt-out cities and the double row of castles set within signalling distance to warn of approaching enemies in days when wars were still in proportion to man.

There was still no post, no telephone, no cars and no trains. No money and no shops. It gave one a surprising feeling of freedom from the tyranny of things, for all assets had melted to nothing overnight and it was an equal start for everybody. It could not last. After a long gasp as if to get one's second wind, capacity, energy and natural gifts set differentiation going once more.

Owing to the complete dispersal of people and the dislocation of all centres of creative activity, every village now boasted of its famous man: doctor, writer or artist, uprooted from his home. With plenty of time and no obligations, there ensued much exchange of thought and a flowering of talent in every field: books and plays were written, theatres sprouted in the most unlikely places, house-concerts assembled artists of world renown in the depths of the country.

Within certain limitations of ordinary politeness towards the occupying forces, there was at last complete liberty of expression and initiative. Under the wise and humane administration of General Clay and the subsequent consolidation of the German Mark, pioneering business talent would also presently break out, enabling Western Germany to soar away like a kite on the wings of prosperity – although we of the war generation could never bring ourselves later to waste bread or soap!

As the exceptionally fine summer turned to a golden autumn, a general effort was made to bring in some sort of a harvest. Hampered by the lack of adequate presses or machinery, twenty-five barrels of the finest vintage were nevertheless finally installed in the cellar, and the wine of 1945 was to become as memorable as the year it grew in.

Although we sighed as we took stock of all we still had to do to get Johannisberg back on its feet again, we were later to realise how lucky we were to be the ones who built and not those who destroyed. As far as we were concerned, the rapid swing backwards and forwards from living in a frame of space and beauty to cramped discomfort and total destitution seemed so inevitable in our time that it had lost its bite. In spite of our exhaustion, there was the incredible relief from lies, betrayal and terror. It was as if Nazism had been a sort of contagious death, and only now could one begin to live again.

It gave me hope for Russia. Perhaps one day they too would make the same recovery as from a mortal sickness.

Part Four

Journey to Austria,
Autumn 1945

1

In exchange for a corresponding amount of wine, we had acquired one of the two cars tucked away all through the war in a shed at Wolfsgarten. It was a blue Opel Super-Six Ford Cabriolet, upholstered in grey leather, and had belonged to Lu's brother, Don, who had perished with all his family in the plane accident of 1937. Wine, again, potatoes and fruit enabled us to reassemble tyres, motor block and permits. Luggage was no problem, for all our things fitted into a small bag. To own a car seemed the height of good fortune, a symbol of liberty, and at last we could leave for Austria to get our papers in order and find Missie.

We meant to return a few weeks later: it was to be two years before we saw Johannisberg again.

Just beyond Wiesbaden, a road block stopped us in our tracks. U.S. soldiers stood signalling a long queue of cars off the main road. The drivers, herded towards an office set up in the middle of a nearby village, looked harrassed and guilty. Most of them were using U.S. Army gasoline, and who could feel above suspicion what with the ever-changing regulations and 'Questionnaires'? We were prepared for any unpleasantness, from arrest to the confiscation of the car. The U.S. officer in charge, on being addressed in English, condescended to answer: 'Line up with the rest. A cow has been stolen!' White with rage, Paul burst out: 'Now get this clear: I could do many things but I would not steal a cow!' He strode back to the car, wheeled it out of line and off we drove, gravel spurting in our wake, while they stared after us, gaping, without attempting to stop us.

We avoided the autobahns, for they were encumbered by the Occupation Armies. Our status was still unclear, we were not too sure of the validity of our car papers, and uneasy as to the cheesy smell of the U.S. gasoline in our tank, which had however been carefully bleached through layers of charcoal.

But we felt alive as if by miracle, strengthened by months of rest as the lovely summer turned to a blaze of autumn foliage. For the first time in years, we were travelling for pleasure, intoxicated by the speed of our progress down empty roads, after all our previous trips on foot or by carriage.

Six months and aeons before, we had entrusted our bags in Bamberg to one of Paul's comrades, who was returning to the Ammersee in Bavaria. They had contained a collection of beautifully painted interiors of rooms intended for the Chancellor's second wife in 1826 which I had taken out of their frames in my Königswart bedroom – a few precious objects, and some essential clothes. We had hoped to pick them up on the way, for winter would be on us soon, and even needle and thread were still impossible to buy. We met with disappointment: they were no longer in his possession, lost or stolen somewhere on his way down.

We avoided Munich, which, although thoroughly destroyed, was now seething with American troops, and Garmisch, which had become a rest centre for the U.S. Army, its approach signalled by a sign marked: 'Boy, it's coming to you!' Beyond the city, another post regretfully commented: 'Brother, you've had it.'

On the Ammersee we found friends who were also hoping to get back to Austria. We stayed with them for a few days, reconnoitring where best to cross the frontier, which had been completely closed. We set off one morning to try it out, and reached the Salzburg autobahn by a roundabout route, bathing in an icy deserted lake on the way. A peaceful heady smell of hay, cow manure and autumn smoke pervaded the intact countryside as we approached the mountains. At the frontier, a CIC man tried to bully Paul into signing a paper by which he decided once and for all whether his interests lay on the German or on the Austrian side of the border. In neither case would he be allowed to return or to own anything in the neighbouring country. We tried two other frontier posts up and down the line without success. Our CIC man had been busy warning his colleagues not to let us through. Night began to fall. There was no chance of finding a room, as every available living space was crammed full of troops or refugees, and no food – but that we had expected. We drove up one hill after another, trying to find somewhere to sleep. It was getting almost too dark to see, so finally, high up on a mountain, Paul broke open the door of a large barn. We got the car in, spread a blanket over the hay, and curled up to sleep with Sherry, the scottie, our indispensable companion, wedged against us.

No sound broke the lovely airy silence, except for the tinkling of bells on grazing cows, and the occasional bleat of a sheep, some-where far down the mountain.

In the morning, we drove back to so-called 'civilisation' in the valley, and returned rather crestfallen to the Ammersee. A visiting U.S. General told us he had to go to Linz the next day, and that if we followed him, we would not be molested: he had a pass for our friend's car, if not for us. A long detour led us to Braunau, Hitler's birthplace, and the last spot we would have thought to visit. The General (who happened to belong to the division stationed there), waved a hand in our direction, saying airily: 'They are all with me.' It worked like a charm: U.S. sentinels saluted, and we were through.

Having heard Missie was there, we headed for Strobl on the Wolfgangsee. It was packed with refugees from Vienna, many friends of ours among them. We were met with the sickening news that Missie had left for Johannisberg to find us. In Red Cross uniform, she was accompanying a train of returning children, and must have crossed the frontier just as we were coming down. She seemed to have had the most adventurous escape from the Soviet Army in Vienna. Having no papers, we could not possibly return, but in comparison with the misfortunes we heard of on every side, I felt ashamed to complain about anything although my disap-pointment was overwhelming.

In one of the larger houses, partly requisitioned by some high-ranking U.S. officers, a small room was nevertheless found for us. Breakfast was taken together with our hosts downstairs, but our situation was embarrassing: no papers meant no food cards. Only potatoes were free but very scarce. Paul went in search of any which might have been overlooked in the harvested fields, and we modestly baked these in the oven, swallowing them with weak tea. No sugar, no milk, no butter. Each 'guest' ate his own food, and we tried to ignore the American delicacies spread before us, refusing offhandedly if some morsel was hesitantly proffered.

We were not far from St. Martin, where the white stallions from the Spanish Riding School of Vienna had been evacuated, whereas the mares and foals were in Hostau in Czechoslovakia. We now heard that the Director of the school, Colonel Podhajsky, a man of great resource and energy, induced General Patton to visit St. Martin, and a show was put on for his benefit. On hearing that the school was condemned if the mares and foals were not retrieved, Patton simply and expediently sent in a few tanks, and the stud was escorted first to Schwarzenberg in Bavaria, and then to Austria, where they rightfully belonged – in spite of howls of rage from the

Czechs, who were fortunately in no position to protest. This gesture brought a wave of genuine goodwill towards the Americans.

One afternoon, returning from a walk past empty boat sheds and balconies dripping with petunias under over-hanging eaves, I found Paul stretched out on the bed, looking green. The Scottie lay on the mat at his side, looking as green as a dog can look when deprived of a good bone since many a month. It was clear that dramatic measures to activate our legitimisation papers should be undertaken without delay, and this seemed only possible in Salzburg. We drove there the next morning past a series of lovely former tourist centres, now over-flowing with refugees, and tried to forget the waves of hunger – as yet a more light-headed than unpleasant feeling. Besides it was always a delight to return to Salzburg. The town spread on the hill towering over the rushing Salzach river, the baroque palaces and churches scattered down its flanks, and the pink and yellow jigsaw puzzle of a city, seemed barely scarred by the war, if in need of refurbishing. The bombers had passed it by. Perhaps the English remembered the famous festivals kindly, Jedermann, Mozart, Hofmannsthal, and the happy-go-lucky Austrian welcome may have struck a chord of pity.

The town was seething with Americans, but this time we were in search of Austrian legitimisation, and with patience and tenacity I plodded from one institution to another, colliding at last with an elderly 'Hofrat' in a minor but key position. His office exuded the cosiness of a much-used private study: books, a worn leather armchair, ledgers piled under a green-shaded lamp. Soft-spoken, polite, conciliating, with his *pince-nez* and clipped white moustache, he was the embodiment of the famous pre-World War I. 'K. und K.' (King and Emperor's) administration, which had for so long contrived to hold the unwieldy Empire together.

'Prince Metternich wants to live in Austria? How natural,' (Aber selbstverständlich) and he produced everything: food coupons, residence permits, Austrian identity cards, and then enquired: 'Have you got a car?' I confessed to this. Uneasily. 'Then you will need a number and gasoline. Just to start with: so much. But we will put through a request for more, for obviously Fürst Metternich will wish to go to Vienna!' I had met with the 'good Fairy' in disguise! and the more immediate problem of living, or rather of being allowed to live, was solved.

Paul was waiting for me when I emerged, but as a dash of cold water on too sanguine hopes, we found no place to sleep in Salzburg: all our friends' homes were packed to overflowing. We wished to avoid the proximity of a huge camp on the outskirts of the city in which many people we knew were still held, until they could prove where they came from and what they had or had not done during the war. For instance, it was considered a heinous crime to have served with the Cossack volunteers fighting in Yugoslavia – as many Austrians had been obliged to do. During the day, we tried to intercede for another friend of ours, assumed to have been trained as a spy, for he spoke three Balkan languages, besides English, French and German. The intricacies of nationality in the ex-Austro-Hungarian Empire seemed unfathomable, even for well-intentioned security officers, and many of these were ex-émigrés who were eager to vent their resentment on those who had stayed at home.

Finally we parked the car unobtrusively in the back yard of the Clary house, distant relations of 'our' Clarys. It was preferable to park within some enclosure, but we did not want to embarrass them by asking for quarters we knew they were not at liberty to dispose of. We tried to curl up in the back of the car and sleep, but it was turning cold; even poor Sherry's furry warmth was of no avail, and we shivered all night through. Next morning the Clarys discovered us and invited us in for breakfast. Mundi, the son of the house, was recovering from wounds: he had been shot after surrendering to the British in France. They had had to move on, so lined up their prisoners and simply shot them. We were almost relieved to hear such things had also occurred individually on the Allied side, if not by higher order, as under Hitler.

We then returned to Strobl, triumphantly independent again. The high road, leading through every village, now devoid of traffic, had become as cheerful a meeting-place as any Mediterranean Corso. We were hailed by Geza and Ali Pejacsevic who had come in search of us. They had escaped from Croatia via Budapest, and were living in a wooden villa near Gmunden, where they had left their two small boys. We decided to join forces and share all, until we could get to Vienna and reorganise our futures. Paul and I crammed into the gabled attic bedroom of their tiny house, perched high on a hill overlooking the Traunsee in a vast sweep from Gmunden to Ebensee, its doors were still chalked with the customary '19 C.M.B. 45' in honour of the Three Kings: Caspar, Melchior and Balthazar, remembered here in spite of that last terrible Christmas.

With pronounced relish for involved intrigue, Geza now plunged into the whirlpool of conflicting rules and black-market possibilities with almost excessive gusto. Paul and he went foraging far afield for essential necessities, helped by the inner grapevine of Croatian and Hungarian refugees, Geza's compatriots. Ali was one of the gay and musical Wilczek sisters from Vienna. She and I looked after the house and the children, visited our neighbours and received a constant flow of guests who sometimes had to sleep in rows on the floor of the sitting-room. We raced each other ironing our husbands' shirts, at first highly inexpert but improving with enforced practice. By and by we acquired some local clothes: silver-buttoned dirndls with knitted white stockings, lodens for the men. I made golliwogs for the little boys, and stuffed animals no zoo had ever seen, while Ali did her mending, and only when the men were away, did we allow ourselves the luxury of regretting our lost homes. In turn, half-laughing, we would describe one room after another, what our wedding presents had been like, and the flowers and trees we had planted that last year. Once we had gone through the list, we both felt better, whereas the men never wanted to refer to what was behind them.

We often heard marauding groups of stateless plunderers shooting in the distance, but one night shots sounded around the house when Ali and I happened to be alone. As the suspicious sounds of running feet and raucous cries drew near, we switched off all the lights and telephoned the nearest U.S. Officers' club in Gmunden for support. Ali would recall years later how I whispered to her urgently: 'Mind you stand in a blind angle where they cannot see you,' for the phone was next to the glass-paned front door. The idea suddenly tickled her sense of humour, and she burst into giggles about the 'blind angle'.

But the message got through, and shortly after a Military Police jeep came wheeling up the drive.

Paul and Geza had left for Salzburg to buy an entire calf from a shady character called Zifferer. He considered himself an honest businessman, bridging the inevitable vacuum in a paralysed economy and would have been deeply hurt if termed a 'fence', but he seemed to be in on every black-market deal up and down the country. He was a weedy-looking individual with a bushy black moustache, and was to be found at all times with his unprepossessing-looking wife or girl-friend fully-dressed in bed – whether from cold or other reasons one could never quite discern. This inevitable inclusion into the intimacy of Zifferer's private life was certainly not a matter of taste or even of policy, but his stronghold seemed to be his bedroom: the stores were kept there, and all transactions took place on or around his vast and lumpy bed.

The calf has been promised and felled, for both Geza and Paul refused to perform this office themselves. They had left early to collect the carcass.

There was a knock on the door of our chalet, and two men – one tall, one short – stood in the living-room. They turned back the lapels of their coats, and quietly said: 'Police!'

The word was disquieting, although it no longer struck the terror it inspired such a short time ago. Trying to appear as unconcerned as possible, we offered them a chair, schnapps, a cigarette and asked to what we owed their visit.

'We are in search of a criminal called Metternich.'

After a weighty pause, the older one added: 'We know he is not your husband.' (Nice to hear they did.) 'But we would like more particulars, and ask him not to leave the house today, as road-blocks have been put up all over the Salzkammergut and Upper Austria to catch our man. We would like to avoid any mistake.'

I ran to get photos of Paul and his identity card. They looked at everything with interest: 'Astounding resemblance, and the same dates, 1917, born in Vienna.' (Oh dear!) 'How tall is your husband?'

'1 metre 90.'

'Ah, there we are! Our man is much smaller: 1 metre 70!'

Before they left, hoping our husbands would avoid all check-points with their slaughtered calf, we asked for more details of the 'criminal'.

It appeared that he had been a soldier stationed in Pilsen at the end of the war. Escaping over the frontier near Königswart, he had by some fluke heard of our departure. From then on, he had dogged our footsteps, robbing, cheating and borrowing money all the way. He must have hung around while we were in Johannis-berg, waiting for our next move, and had then followed us on to Austria. He had declared himself to be Paul, and obtained a pension from the local Government, to start off on a renewed and fruitful career of larceny and embezzlement. He had even forged the stamps of all the Military Governments, and was now armed as well.

We had seen for ourselves how helpful it was to be called Metter-nich in Austria and we also lived on the fringe of rules and regu-lations, if scrupulously paying our way. Indeed it would seem that well-known names often suffered from a host of imposters. The Hessens were plagued by pseudo-relations, including the false Anastasia. There was a spurious Prince Wiazemsky in London, and my mother's family were not edified to hear that a GPU agent in Soviet Russia called herself by their name. We were comparatively lucky that our man should have been tripped up so soon, but it was startling to realise how easily a gangster could put these over-regulated and therefore almost lawless times to use.

To our relief, Paul and Geza soon returned, lugging the calf. They had come by back roads and never seen a single control.

With axe, saw, knives, and a total ignorance of the animal's anatomy, they set to work in the cellar, while we entertained the usual stream of visitors, trying to stifle the grunts and bangs coming from below stairs by lively conversation. Only a few intimates peeped down over the bannisters, and collapsed in mirth at the sight. We had begged for schnitzels, côtes de veau, blanquette, but the final result of their labours was a great quantity of chopped meat, suitable for goulasch only. 'Not a single schnitzel!' we sighed. But it all turned out for the best, as the news that we had more than enough to eat spread rapidly, and Hungarian, Czech, Yugoslav and Austrian friends followed in close succession. It was easier to keep a pot of goulasch cooking than to improvise a menu. Even Sherry began to take on the rotund aspect of a sleek and prosperous scottie.

In the local theatre of Gmunden first-rate plays were staged, acted by refugee Burgtheater actors from Vienna living in the vicinity along the lake. We made friends with many of them, and heard that they too had suffered from Nazi intrigues under Hitler, as my friend Neugebauer had intimated in Prague.

Baron Jeszensky kept open house for a number of Hungarian refugees in Schloss Kammer on the Attersee. Although handicapped by emigration and sudden poverty – many had crossed the frontier in the clothes they still wore – they managed to recreate the proverbial gaiety of Budapest night-life, and soon unearthed gipsy musicians to whom they listened with what they termed themselves 'émigré expressions' – a look of nostalgia mixed with slightly maudlin rapture. Charming and feckless, chivalrous and unreasonable, Hungarians would share their last crust and tip a waiter with the cuff-links they happened to be wearing. As for Spaniards, the 'geste gratuit' seemed more important at the moment than any consideration of what the next day might bring, but their fundamental solidarity helped them to find a new footing in an often hostile world.

How different all the 'K. und K.' (King and Emperor's) concomitants were! The Catholic Croatians seemed in fact much more akin to the Hungarians on one side and to the Italians on the other, than to their present compatriots, the Orthodox Serbs. And yet they had all found their place in the flexible structure of the Empire. Placed in a key position in Central Europe, Austrians are by tradition and character tolerant, kindly, at all times ready for negotiation and compromise – except incomprehensibly in 1914, and it was to be their downfall! They wait patiently for time to ripen, and perhaps even owing to their lack of passionate involvement, they seem to have been predestined to be the peacemakers of Europe.

Extreme nationalistic tendencies have given a distorted picture of their careful handling of the incredibly complex possibilities of explosion between the peoples around them. Their patience, tact and nonchalance: 'Die Türken sind auch einmal weggezogen . . .' (The Turks also left one day) now stood them in good stead when dealing with the Russians, whom they had unobtrusively set out to tame.

The terror caused by the invasion of the Soviet Army had abated. With their inborn talent for diplomacy, the Austrians had succeeded in coming to terms with their oppressors, becoming adept at handling them drunk or sober. In spite of occasional outbreaks of looting and raping, such unexpected nominations as that of the Duke of Hohenberg, (son of the Archduke Franz-Ferdinand murdered in Sarajevo in 1914, and recently freed from a Nazi concentration camp), to the post of Mayor of his home town of Amstetten, had brought some measure of reassurance.

On setting out for Vienna, we had been warned that a moody or drunken Soviet frontier guard was liable to tear up or keep our papers. We therefore hid our precious identity cards and car licence, holding photographed copies in readiness for eventual controls. The weather was turning bitterly cold, and Ali and I, padded in onion-like layers of clothing, huddled in the back of the unheated car, Sherry, warm as a bed-brick, between us. We tried to look as inconspicuous as possible, but as we approached the Russian Zone frontier post of Enns, near Linz, Ali whispered urgently to our husbands: 'If it comes to the worst, please don't intervene!' for this always led to immediate violence. In fact we did not really expect 'the worst' at a place where a number of Allied cars were bound to cross every day. However, we were all from suspicious regions: Yugoslavia or Czechoslovakia; I was born in Russia and Paul had fought there: nothing to feel too secure about.

The men were gruffly required to get out and enter a small wooden hut at the side of the road. An armed sentinel walked around the car, peeped in through the blurred panes, and grinning broadly, pointed at Sherry: 'Passagir!' (Passenger).

After a long wait, Paul and Geza returned accompanied by a

gesticulating, shouting Russian soldier. I translated in undertone: 'He wants to know how fast the car can go.' We had decided that it was better if I did not appear to speak Russian, for that brought on either excessive friendliness or sudden suspicion, but it was essential to know what they meant, as the most harmless question, blurted out in that rough way, sounded as if someone was going to be shot out of hand. The average soldier expressed a childlike fascination for any mechanical device, from a musical toy to a watch, or a car, and was more than ready to relieve one of its possession on the flimsiest (if any) pretext. They were, however, easily diverted by a friendly offer of cigarettes or schnapps. Our friends turned to me for an explanation but I was equally at a loss. I did not know my ex-compatriots in the mass. The Soviet prisoners we had met: the boys singing in the Marienbad church, the two Ukrainian girls who came walking for miles to see me only because they had heard I was Russian, the Cossack troops so loved by their Austrian officers, were warm, simple, earthy people, but not brutish.

We now faced a sort of 'mass' man. Was it the Army, or the excesses of war which brought out this primitive, completely unaccountable Neanderthal type of fellow? Wellington said there were no bad soldiers – only bad officers. Stalin had eliminated a great number of them just before the war, and losses during the German campaign added up to a daunting whole, resulting in a breakdown of discipline and lack of moral leadership. It was impossible to assess what turn any interchange would take, and every new confrontation with a Soviet Russian was like taming a potentially dangerous, but not ill-natured wild bear. When drunk, the wider the berth given them, the better.

An ex-Austrian American officer, on his way to Vienna in a smart roadster, found himself followed by a Soviet Army car. He pressed his foot down on the accelerator, not wishing to be held up on that deserted road, leading right through the Soviet occupation zone. The car behind him kept close on his heels, its driver making wild signs to him to stop. On reaching the centre of Vienna, our friend had to halt at a traffic light. His pursuer wheeled round to stop in front of him, and out jumped a Soviet officer, joyfully brandishing a bottle of schnapps: he only wanted to drink to the marvellous race they had had!

Driving towards the capital, we were relieved to find an American Army car on the road, and kept well in its wake through the sad and lifeless wintry landscape, blending into a leaden sky. The country seemed numbed by war and occupation. Metternich had said Asia began in his back garden. It now seemed to begin at Enns.

At last we reached the bruised and battered city, and headed straight for the Wilczek 'Palais' in the Herrengasse, next to the Hofburg.

The great front door was pulled open by the old doorman, beaming at the sight of Ali, and hastily barred behind us. Our car seemed safe in the courtyard. A single set of rooms was still at the disposal of the family, and Ali's uncle, Count Cari, who had stayed on in Vienna right through the siege, was living in it. He made room for us, and we squeezed into what had been the childrens' rooms in the old family palace. We slept fully dressed, for at night the temperature dropped far below freezing point. There was no heating, except for a small stove in the bathroom and another in the kitchen, which became the centre of social gatherings, cheered by a few bottles of wine Ali had wheedled from the porter: jealously guarded remains of the family cellar. Her brother, Hansi, had survived a near-lethal shot through the neck, which had prevented his return to the Front during those last murderous months. He was now trying to get in touch with their ravaged estate near Vienna. His brother-in-law, Ferdinand Traun, attempting to plan some future for his lovely wife and six children, tucked away in boring safety on some mountain top, soon also joined our small group in the Herrengasse. The news that we had arrived spread rapidly, and before long we were in contact with a number of friends and acquaintances, trying to find their footing among the quicksands of the 1946 winter in Vienna. Among them were artists and musicians, such as Herbert von Karajan, who having no choice but to persevere in their profession, turned to 'entertainment' for troops and country during the war, and now found themselves 'compromised' by having done so. The Allies, however, were much more friendly than on the German side, since their policy for Austria seemed to go under the heading of 'liberation'.

We met in small groups all over the 'Erster Bezirk', – the first district – feeling safer there than on the outskirts of the town, for Vienna had been cut into four administrative zones: Russian, American, British and French, whereas the centre, the 'Erster Bezirk' was common ground, occupied by all four nations, each in turn taking the chair for a month. A Military Police Jeep, symbolically containing one Soviet, one American, one English and one French solider, toured the centre at all times. The large hotels had also been equitably distributed: the Grand Hotel and Imperial to the Soviets, the Bristol to the Americans, and the Sacher to the English. The French, however, were far less in evidence although General Béthouart, occupying the Tyrol, was to become the most popular of the Allied Commanders. His humane administration would be remembered gratefully for many years to come.

It was still too soon to venture into the surrounding country, which was entirely in Soviet hands, although some more enterprising friends did so every now and again, foraging for food, or trying to ascertain what had survived the invasion (or liberation, as it should now be called.) At last we heard at first hand what had happened during and since the siege.

We had been in Vienna frequently all through the war, and had witnessed a number of Allied air attacks. During one of them a bomb had obliquely entered the cellar of the Liechtenstein Palace just behind the Burgtheater, killing all its occupants except Constantin Liechtenstein's little girl. She had jumped off her mother's lap to run to him, as he stood talking to his father under the vaulted entrance. They were to be the only survivors.

Some time later, an Allied plane crashed on to the roof of the same building, destroying the baroque staircase and courtyard. The pilot hung clinging to the roof's edge, and although people dashed to help him, he could not be reached in time.

Those who had rushed into burning houses to save people or objects would say that the first moment of instinctive unwillingness to do so would soon be replaced by a sort of mad attraction for danger, an irresistible impulse to see how far one could go; but it appeared to be a major decision to start breaking open drawers or cupboards, as if plundering, even with the intention of salvaging someone's belongings.

The raids had become ever more murderous, indiscriminatly destroying hospitals, monuments and churches, and trapping hundreds in shelters, as under the Jockey Club in the centre of the city. The cellars were then opened up to communicate with each other through the catacombs, and there the Soviet Army, breaking into the capital, stumbled over vast stores of wines and spirits. Riotous drinking ended in a wild splurge of plunder and rape.

The stunned population fled, hid, or was forced to submit in the most brutal way. The procedure was expedient: the first two or three women who resisted were shot 'to clear the way'. The owner of an umbrella shop down the street told me she and her young daughter had hidden, crouching on the floor of an outdoor telephone booth for forty-eight hours.

Girls rubbed their faces with nettles, or took refuge in the most unlikely places, but soon it appeared that no woman of any age was safe, for Soviet soldiers laboured under the superstition that old women brought luck against bullets.

Next to dramatic cases, there was of course the usual crop of 'funny' stories. The 'char' of the Wilczeks, Frau Herzinger, a typical Nestroy Operetta character, related with relish how a young boy had tried to attack her, but she belaboured him with a rolling-pin, screeching: 'Get going, get going! Shame on you, you could be my son' (Geh ma, geh ma! Schäm Dich, könntest mein Sohn sein), at which he beat a hasty retreat.

A group of friends were held at gun-point in a Vienna 'palais', and a spinster of uncertain age was ordered to step outside. She had been of non-descript appearance – 'ein Popo-Gesicht', but after they had sat for some hours, praying for her to be sustained by fortitude in this hour of tribulation, the door opened, and in came a radiant beauty. In answer to urgent questions, she remarked nonchalantly: 'He only talked about his home,' and with that they had to be content.

After a few days, a sort of discipline set in again and taking heart, the Viennese began to counter incursions of drunken soldiers by a bush-telephone system of frantic screams. A Russian only had to appear, for every woman in the house to start caterwauling. This was immediately taken up by the next house, up and down the street, resulting in the prompt intervention of the Military Police.

Professor Knaus, the famous gynaecologist, who had moved from Prague to Vienna, told me that after those first days of general rape, the clinics of Vienna had thrown open their doors, bypassing all regulations, begging every woman who had cause to do so, to come free of charge: no names or questions would be asked. It was a pitiful sight: endless queues from every walk of life, some in a desperate state. 'At least there were hardly any men here at the time,' he had added. 'Not like in Budapest . . .' where when the men intervened, they would be shot out of hand.

If they had no one to look after them, elderly people died in great numbers from hunger or neglect. The sad death of our old friend Ambassador Count Mensdorff was no exception.

People would be suddenly grabbed off the street and mobilised for some chore, or marched off to Siberia: it was impossible to know which until a heavy guard surrounded them and by then it was too late to get away. Weeping wives ran alongside, offering jewellery or schnapps in exchange for their husband or son, and frequently the soldier in charge would let him go, only to grab some chance passer-by to replenish his quota. A sophisticated friend of ours was forced to carry a huge sack, but surreptitiously widening a hole in it as he went, he had succeeded in losing a great deal of the sugar he was transporting. He found this a minor irritation, compared to wielding a 'Panzerfaust' during the siege: 'Cet engin dont j'ai horreur!' that detestable contraption, he sniffed with disgust.

The average Soviet soldier, and even many officers, appeared unused to the most elementary sanitary system. On occasion butter would be cooled in W.C.s, or broken glass piled into the cavity, as if expecting aggression from that quarter. Cupboards would be stacked with newspaper parcels, later traced by the stink; and yet to be termed 'ne kulturni' would have been considered the greatest insult.

Another of those icy, biting 'war' winters was upon us, and we had no winter clothes. Peter Habig, head of a well-known firm, offered to re-make the suit and coat he had sent me two years before, lost with so much else, and I then went to fittings in the workshop in the Soviet Zone. One evening, two Soviet officers strode into the back room, and jostled in between me and the long mirror, trying on felt hats which looked like overturned puddings, for they omitted to dent the crown. The dress-maker and I fell back a step, but they meant no harm. Night fell early, and not noticing how late it was, I ran down several ill-lit floors passing three Soviet soldiers on their way up. Pungent comment in Russian making their intentions clear, they turned and clattered down after me, but I dashed for the street before they had time to reach the front door. We were more careful after that, especially during the 'Soviet' month in the 'Erster Bezirk', for one night we had to flee like pursued deer.

We were returning down the Augustinerstrasse, when suddenly: 'Davaf!' 'Davaf!' the plunderer's cry, resounded down the empty streets. Paul grabbed my elbow and we ran for our lives – or at least for our coats!

With a roar, three Soviet soldiers burst out from behind the monument on the Josefsplatz to our left: they had been lying in wait of likely prey. Brandishing sawn off machine guns, our pursuers galloped after us: through the shadowy arch under which satin-smooth white Lippezaners, harnessed in scarlet and gold, used to cross over from their stables to the Hofburg; on we dashed across the Michaelaplatz, down the Herrengasse. The old porter had been waiting for us, and, hearing the yells and clatter of running feet, he instantly opened the door to our call. We slipped through, and all three panting and straining, threw our weight against it. The heavy bar fell into its sockets as the soldiers battered on the other side, seconds too late.

The great capital was in a sorry state: gutted houses, peeling remains of paint, broken panes patched with cardboard, deficient plumbing, twisted ironwork, loose slates, banging shutters hanging askew between gaping holes and piles of rubble. There was not an object or a building which did not require urgent repair. Incongruous names in chipped lettering were still discernible over some doorways: 'Dentist Jammer' (Howls), pawn shop 'Ehrenfest' (Honourbound), cleaners 'Habsburg', and 'Macalka und Peinlich' (Distress) roofers, who could at least all be sure of a flourishing trade. They sounded like the card game of 'Happy Families' we had played in our childhood.

The roof of the beautiful cathedral of St. Stephen bombed by the Allies, had caved in, and postcards were now put into circulation picturing the mosaic of many-coloured tiles. Each one was numbered, and on paying a modest sum, one received a receipt confirming which tile one had paid for. It was an expedient and satisfying arrangement, but the Viennese were still resentful about its destruction, and when an Allied airman asked his way to the Cathedral, he was told tartly: 'If you could find it alone from the air, you can jolly well find it alone on foot!'

Paul intended to enter the Austrian Foreign Service, and at first he met with much encouragement. But soon it appeared that the moment was inopportune: there could be no room for a Metternich in the administration of a country occupied by the Soviets. We then embarked on endless 'démarches' to obtain a valid travel document and the corresponding visas, which could only be awarded by each occupation Army in turn. Passports were not issued as yet, so we erased the forbidding sentence 'not for travel abroad' from our Austrian identity card, and added a number of pages. It would become an impressive document, accumulating innumerable stamps, for nothing would deter Paul from travelling after eight years of war. But for the time being, we waded through a quagmire of 'Fragebogen' (questionnaires).

Among all the plagues invented to pester mankind, that of the 'Fragebogen' was one of the most irritating. A Russian friend once told me that he considered any personal question an unbearable impertinence, starting with 'How do you do.' 'It does not concern anyone how I do!' But he was a pre-revolutionary white Russian, quite out of touch with modern times.

Probing, prying questions delved into one's private life. This had already begun under the Nazis, and alas, with the advent of the Allied Forces, it acquired the impetus of an avalanche. Ever longer lists of questions rained down on all and sundry, producing a feeling of guilt for having brown or fair hair, for having travelled, for not having travelled. And why? For how long, and where have you lived for the last ten or twenty years, with the exact address?

'I have travelled out of curiosity. For pleasure.' No, this would never do. Such terms were a luxury. In a destroyed and ravaged Europe, where waves of refugees were hurled from one country to another, how was one ever to explain on one line why one had had five nationalities, or rather five passports, and possibly no birth certificate? One must apologise for existing at all, and especially for surviving. A chance employee could decide with one stroke of the pen, whether a person belonged to one country or another, and in which zone he was to live. Free improvisation was the only possible answer, but how was one to remember what had been written last time?

It soon transpired that they now slipped these answers into a machine, typed the name, pressed a button, and out came all corresponding war-crimes. Should one have the misfortune of bearing the name of Schmidt or Müller, what vast possibilities there were for confusion.

The Americans considered the French sinfully preferential for still assessing a person by looks, manners or credentials, yet in the long run this seemed more dependable than the machine.

To get in touch with one authority after another was the 'wives' ' job, for the men were averse to asking for anything, and would be turned down if they did. Friendly relations having been established, Ali and I would be invited to some dinner or party, and then disappointed our hosts by bringing our husbands along as a matter of course, and often some friends as well. Invited once to the British Officers' Club, we arrived with four men. All the food came from the famous pastry-cook Demel, to which we had no access. We had tried not to seem too ravenous, but as we were leaving, Ali and I found ourselves in a cloakroom lined with tables, piled high with Demel pastries. I am ashamed to say we barely hesitated, and filled our pockets, rearranging the heaps so as to veil the theft. We were offered a lift home in a Military Jeep, and there ensued an embarrassing moment, as we climbed in, clutching our coats so as not to strew a ring of telltale pastry around our feet. For the next few days our men got one each for breakfast.

Our normal fare was heated weak tea and baked potatoes. Bread and butter in thin slices induced sudden euphoria, and lard, when forthcoming, could be eaten in lumps without disgust. Sometimes corned beef or a piece of sausage appeared, 'bought' at the corner antique shop in exchange for coffee, the new gold standard.

To obtain some foreign currency for our journey to Spain, a box of silver cutlery which we had left in Vienna now found its way to Hungary to be sold to Käthe von Nagy, a well-known Hungarian actress, apparently high in favour with a Soviet Marshal. The transaction went through many hands, and the final result for us was a few English five-pound notes. We knew we had been cheated, but were relieved to have them. Hungarian friends had exchanged silver plate or precious stones for a chunk of ham. Precious stamp collections went for a song: nobody seemed to mind.

The black market had in fact come out into the open, and was centred around the Karlskirche, the church in which Paul had been baptised. Anyone could take anything there, keeping a wary eye open for Military Police of any denomination. Soviet Army soldiers and officers came with looted goods, watches from wrist to elbow; peasants brought food smuggled in from the country; one could find telephone cables, electric bulbs, taps – anything liable to be screwed or prised loose in a plundered city, but the exchange served its purpose and enabled many to survive that cold and hungry winter.

However in its shade, criminals took over too: medicines, especially the new and precious penicillin, were diluted and mixed, with lethal results. Passports, money and stolen goods, treasures from looted museums, changed hands here, and many a doubtful 'deal' could be 'fixed' in no time.

Gradually the mounting tension between the Allies began to be felt. The contrast between the American and Soviet way of life at close quarters was too blatant to be over-looked by any 'appeasement' illusions, fomented since Yalta. Here at least it was common knowledge, that the 'repatriated' Cossacks, Vlassov volunteers and Soviet prisoners of war had been met with firing squads or deported to Siberian camps. Stalin's iron hand fell on all within reach. Spying and counter-spying, illegal frontier crossings and kidnappings were also just on the edge of our daily lives.

The administration of the country being entirely in the hands of the soon not-so-united Allies, we existed in a No-Man's-Land between duty and lawlessness, freed from all sense of possession and any civic responsibility. Unexpectedly, this state produced a tendency to naughty tricks, like children when teacher's back is turned.

An enterprising friend had discovered the code of Allied Military telephone relays, and it became a favourite pastime to use it illegally. It gave us the illusion of not being so cut off from the outer world. With a rosary of magic words: 'Antonia . . . Blackbird . . . Peanut' we would order a tie from London, or indulge in a chat with relations in Rome or Paris. However, we could not get through to Germany or Spain. Nearly two years earlier, I had tried to get in touch with Paul, lost in the depths of Russia, just as illegally. It was disquieting to think to what far less innocent use this chain of names evoking girls and spring may have been put to on both sides, during the war.

And yet, in spite of intense privation, personal material loss, distressing news from all sides, regulations and 'Fragebogens' hemming us in, but affording no protection or defence against abuse, there was a strong feeling of fraternal solidarity between us all, and such sincere joy in reunion with friends one never thought to see again, that the general mood was unjustifiably carefree.

Having been for so long so close to death, there was the tremendous lift of life starting off once more – perhaps also a certain light-headedness through being so often hungry. The most blood-curdling adventures were related as a joke, and one was later tempted to say: 'It was all awful, but we had such fun!'

After American and English permits, we had at last even acquired the Soviet one. The French only delivered theirs in their zone, the Tyrol. Plans had to be readjusted, but winter was setting in and the Tyrol was a pleasant place in which to ignore its icy grip. In the U.S. Zone at Linz, a gum-chewing G.I. carelessly sprayed us with D.D.T., to the disgust of self-respecting and clean Austrian citizens queuing up with us, who felt they were being treated like cattle. No soaping or brushing had eliminated the hen-lice which our Scottie had picked up on some visit to a girl friend of low degree. I now held him up gratefully for a generous squirt of this magical and hitherto unknown powder. A small bag of it was added for good measure, with much joking and the usual offer to buy our dog, in exchange for any amount of cigarettes.

On our return to Gmunden, where we were to spend Christmas, we at last got news of Missie, who would join us in Kitzbühel: she was unexpectedly engaged to an American officer. This was startling news.

On reaching Johannisberg after many tribulations, Missie had been met with the news that we had just left. Between Austria and Germany, all communications had been severed, as we had ourselves experienced when trying to cross the frontier without any possibility of returning at the time. I was deeply disappointed to have missed her, for we had shared all our joys and sorrows during these turbulent years and had remained as close as all through our childhood.

While Missie was recovering from the last strenuous months in Johannisberg, she met her future husband, Peter Harnden, an American officer, who had been sent to us by mutual friends. He was an architect by vocation, a man of warm heart and great vitality. Some months later, she at last succeeded in joining us in Kitzbühel to introduce her fiancé. Peter's first preoccupation before settling into the primitive inn in which we had found rooms, was to saw off the legs of a number of tables, and line the walls of the 'common room' with mattresses, discreetly concealed by U.S. army mattresses. He then produced candles, egg powder and peanut butter, while we looked on, bemused.

Missie and I slept on mattresses on the floor of the only bedroom. Peter had vetoed the high wooden bedsteads. At last we could talk over all our adventures.

Missie and Peter were married in the old church of the village, a Russian priest, a choir, crowns and requisites having been produced like rabbits out of a conjuror's bag from refugee camps in the surroundings. The religious ceremony was followed by a cheerful reunion of French officers, the future Ambassador in London, Johnny von Herwarth and his wife, who were pre-war friends of Peter's, and our aged uncle Serge Issakoff, our Grandmother Wassiltchikoff's brother, who had recently joined his family emigrating from Eastern Europe.

Peter wore his uniform as a temporary disguise. Generous and full of cheer, he was to say that his only spoils of war were his wife and an ancient sports car, a BMW he had fished out of the Rhine. He was to become one of the most energetic promoters of the rehabilitation of Western Europe before returning to his profession as an architect.

Her new life, so different from all she had gone through, was to cure Missie from the moral shock of the war and the 20th July plot. Although this marriage had seemed to us a hasty decision, it was to be the foundation of a numerous and united family and twenty-five years of happiness.

The snow began to melt, brooks and rivers breaking loose; young people in becoming dirndls and lederhosen sat playing the zither outside their wooden houses, the window-boxes overflowed with plants, shutting out the light from low zirbel-panelled rooms. We skied ever higher up the mountain and waited, until, at last, our French permit arrived.

In a splurge of wild and riotous living, we ate up our monthly ration cards in three days: the single egg per head, the quarter-pound of butter and bits of sausage, distributing dried peas, bread and oatmeal. At the last moment the car broke down, but the missing part was exchanged for my dirndl jacket and we were on our way!

On leaving the Austrian frontier of Feldkirch, the guard asked to see what I had in my handbag. I travelled with my jewels packed tightly into a small red leather case, marked 'travelling slippers' (which it had once contained). A tray was fetched, and the contents emptied out on to it. Fumbling among the stones shimmering in the dark backroom, he extracted a tie-pin, topped by a tiny diamond-encrusted cock. Holding it to the dim light, he enquired: 'Real gold?'

Too dumbfounded for comment, I mumbled: 'Possibly . . .'

'All right, take it along,' he said kindly, as he swept the glittering heap together again. He had thought it was all junk! We were simply dressed, and carnival jewellery (much used in these parts) tended to be gawdy. Remembering belatedly that one of the Fragebogens enjoined: 'No objects of value', I had mentally taken leave of the whole lot.

The sudden impact of prosperity in Liechtenstein was intoxicating! The streets were so clean, one could sleep on them; the houses and cars as immaculate as toys just removed from a cardboard box; the shops bursting with watches, mink-coloured cows grazed undisturbed in salad-green fields; smooth-faced stout burghers seemed to lift an eyebrow to unruly intruders, hypnotically inducing immediate good behaviour.

We felt law-abiding citizens again.

We stayed for a few days with the Liechtensteins at their fairy-tale castle of Vaduz, packed with unbelievable treasures. Our hosts had left Vienna after bombs hit their palace two years before. We were warmly welcomed, for Josef used his exceptional status as Chief of this tiny state to help as many of his friends and relations as possible. Gina, born Wilczek, had all the charm and grace of her family, and was now naturally eager for news of her cousins.

In Zürich we stayed for one night in the Hotel Baur au Lac. We were given the Royal Suite with a huge drawing-room, and an equally huge sheaf of flowers shading a basket full of every sort of fruit, not just the monthly orange: we hardly dared think of the cost. In the Bank where we then went to change our precious five-pound notes from Budapest, the clerk coldly announced: 'They are forged.' Our look of consternation must have reassured him, for he then explained that the Nazis had forged foreign currency on a grand scale, even paying their spies with it.

As we drove on through France, our spirits soared again. At last we reached the Spanish frontier. The official gathered up our odd-looking documents and disappeared for a while: they had never seen anything like them before, and could not be responsible for letting us in. But we had left France, and could not return there on a transit visa. It was too late to phone Madrid, and Spanish telephones would lose the race against Congo bush-drummers. 'Demora' (delay) was the explanation, with a vague gesture.

We felt like a runner jerked back by a cord, for we had expected difficulties everywhere except here.

But next morning, after a miserable night in a 'fonda', the local inn, the call to Madrid got through and the entire frontier-post buzzed with profuse apology as they waved us on our way.

We were received with open arms and treated at first as if we had come from the moon. Soon life resumed its usual rhythm in spite of our much changed circumstances. I had thought never to need evening clothes again, but soon there was a ball, and the outstanding dressmaker Balenciaga, who owed his career to a cousin, lent me a wonderful dress.

Entering the red drawing-room of the old Madrid Palace I once found Marysia rather absent-mindedly saying her rosary.

'Whom are you praying for, now that this nightmare is over?' I asked.

'The Primate of Poland, Cardinal Wyszinsky, has declared that the Polish people cannot live with the hate they bear the Germans. He told us to choose the worst one and to pray for him. The worst was Frank, the "butcher of Cracow". So now we all pray for him.'

The days went by, and we heard that among those condemned to death at the Nürnberg trials, Frank alone repented and returned to the Catholic Faith.

'You see,' said Marysia, showing me the paper. 'It refers to our Frank.'

The fact, that she could say 'our' was like a breath of mercy over the murderous waves of hate still rolling over Europe.

Many years later in Johannisberg, we received a telegram: 'Passing through Germany, may I visit you? Arthur Mullin ex-Commander of Marienbad.'

So much time had gone by since our two dramatic interviews in May 1945; the young officer had turned into a lawyer with greying temples, accompanied by his charming wife, Leinie. An article in the American magazine 'Holiday' had inspired him with the wish to see how we were doing. On our side, we were curious to know what had happened after our departure.

'Well, you left me a comprehensive shopping-list,' he said.

'What could you do about it?'

'Everything. I emptied the hospitals and evacuated the wounded as well as the Russians, the frontier being so close. As to the babies, we could not save them all, for we did not have the right food or care. But we did our best. We let you go and put a guard on your house. We lacked bandages. That was quite a problem.'

'Our house was packed with Red Cross stores!' I cried. 'Ten minutes more, and I would have told you about it.'

'We managed as far as possible with linen and Kleenex.' he said.

We were amazed, for our illusions as to Allied Governments had melted rapidly under the icy wind of Teheran and Yalta agreements, handing over whole nations and millions of Russians to Stalin's vengeance. Even my father's old friend, General Krasnoff, who had emigrated after the Revolution and was a writer of merit, was delivered to Soviet troops, although he was in the zone occupied by the British. He was then hanged on a square of Moscow. Only the reigning Prince of Liechtenstein, General Patton and the French Generals de Lattre de Tassigny and Béthouart opposed these measures, without even incurring any unpleasant consequences.

'Why did you do it?' I asked Mullin.

'You were rather persuasive.' (At the time, I was indeed sure everything would now be for the best.) 'And then,' he added, 'Patton's Army was an offended Army. We had been held back all the way. We thought we were going on to Berlin, for there was no opposition to speak of . . . and were turned back instead. There was a strong feeling right up to the top of "Don't add to the mess." '

He was then entrusted with a camp of over fifteen thousand German prisoners of war. The Americans only disposed of their own rations. Mullin then chose four or five highly decorated young German officers out of the camp. 'Seeing their Ritterkreuzes and all the rest, I thought that they had more experience than we had, after six years of war and the Russian campaign; and these were the ones who ran it ... I gave them 'laissez-passers' like yours, two jeeps with our drivers and told them to run the camp. I thought they would not ruin their own countrymen. They first gave their word not to run away. They did a good job, finding hams like maize cobs hanging under the rafters of the peasants of Northern Bavaria ... Meanwhile, I sat in my little office and trembled ... But we didn't lose a man, and they were dying like flies in other camps. After three weeks, we got our food, but it takes less than three weeks for fifteen thousand men to starve.'

'How old were you?' I asked gently.

'Twenty-seven.'

By chance that day in Johannisberg, I was supposed to inaugurate a competition of Rhenish choir-singing. I climbed on to the platform with Mullin and said: 'This guest of ours was a young officer in Patton's Army. In spite of contrary regulations, he saved a great number of people by evacuating them in the teeth of the Soviet Army, and then through sheer good sense and kindness saved thousands of camp inmates from hunger. I would like you to cheer him.'

The ovation which then burst out in resonant Rhenish voices, was all the more joyous owing to generous libations of Johannisberg wine.

Part Five

Twenty years later:
Königswart and Plass revisited

2

I would have preferred never to return. In dreams I had often wandered from room to room, each door opening with its characteristic creak. Sometimes the dream became nightmarish and it seemed as if we were living those last days of April 1945 in Königswart again, oppressed and harrassed on all sides. But never did it appear as I remembered it: shimmering white, nestling among tall feathery trees, translucent in the sunshine.

I did not want to see it again, but Paul felt he had to go there once and be rid of nostalgic regret.

It seemed best to cross the border in the morning, so we slept in Markt Redwitz next to the frontier, and that night I dreamt of Königswart for the last time in a strange preview of our visit a few hours later: everything was exactly as it turned out to be – like a projection of the mind before the feet could follow.

We were quite alone at the frontier. There was an endless wait in the little shack while Paul's papers were inspected and a one-day transit visa awarded. When he said he needed a second day, the answer was: 'Quite all right: it is also valid for two.'

But they would not change it on the paper. Probably it puts one always in the wrong, so as to trip us up more easily, should they wish to do so.

While Paul was in the shack a man had come up to the car and asked for a lift, but I said we were not going to Prague directly.

'I am not in a hurry and could show you the region.'

'Thank you, we know our way.'

'I would not disturb you.'

'We prefer to be alone.' I said at last firmly. Looking back as we drove off, I saw him go straight back into the frontier office. As I had thought, he was no hitchhiker.

Absorbed by our first sight of the country we had loved after so
many years, we turned off the main road towards Sandau, shocked
at the change: empty houses, nothing repaired, shutters flapped
on broken hinges, the roofs gaped open.

It has been such a neat little village, famous for handmade lac-
quer boxes and leather travelling-bags which found their way to
the best shops in Carlsbad and Vienna. The window-boxes were
always full of flowers, petunias in summer and fir and pine twigs in
winter. More effectively than any traffic sign, herds of cackling
geese, meandering in the middle of the road, would slow one down
just before the sharp curve leading straight for the pond.

Now all was quiet and deserted in the warm June sunshine.

The golden roads had turned grey-black, powdered with coal
dust they must have gone far to fetch. Paul was more unhappy at
this than at anything else as yet.

We passed the pile of rocks near the brook, where the first lilies
of the valley sprouted, crossed the railtrack and drove past the
farm: every building sadly in need of repair.

We turned the last corner, and there lay the house.

In marked contrast to everything we had seen on the way, it had
been repainted in a uniform yellowish tone. All the creepers had
been torn off, and the rhododendron bushes I had been at such
pains to plant removed. The two large Thorwaldsen marble
medallions encrusted into the wall at the end of each wing had
vanished.

Military cars were parked near the entrance outside the gates.
Wondering why, we parked there too and walked into the wide
courtyard, past a group of rather skinny pale young girls in scanty,
faded bikinis, and young men in checked shirts lolling – faces tilted
to the warm June sun – on gilded drawing-room chairs, forlorn out-
casts of sets of chairs I recognised at once. They did not take the
slightest notice of us.

We joined a nondescript group of tourists standing in front of
the main entrance: 'You must buy tickets. The guide will come
at once.'

The ticket office had been built into a recess leading to the
kitchen on the right of the lower hall, now filled by Metternich's
State Coach, battered and faded. It had been in impeccable condition, but we had heard that in 1945 the U.S. Army amused themselves driving around in it after our departure. Later it had been a
playground for the refugee children and was used for proletarian
weddings, until finally reinstated as 'Exhibit A'.

I tried to re-charge my camera on the steps let down from its open door, but my hands trembled and the reel was irretrievably lost.

We went upstairs with the rest, feeling like our own ghosts, come back to haunt the marvellous old house again.

Nothing seemed to have changed here: the same pictures gazed down at us, the alabaster vase was still in its niche, the then already shabby green carpet had become a little more threadbare, the mahogany letter-box at the top of the stairs was gone, and of course also the coats and walking sticks which lay on the stand next to it.

We turned in docile file towards the guest-room wing. Shooting trophies still lined the corridor – branching antlers or boar tusks, mounted on small boards neatly marked with name and date. Below them ran the traditional series of Riedinger engravings depicting aberrations of nature: mossy antlers in capricious array, a white stag with the caption 'aus dero hoher Hand erlegt' as some royal guest accounted for it. One would almost have expected the line of sandbags, placed at every door during the war.

We were herded through the green-padded door into my dressing-room. It was quite empty: all the French Empire furniture gone, only the lamp still hanging. My writing-room next door was stipped bare too, as if it had shrunk. (Where could all my papers and books have gone?) I remembered again Fritzi Fürstenberg describing how he felt when he thought of all his personal belongings, even schoolboy butterfly collections, being pored over by thoughtless, inimical, faceless people, 'as if one had zipped him up and looked into his stomach.'

As we moved into the red corner drawing-room, Paul and I whispered together, while the guide pattered on. She kept glancing in our direction: an elderly woman, grey hair drawn into a tight bun, speaking German for the benefit of the East German tourists with us. Unexpectedly she said:

'If you would like to see pictures of the last owners, here they are!' and from behind a sofa she extracted our portraits done by a Viennese artist just before our marriage. I had left them behind on purpose, hoping to leave some trace of us in the house.

With a coy smile she added: 'You see, I recognised you at once!'

Recovering from shock, I asked: 'If you don't hang them up, couldn't we have them back again?' (That of course would not be possible, but called for some explanation.)

'I put them away because people said unkind things about you. Untrue things.'

Now this was also not quite true. A friend of ours, the racing driver Louis Chiron, had been here and said the tourists were treated to a 'boniment' (rigmarole) on 'the previous exploitation by capitalist reactionaires', to which there had been laughs: 'They don't look like it!' and Louis promptly said: 'What nonsense, I know them well.'

Shortly after, one of our Soviet friends told us he had been to Czechoslovakia and asked to visit our house in Königswart. The guide started off on the ritual litany of 'Bloodsuckers of the People', which he probably didn't believe in himself, but thought appropriate for his audience.

Our friend lifted a majestic hand: 'Stop! All lies. Proprietor is friend!' greatly enjoying the effect of this statement on subservient Czech communists accompanying him.

Our guide now added playfully: 'I know all about you! I have read all your letters!'

I answered drily: 'Even I would hardly know now which letters were mine and which not, since so many were given to me to keep here for safety at that time.' (They were love-letters for the most part, starting with a term of endearment – they must have acquired a distorted notion of my consumption of admirers if they attributed them all to me.)

In an aside, perhaps wishing to conciliate, she said: 'We also know from your letters, whatever "they" may say, that your husband was no Nazi.' (And yet for years after they went on repeating these false allegations, until Paul wrote an official letter of protest, which produced some effect.)

From then on, she only talked to us, well-meaning in a clumsy way. The other tourists stared blank-faced, uncomprehending, then wandered on in shuffling felt slippers, getting their money's worth, while we glanced around, noticing all that was missing in the emptying rooms. We had heard numerous accounts which gradually pieced the whole story of depredation together.

Under American custody during the first years after the war, the house escaped looting, except for the understandable distribution of my clothes and the linen among the girl-friends of the U.S. soldiers in charge. Then U.S. Ambassador Steinhardt restored order, and established a new inventory.

When the Czech authorities took over, the safe in Paul's room was opened by two criminals brought in from the prison in Pilsen for the purpose, but we had left nothing of value inside. It was then that they chopped down the great tree in front of the lake for firewood, and the bridge to the island collapsed, never to be repaired.

We had reached Metternich's study, which could not be dis-
mantled so easily. It was still lined from floor to ceiling with filled
bookcases, but many pieces of lovely furniture were missing: the
map stand, the document cases and even one writing-table. No
carpets anywhere.

In the green salon I exclaimed in surprise: 'But these did not
belong to the house!' A set of heavily gilt late Empire chairs were
set in the middle of the room like in an old-fashioned dentist's
waiting-room. Metternich would never have had such ugly things
around him.

'We are collecting everything belonging to "that" period,' the
guide said primly.

What can 'that' period be, one wonders. The Chancellor lived
for a very long time. Although he rebuilt the house, there were
many things of interest for family and European history before and
after his time, besides the charm of all the not necessarily
'precious' objects, collected from generation to generation. We
had heard that a steady stream of small pilfering had set in: officials
would arrive in cars and carry away carpets, the mediaeval tapestry
from the red drawing-room or smaller objects which happened to
have caught their roving eyes. The official excuse would probably
be: 'Not relevant to the period.'

With the elastic justification of whittling away a decade here, a
decade there, bureacratic veneer covered arbitrary measures. No
one would dare to gainsay them.

After the unchanged billard-room came the central main
drawing-room, with windows on both sides of the house leading
out on to wide balconies we had sometimes dined on in summer. It
was quite empty except for the Canova statues and a few pictures.
Where were the stone inlaid Italian consoles, Chinese chests, the
writing table, the great carpet which were still to be seen on recent
photos sent us by passing friends?

But the huge portrait of Nicholas I of Russia still hung in its
place.

'It is not a good work of art,' chided the guide.

'It was never considered to be so.' I agreed.

'But how could the Emperor Nicholas have sent such a bad picture to Metternich?'

'At that time, he probably had no better artist at hand.'

'But how surprising that the Emperor of Russia should give such
an inferior portrait to the Chancellor of Austria!'

Slightly exasperated, I said: 'If it was good enough for Emperor

Nicholas and good enough for Metternich, it should be good enough for you.'

But Paul, with usual detachment rightly remarked: 'They don't mean it badly. At least they try and look after the house as well as they can.'

The dining-room with the portraits of Rhine Electors still inserted in the panelling, was filled with a display of the bronze 'Thomire' set, given to Metternich by the town of Brussels. I had tried to send it to Johannisberg, before the local Nazi authorities prevented me from doing so, but many pieces seemed to be here still.

The rooms beyond were crammed with strange Chinese vases, distributed over steps draped in velvet, as in a shop window: none of them were ours, or rather 'had been' ours.

The museum seemed more or less in order, the famous library so vast, it was impossible to see at a glance if it was still intact, but we had heard that rolls of parchment maps had been pushed down a chute into an open lorry under pouring rain without any measures of protection. The Chapel was crammed with furniture: some of it belonged to the house, and some also to Johannisberg, and had been sent here after its destruction in 1942.

Before leaving I asked the guide to show us our bedroom, which she kindly did: everything seemed still to be there, piled with dust and faded of course. She would not let me glance into the bathroom, and later we heard that every appliance had been torn out, including the tiles and electric wiring.

One of Dubcek's justified claims shortly after, was the total dishonesty of the previous régime, as of all such régimes. And yet Königswart is still considered one of the best kept 'State museums' in Czechoslovakia!

As we drove away down the avenue leading away from the house we glanced back and saw a sheet stretched out on the uncut lawn in front of the facade facing the park. The girls previously seated in the courtyard were dancing on it. They were apparently making a film, and had been lodged in the guestrooms at the end of the wing we had visited. The military cars we had seen on entering, had transported the cameras and other requirements.

The incongruous scene was quite in keeping with the unreality of it all.

The guide in Königswart had told us 'sotto voce' that our old Czech gardener would be so happy to see us. We went to his little house on the outskirts of the village, and took him up to the local inn for lunch. With tears in his eyes, he grasped Paul's hand, and proudly waving his arm around the modest back-room we sat in, said: 'This also belongs to Your Highness!' He told us his son had emigrated, but he was too old to move.

We heard later that a day or two after our departure the police came to question our poor friend, and we were glad we had not returned that way again, as the last thing we wanted was to compromise him in any way.

As the short-lived Dubcek era broke out, we received packets of photos and letters sent anonymously, and the oil portrait Kossuth had begun to paint of me in Prague during the war.

We drove on through the woods feeling rather shattered, climbing towards Glatzen high on the hill to find it had recently burnt down entirely owing to the negligence of the people who had used it for shooting purposes in exchange for dollars.

Paul was particularly interested to see the woods, finding them unchanged except for the blackened roads, flying dust also throwing a grey veil over the trees lining the road.

Marienbad seemed to have been thrust into the same uniform pail of yellow paint used for Königswart, apparently the Communist luxury dye. Drab-looking people wandered up and down, glasses of the famous bitter water in their hands. Some flower-beds had been thinly planted, but the lawns looked like fields for cattle. No shops, and they used to be so smart, even in wartime. Luckily no buildings had been added to the little town, and as it did not suffer during the war, it had at least remained outwardly the same, as if waiting patiently for happier days.

We soon passed the Berchem castle of Kuttenplan, in which a garrison was installed, although the castle looked on the verge of collapse. This part of the country appeared entirely depopulated. The four million Sudetes ejected in 1945 with eight pounds of luggage a head, had not been replaced. Grass grew between the cobbles on the main squares of the villages, punctuated by their Maria-Theresia 'Plague' columns, still topped by their Virgins. Precariously perched on unrelated swirling draperies, they looked as if they would totter and fall at the slightest push.

Skirting Pilsen, we reached Plass rapidly, the countryside as beautiful as ever.

It was oppressive to remember the Czech takeover in these parts. They had murdered their own countrymen: cosy plump Prohaska, the brewer, and so many others. Then the Soviet Army had plundered the Prälatur where we lived and thrown everything out of the windows, except for the immured archives. Now there was a pall of shabbiness over everything. The roof of the 'Konvent' was patchworked with single new tiles. We had had the painted baroque ceiling of the main hall in the Prälatur restored during the war, and found tourists could now visit it for a modest sum. The entire building was distributed into small dwellings, and chimneys curled unexpectedly out of the window-panes.

To our surprise the baroque Church and Metternich Family Mausoleum were freshly repainted and in good order. This must have been due to an energetic priest, so we thought it better not to visit him and perhaps cause trouble.

In Königswart we had heard: 'The Chancellor apparently included his illegitimate children in the family Mausoleum of Plass.'

'Whom for instance?'

'Count Roger Altenburg.'

'But he was Victor Metternich's son, and his grandfather the Chancellor always treated him as a member of the family.'

'A very interesting new version.'

'Not a "new" version but fact. We *know* this.'

The guide's glassy stare was unconvinced, and one realises how history gets distorted if every pseudo-historian insists on discovering his own 'new version'.

We drove and walked around, but not for long.

It had become even more alien than Königswart, owing to the expansion of the village, crowded now with new inhabitants from Pilsen.

Some months later, following our advice, our Forester Dobner returned to Königswart and Plass with his Czech wife. We had told him he would find it painful at the time, but feel all the better for it afterwards.

His wife's family lived in Pilsen, and they wept to see them again. Dobner had left on foot in 1945 and now returned in his own large new car, a prosperous gentleman, looking many years younger than his contemporaries.

He told us sadly how much he regretted not to have torn down some houses we had no longer used for any purpose, as now people who had worked on the estate had been shoved back into them, without any previous repairs. On reaching the age of retirement they were discarded like useless garbage.

Paul had been right: seeing it once again was like closing a book.

Books of related interest in Century Classics

Autobiography of Lady Diana Cooper

Lady Diana Cooper's autobiography offers a wonderfully vivid and entertaining kaleidoscope of society, politics, diplomacy and the world of letters over the first five decades of the century. Asquith and Baldwin, Belloc and Waugh, Noël Coward and Vivien Leigh, Hitler and Roosevelt, Margot Fonteyn and Freya Stark are just a few of the huge cast in this extraordinary life.

The Diaries of Lady Cynthia Asquith

Wife to Herbert, second son of Prime Minister Asquith, Lady Cynthia was one of the most intelligent and beautiful women of her time, painted for love by McEvoy, Sargent and Augustus John. Her sequence of diaries began in 1915 and she wrote extremely frankly about major political issues and characters of the day, which merge into the intimacy of family gossip.

Enid Bagnold Autobiography

Enid Bagnold, author of *National Valvet*, was born in 1889. Her vivid memoirs cover her childhood in Jamaica, then 'finishing and burnishing' in Switzerland and Paris, before 'coming out' in pre-First World War London when she formed part of the artistic 'zinc bath circle' in 1912 Chelsea – mixing with artists and poets such as Walter Sickert and Edward Thomas. She tells of the three-day love of Prince Antoine Bibesco; her first book (of many); marriage at 30 to Roderick Jones, the very powerful Chairman of Reuters; the birth of her children, as well as of more books and plays.

A Grand Tour
Letters and Journeys 1794–1796
J. B. S. Morritt

Not published until 1914 and unjustly neglected since, the letters of John Morritt of Rokeby Hall in Yorkshire describe a fascinating tour through Austria, Hungary, Constantinople, Greece and its islands, and Italy. The revolutionary upheavals in France barred him from visiting many of the more conventional European landmarks, and diverted him to more exotic locations in Eastern Europe and Asia Minor.

Harriette Wilson's Memoirs

Harriette Dubochet was born in Mayfair in 1786, one of fifteen children, and under the professional name of Harriette Wilson she was to become the most famous and sought-after courtesan among the dandies of Regency England. Her confessions were penned with the aim of raising blackmail money from the well-known admirers they feature – the Lords Worcester and Ponsonby (whom she truly adored), Beau Brummel and the Duke of Wellington, whose response was 'Publish and be damned!'. In her heyday, along with her sister Fanny and friend and rival Julia Johnstone, Harriette was known in London as one of 'the Three Graces'. She flourished at a time when to be elegant, witty and available, the possessor of personality, style and beauty was a sufficient currency in itself and her memoirs recall those days.

Journey Into the Mind's Eye
Lesley Blanch

This amalgam of autobiography, travel and history is also an extraordinary love story – of the author's life-long love for Russia and its people. It is the tale of how Lesley Blanch finally achieved her dream to visit the mysterious frontiers of Outer Mongolia and Siberia.

Memoirs of Madame de la Tour du Pin

Madame de la Tour du Pin, born Henrietta Lucy Dillon in 1770, had the good fortune to survive the French Revolution and record a life crammed with enough adventure to fill a dozen novels. She escaped the Terror in a ship to Boston and settled with her husband and four negro slaves on a farm in New York State. Returning in 1796, they were forced into exile – this time in England – a year later. In 1800 they went home once more and Henrietta was taken up by Talleyrand, Mme de Staël, the Empress Marie-Louise and by Napoleon himself.

Princess
Vijayaraje Scindia with Manohar Malgonkar

The autobiography of one of India's most remarkable women, the Dowager Maharani of Gwalior, who has made the rare transition from the opulence of a palatial lifestyle to become a radical and popular political leader. Eschewing a life of luxury in a safe tax haven, her political career has resulted in fines, tax-raids and even imprisonment.

A Princess Remembers
Gayatri Devi and Santha Rama Rau

This is the story of the daughter of the Maharaja of Cooch Behar and widow of the Maharaja of Jaipur. Raised in a sumptuous palace staffed with 500 servants, she shot her first panther at the age of twelve, in later life won a seat in the Parliament of India with a staggering majority and has appeared on lists of the world's most beautiful women. Politically successful and a leading figure in India's women's movement, Gayatri's later life was marred by tragedies which are movingly described in this book.

Scrambles amongst the Alps 1860–1869
Edward Whymper

An epic account of Alpine exploration, *Scrambles* is an acknowledged masterpiece of mountaineering literature by one of the great pioneers of alpine climbing. His account of the first assault on the Matterhorn includes the human drama associated with it, and describes the immediate dangers of the rock face.